Naming Race, Naming Racisms

Defining racism is like nailing jelly to the wall. Eschewing social scientific approaches, which tend to examine race and racism in terms of quasi-static ideal types, this volume surveys differing historical contexts from the advent of scientific racism in the late eighteenth-century to the post-racial racism of the post 9/11 period, and from Europe to the United States, in order to understand how racism has been articulated in differing situations. It is distinguished by the attention it pays to the on-going power of racial discourse in the contemporary period as a legitimating factor in oppression. It exemplifies methodological openness, combining the work of historians, philosophers, political scientists, and literary critics, and includes differing theoretical models in pursuing a critical approach to race: cultural studies; trauma theory and psychoanalysis; critical theory and consideration of the "new racism"; and postcolonialism and the literature on globalization. It brings together the work of leading academics with younger practitioners and is capped off by an interview with world-renowned intellectual Cornel West on black intellectuals in America.

This book was previously published as a special issue of *Patterns of Prejudice*.

Jonathan Judaken is an associate professor of intellectual and cultural history at the University of Memphis.

Dedication

To Joelle

Know that the answers make you wise, but the questions make you human

Naming Race, Naming Racisms

Edited by Jonathan Judaken

Routledge
Taylor & Francis Group

LONDON AND NEW YORK

First published 2009 by Routledge
2 Park Square, Milton Park, Abingdon, Oxon, OX14 4RN

Simultaneously published in the USA and Canada
by Routledge
270 Madison Avenue, New York, NY 10016

Routledge is an imprint of the Taylor & Francis Group, an informa business

© 2009 Edited by Jonathan Judaken

Typeset in Palatino by Value Chain, India
Printed and bound in Great Britain by MPG Books Group

British Library Cataloguing in Publication Data
A catalogue record for this book is available from the British Library

ISBN10: 0-415-45161-2
ISBN13: 978-0-415-45161-1

Table of Contents

Notes on Contributors

Robert Bernasconi has been the Moss Professor of Philosophy at the University of Memphis since 1988, and will join Pennsylvania State University in 2009 as the Sparks Professor of Philosophy. He has written extensively on continental philosophy and the critical philosophy of race, and edited numerous books on race, including *Race, Hybridity and Miscegenation* (Thoemmes 2005). His most recent book is *How to Read Sartre* (W. W. Norton 2007).

Richard Francis Crane is Professor of History at Greensboro College, Greensboro, North Carolina. He is the author of *A French Conscience in Prague: Louis Eugene Faucher and the Abandonment of Czechoslovakia* (East European Monographs, 1996), as well as the forthcoming book *Passion of Israel: Jacques Maritain, Catholic Conscience, and the Holocaust* (University of Scranton Press, 2009).

Leigh Anne Duck is Associate Professor of English at the University of Memphis. She has published articles on American modernism, film and the study of post-plantation literatures in various journals, including the *Journal of American Folklore, American Literary History* and *American Literature*. Her book *The Nation's Region: Southern Modernism, Segregation, and U.S. Nationalism* was published in 2006 by the University of Georgia Press.

Damon Freeman is Assistant Professor in the School of Social Policy and Practice at the University of Pennsylvania, Philadelphia. He is working on a monograph on the life and thought of Kenneth B. Clark entitled *Not So Simple Justice: A Biography of Kenneth B. Clark.*

Jonathan Judaken is Associate Professor of History and Director of the Marcus W. Orr Center for the Humanities at the University of Memphis. He is the author of *Jean-Paul Sartre and the Jewish Question: Anti-antisemitism and the Politics of the French Intellectual* (University of Nebraska Press 2006), and editor of *Race after Sartre: Anti-racism, Africana Existentialism, Postcolonialism* (SUNY Press 2008).

Mark Larrimore is Associate Professor of Religious Studies at Eugene Lang College The New School for Liberal Arts, New York. He is the editor of *The Problem of Evil: A Reader* (Blackwell 2001) and, most recently, co-editor (with Sara Eigen) of *The German Invention of Race* (SUNY Press 2006).

Alfred J. López is Associate Professor of English and American Studies at Purdue University in Indiana. He is founding editor of *The Global South,* an Indiana University Press journal. His most recent book is *José Marti and the Future of Cuban Nationalism* (University Press of Florida 2006). He is also the author of *Posts and Pasts: A Theory of Postcolonialism* (SUNY Press 2001), and editor of *Postcolonial Whiteness: A Critical Reader on Race and Empire* (SUNY Press 2005). His works in progress include a trade biography of José Marti and a project tentatively entitled 'The (post)global South'.

George Michael is Assistant Professor in the Department of Political Science and Administration of Justice at the University of Virginia's College at Wise, Virginia. He is the author of *Confronting Right Wing Extremism and Terrorism in the USA* (Routledge 2003) and *The Enemy of My Enemy: The Alarming Convergence of Militant Islam and the Extreme Right* (University Press of Kansas 2006).

D. J. Mulloy is Associate Professor in the Department of History at Wilfrid Laurier University, Ontario, Canada. He is the editor of *Homegrown Revolutionaries: An American Militia Reader* (Pen and Inc 1999) and the author of *American Extremism: History, Politics and the Militia Movement* (Routledge 2004) and *Willis Carto and the American Far Right* (University Press of Florida 2008).

Brigitte Weltman-Aron is Associate Professor of French in the Department of Romance Languages and Literatures at the University of Florida. She is currently writing a book about Hélène Cixous and Assia Djebar, and her articles on these writers and postcolonial Algeria have appeared in journals such as *parallax* and *Yale French Studies*. She has also written several articles on the French eighteenth century and is the author of *On Other Grounds: Landscape Gardening and Nationalism in Eighteenth-century England and France* (SUNY Press 2001).

Acknowledgements

The seed for this book began as the first conference of the Scholars in Critical Race Studies group at University of Memphis. While its appearance in print is dramatically different from the original symposium, the spirit that nourishes the group is here contained. For the contributors to this volume are all working at the intersection of theoretical and empirical concerns, which is where the real work in unworking racial matters happens. I am grateful to Robert Bernasconi and Leigh Anne Duck as co-founders of this endeavor, and to Bill Lawson and Leigh Johnson, as well as Daphene McFerren, Director of the Hooks Institute for Social Change, who have all embraced this effort as an ongoing calling. I am also indebted to another colleague, Scott Lerner, who greatly assisted me in the Introduction, conveying what was needed as economically as possible.

This volume would simply not have the form it does without the immeasurable efforts of Barbara Rosenbaum. I have learned much about the rigors of the editorial process from her. Two top-notch anonymous readers who Barbara solicited vetted each chapter for this book, so in toto there are many unacknowledged contributors to the final product. Barbara then carefully aided each of the writers in navigating the details and the discussion as a whole as we solidified the final form, not least in my own contribution.

I am appreciative also to Jennifer Geddes for first asking me whom I would want to interview for an issue of *Hedgehog Review* focused on the role of intellectuals and then for joining me in the dialogue with Cornel West published here in its entirety as the last chapter. I am thankful to *Hedgehog Review* for their permission to republish it. Jennifer and I met as fellows at the Center for Advanced Holocaust Studies (CAHS) at the United States Holocaust Memorial Museum, where my 2006-2007 tenure enabled me to complete a lot of the work for this collection.

This book is dedicated to the newest member of the J-crew, who arrived on the scene while the book was in labor. It was nourished daily by all the J-girls who give a larger purpose to what might otherwise turn into merely an academic endeavor.

Naming race, naming racisms: an introduction

To better understand the protean concept of race, we might consider it in light of what Friedrich Nietzsche said about truth: 'It is a mobile army of metaphors, metonyms, and anthropomorphisms—in short, a sum of human relations, which have been enhanced, transposed, and embellished ... and which, after long use seem fixed, canonical, and binding to a people.' Races are 'illusions which we have forgotten are illusions. They are metaphors which have become worn out and no longer have the power to carry meaning.' The historians, literary theorists, political scientists and philosophers included in this volume seek to analyse some of the key debates since the eighteenth century that have helped shape how concepts of race have served as metaphors, as carriers of meaning, in the shifting contexts of modernity.

Eschewing social scientific approaches and their reliance on quasi-static ideal types, this volume provides an overview that ranges from the consolidation of 'scientific' conceptions of race in the late eighteenth century to today. Its essays range transnationally in order to understand how racism has been articulated in differing situations. With four essays focused on the post-9/11 period, and all of them engaged with contemporary discussions about race, the volume is distinguished by the attention it pays to the ongoing power of racial discourse and the institutionalization of racism. It exemplifies methodological openness, employing differing theoretical models for a critical approach to race: the history of philosophy and systems of thought; trauma theory and psychoanalysis; critical theory; cultural studies and intellectual history; and postcolonial and globalization literature.

Mark Larrimore's essay on Immanuel Kant offers a novel perspective on modern racism's origins. He maintains that the renowned philosopher was not only an originator of the scientific concept of race and a key figure in the central role of anthropology in the development of scientific racism, but also a founder of the category of 'whiteness'. 'Kant had invented not only race but "whiteness" as an escape from it,' writes Larrimore. 'Whites were at once a race and beyond race, the summation and circumvention of race, an uncertainty' that Kant would 'sharpen into an antinomy with his critical philosophy'. The challenge of Larrimore's piece is his location of Kant's marginal writings on race and whiteness firmly within the development of his overall system of thought, drawing attention to the formative role these played *throughout* Kant's philosophical project and, in turn, in the history of the theorization of race. Larrimore also positions Kant's writings on race within the wider discourse of race theorizing in the eighteenth century. He correlates Kant's position with those of Buffon and Blumenbach, situates his writing in relation to Lavater's physiognomy, and counterposes Kant's interventions to the polygenetic theories of Lord Kames and Voltaire, just as systems of racial classification were beginning to coalesce.

Robert Bernasconi picks up this thread by contextualizing Anténor Firmin's *De l'égalité des races humaines* (1885), a remarkable 650-page tract written by a young Haitian to oppose the doctrine of racial inequality. He situates Firmin's intervention at the centre of circulating nineteenth-century discussions of racial science. Bernasconi takes up where Larrimore leaves off, with the debate between polygenesis and monogenesis as it was played out under the auspices of the the Société d'Anthropologie de Paris, 'the most important anthropological society anywhere in the world', founded in 1859, the same year that Darwin's *The Origin of Species* was published. Firmin's *De l'égalité des races humaines* was, as its title suggests, a counterpoint to Joseph Arthur, Comte de Gobineau's *Essai sur l'inégalité des races humaines* (1853–5), which argued that race was destiny and race-mixing led to the decline of civilizations. Firmin was also responding to the leading racist anthropologists of the nineteenth century, like Paul Broca, who founded the Sociéte. His main target, however, was the importation of evolutionist theories as applied to the human races, especially those of Clémence Royer, 'Darwin's bulldog in France'. Firmin would mobilize his own version of Auguste Comte's positivism in order to dismantle these racist viewpoints. But he also imbibed aspects of the racialist presuppositions of French Republican ideology, which was busy legitimating colonial empire under the auspices of the *mission civilisatrice*. Bernasconi thus reveals the limits—but more importantly the possibilities—of an anti-racist perspective, as scientific racism was becoming a fixture of European's self-understanding.

If Larrimore and Bernasconi reveal just how wide ranging discussions of race were during the long nineteenth century, then Richard Francis Crane's focus on France's most important twentieth-century Catholic intellectual, Jacques Maritain, makes evident that this was also the case for discussions of the Jewish Question in the period between the Dreyfus Affair and the rise of National Socialism. Crane chronicles the shift in Maritain's perspective from his close association with the radical-right Action Française, then the foremost antisemitic group in France, to his emergence in the 1920s as a leading voice opposed to antisemitism. Even as Crane sensitively treats the polysemic discussions of Jews and Judaism in interwar France, he shows nonetheless that

> Maritain strove to advance a metahistorical understanding of what might be called the Sacred Jew in an era when the racially hygienic construct of the Dirty Jew threatened to prevail ... But Maritain's recasting of the timely Jewish Question as the timeless Mystery of Israel amounted to just as clear an expression of the political-cultural anxieties of the interwar period as its racist and ever more eliminationist counterpart.

Larrimore, Bernasconi and Crane therefore demonstrate the paradoxes at work in discourses on the racial question: ostensibly cosmopolitan and universalist rationalists who were at the origins of race-thinking (Kant); anti-racism that articulated a vision of equality within a progressive teleology but that reiterated some of the suppositions of racial hierarchy (Firmin); and anti-antisemites whose commitments to an eschatological theology continued to fix Jews and Judaism within a pre-scripted role in the drama of Christian salvation (Maritain).

These tensions did not end with the civil rights era. Damon Freeman focuses on the conflict between Kenneth Clark and Adam Clayton Powell, two prominent African American leaders of the 1960s. Their intra-racial struggle, Freeman argues, does not fit neatly into narratives about either the civil rights or black power movements, and poses difficult questions about the politics of race and the transformations of racial thought. 'The Clark–Powell split symbolized both the promises and the perils of the black freedom struggle', Freeman notes. He explores how the conflict helped Clark to rethink 'the nature of power, the civil rights movement and the prospects for African American leadership' and how Powell came to argue that the dilemmas of race were, in fact, subsumed within power relations in ways that anticipated the critical race theorists of the 1980s.

In turn, Leigh Anne Duck reads Alice Walker's post-civil rights novel *Meridian* (1976) as an exploration of the political significance of suffering. She interrogates Walker's text to explain how the psychoanalytic concepts of mourning and melancholia help render more intricate the relationship between racial/gender oppression and psychic trauma. She also examines how the eponymous protagonist of *Meridian* can sensitize critical race theorists to a more complex understanding of the damaged racial pasts they examine, offering 'insight into problems that are simultaneously social and psychological'.

The remaining contributions all focus in different ways on race and racism today. George Michael and D. J. Mulloy's 'Riots, Disasters and Racism' surveys how some key journals and figures on the extreme right in the United States represented Hurricane Katrina, the November 2005 riots in Paris, and the inter-ethnic mêlée on Cronulla Beach in Sydney between native Whites and Middle Eastern immigrants in December 2005. We learn about the ways in which these groups oppose a multicultural society, racialize the politics of immigration and feed on current events for an affirmation of their racist perspective. Michael and Mulloy ultimately reveal that the very media mechanisms that disseminate the diatribes of this white supremacist community are a function of how essentialist and exclusionary nationalism has become transnational. White supremacy is today defined more in terms of a crisis of European and western civilization (read as white) rather than in narrower nationalist terms. Since the very events Michael and Mulloy survey are the result of global forces, it indicates how globalization is transforming the discourse of extreme nationalism and racism.

This conjuncture of racism, nationalism and globalization is explored in more detail in the final three pieces. Brigitte Weltman-Aron shows how the postcolonial resides at the intersection of the global and the local. She considers Assia Djebar, the first Algerian woman writer ever elected to join the Académie Française, an institution founded in 1635 to define the French language by writing its dictionary. Djebar is one of several francophone, and specifically Mahghrebian, writers who have analysed the relationship between the French language and racialization, a relationship Frantz Fanon made clear in *Black Skin, White Masks*: 'The Negro of the Antilles will be proportionately whiter', he wrote, 'that is, he will come closer to being a real human being—in direct ratio to his mastery of the French language'. Weltman-Aron examines how Assia Djebar's inclusion of idiomatic terms in her writing is an index of a dual poetics of resistance. On the one hand, Djebar dismantles the cultural racism at work in the discourse on assimilation that underpinned the French model of colonialism, since the *mission civilisatrice* was founded on the notion that mastery of the language was the sign of whiteness. On the other hand, she opposes

Algerian claims to any unproblematic and 'authentic' self-recovery after colonialism.

A similar nexus of globalization, racialization and resistance is considered in Alfred López's work, as his subtitle, '9/11, Race and the New Postglobal Literature', makes evident. López explores how the forces of globalization affect those at the bottom, the subalterns of the new global economy: migrants and workers in the postcolonial metropole. He develops the concept of the 'postglobal' through a close reading of Monica Ali's novel *Brick Lane*, which exemplifies a 'new postglobal literature' that depicts the experience of aliens and minority labourers as symptomatic of the confines of a neo-liberal order defined by the global expansion of capitalism.

Finally, my own effort to rethink antisemitism in a global age explores the postglobal from the vantage of the debate on what has been named the 'new antisemitism'. I argue that it is not new in at least two senses. First, none of the elements that characterize the new antisemitism are actually new: Holocaust denial, Islamic Judaeophobia, antisemitism on the left, anti-racism as antisemitism, and anti-Zionism each have a long history. Second, the extensive historiography on the 'new antisemitism' mitigates the claim that something novel is afoot. But the forces of globalization have transformed discussions of antisemitism into a battleground with the rhetorical warfare played out on the Internet both a symptom and cause of the ways representations of Jews and Judaism are being altered in the age of the new media. Here, I draw on works by Léon Poliakov, Judith Butler, Jean-Paul Sartre and the Frankfurt School, among others, to critically re-evaluate the phenomenon of the new Judaeophobia in our era of globalization.

So what does the genealogy of 'race' and 'racism' presented in this volume reveal? It shows how race has functioned as a metaphor in different historical contexts: a means to point to a fixed origin and stable cause of meaning for historical phenomena that are constantly in flux. Race seeks to stabilize discourse, to provide its knowable ground, but is not itself stable and so cannot be easily defined or named. It is, rather, a symbolic and imaginary way of attempting to anchor meaning given the changes engendered by modernity. Most importantly, this collection of essays shows that this slippage of meaning can be historicized. To do so involves situating forms of racial categorization in relation to other discursive constructs that are posited as transcendental signifieds, including the technologies of power at work in gender formation, class structures, regimes of normativity and respectability, religious conceptions and configurations of epistemic truth. 'Race' and 'racism' are therefore useful as vectors of historical change that help to trace the effects of racial discourses and how these are projected on to racialized bodies within the dynamic of power relations played out in the body politic. This forensic exercise is ultimately undertaken in order to demythologize, destabilize and deconstruct the mutations of racism in modernity.

The book ends with an interview with Cornel West about "Black Intellectuals in America." In his inimitable fashion, West's ruminations knit together the concerns of the work as a whole. For West locates himself as a black intellectual within both a Socratic and Jewish tradition of prophetic critique whose sights are sharply honed in on both anti-Jewish demonization and anti-black racism. The discussion with West ranges from how the itinerary of black intellectuals overlaps, but also differs from those of the New York Intellectuals, many of whom were Jewish. Their agenda was defined after Auschwitz and with the onset of the Cold War and was attentive to the issues of mass murder, Marxism, and modernism. 'Whereas the black intellectuals,' West avers 'are actually dealing with the night side of American democracy. They're dealing with the problematic of the forms of death—social death and civic death, spiritual death and psychic death in America—and so it's a very different context in which they're working.' Parsing his own demarche from *Race Matters* to *Democracy Matters*, West reconsiders the possibilities of resistance to the anti-intellectualism in American life, including the role of the academy, as well as the interconnections of imperialism, racism, and democracy in a post-global age: 'Every democracy we know has been predicated on some kind of imperial project,' he stipulates, 'So the question becomes how does one engage in a critique of democracy with democratic ideals that are suspicious of the imperialism which often are the preconditions for your democracy. It's a real paradox.' This paradox is at the heart of the project of *Naming Race, Naming Racisms*.

Jonathan Judaken
University of Memphis

Antinomies of race: diversity and destiny in Kant

MARK LARRIMORE

Immanuel Kant, the inventor of autonomy, was also the inventor of race.[1] Understanding the *invention* of a concept is a challenging business, however, especially when the concept has played so fateful a part in

1 See Robert Bernasconi, 'Who invented the concept of race? Kant's role in the Enlightenment construction of race', in Robert Bernasconi (ed.), *Race* (Oxford: Blackwell 2001), and the essays by Bernasconi, Susan Shell, John Zammito and myself in Sara Eigen and Mark Larrimore (eds), *The German Invention of Race* (Albany: State University of New York Press 2006).

subsequent history. Even histories of race as a construction risk reifying what they seek to dismantle by treating it from the start as *explanandum* rather than *explanans*. When first invented, race was an answer to questions we no longer ask, and conceived in terms of schemes of human diversity we barely remember. Kant lectured on human diversity against the backdrop of geography and history throughout his career out of an eighteenth-century sense of diversity as real and inevitable as well as potentially meaningful. The critical turn and his mature ethics did not displace these concerns. They reframed them and, as they did, 'race' became a term claiming at once scientific, providential and pragmatic significance. In this essay I will explicate Kant's writings on race of the 1770s, 1780s and 1790s, not in terms of the disingenuous 'science' his work helped make possible, but rather in relation to the concerns of Kant's practical thought in their true home.

Scholarship on Kant's contributions to race theory tends either to focus on his appalling views of non-Europeans, especially Africans, or to see him as engaged in a classificatory exercise, albeit one connected to understanding man's place in nature and history. But Kant didn't need the concept of race to maintain noxious views of non-Europeans, and classification of human varieties is never innocent. Scholars also often fail to distinguish between writings from different stages of Kant's career, allowing others to draw false comfort from the possibility that Kant dropped his hateful views with the critical turn of the 1780s or his theory of race with the cosmopolitan turn of the 1790s.[2] Kant's views did change in important ways. Once invented, however, the race concept only became more complex and ambitious, moving from geography to anthropology and from discussions of 'what nature makes of man' to those concerning 'what man can and should make of himself'.

Kant's theory of race shows the importance of reading together elements of his *oeuvre* that tend to be studied in isolation: practical philosophy, philosophy of history, anthropology, physical geography. But race is more than an instance of their interrelation. Both before and after the critical turn, Kant was committed to race for its potential to anchor his larger understanding of human diversity and destiny, and reserved a special place for Whites beyond

---

2 Important arguments that fail to distinguish pre-critical from critical works by scholars such as Emmanuel Chukwudi Eze (*Achieving Our Humanity: The Idea of the Postracial Future* (London: Routledge 2001), ch. 3) and Charles W. Mills ('Kant's *Untermenschen*', in Andrew Valls (ed.), *Race and Racism in Modern Philosophy* (Ithaca, NY: Cornell University Press 2005), 169–93) allow scholars like Thomas E. Hill and Bernard Boxill ('Kant and race', in Bernard Boxill (ed.), *Race and Racism* (New York: Oxford University Press 2001), 448–71), and Robert B. Louden (*Kant's Impure Ethics* (New York: Oxford University Press 2000), 93–106) to claim that Kant's racism was confined to his pre-critical thought. Pauline Kleingeld has recently shown that Kant's racial views persist well into the critical period (she goes so far as to assert that he supported slavery during this time), but argues that he renounced his view of race in the 1790s; Pauline Kleingeld, 'Kant's second thoughts on race', *Philosophical Quarterly*, vol. 57, no. 229, October 2007, 573–92.

race. In a manner paralleled by his characterizations of the German national character and one of his accounts of moral autonomy, Kant argues not that Whites are a superior race but that they are the pre-emption and redemption of race: Kant's invention of race was attended by the simultaneous invention of 'whiteness' as an escape from it. Seeing in Kant race's pivotal role linking nature, diversity and freedom raises difficult questions for Kant scholarship. It can also help us understand the appeal of this pseudo-concept and why it was able to exert such widespread influence throughout western culture in the nineteenth and twentieth centuries.

Races and not-quite races

Kant's first essay on race, 'Von den verschiedenen Racen der Menschen' ('On the Different Races of Men') of 1775,[3] was one of only two works he published during the 'silent decade' when the *Kritik der reinen Vernunft* (*Critique of Pure Reason*) was germinating. It announced his upcoming lectures in physical geography. Kant thought he had identified an exception-less law in human heredity that for the first time promised a truly scientific natural history of man. Establishing a precise concept of race offered Kant the opportunity to assert himself as a scientist, indeed as the philosophical policeman among scientists.[4] As important was the fact that it showed that physical geography, a field Kant had introduced and thought vital to understanding human destiny, could be a science.

The word 'race' (*Race*) was an import into German from English and French with no precise meaning; it didn't become the German word *Rasse* until the 1780s.[5] Like *Geschlecht*, *Art*, *Stamm* and *Gattung* it was used to refer to genetically related communities or lineages. If it had any particular resonance

3 With the exception of this essay, references to Kant's writings will be given in the text to the standard edition, the Akademie-Ausgabe: Immanuel Kant, *Gesammelte Schriften*, ed. Königliche Preußische Akademie der Wissenschaften, 29 vols (Berlin: Walter de Gruyter and predecessors 1902‒). The important differences between the 1775 and 1777 versions of this essay are easier (if still not easy) to see in Immanuel Kant, *Werke*, ed. Wilhelm Weischedel, 12 vols (Frankfurt-on-Main: Suhrkamp 1968), xi:9–30, which I will cite in the text as 'W'. English translations by Jon Mark Mikkelsen of both the 1775 and 1777 versions of 'On the different races of men' will soon be available. In general and with some modifications, I use the English translations in the multi-volume series, the Cambridge Edition of the Works of Immanuel Kant in Translation (1995‒), and Immanuel Kant, *Observations on the Feeling of the Beautiful and the Sublime*, trans. John T. Goldthwait (Berkeley: University of California Press 1960). Some texts discussed in this essay have not been published in English; translations of such texts here are by the author.
4 John H. Zammito, 'Policing polygeneticism in Germany, 1775: (Kames,) Kant, and Blumenbach', in Eigen and Larrimore (eds), *The German Invention of Race*, 35–54 (36–7).
5 Antje Sommer, 'Rasse II. Entstehung und Entfaltung des Rassebegriffs', in Otto Brunner, Werner Conze and Reinhart Koselleck (eds), *Geschichtliche Grundbegriffe*, vol. 5 (Stuttgart: Klett-Cotta 1984), 149.

of its own, it referred not to natural variation but to husbandry and breeding. As in other languages, one main use was in reference to dogs and horses (and aristocrats). A race in this sense was an artefact, the development of the potential in an animal (or plant) species brought out through careful breeding. It used knowledge of natural processes to improve on nature, but could be undone through neglect and an unguided mixing with other stocks. In using the word 'race' Kant suggested that *Menschenracen*, too, were products of something like the process of breeding, or could be.

Kant followed Buffon in defining a 'species' in terms of the limits of viable hybrid offspring. All the different kinds of human beings were, by this definition, members of the same species. But Kant departed from Buffon in seeing races as more than accidental 'degenerations' caused by climate. Some heritable differences among human populations seemed permanent. Unlike 'varieties', 'variations' and 'stocks', terms Kant proposed to name various traits that were transmitted less deterministically or only for a few genera-tions, Kant proposed restricting the term 'race' to populations characterized by inevitably heritable and perdurable traits (W12). Mixed-race children thus inevitably bore the marks of both parents. The necessity Kant claimed to find here showed something non-accidental in the unfolding of human diversity. It presaged a study of nature that could move beyond mere 'description of nature' (*Naturbeschreibung*) to a true 'natural *history*' (*Naturgeschichte*).

Kant proposed that human nature contained within itself 'seeds' (*Keime*) and 'predispositions' (*Anlagen*) for the races, which were triggered but not caused by climate in the same way that different climes trigger thicker husks in wheat or a second layer of feathers in birds (W17). The full unfolding of *Keime* takes time. 'Natural cataclysms', like the seas that isolated the Indian subcontinent and sub-Saharan Africa 'in those times of floods', helped keep human populations apart long enough for the different races to take form (W24, 25n). In all only four races needed to be posited to account for the appearance of all of the people across the globe: '1) the race of the *Whites*, 2) the *Negro race*, 3) the *Hunnish* (Mongolian or Kalmuck) race, 4) the Hindu or *Hindustani* race' (W14). The supposed permanence of race traits led Kant to conclude that, once the potentiality for a race was precipitated by a climate, the potentialities for other races were disabled.

Kant's contemporaries, too, thought that human beings had changed in response to different climates as they radiated out from a place of origin in southwest or central Asia, but thought that these changes were accidental and generally harmful, though reversible, at least in theory.[6] For Kant, race

---

6 For climate theory, see Clarence J. Glacken, *Traces on the Rhodian Shore: Nature and Culture in Western Thought from Ancient Times to the End of the Eighteenth Century* (Berkeley: University of California Press 1967); Roxann Wheeler, *The Complexion of Race: Categories of Difference in Eighteenth-century Britain* (Philadelphia: University of Pennsylvania Press 2000), 21–33; and David Bindman, *Ape to Apollo: Aesthetics and the Idea of Race in the 18th Century* (Ithaca, NY: Cornell University Press 2002), 58–70.

was an achievement: the unfolding of a seed or predisposition put there precisely for the occasion. Race was an *Abartung* (deviation) rather than an *Ausartung* (degeneration), a modification that did not imply decline.[7] Defined in terms of its terminus as well as its point of departure, race seemed to confirm that human beings were meant to populate the whole globe without degeneration. Nature's cataclysms functioned like good husbandry.

Four 'base races' (*Grundrassen*) sufficed to account for all mixtures, Kant argued, but not all peoples were fully raced. The ancestors of (Native) Americans had apparently migrated too fast. Americans' supposed congenital weakness could be explained by the incomplete achievement (*Einartung*) of the 'Hunnish' *Keim* exacerbated by a further degeneration (*Ausartung*) as they moved south from one climate to another. Races were not 'degenerations' but the 'half-degenerated' (*halb ausgeartet*) Americans very nearly were (W22). Like Buffon, Kant had long seen nature as an orderly but indifferent system in which many got lost. Indeed, he seems to have seen the dying out of some populations as inevitable, a sublime spectacle of the grandeur of nature and the fragility of humanity.[8]

There was another anomalous population, however. Whites, too, were not fully *eingeartet* (achieved). In this case, however, the consequence was not weakness but strength. If the ancestors of the Americans had moved too quickly for any *Keim* fully to unfold, those of Whites had moved slowly enough not to trigger the development of one *Keim* at the expense of the others. 'If one asks with which of the present races the first human stock (*Menschenstamm*) might have had the greatest similarity, one would, though without any prejudice, pronounce in favour of the Whites because of the evidently greater perfection of one colour over others' (W25n). While supposedly one of the 'base races', Kant in fact referred to Whites using all the terms *against* which he had defined race. As Peggy Piesche has argued, the less deterministic terms used in describing Europeans, especially *Spielart*, suggest that development may be expected here alone.[9]

---

7 In 1788 Kant suggested that 'race' should be rendered *progenies* rather than *degeneratio* in Latin (8:163–4).
8 In the undated "'Reflexion" 1520', Kant writes: 'All races will be wiped out (Americans and negroes cannot govern themselves. Thus are good only as slaves.), except for the white' (15.2:878). I suggest that this view, if not perhaps Kant's considered opinion, is consistent with his published views in Mark Larrimore, 'Sublime waste: Kant on the destiny of the "races"', in Catherine Wilson (ed.), *Civilization and Oppression*, supplementary vol. 25 of the *Canadian Journal of Philosophy* (Calgary: University of Calgary Press 1999), 99–137.
9 Peggy Piesche, 'Der "Fortschritt" der Aufklärung—Kants "Race" und die Zentrierung des *weißen* Subjekts', in Maureen Maisha Eggers, Grada Kilomba, Peggy Piesche and Susan Arndt (eds), *Mythen, Masken und Subjekte: Kritische Weißseinsforschung in Deutschland* (Münster: Unrast 2005), 30–9 (34).

That neither Americans nor Whites were fully a race didn't weaken Kant's theory. Indeed, race unified human natural history by explaining not only races and their mixtures but anomalies and their relative strength or weakness. It is no surprise that Whites should be the happy anomaly. By tucking into his theory of race an idea of Whites distinguished by a completeness no other race could attain, Kant invented 'whiteness' at the same time and by means of his theory of race.

Kant's was one of three essays published in 1775 that seem simultaneously to inaugurate the discourse of race[10] but it alone invoked a concomitant invention of 'whiteness'. All were probably provoked to some degree by the eloquent restatement of the polygenetic argument in Lord Kames's *Sketches of the History of Man*. The idea that the various human communities spanning the globe were not descendants of a single original set of parents wasn't new; Voltaire and Hume had argued that climate theory could not explain the variety to be found within climatic zones or the endurance of certain traits as populations moved. Kames's case was less polemical. Had an original monogenesis perhaps been fractured by divine decree after the building of the Tower of Babel?[11] In the terms of four-stage theory he argued that non-Whites were stalled but could be helped. Africans were prevented by their climate from developing 'judgement' and 'prudence', but 'who can say how far they might improve in a state of freedom, were they obliged, like Europeans, to procure bread with the sweat of their brows?'[12]

Monogenesis has no intrinsic connection to egalitarianism or universalism, in science or religion, as the example of the relation of 'degeneration' to monogenesis in Buffon shows.[13] Belief in degeneration was widespread; the real issue was whether or not 'regeneration' was possible. On this question Kant's monogenetic view was more unforgiving than polygenetic ones like Kames's. There was no contradiction between Kant's view and the biblical monogenesis that was one of its distant sources. In its very rigidity it may even have been more theologically correct than universalistic monogenetic views. Everyone's ancestors may have been in Eden, but few biblical traditions have believed that all or even most would be gathered again in Paradise.

10 For the other two, see Johann Friedrich Blumenbach, *The Anthropological Treatises of Johann Friedrich Blumenbach … and the Inaugural Dissertation of John Hunter, M. D. on the Varieties of Man*, trans. and ed. Thomas Bendyshe [1865] (Boston: Milford House 1973).

11 Henry Home, Lord Kames, *Sketches of the History of Man*, 4 vols (Dublin: printed for James Williams 1774–5), 43–4 (available in 'Eighteenth Century Collections Online'). This work was immediately translated into German after it was published.

12 Ibid., 35.

13 See Phillip R. Sloan, 'The idea of racial degeneracy in Buffon's *Histoire Naturelle*', in Harold E. Pagliaro (ed.), *Racism in the Eighteenth Century* (Cleveland and London: Case Western Reserve University Press 1973), 293–321.

At this stage Kant's interest in establishing the unity of the human species through a theory of race had more to do with the project of physical geography than with religion or ethics. As Kant had made clear in an important 1765 description of his courses, encountering the theoretical sciences without having first learned to exercise the understanding in empirical judgements led to 'the precocious prating of young thinkers which is blinder than any other self-conceit and more incurable than ignorance' (2:305). The lectures in physical geography that Kant gave throughout his career provided a sort of place-holder for life experience his students were too young to have.[14] But it was not theoretical as opposed to practical knowledge Kant was hoping to ground. The 1775 announcement advertised physical geography as 'anticipatory practice in a *knowledge of the world*' that added 'the *pragmatic*' to all other knowledge and abilities 'so that they are useful not only in *school* but in *life*, and through which the finished apprentice is introduced to the place of his destiny, namely the *world*'. Its two components '*nature* and *man*' must be appraised '*cosmologically*', not in terms of isolated differences in but in terms of 'their relation in the whole, within which they stand, and wherein each takes its place' (W26, cf. 9:157).

Physical geography afforded students a sense of a bounded and thus knowable set of phenomena, the 'unity without which all our knowledge is nothing but fragmentary patchwork' (2:313). The most basic fact about the earth was that it was spherical with a tilted axis. Since its surface area was limited and continuous, its varied geological and other phenomena could and must be understood as part of a single system. The diversity of human populations could and must be understood in this context too. The physical geography lectures expanded into a companion course on anthropology in 1772, but long before that Kant had offered a '*physical, moral* and *political* geography' (2:312) that included 'cosmological' discussions of the peoples of the world.

A taste of the kind of material Kant offered his students may be found in *Beobachtungen über das Gefühl des Schönen und Erhabenen* (*Observations on the Beautiful and the Sublime*) of 1764, a popularizing work less interested in aesthetic objects than in the utility of aesthetic concepts for illuminating the differences and synergies of various sorts of human difference, from varieties of moral sensibility and temperament to gender and national character. These categories of difference remained central to Kant's lectures on human diversity to the end. The same discussions appeared in 1798 under the title 'Anthropologische Charakteristik' in *Anthropologie in pragmatischer Hinsicht* (*Anthropology from a Pragmatic Point of View*). *Charakteristik* was a specifically eighteenth-century genre concerned with 'the way of cognizing the interior of the human being from the exterior' (7:283) to which

14 See Michèle Cohen-Halimi and Max Marcuzzi's valuable introduction to Immanuel Kant, *Géographie = Physische Geographie*, trans. into French by Michèle Cohen-Halimi, Max Marcuzzi and Valérie Seroussi (Paris: Aubier 1999), 9–55, esp. 23–33.

Observations already recognizably belonged. Also known as *Moralistik*, its point was pragmatic, teaching how best to make use of other people: whom to trust, whom to entrust with different kinds of work, what sort of couplings produced the best offspring.[15]

The understanding of diversity displayed in *Observations* showed that things fit together as a whole. The conclusion of the chapter on different kinds of virtue and their correlates among the four temperaments can speak for the whole work: 'the different groups unite into a picture of splendid expression, where amidst great multiplicity unity shines forth, and the whole of moral nature exhibits beauty and dignity' (2:227). Yet this unity was more an article of faith than something Kant could demonstrate.

> If I examine alternately the noble and the weak side of men, I reprimand myself that I am unable to take that standpoint from which those contrasts present the great portrait of the whole of human nature in a stirring form. For I willingly concede that so far as it belongs to the design of nature on the whole, these grotesque postures cannot give anything but a noble expression, although one is indeed much too shortsighted to see them in this relation (2:226–7).

Human diversity posed a kind of theodicy problem for Kant. At this point the unity was assured, whether we could see it or not. In the ensuing decades Kant would make this postulated unity first an article of moral faith, and then a project for human beings.

Observations offered several models for unity in multiplicity but the underlying template was the bounded whole formed by the sanguine, choleric, melancholy and phlegmatic temperaments.[16] This was not unusual for the 1760s; temperament was the mainstay of western anthropology and psychology until the nineteenth century. Seeing all types as different mixtures of the same few elements was a helpful way of reconciling unity and diversity, and articulating as natural various kinds of social complementarity and hierarchy. Like many of his contemporaries, Kant explained national characters in temperamental terms. The nations of Europe made a kind of whole like that of the temperaments: the French sanguine, the Spanish choleric, the English melancholy, the Dutch phlegmatic. The nations of Asia were then explored as analogies of Europe. Persians were the French of Asia, Japanese the English and so on (2:252). Finally, the 'savage' nations

---

15 *Characteristik* overlapped with *Popularphilosophie*, Lavater's revival of physiognomy *Erfahrungsseelenkunde*, Ernst Platner's *Anthropologie* and Knigge's radical etiquette. See Hans Robert Jauß, 'Zur Marginalität der Körpererfahrung in Kants *Anthropologie* und der in ihr vorgegebenen moralistischen Tradition', in Rudolph Behrens and Roland Galle (eds), *Leib-Zeichen: Körperbilder, Rhetorik und Anthropologie im 18. Jahrhundert* (Würzburg: Königshausen & Neumann 1993), 11–21.

16 I have traced Kant's commitment to the temperaments in Mark Larrimore, 'Substitutes for wisdom: Kant's practical thought and the tradition of the temperaments', *Journal of the History of Philosophy*, vol. 39, no. 2, April 2001, 259–88.

were described in terms resonant again with the temperaments: this is where Kant's shocking and widely quoted lines about Africans (whom he, unusually, describes as phlegmatic) appear. Human variety was a problem of meaning and order to which *Observations* provided a somewhat wavering hope for a solution.

Kant revised the 1775 announcement for the collection *Der Philosoph für die Welt*, edited by *Aufklärer* J. J. Engel in 1777, and made changes that strengthened race as a kind of theodicy of diversity. Terms were tidied up. All references to partial or incomplete *Einartung* were removed, as was all reference to *Ausartung*. The irrevocability of race was affirmed: 'A race, when once it has taken root and extinguished the other seeds, resists all further transformation because the character of race at one point became dominant in the generative power' (W29). Kant added a table reminiscent of Linnaeus that suggested only four races were possible; it also made the loophole for the not-quite race of Whites explicit.

Stem Genus:
Whites of brunette colour
First race, very blond (northern Europe) of damp cold.
Second race, copper-red (America) of dry cold.
Third race, black (Senegambia) of damp heat.
Fourth race, olive-yellow (Indians) of dry heat (2:411).

These four races—defined now in terms of colour as well as geography—didn't match those still discussed in the body of the essay. But the purpose of the summary was not to account for the four posited races so much as to show that they fit together as a whole, and that no others were necessary (or possible). The grid of heat and cold, and dry and damp was the template of temperament theory. By correlating them with the temperaments, Kant locked the races into one of the most familiar and closed schemes of differentiation available in western culture.

The apparent chaos of diversity was safely contained, but counting the weak Americans a full race made race no longer a guarantee of fitness. Correspondingly, Whites' circumvention of race was affirmed; already in 1775 Kant had written that white 'brunettes' and 'blondes' differed only as *Spielarten* (W13). 'Whiteness' was explained in a different way than 'blackness', which Kant had argued resulted from iron in the blood precipitated by tropical climate. 'Among the Whites (*Geschlechte der Weißen*), however, the iron dissolved in these juices is not precipitated at all, demonstrating both the perfect mixing of juices and the strength of this human stock in comparison to others' (W27). A race emerged as a single *Keim* unfolded, stifling the others. But among Whites the story was one of balance, of a perduring and dynamic mixture in which no possibilities were lost. The temperate zone between 31 and 52 degrees latitude in the old world ... can justifiably be thought of as that with the most fortunate mixture of influences of colder and hotter regions, and the greatest wealth of creatures; where man too, because from there he is [*sic!*] equally well-prepared for every transplantation, must have diverged least from his original form (W27).

It seems that by not moving too soon or quickly, Whites had outlasted the danger of becoming a race, and now could survive transplantation anywhere.

Whites' escape from the one-sidedness that constituted race through a balance of forces paralleled arguments in other areas of Kant's thinking. In the roughly contemporary *Über Pädogogik* (*Pedagogy*) Kant wrote: 'There are many seeds (*Keimen*) lying undeveloped in man. It is for us to make these seeds grow, by developing his natural dispositions (*Anlagen*) *in their due proportion*, and to see that he fulfils his destiny' (9:445, emphasis added). Around the same time as his invention of race, Kant's view of the temperaments underwent a significant and related shift. The once contemptibly weak phlegmatic was joined by a 'phlegma as strength', which was superior not only to 'phlegma as weakness' but to all (other) temperaments, as it contained within itself all motives. 'Phlegma as strength', which was henceforth the temperament of the German national character, reappeared as a trait of the autonomous agent in Kant's mature ethics. Freedom cannot by definition be accounted for, but is attended by a mastery of inclinations constituted not by their absence or suppression but by the tranquil equipose resulting from their due proportion. It is composed of every inclination but determined by none (6:408).

With 'Of the Different Races of Men' and physical geography, Kant claimed to have laid the foundation for a 'natural history' of humanity that could move beyond the imprecision of mere 'description of nature'. It offered a way to see (at least some) human varieties as teleological achievements rather than accidental degenerations, in the process confirming that man was destined to spread over the whole earth. Kant's account of the nature and emergence of race out of *Keime* that unfolded irrevocably in the distant past also assured a limit to diversity, a limit already reached. But Kant had invented not only race but 'whiteness' as an escape from it. Whites were at once a race and beyond race, the summation and circumvention of race, an uncertainty that we will see Kant sharpen into an antinomy with his critical philosophy. To those whose ancestors moved far from the place of the original *Stamm*, race in its necessity was destiny. The white students of Kant's lectures on physical geography and anthropology learned that they were well prepared even then to make the whole world their home. Prepared for transplantation anywhere, they must and could make something of themselves.

Race a priori

Discussions of Kant's racial views quote mainly from pre-critical works like the *Observations on the Beautiful and the Sublime* and from the *Physische Geographie* (*Physical Geography*), which, while published in 1801–2, was based on notes long predating Kant's theory of race (see 9:509ff.). This can leave the impression that the Kant of the *Critiques* had outgrown an interest in race and diversity. Indeed, as conventionally understood, Kant's mature ethics should certainly have led him to repudiate it. Yet the critical turn did not displace diversity from Kant's concerns. The critical turn changed the status of all knowledge claims, but the relationships described in Kant's works in geography and anthropology remained substantially intact. His rigorously abstract mature ethics was developed against the backdrop of a continued commitment to the importance of understanding deep human differences like gender, temperament and race, and may indeed presuppose them.

Kant wrote two essays on race in the very midst of elaborating the critical philosophy. 'Bestimmung des Begriffs einer Menschenrace' ('Determination of the Concept of a Human Race') appeared in 1785 less than a year after the *Grundlegung zur Metaphysik der Sitten* (*Groundwork for the Metaphysics of Morals*) and 'Beantwortung der Frage: Was ist Aufklärung?' ('Answer to the Question, "What Is Enlightenment?"'). The second, 'Über den Gebrauch teleologischer Principien in der Philosophie' ('On the Use of Teleological Principles in Philosophy'), an important step towards the analyses of the *Kritik der Urtheilskraft* (*Critique of Teleological Judgment*), appeared in 1788 just after the B version of the *Critique of Pure Reason* and a few months before the *Kritik der praktischen Vernunft* (*Critique of Practical Reason*). Wedded to the ambitions of the critical philosophy, Kant's thinking on race took flight.

Human beings still needed to understand themselves as part of a unified whole, but with the critical turn the whole could no longer be discovered or confirmed empirically. Where human nature and destiny were concerned, the relevant whole—the 'kingdom of ends'—was not found in phenomena but posited by practical reason. In the 1770s race had been discovered by assembling empirical reports, and demonstrated a necessity not otherwise known in human heredity. If only in theory it had confirmed that human beings could indeed populate the whole globe without loss of their humanity. With the critical turn things went the other way round. The idea that humanity was destined to spread free republics all over the globe was posited by practical reason rather than gleaned from theoretical reason. The idea of a mechanism like 'race' suggested itself as a way this end could be achieved in a climatically varied world. If it could also be confirmed empirically, race would demonstrate the value of a practical-reason-shaped understanding of human destiny for all the human sciences.

The immediate occasion for these two essays was the public quarrel with J. G. Herder that was so important for the development of Kant's thinking.[17] Herder had attended Kant's pre-critical lectures in the early 1760s, including the lectures in physical geography and moral philosophy. In 1784 Herder published the first part of his *Ideen zur Philosophie der Geschichte der Menschheit* (*Ideas for a Philosophy of the History of Humanity*), a work he thought consonant with Kant's geographical and anthropological project and even a sort of consummation of it. Kant's frosty reviews are well known. Less well known is the effect this quarrel had on Kant's ideas of race. Herder had rejected the concept of race as 'ignoble', inappropriate to humanity.[18] Human history unfolded in harmony with nature, he felt, but needed to be understood in specifically human terms, in terms of culture. Kant retorted that it was Herder's view that sold short the as yet unrealized potential of human existence for true freedom and reason.

'Determination of the Concept of a Human Race' was the second of three anti-Herderian essays Kant published in 1784, 1785 and 1786 in the *Berlinische Monatsschrift*, a central organ of the *Aufklärung*. The first, 'Idee zu einer allgemeinen Geschichte in weltbürgerlicher Absicht' ('Idea for a Universal History with Cosmopolitan Intent'), had offered Kant's view on what a truly human history would have to look like. It did not concern itself with actual history at all. On available evidence, Kant reasoned, human history—a history of human beings achieving their 'end'—had yet to take place. Since everything else in nature achieved its end, however, one could hope that humanity's 'seeds and predispositions' (*Keime* and *Anlagen*) for reason would unfold and achieve their end too (8:18). But nature had willed that man 'should produce entirely by his own initiative everything which goes beyond the mechanical ordering of his animal existence, and that he should not partake of any other happiness or perfection than that which he has procured for himself without instinct and by his own reason' (8:19). Somehow nature—still the wise breeder—was nevertheless needed to push man through 'antagonism' (8:20) out of the 'arcadian, pastoral experience of perfect concord, self-sufficiency and mutual love' in which he might otherwise stagnate (8:21). This essay opened up a new kind of historical enquiry, which looked beyond the surface of events to see the underlying processes and clues that humanity might yet make good as a species, but also insisted that a history of freedom was a necessarily paradoxical project (cf. 8:41).

This could not be more different from Herder, whose *Ideas* (like Kant's pre-critical geography) worked from empirical knowledge of nature and travel reports. Herder's was a cosmos in which everything reflected and influenced

---

17 See John H. Zammito, *The Genesis of Kant's 'Critique of Judgment'* (Chicago: University of Chicago Press 1992) and John H. Zammito, *Kant, Herder, and the Birth of Anthropology* (Chicago: University of Chicago Press 2002).

18 Johann Gottfried Herder, *Ideen zur Philosophie der Geschichte der Menschheit*, 4.5, in Johann Gottfried Herder, *Sämmtliche Werke*, ed. Bernhard Suphan, 33 vols (Berlin: Weidmann 1887–1913), xiii.151.

everything else; the best method for understanding it was 'analogical', a kind of *Naturbeschreibung* on speed. Inspired rhapsody seemed the likeliest way to discern the significant features of human nature figured analogically throughout nature. Man achieved his end everywhere in cultures developed in harmony with a nature articulated in a spectrum of microclimates. Herder reveled in the thought of ever new forms emerging, filling out the continuum of possibilities, and thought any effort to set a limit to this variety pernicious.

> There are neither four nor five races, nor are there exclusive varieties on earth. The colors run into one another; the cultures serve the genetic character; and overall and in the end everything is only a shade of one and the same great portrait that extends across all the spaces and times of the earth.[19]

What was needful was not a 'systematic history of nature' but a 'physical-geographical history of humanity'.[20]

In critical reviews of the first two volumes of *Ideas*, Kant sniffed at Herder's enthusiastic method. By claiming to find human potential achieved in every individual, era and culture, Herder proved incapable of distinguishing human from animal happiness and so missed the true destiny of man. 'Does the author really mean that, if the happy inhabitants of Tahiti, never visited by more civilized nations, were destined to live in their peaceful indolence for thousands of centuries, it would be possible to give a satisfactory answer to the question of why they should exist at all ...?' (8:65). Kant's asking the question reveals more than Herder's failing to consider it. His own answer to the question is not immediately obvious: did 'antagonism' fail to jostle people out of indolence in some climates, or does antagonism in some cases require the antagonism of peoples?

Kant thought the very poetic lengths to which Herder had to go confirmed that human history was shapeless and meaningless as it stood. He quoted Herder's hope that someone might 'gather together the faithful paintings which are scattered here and there of the different branches of our species, and would thereby lay the foundations of an *explicit natural science and physiognomy of the human species*' (8:59). This sounded a lot like what Kant endeavoured to do in his lectures, but he now asserted that travel narratives were inconclusive. It would be far more useful to the writing of a 'general natural history of mankind', he opined, if 'a historical and critical mind ... select[ed] from the boundless mass of ethnographic descriptions or travelogues, and from all the reports in these which can be presumed to

---

19 Herder, *Ideen zur Philosophie der Geschichte der Menschheit*, 7.1, in Herder, *Sämmtliche Werke*, xiii.258; English translation by Tom Nenon in Robert Bernasconi and Tommy L. Lott (eds), *The Idea of Race* (Indianapolis, IN: Hackett 2000), 26.
20 Ibid.

shed light on human nature, those in particular which are mutually contradictory' (8:61–2). What follows is a sort of antinomy of ethnography.

> As it is, one may prove, if one wishes, from numerous descriptions of various countries, that Americans, Tibetans, and other genuine Mongolian peoples are beardless—but also, if one prefers, that they are naturally bearded and merely pluck their hair out. Or one may prove that Americans and Negroes are races which have sunk below the level of other members of the species in terms of intellectual abilities—or, alternatively, on the evidence of no less plausible accounts, that they should be regarded as equal in natural ability to all the other inhabitants of the world. Thus, the philosopher is at liberty to choose whether he wishes to assume natural differences or to judge everything by the principle *tout comme chez nous*, with the result that all the systems he constructs on such unstable foundations must take on the appearance of ramshackle (*baufällige*) hypotheses (8:62).

In 'Die Antinomie der reinen Vernunft' ('Antinomy of Pure Reason') theoretical reason stalemates itself, freeing us to take the biddings of practical reason into account. Is the question of the unity of the human species something as impossible to confirm or disconfirm as freedom or God? Kant immediately turned to Herder's objections to the concept of race (the examples mentioned above all relate to claims about race) and clarified his own view. The explanation of what or how an understanding of race could tell concerning the intellectual capacities of Americans and Africans—and its kinship to the presentiments of practical reason—would however have to wait until 1788.

In 'Determination of the Concept of a Human Race', which appeared the same month as his second Herder review, Kant reiterated his theory of race in a newly philosophical way. 'One finds what one needs in experience only when one first knows what to look for' (8:91). Readers of his 1775/7 essay had focused on the implied historical claims but the 'hypothetical application of the principle' was secondary to the principle's potential to found a *Naturgeschichte* (8:91). Kant instead asked the theoretical question what if anything might qualify as a 'class difference' within a species. Race, defined as *'the class difference of animals of one and the same line of descent in so far as it is invariably heritable'* (8:100) and identifiable by the 'law of necessarily half-bred generation' (8:95), met the specifications. Race was not specific to humanity—the wolf, fox, jackal, hyena and domestic dog were 'races of dogs' (8:100n)—but in the human case it was made easy to visualize by an exclusive emphasis on colour. Skin colour had been dismissed as a marker of variety by Johann Friedrich Blumenbach, but Kant insisted skin was the most important organ of climatic adjustment (8:93, 95). One could read people's racial history in their faces, at least in the moderate climate of Europe.

The 1785 essay makes race seem like a matter only of classification, innocent of any interest in establishing the superiority or inferiority of different human populations. 'Even the character of the Whites', Kant closed the essay, 'is only the development of one of the original predispositions' (8:106).[21] Some scholars argue that Kant's theory of race is detachable from his views on particular races, and this essay, presenting the concept as the answer to a theoretical puzzle in classification, is their favourite. 'Necessity' appeared only in the case of those traits at one time indispensable to human survival (8:99), and one could see which traits those were by examining patterns of inheritance. But even the traits that are not transmitted exceptionlessly could come only from seeds in the species as a whole. Kant's experimental method for rendering the processes of human variety visible seems a picture of scientific rigour and detached objectivity. Kant's next essay filled in the background that these interpretations, ignorant of the project of physical geography, overlook.

'On the Use of Teleological Principles in Philosophy' (1788) was provoked by an attack on Kant's race theory by Georg Forster, a celebrated young ethnographer (he'd visited the Tahitians with Captain Cook) and admirer of Herder.[22] Forster accused Kant of ignoring empirical data to make way for unacknowledged theological commitments. He appears to have known little of Kant's other work besides the tongue-in-cheek 'Conjectural Beginning of Human History' (the third of the anti-Herderian essays in the *Berlinische Monatsschrift*) in which Kant had suggested that a practical-reason-informed idea of human beginnings could make as much sense of the text of Genesis as Herder had, if not more. To Forster, both essays arrived swiftly at a monogenesis he thought was disconfirmed by empirical experience. Africans seemed to him to belong to a different human 'family' or 'species'.[23] The scientific as well as the Christian thing was to acknowledge this. Had 'the thought that Blacks are our brothers anywhere even once led a slaver to put down his whip'?[24] Far better to think that God, who fills out the whole chain of being, had created Africans as the highest task for Whites. Cultivating the capacities of Africans might be the role of Whites in creation, developing latent capacities of their own too.[25]

---

21 Even in this essay it is only the non-white races whose colour is explained however. Kant's account of blackness as an effect of iron precipitation implies that people started as white.

22 Georg Forster, 'Noch etwas über die Menschenrassen' and 'Beschluß der im vorigen Monat angefangenen Abhandlung des Herrn G. R. Forsters über die Menschen-Rassen', *Teutsche Merkur*, October 1786, 57–86 and November 1786, 150–66, respectively. In 'Noch etwas über die Menschenrassen', Forster praises Herder for articulating the 'noble thought that a common structure underlies all diversity' (77–8).

23 Forster, 'Noch etwas über die Menschenrassen', 71 and 'Beschluß der im vorigen Monat angefangenen Abhandlung', 165–6.

24 Forster, 'Beschluß der im vorigen Monat angefangenen Abhandlung', 163.

25 Ibid., 165.

The 1788 essay is the richest and strangest of Kant's essays on race. In response to the double attack of Herder and Forster, Kant revealed both the philosophical ambition of his concept of race and its abiding relationship to his derogatory views of non-Whites. The essay argued that teleological principles were sometimes indispensable both in metaphysics (defined as concerning the world and God) and physics (which only concerned the world). In the former case, the idea of the highest good derived from 'pure practical reason' alone allowed us to speak of God (8:159). In the latter, the relationship with 'theoretical' knowledge was more complicated. One can't know a priori that there are elements of nature that demand teleological understanding. However, the situation offered a 'similar permission, indeed need, to proceed from a teleological principle where theory abandons us' (8:159). The only thing more stunning than the parallel between the ideas of God and of 'race, as *radical* peculiarity' (8:163), is the suggestion that race might offer experimental confirmation of the critical philosophy as a whole.

The issue was the same as before: putatively exceptionless half-breed generation. Systems of nature like Linnaeus's hadn't noticed race, but the '*concept* which this expression designates is nevertheless well established in the reason of every observer of nature', even should it never be found in nature (8:163)! The spread of peoples all over the earth was no longer the key. Instead, race was an 'idea of the way reason might unite the greatest diversity in generation with the greatest unity of descent' (8:164) given nature's concern that 'all the multiplicity implicit in a species' *Keime* should unfold' (8:167). For Kant this claim about nature is really a claim about what we are entitled to assert about nature in a regulative way; its warrant comes not from empirical experience (recall the antinomy of ethnography) but from practical reason.

As Kant explained the teleology, however, race shared the spotlight with 'variety'. Already in 1775, 'variety' was defined as *lacking* the necessity characteristic of race, but here the very lack emerged as purposive. 'The variety among people of the same race was in all probability laid just as purposively in the original genus to develop the greatest multiplicity to the end of infinitely different purposes, as race difference was to achieve fewer but more essential purposes' (8:166). Race differences, which must have unfolded in ancient times, would give rise to no new forms, but variety revealed a nature inexhaustible in producing 'new characters (external as well as internal)' (8:166). 'Variety' was specifically human. In animals all traits were transmitted exceptionlessly, as they 'have value only as means', and so must have predispositions in place for various human uses (8:168).

As Kant's students would already have known, race also affected 'external as well as internal characters'. Africans and (East) Indians had no more 'drive to activity' than was required by the climate in which they were at home (8:174, 174n). This was a standard argument, shared by climate theorists and Kames. Kant's *Keim* theory alone made the loss of 'drive to activity' permanent. Kant also revived his argument from the 1770s about the congenital weakness of Americans. His view alone was able to explain—without faulting providence—'why this race is too weak for heavy labour ... incapable of all cultivation, for all the example and encouragement nearby', and so 'stands far below the negro, who occupies the lowest step of all others which we have called racial differences' (8:176). These views, mainstays of Kant's lectures, seem extraneous to the argument only if we accept that race can be a mere philosophical puzzle.

Kant had kept the promise made in his reviews of Herder's *Ideas*. His 'natural history' informed by a practical-reason-inspired concept of race had shown that there were permanent differences between races, including permanent inferiority for all races but the Whites, the only ones with the 'drive to activity' required to make themselves over in the image of freedom.[26] The place of the non-white races in history is uncertain but surely grim. The arrival of white colonists seemed the only hope for the Tahitians. Robert Bernasconi notes that Kant explicitly quotes from a pro-slavery pamphlet in this essay (8:174n), and detects an argument against race-mixing here.[27] As implied already in earlier essays, *Keime* and *Anlagen* were meant to mature together, not one at the expense of the others. Unluckily for the (non-white) races, nature—less stepmotherly than extravagant—spread their ancestors too quickly into distant climates and then isolated them there. Whites, nature's intended if only by default, have all seeds and predispositions at their disposal, and are now ready for transplantation to every climate.

It is in Kant's essays of the 1780s that race gets philosophical traction. We may think that the critical philosophy should have turned Kant's gaze away from empirical human differences, but he remained committed to geography and anthropology, and to race. In its new critical form derived from a priori understandings of human destiny proffered by practical reason, race could even serve as a test of the efficacy of an anthropology structured by the needs of reason. Indeed, empirical confirmation of race would show the critical project as a whole to be viable and indeed necessary. Allied with the philosophy of freedom and the idea of God, race was ready to assert metaphysical and world-historical significance.

What man can and should make of himself

The last chapter in Kant's race thinking presents a textbook case of the need for contextual work in the history of ideas. Kant wrote no further essays on

26 See Susan Shell, 'Kant on race', in Eigen and Larrimore (eds), *The German Invention of Race*, 55–72.

27 Robert Bernasconi, 'Kant as an unfamiliar source of racism', in Julie K. Ward and Tommy L. Lott (eds), *Philosophers on Race: Critical Essays* (Oxford: Blackwell 2002), 145–66.

the subject, and race was not mentioned where it might be expected in the *Critique of Teleological Judgment* (1790),[28] and when Kant described how nature had 'taken care that men can live in all regions of the world' in *Zum ewigen Frieden* (*Towards Perpetual Peace*, 1795) (8:363). The only discussion of race is a section in the 'Anthropological Characteristic' of *Anthropology from a Pragmatic Point of View* (1798), which is barely a page long and devoted mainly to discussing 'family kinds'. It has recently been argued that Kant, inspired by new cosmopolitan insights, dropped his race theory in this period.[29] In fact it was in the 1790s that Kant's view of race came into its own. Kant did not lose interest in race, let alone repent of this interest.

Kant wrote no more essays on the subject because he didn't have to. All three race essays were republished numerous times in collections of his works starting in 1793.[30] More importantly, they were cited and recommended by Blumenbach in the 1795 edition of *De generis humani varietate nativa* (*On the Natural Variety of Mankind*), who now accepted the centrality of skin colour.[31] In 1796 the young chemist Christoph Girtanner published *Über das kantische Prinzip für die Naturgeschichte* (*The Kantian Principle for Natural History*), a book-length synthesis of Kant's three essays together with some ideas from Blumenbach.[32] By 1797 Herder again saw the need to denounce race as inimical to a 'human' understanding of humanity.[33] And in 1799 Schelling integrated Kant's theory of race into *Naturphilosophie*.[34]

The section on race in *Anthropology* was abbreviated, but this is because race was the one part of his anthropology that Kant could assume his readers already knew. Indeed, Kant built on this familiarity in explaining what a 'pragmatic' understanding of diversity was more generally. Not knowing what to look for, scholars have not seen the structural and structuring part race plays in the work. Race was mentioned at the beginning and at the end of the *Anthropology*. Those few who notice the section on race wonder why it is there.[35] Surely race belongs not to 'pragmatic' anthropology but to

28 All of Kant's race theory except the word itself appears in §§66 and 80.

29 Kleingeld, 'Kant's second thoughts on race'.

30 The 1785 and 1788 essays were reprinted in Immanuel Kant, *Zerstreute Aufsätze* (Frankfurt and Leipzig 1793) and Immanuel Kant, *Kleine Schriften* (Neuwied 1793). Immanuel Kant, *Immanuel Kants frühere noch nicht gesammelte kleine Schriften* (Lintz 1795) reprinted the 1785 essay. All three essays were reprinted in Immanuel Kant, *Immanuel Kants sämmtliche kleine Schriften*, 3 vols (Königsberg and Leipzig 1797/8) and Immanuel Kant, *Immanuel Kants vermischte Schriften*, vol. 1 (Halle 1799).

31 Blumenbach, *The Anthropological Treatises*, 207.

32 Christoph Girtanner, *Über das kantische Prinzip für die Naturgeschichte* (Göttingen: Vandenhoek und Ruprecht 1796); reprinted as vol. 7 of Robert Bernasconi (ed.), *Concepts of Race in the Eighteenth Century*, 8 vols (Bristol: Thoemmes 2001).

33 Johann Gottfried Herder, *Briefe zur Beförderung der Humanität*, no. 161, in Herder, *Sämmtliche Werke*, xviii.246–9.

34 F. W. J. Schelling, *Erster Entwurf eines Systems der Naturphilosophie. Zum Behuf seiner Vorlesungen* (Jena and Leipzig: Christian Ernst Gabler 1799), 56.

35 See, e.g., Louden, *Kant's Impure Ethics*, 94.

'physiological' anthropology? Indeed, wasn't race covered in *Physical Geography* (9:311–18)? But that part of *Physical Geography* was based on pre-critical notes, and recently edited student notes confirm that the races were regularly discussed in Kant's anthropology lectures (25.2:843, 1187–8).

In the preface, Kant seemed to say as much: 'even knowledge of the races of human beings as products belonging to the play of nature is not yet counted as pragmatic knowledge of the world, but only as theoretical knowledge of the world' (7:120). Taken in isolation from the rest of the work, this seems to say that race has no place in pragmatic anthropology. But of course there *is* a section on race. The contrast Kant was making was not between anthropology and geography (with race relevant only in the latter), but between two kinds of anthropology, *both* of which have things to say about race. Kant's concern is race, but precisely *not* as a mere play of nature.[36] Scholars today don't see that interest in what Kant called 'race' had always been practical as well as theoretical, 'concerned with what man can and should make of himself' as much as 'what nature makes of man' (7:119).

Immediately before this reference to race Kant had prepared readers for the 'Anthropologische Didaktik' ('Anthropological Didactic'), the first part of *Anthropology*, by contrasting a merely 'physiological' knowledge of memory with a 'pragmatic' one that 'uses perceptions concerning what has been found to hinder or stimulate memory in order to enlarge it or make it agile, and ... requires knowledge of the human being for this' (7:119). The contrast between a merely physiological and a pragmatic knowledge of race was analogous, and suggested a breeder's knowledge of racial possibilities as the model for 'Anthropological Characteristic' as a whole. This should not be surprising. It had always been a point of *Charakteristik* to determine suitable matches and chart the destinies of the offspring of well-matched and ill-suited pairings. The chapter 'Vom Charakter des Geschlects' ('On the Character of Sex') ends with a whole section of just such 'pragmatic consequences' for marriage (7:308–9), and 'Vom Charakter des Volks' ('On the Character of the Nation') ends with the observation: 'that the mixture of tribes ... which gradually extinguishes their characters, is not beneficial to the human race—all so-called philanthropy notwithstanding' (7:320). Reproduction wasn't the only concern of the 'Anthropological Characteristic', but it made the importance of the project clear in the baldest terms.

Of course the 'Anthropological Characteristic' was 'pragmatic' in a different way than Kant's pre-critical physical geography and anthropology. In the *Observations*, the meaning and harmony of diversity were posited, though one could not yet make them out. Now the meaning of diversity was something human beings must make their own, transforming physiological knowledge of characters and their interactions into pragmatic knowledge by

---

36 Reinhard Brandt obscures this by erroneously asserting that races are *Spielarten*; Reinhard Brandt, *Kritischer Kommentar zu Kants Anthropologie in pragmatischer Hinsicht (1798)* (Hamburg: Meiner 1999), 119.

reference to the needs of practical reason. One could and should learn from the physiology of race to work with nature for the end of the highest good. Knowledge of temperament, gender, national character could and should be analogously functionalized for the good of the species.

The pragmatic upshot of physiological knowledge of race—one could call it human self-husbandry—was implicit in the *Anthropology*. 'Vom Charakter der Rasse' ('On the Character of Race') referred readers to Girtanner's *Kantian Principle for Natural History*, which is not a pragmatic work. To illuminate what the pragmatic upshot would be, Kant instead dilated on 'family kinds' in a manner reminiscent of the discussion of 'variety' in 1788.

> Instead of *assimilation* (*Verähnlichung*), which nature intended in the melting together of different races, she has here made a law of exactly the opposite: namely in a people of the same race (for example, the white race), instead of allowing the formation of their characters constantly and progressively to approach one another in likeness—where ultimately only one and the same portrait would result, as in prints taken from the same copperplate—rather to diversify to infinity the characters of the same tribe (*Stamm*) and even of the same family in mental and physical traits (8:166).

Mental and physical traits were once again linked, but it didn't seem to occur to Kant that the mixing of races might help achieve his infinity of characters. The determinism of race had its place in nature, but a pragmatic anthropology showed it to be a threat to the human future, closing down rather than opening up possibilities. 'Assimilation' of races was to be avoided not for 'natural' but for 'pragmatic' reasons.[37] The achievement of man's end was in his own hands.

'On the Character of Race' needs to be understood also in terms of the larger argument of which it is part. Following it was the section 'Vom Charakter der Gattung' ('On the Character of the Species'), something on which Kant insisted not much could be said in the absence of knowledge of *non-terrestrial* rational beings' with which to compare ourselves (7:321). But Kant nevertheless made several observations. He closed the section (and the 'Anthropological Characteristic' and the *Anthropology* as a whole) with a discussion entitled 'Schilderung des Charakters der Menschengattung' ('Main Features of the Description of the Character of the Human Species'), and here he described a way in which the human species could be seen as one member of a larger set of beings after all.

37 Kleingeld ('Kant's second thoughts', 591) interprets this passage as saying the opposite: '"*fusion*" of races is seen as at least part of Nature's design', but this identification of nature's aims with our own collapses the distinction between physiological and pragmatic anthropology.

If one now asks whether the human species (which, when one thinks of it as a species of rational *earthly beings* in comparison with rational beings on other planets, as a multitude of creatures arising from one demiurge, can also be called a race)—whether, I say, it is to be regarded as a good or a bad race, then I must confess that there is not much to boast about in it (7:331).

This extension of the concept of race was something new. (Note also the reference to good and bad races!) It might seem that Kant's theory of race should not have been available for this extension: a race is a historically emerged subgroup of a species with a common origin whose particularity was triggered by a particular climate. The populations of various planets did not share a common genetic origin or (for all one knew) produce fertile hybrids. And yet this analogy with race makes sense: the foundation of Kant's anthropology is still physical geography. We are *earthly* or *terrestrial* beings, affected one and all by the particularities of the earth.

Suggesting that we think of our species in terms of a *Keim* in 'rational beings' triggered by the particularities of our planet is a good way of emphasizing our dependence on the earth, and the difficulties our embodied existence sets for our lives as rational beings (finite, and so required to arrange for reproduction). It is also a challenge. Are there other *Keime* forever extinguished in us by the requirements of earthly life? Some, perhaps most, races are 'bad': what reasons have we to think we'll make good? This is a cosmopolitan moment but a bittersweet one. All human beings might be only one race of this species; even if not a 'real race' in the terrestrial scheme, Whites might turn out to be a race (or a 'bad race') after all in the cosmic scheme, unable to achieve their end. 'Pragmatic' use of knowledge of human diversity might make the difference here. Whites might yet redeem the terrestrial race. What this meant for other races of human beings was not clear. It could lay the groundwork for human solidarity across races (though not mixing), or for the white man's burden.

From theoretical to practical

Immanuel Kant was not singlehandedly responsible for the spread of the ideology of race, but his work giving scientific and philosophical cachet to this term with roots in the world of breeding was indispensable. Developed and elaborated as a response to worries about human prospects raised both by questions of human diversity and, later, by his critical understanding of human destiny in freedom, Kant's concept of race was never just a classificatory term in a physiological anthropology. We will not understand its continuing appeal if we accept the anachronistic idea that race was a 'theoretical' or 'scientific' issue rather than a 'practical' or 'pragmatic' one: it was and is both. We will better understand the abiding appeal of race if we see it in the context of the interconnections of geography, anthropology, philosophy of history and practical philosophy, and if we recognize the promise of 'whiteness' that attended it from the start: to escape from race just as autonomy does from nature.

Kant's theory of race changed significantly over the course of his career. Each iteration was more ambitious and, as empirical counter-evidence arose, more dangerously ideological. Race was first offered as proof that a scientific understanding of human experience in the context of our varied terrestrial existence was possible. The template for race was temperament, itself an uneasy theodicy of human diversity. From the first, Whites were described not as one race among others but as qualitatively different, distinguished from the others as balance is from imbalance. The question whether Whites were 'raced' in the operative sense would persist until Kant's last references to race in 1798.

Challenged by Herder and Forster in the 1780s, the critical Kant described a kind of antinomy of ethnography from which only a practical-reason-informed understanding of human destiny could offer a responsible way out: race became an a priori concept, its teleology evident independently of empirical data. In 1788 Kant likened the 'permission' practical reason granted for approaching human experience with race as a category to that it gives for faith in God, and made clear that the hierarchy of races he had been lecturing about for decades had not been forgotten or revised. But, while developed independently of evidence, race looked to be empirically confirmed, and in this way legitimized Kant's whole project.

In the 1790s Kant's theory of race came into its own, making important converts in physical anthropology and *Naturphilosophie*. Race provided the template for explaining the nature of a 'pragmatic' understanding of human diversity, and the need for it. 'What man can and should make of himself' involved a kind of self-husbandry of humanity; nature still has a hand, but humans must use knowledge of themselves as part of nature to make and keep themselves free. As rational beings shaped by the exigencies of life on earth, they must recognize the power of geography to trigger fatal imbalances in human potential, and hope that the least 'raced' of earth-lings—Whites—might yet attain their end.

It is beyond the scope of this essay to assess the possibly constitutive place of race in Kant's philosophical system, but we can say this much. Kant did not think you could responsibly do practical philosophy without physical geography and pragmatic anthropology, and wasn't trying to. We misread his ethics if we do not also read his accounts of human diversity and their implications for respecting the humanity in everyone, treating none as a means only. We misunderstand his philosophy of history and politics if we forget the potentially fatal imprint of the earth and its regions on human populations, first through climatic *Einartung* and later (and still) through reproduction. Kant thought one could not live out his practical philosophy without the kind of pragmatic knowledge of which his theory of race was the emblem and first fruit. We may not be able to uproot the ideology of race he helped legitimate without tracing its connections to practical reason and providing pragmatic as well as theoretical counter-knowledge.

A Haitian in Paris: Anténor Firmin as a philosopher against racism

ROBERT BERNASCONI

Imagine the scene. This is Paris. It is 17 July 1884 and Anténor Firmin, a black man newly arrived from Haiti, only thirty-three years old but already qualified as a lawyer, is elected to membership of the Société d'Anthropologie de Paris, the most important anthropological society anywhere in the world. He is not the first black member. Indeed, his fellow countryman Louis-Joseph Janvier is one of the three members of the Société that propose him for membership, as the rules of the society require.[1]

After a year he publishes a book of over 650 pages inspired by a need to intervene in the debates he hears at the meetings of the Société. The book,

---

1 Janvier had been elected in December 1882. Another Haitian, J. B. Dehoux, who had been director of the medical school in Port-au-Prince, was elected a member on 21 June 1883; *Bulletins de la Société d'Anthropologie de Paris*, 3rd Series, vol. 6, 1883, 599.

De l'égalité des races humaines,[2] is announced, as is the custom in the Société, on 1 October 1885, at the first meeting after the summer recess, but this seems to have been almost the only notice taken of it.[3] It was virtually ignored in Europe and in the United States until the publication in 2000 of an English translation.[4] In the preface Firmin apologizes for the signs of haste in the book, which are indeed clearly visible at various points.[5] However, it is obvious today that it is a major statement in favour of the equality of races. The book includes a rich account of the intellectual life of Haiti in the nineteenth century, but my focus here will not be on Firmin as a forerunner of pan-Africanism, negritude or postcolonial theory. Instead, I will concentrate on what he can tell us about the science of race at the end of the nineteenth century.[6]

Even academics who should know better tend to work today with a highly simplified picture of nineteenth-century racial essentialism. In consequence, there is a great danger that readers of Firmin today will misstate his contribution. Indeed, one sees this in some of the claims that are now being made on his behalf. I will also make a concerted effort to situate him in the context of the science of his day. Because Firmin was a vigorous and insightful, if largely unheard, opponent of many of his more illustrious contemporaries, a study of his books helps to clarify not only what eminent scientists thought at that time, but also indicates other

2 Anténor Firmin, *De l'égalité des races humaines* (Paris: Cotillon 1885), hereafter referred to as *ERH*.

3 *Bulletins de la Société d'Anthropologie de Paris*, 3rd Series, vol. 8, 1885, 599. Firmin may or may not have been present at the meeting. In any event he did not take the opportunity of which some authors availed themselves of introducing the work in detail. See also the review by L. Manouvrier in *Revue Philosophique de la France et de l'Étranger*, January 1886, 180–2. The review is discussed by Ghislaine Géloin in her informative introduction to Anténor Firmin, *De l'égalité des races humaines*, ed. Ghislaine Géloin (Paris: L'Harmattan 1993), xiin1.

4 Anténor Firmin, *The Equality of the Human Races*, trans. from the French by Asselin Charles (New York: Garland 2000), hereafter referred to as *EHR*. A photomechanical reprint of the original edition was published as the eighth volume of Robert Bernasconi (ed.), *Race and Anthropology*, 9 vols (Bristol: Thoemmes 1993). In the same year, the new French edition, published by L'Harmattan under the editorship of Ghislaine Géloin, appeared.

5 Some are obvious. A well-known passage from Kant's *Observations on the Beautiful and the Sublime* is attributed to the *Critique of Pure Reason* (*ERH* 471, *EHR* 325); a book by Bowdich is attributed to Bosman, who lived a century earlier (*ERH* 355n2, *EHR* 253n28) and so on. Unfortunately, matters are much worse in the English translation, which, so far as I can see, corrects none of Firmin's errors but introduces a number of new ones that went uncorrected when it was reprinted by the University of Illinois Press in 2002. However, the fact that the work is in translation at all is to be celebrated.

6 For Firmin as an early advocate of pan-Africanism, see Carolyn Fluehr-Zobban, 'Anténor Firmin: Haitian pioneer of anthropology', *American Anthropologist*, vol. 102, no. 3, 2000, 449–66.

options that were open to them; he makes explicit what they could have thought, but did not think, and so saves us from anachronism in our judgements of them.[7]

The French debate between monogenesis and polygenesis

What was the Société d'Anthropologie de Paris? It was founded in 1859, the year of Charles Darwin's *The Origin of Species*. Before long, Darwin would be a point of contention between the members of the Société. However, the circumstances surrounding the foundation of the Société had nothing to do with Darwin. The Société d'Anthropologie arose out of the growing resurgence of polygenesis, the theory that at least two human species were created separately. In May 1858 Paul Broca had presented to the Société de Biologie evidence that the offspring of a female rabbit and a male hare had been prolific over successive generations. He argued that this animal represented a challenge to Buffon's rule of species identification, according to which only animals of the same species could procreate. Broca also saw that this represented a challenge to monogenesis, understood as the theory that the human species had a single origin. For this reason, the founding president of the Société de Biologie, Pierre Rayer, persuaded Broca to withdraw his article from the publication of the proceedings of the Société and to agree not to present such ideas in the future.[8]

Nevertheless, Broca, who was only thirty-four at that time, could not be silenced. He immediately began publication of his views on heredity in the *Journal de la Physiologie*. He also organized a small gathering of polygenists. This was the start of the Société d'Anthropologie de Paris, which soon began to expand its numbers and intellectual orientation. Among those who accepted the invitation to join in the second year of its existence was Jean-Louis Armand de Quatrefages, the foremost monogenist in France at that time. The French debate between monogenesis and polygenesis was thus conducted within the confines of the Société itself, though the majority of its members were sympathetic to polygenesis.

The debate between monogenesis and polygenesis had been at the heart of the scientific discourse about race since Immanuel Kant had provided the first definition of 'race' in 1775 in reply to the polygenetic theories of

7 Consider the comment by Francis Schiller: 'we must not expect a Broca, a Lincoln, indeed any enlightened minds, to have believed in racial equality'; Francis Schiller, *Paul Broca* (Berkeley: University of California Press 1979), 137. Reading Firmin makes such easy excuses more difficult to sustain.

8 See Paul Broca, 'Introduction aux mémoires sur l'hybridité', in Paul Broca, *Mémoires d'anthropologie*, vol. 3 (Paris: Reinwald 1877), 321–5.

Voltaire and Henry Home, Lord Kames. Kant defined 'race' in terms of inheritable characteristics that derived equally from both parents. Although skin colour was the only clear example he ever gave of such a shared inheritance, he extended it to other features, including intelligence. He fastened on the term 'race' in an attempt to find a new way of defending monogenesis. His leading argument was simply that, because all varieties of human beings could interbreed, they satisfied Buffon's rule of species identification.[9]

However, Kant and all monogenists that came after him were left with the problem of having to explain the permanence of racial characteristics. Primarily, it was a question of why Whites did not become Blacks if they moved to sub-Saharan Africa and why Blacks did not turn into Whites in Northern Europe. As late as 1762, Buffon still believed that these transformations would occur, albeit over a number of generations.[10] Kant's solution, which later generations had difficulty accepting, involved positing the existence of four seeds or germs in the original human being, one of which was actualized to varying degrees at the expense of the others as a result of the climate and other environmental factors. However, in the late 1840s, monogenesis was threatened by a challenge more serious than its difficulty in explaining how permanent differences could arise from a common origin. The so-called American school of polygenesis, led by Josiah Nott, changed the terms of the debate by arguing that Buffon's rule of species identification applied even when sterility was only gradual, in the sense of emerging only after a number of generations. Indeed, Nott argued that, in the absence of sterility, a greater susceptibility to disease or a shorter life expectancy might also be evidence that two species had crossed.[11] When Broca wrote his essay on hybridity, he referred to Nott's early discussions of hybridity, as did other polygenists like Georges Pouchet.[12] However, as Firmin himself noted, Broca and other French anthropologists were drawn to polygenesis on account of

---

9 Immanuel Kant, 'Von den verschiedenen Racen der Menschen', in Immanuel Kant, *Werke* (Berlin: Walter de Gruyter 1968), vol. 2, 429–43; English translation as Immanuel Kant, 'Of the different human races', trans. from the German by Jon Mark Mikkelsen, in Robert Bernasconi and Tommy L. Lott (eds), *The Idea of Race* (Indianapolis, IN: Hackett 2000), 8–22. See also Robert Bernasconi, 'Who invented the concept of race?', in Robert Bernasconi (ed.), *Race* (Oxford: Blackwell 2001), 11–36.

10 Georges Louis Leclerc, comte de Buffon, *Histoire Naturelle* (Paris: Imprimerie royale 1762), 314.

11 For a selection of Josiah Nott's writings and other related documents, see Robert Bernasconi and Kristie Dotson (eds), *Race, Hybridity, and Miscegenation*, 3 vols (Bristol: Thoemmes 2005).

12 Paul Broca, *Recherches sur l'hybridité animale en général et sur l'hybridité humaine en particulier* (Paris: Claye 1860), 626–7; English translation in Paul Broca, *On the Phenomena of Hybridity in the Genus Homo*, trans. from the French by C. Carter Blake (London: Longman, Green, Longman and Roberts 1864), 33–4. Georges Pouchet, *De la pluralité des races humaines* (Paris: Baillière 1858), 138.

their anti-clericalism, whereas Nott and George Gliddon advocated it in an effort to support slavery.[13]

After Broca died in 1880, his former student Paul Topinard was elected to succeed him as Secretary-General of the Société d'Anthropologie. He was still the Secretary-General when in 1884 Firmin was elected to membership but, during 1886, he was ousted by Charles Letourneau, who had presided over the meeting at which Firmin had been elected. It was a victory of the scientific materialists over the positivists.[14] In that way, as in many others, Firmin, as a positivist himself, was swimming against the tide. The late nineteenth century saw an intensification of racism, motivated by the demands of imperialism and justified by social Darwinism. This no doubt helps to explain why Firmin's book was stillborn.

The *Bulletins de la Société d'Anthropologie* provides a record of the discussions that took place at the meetings of the Société, and on that basis it seems that Firmin never made an intervention of any kind until much later. This happened only after he returned to Paris in 1892, following the failure of his political ambitions in Haiti, including a brief period as Minister of Finance, Commerce and Foreign Relations in Florival Hyppolite's government. During meetings in April 1892 Firmin twice intervened to put into question the tendency to characterize certain races as irrevocably inferior without reference to environmental conditions.[15] Nevertheless, even in 1884, he was far from overawed by the famous scientists who attended these meetings. The book he decided to write soon after joining was critical to the point of outright hostility towards many of the luminaries of the Société d'Anthropologie. For example, he said of Broca, its founder and the teacher and sponsor of many of its current members, that 'the eminent professor, the great anthropologist, who spent all his life measuring crania and discoursing on the human types, was more often than not totally ignorant about what he was talking about with the self-assurance of an expert'.[16]

13 *ERH* 48–51, *EHR* 36–8. Firmin's observation is supported by scholars today. Claude Blanckaert, 'L'esclavage des Noirs et l'ethnographie américaine: le point de vue de Paul Broca en 1858', in Claude Blanckaert, Jean-Louis Fischer and Roselyne Rey (eds), *Nature, Histoire, Société: essais en homage à Jacques Roger* (Paris: Klincksieck 1995), 391–417; Luc Forest, 'De l'abolitionnisme à l'esclavagisme? Les implications des anthropologues dans le débat sur l'esclavage des Noirs aux États-Unis (1840–1870)', *Revue française d'histoire d'outre-mer*, vol. 85, no. 320, 1998, 85–102.
14 See Joy Harvey, 'Evolution transformed: positivists and materialists in the *Société d'Anthropologie de Paris* from Second Empire to Third Republic', in David Oldroyd and Ian Langhan (eds), *The Wider Domain of Evolutionary Thought* (Dordrecht: D. Reidel 1983), 289–310. Harvey identifies the scientific materialists in terms of their insistence on 'physical explanation in terms of matter imbued with force' (291), and she highlights their indebtedness to Carl Vogt, but more still needs to be done to clarify the differences between the two groups.
15 *Bulletins de la Société d'Anthropologie de Paris*, 4th Series, vol. 3, 1892, 236 and 329.
16 *ERH* 58, *EHR* 42 (translation modified).

In his book Firmin recalls a debate that took place during the meeting at which he was elected.[17] An examination of the record of this session offers some clues as to what led Firmin to write his book. De Quatrefages, by then, at seventy-four, the grand old man of French anthropology, discussed some observations Paul Lévy had made on the impact that the American environment had had on the European races. The report was more amateurish than scientific: it included such gems as the idea that the sweat of a pure Negro had a different smell from that of a creole.[18] Janvier, Firmin's compatriot and himself the author of a pamphlet with the title *L'égalité des races*,[19] responded at some length, arguing that to understand the creolization of the black race, one would do well to look to Haiti. His intervention can be understood as an attempt to make the point that one hardly needed to rely on reports of the testimony of Paul Lévy to find out about creolization in the Caribbean with Janvier and now Firmin present at the meetings. However, if that was Janvier's point, it seems that it was lost on his audience. Nevertheless, it may well have framed Firmin's reaction to the exchange that took place between André Sanson and de Quatrefages immediately after Janvier's intervention, and that he subsequently recalled in his book. Firmin remarked on how both men saw the question of species in terms of monogenesis and polygenesis: 'It is curious to see how passionate and vehement these usually calm men become whenever these issues are broached.'[20] De Quatrefages believed that Sanson was confusing race, a matter of hereditary descent, with species, a matter of origin. In response, Sanson rehearsed the familiar puzzle with which the polygenists loved to taunt the monogenists: a white person cannot become black, so how can the races all be said to have the same origin?[21]

Firmin the philosopher

To be sure, by 1884 many members of the Société would have considered the debate between monogenesis and polygenesis a dead issue. For example, Topinard had written in his *L'Anthropologie* in 1876 that the

---

17 *ERH* 47nl, *EHR* 84nl.
18 Armand de Quatrefages, 'Observations à propos d'un passage d'une lettre de Paul Lévy', *Bulletins de la Société d'Anthropologie de Paris*, 3rd Series, vol. 7, 1884, 580.
19 Louis-Joseph Janvier, *L'égalité des races* (Paris: G. Rougier 1884). Janvier's pamphlet, which was mainly a response to some remarks denying the equality of Blacks by Ernest Renan in *Dialogues philosophiques* (1871), appeared on 1 August 1883 in the journal *Revue de la jeune France* under the title 'M. Renan et l'égalité des races: Bretons et Nègres'.
20 *ERH* 47nl, *EHR* 84nl.
21 André Sanson, 'Discussion sur l'influence des milieux', *Bulletins de la Société d'anthropologie de Paris*, 3rd Series, vol. 7, 1884, 584–7.

debate no longer held any interest.[22] Darwinism had changed the intellectual context. Firmin seems to have been equally convinced that the debate between monogenesis and polygenesis was an irrelevance, but he suspected that the passions that it aroused were a consequence of the underlying agendas of each camp. So far as he was concerned, this passionate response was evidence that they were not true scientists. Firmin was particularly upset that de Quatrefages, in *L'Espèce humaine*, had quoted approvingly Thevenot's remark that 'The mulatto can do all that the white man can do; his intelligence is equal to ours', while nevertheless continuing to uphold the idea of the inequality of the races.[23] De Quatrefages was forced to argue that the mulatto inherits his or her intelligence from his or her white parent, while sharing equally in the physiological characteristics of both parents. Firmin suggested that the evidence pointed rather to the idea that race-mixing concerned physiological characteristics alone and that the source of intelligence of the child was unpredictable.[24]

In this regard, Firmin clearly saw himself upholding true positivism against both the scientific materialists and the false representatives of positivism in the Société, like Topinard. Firmin presented himself as a positivist in anthropology.[25] He even subtitled his book *Anthropologie positive* (Positivist Anthropology). But it would be a mistake to think that this made him an upholder of scientific facts at the expense of philosophy. In the opening chapter of his book Firmin made clear his belief in the significance of philosophy. According to him, changes in scientific theories that eventually transform prevailing currents of thought are brought about by philosophical innovation.[26] This led him to begin his account of anthropology by considering Kant, whom he clearly appreciated, and Hegel, whose works he regarded as somewhat confused but sometimes brilliant.[27] However, it is clear that Firmin's philosophical sympathies lay with the positivism of Auguste Comte,[28] which he understood as opposed to 'the metaphysical doctrines that have too long subjugated the human mind, from Plato to Hegel'.[29] Comtean positivism is not only explicitly visible in Firmin's endorsement of

22 Paul Topinard, *L'Anthropologie*, 2nd edn (Paris: Reinwald 1877), 546; English translation in Paul Topinard, *Anthropology*, trans. from the French by Robert Bartley (London: Chapman and Hall 1878), 561.

23 Armand de Quatrefages, *L'espèce humaines* (Paris: Germer Baillière 1877), 211; English translation in Armand de Quatrefages, *The Human Species* (New York: Appleton 1879), 283. Quoted in *ERH* 303–4, *EHR* 204.

24 *ERH* 308, *EHR* 207.

25 *ERH* ix, *EHR* liv.

26 *ERH* 14, *EHR* 9.

27 *ERH* 6, *EHR* 5.

28 *ERH* 248, *EHR* 166.

29 *ERH* 254, *EHR* 171.

the idea that 'the fetishistic stage is more conducive to the development of positivist philosophy than the theological stage',[30] but is also implicit in Firmin's frequent appeals to progress, perfectibility and humanity.

For Firmin positivism is not only a method, but also a philosophy. He understood Comtean positivism to culminate in 'a healthy philosophy [that] consists in following the laws of nature as we contribute intelligently to reinforcing the harmony of all elements, human beings and planets, on the immense expanse of our planet'. He continued: 'This need for harmony underlies the altruistic sentiments which make of humanity a concrete entity whose interdependent parts act, work, and progress toward a common destiny.'[31] Firmin was so persuaded by this broad positivism that he called the doctrine of the inequality of the races not only anti-scientific, but also anti-philosophical.[32] One can see that conviction at work in his response to Georges Pouchet's claim that scientists must set aside 'those infinitely honorable sentiments of equality and brotherhood which a noble heart must feel toward all human beings regardless of their origin and their color'.[33] Firmin simply dismissed Pouchet's statement on the grounds that it exhibited 'a regrettable absence of any philosophical thought'.[34] Indeed, Firmin rejected all theories that contradicted progress and justice.[35] So far as he was concerned, the harmony of science and progress was so firmly established by Comte that a theory that was not 'consistent with humanity's highest aspirations' could readily be rejected as false.[36]

Firmin's Gobineau

The title of Firmin's book might lead one to believe that it was written as a refutation of Gobineau's idea of a racial hierarchy, as set out in his *Essai sur l'inégalité des races humaines*, but Gobineau was not Firmin's primary target. This was because Gobineau was not as influential at that time as he would later become. It is true that at one point Firmin wondered whether 'anthropologists have found in Gobineau's fantastic notions and equivocal

---

30 *ERH* 504, *EHR* 343. See Auguste Comte, *Système de politique positive*, 4 vols (Paris: Carilian-Goeury 1851–4), IV.42–3 and 517–18; English translation in Auguste Comte, *System of Positive Polity*, trans. from the French by Richard Congreve, vol. 4 (London: Longmans 1877), 39–40 and 450–1.

31 *ERH* 248, *EHR* 167.

32 *ERH* 204, *EHR* 140.

33 Quoted in *ERH* 65, *EHR* 146. I have not found this quotation in Pouchet, but he expresses similar sentiments in *De la pluralité des races humaines*, 203–4. However, it is noteworthy that, even after having liberated anthropology from all humanitarian tendencies, Pouchet insists that whatever is true is good.

34 *ERH* 65, *EHR* 46.

35 *ERH* 644, *EHR* 437–8.

36 *ERH* 444, *EHR* 438.

paradoxes such a bright light source that they take his conclusions for Gospel truth', but he had to admit that, if they did so, it was without actually saying so.[37] In fact, I have found little evidence of a deep commitment to Gobineau on the part of anthropologists of the time, although he was certainly read.[38] Gobineau's racial theories began to be genuinely popular at the end of the nineteenth century, although even then they were eclipsed by writers such as Houston Stewart Chamberlain.[39] Gobineau's importance was only fully established in the 1920s and 1930s. It would be a serious mistake to be convinced by Firmin to overestimate the significance of Gobineau's essay in the 1880s. Indeed, Gobineau, who died in 1882, had four years earlier been forced to give up his plan to publish an expanded edition of his work that took into account Darwin's theories, for lack of a willing publisher. Nevertheless, a virtually unchanged edition of the *Essai* appeared in France in 1884, the same year that Firmin began preparing his own book, and this was the edition Firmin used. Its publication had only been possible by a subvention from Bayreuth, where Richard Wagner's circle continued their master's idiosyncratic enthusiasm for Gobineau's works.[40] Firmin's focus on Gobineau was more an accident of timing than a reflection of the book's reputation among scientists.

Even so, it is still worth trying to be clear about Gobineau's argument. Although the title of Gobineau's book, *Essai sur l'inégalité des races humaines*, might lead one to suppose it was a book primarily rehearsing familiar claims concerning the hierarchy of the races, it was in fact a novel attempt to write a philosophy of history organized around the relatively new obsession with race-mixing as posing a biological threat to a people or nation. What was so distinctive about Gobineau's classic work was not his belief in the inequality of races, which was widespread, but his belief that civilization arose only through a process of racial intermixing that would eventually lead to the decline of humanity as a whole. According to Gobineau, although all civilizations derive from the 'white race', clear advantages for civilization

37 *ERH* 213, *EHR* 145. It should be noted that Gobineau is fully aware that his theories appear paradoxical. Joseph Arthur, comte de Gobineau, *Essai sur l'inégalité des races humaines*, 4 vols (Paris: Firmin-Didot 1884), i.18; English translation in Joseph Arthur, comte de Gobineau, *The Inequality of Human Races*, trans. from the French by Adrian Collins (London: William Heinemann 1915), 19.

38 In 1859 Broca had already begun that portion of his long study of hybridity that dealt with a rejection of Gobineau. Paul Broca, 'Des phénomènes d'hybridité dans le genre humain', *Journal de la physiologie de l'homme et des animaux*, vol. 2, 1859, 601–2; English translation in Broca, *On the Phenomena of Hybridity in the Genus Homo*, 1.

39 Paul Fortier, 'Gobineau and German racism', *Comparative Literature*, vol. 19, no. 4, 1967, 344–6.

40 Since 1876, when Gobineau first made the acquaintance of Richard Wagner, the latter had shown an interest in his racial theories and, by the early 1880s, essays by and about Gobineau appeared in the *Bayreuther Blätter*. Michael D. Biddiss, *Father of Racist Ideology: The Social and Political Thought of Count Gobineau* (London: Weidenfeld and Nicolson 1970), 246–7 and 255–6.

came from mixing with other races. Thus artistic genius arises only from the mixing of Whites and Blacks.[41] This is a very different theory from that of the French anthropologists who were Firmin's intended audience and main target. It also shows that Firmin was only telling half the story when he attributed to Gobineau the thesis that 'the human races degenerate through certain [racial] crossings'.[42]

Royer's Darwin

Whereas Gobineau would not become a central reference point in French discussions of race until the twentieth century, there is no doubt that Darwin's theory of evolution was just that, particularly as the result of speculation about the application of this theory to the human races. This debate had begun almost as soon as *The Origin of Species* was published in 1859. The book's full title—*On the Origin of Species by Means of Natural Selection, or the Preservation of Favored Races in the Struggle for Life*—already suggested its application to human races. Darwin did not address these issues specifically until the publication of *The Descent of Man* in 1871, but Firmin dismissed the latter book in a couple of sentences on the grounds that the focus there fell more on developing a theory of sexual selection than on an in-depth ethnological study.[43] He was more interested in the speculation of Darwin's contemporaries as to the application of his theories to the human races. Even though Darwin had decided to omit any such discussion from the work, his readers wasted no time in trying to work out its implications. In Britain, Alfred Russel Wallace and Thomas Henry Huxley were the most prominent among those who took up the topic; in Germany, Ernst Haeckel did so; and in France, Darwin's first translator, Clémence Royer, already prefaced her translation of *The Origin of Species* with a long introduction, part of which addressed the possible application of Darwinism to racial questions.

The growing reputation of Darwin in France and Clémence Royer's role as the translator and main spokesperson of Darwinism meant that Firmin had no choice but to confront her work. Just as Huxley was Darwin's bulldog in England, Royer was Darwin's bulldog in France. Nevertheless, Darwin had complained about her successive translations of the various editions of *The Origin of Species*, and particularly the prefaces and notes that she added.

41 Gobineau, *Essai sur l'inégalité des races humaines*, I.217–23; English translation in Gobineau, *The Inequality of Human Races*, 208–11.
42 *ERH* 303, *EHR* 204 (translation modified).
43 *ERH* 398, *EHR* 270. Firmin was not saying that Darwin was not interested in the question of the philosophical study of the development of the human races. Indeed, he quoted a sentence from *The Origin of Species* to show that, from the time of the first publication of the book, Darwin was indeed interested in the issue. Unfortunately, the sentence he chose was first introduced only in the sixth edition in 1872.

Darwin's dissatisfaction might not have been common knowledge, but there was no mistaking the fact that he arranged for a new translation to appear in 1873. Firmin was not alone in preferring the old edition.[44] Even though Firmin was faced with a distinguished author who had come to markedly different conclusions about racial equality and race-mixing from his own, he recognized that they both drew on Darwin and Comtean positivism.[45] That was why Royer was a necessary as well as a convenient target for Firmin.

Royer became a member of the Société d'Anthropologie de Paris in 1870. Although her election was controversial, both because she was a woman and someone strongly identified with Darwin's theories, she had the support of de Quatrefages, the Société's strongest critic of Darwinism.[46] However, the *Bulletins de la Societé* show that she was an extraordinarily active member. Indeed, in December 1885 she was elected an honorary member, making her only the seventh person to be recognized in this way.[47] This was a singular honour, especially given the fact that she had a record of distorting the Société's positions and being openly critical of the Société in general.[48]

In her introduction to the French translation of Darwin's *The Origin of Species*, Royer presented it as a work dedicated to the idea of racial inequality. She believed that Darwin's theory of natural selection left no doubt that the superior races would progressively supplant the inferior races. The idea of the equality of human beings was to her a dangerous, impossible idea.[49] The passage in which Royer made these claims was quoted at length by Firmin and, given that they ran entirely counter to the thesis of his book, it is no surprise to find that he directed some of his usual invective towards her.

Nevertheless, the precise character of the tirade is extraordinary. Here are some extracts:

> Clémence Royer is a scholar and a scientist, but she is a woman. There are problems of such complexity that they can be properly studied only by men, for only men, because of their education and their temperament as males, can see

---

44 Linda Clark, *Social Darwinism in France* (University: University of Alabama Press 1984), 15–16. Joy Harvey, *'Almost a Man of Genius': Clémence Royer, Feminism, and Nineteenth-century Science* (New Brunswick, NJ: Rutgers University Press 1997), 100–1.

45 She may not have been a self-confessed follower of Auguste Comte, but her thinking at various points owes a great deal to his method and to his formulations.

46 Harvey, *'Almost a Man of Genius'*, 105.

47 *Bulletins de la Société d'Anthropologie de Paris*, 3rd Series, vol. 6, 1883, xvii and 702.

48 Harvey, *'Almost a Man of Genius'*, 79. See also Royer's comments quoted by Firmin (*ERH* 17, *EHR* 12) from *Congrès International des Sciences Ethnographiques tenu à Paris du 15 au 17 juillet 1878* (Paris: Imprimerie Nationale 1881), 438.

49 Clémence Royer, 'Préface de la première édition', in Charles Darwin, *De l'origine des espèces*, 3rd edn (Paris: Victor Masson 1870), lxix. Firmin quotes the 4th edn in *ERH* 399, *EHR* 271.

them from every angle. . . . Despite the high esteem in which I hold Darwin's translator, I cannot help but point out that she remains a woman.[50]

The depth of these misogynic sentiments is remarkable. Even if Firmin had been persuaded by the scientific discourse about the inequality of women that he must surely have encountered, one might have expected him to grant that Royer was an exception, just as scientific proponents of racial inequality were often willing to acknowledge exceptions, which might well have been how Firmin was regarded within the Société d'Anthropologie de Paris. One is therefore left wondering whether Firmin and the outspoken Royer had not had words with each other at one point or another. Even so, it is still hard to understand why Firmin devoted so much of his criticism of her not to her main book, nor to her introduction to Darwin's *The Origin of Species*, but to some improvised remarks about race-mixing she made at the Congrès International des Sciences Ethnographiques in 1878.[51] It was not because these remarks were any more controversial than her considered writings. Had Firmin cited Royer's book he could have addressed her claim that race-mixing between inferior and superior races was immoral.[52]

Nevertheless, it has to be admitted that there is nothing in Darwin's text to support Firmin's claim that Darwin's theory of natural selection authorized a belief in the equality of races. On a couple of occasions Firmin actually conceded this, so it seems that his goal was to subtract the more vicious aspects of social Darwinism from the theory of evolution. The European view of so-called inferior races was, according to Firmin, as follows: 'These races were thought then to be ignorant and stupid, and so they are still and will be until the day they disappear from the earth, as Darwin's law decrees they must.'[53] One can see those consequences clearly in a remarkable passage from Herbert Spencer that is quoted in part by Firmin:

> It is said that as the Hebrews thought themselves warranted in seizing the lands God promised to them, and in some cases exterminating the inhabitants, so we, to fulfill the 'manifest intention of Providence,' dispossess inferior races whenever we want their territories; it may be replied that we do not kill any more than seems needful, and tolerate the existence of those who submit.[54]

---

50 *ERH* 400, *EHR* 271.
51 *ERH* 305, *EHR* 205.
52 Clémence Royer, *Origine de l'homme et des sociétés* (Paris: Guillaumin and Masson 1870), 532.
53 *ERH* 395, *EHR* 267.
54 Herbert Spencer, *The Data of Ethics* (New York: D. Appleton 1879), 240. Quoted by Firmin in *ERH* 571–2, *EHR* 385 from the French translation, Herbert Spencer, *Les Bases de la morale évolutionniste* (Paris: Germer Ballière 1880), 206.

Were it not for these two passages, it might be tempting to suppose that Firmin did not recognize the vicious role of natural selection in Darwinian accounts of racial progress.

Ideas of evolution

Firmin's account of Darwin's theory highlighted climate and environment as the primary causes of evolution at the expense of natural selection. Firmin's neglect of natural selection is apparent when he writes that Darwin's theory showed that reference to environment and heredity is sufficient to explain 'the difference in development of each ethnic group in the relatively short historical evolution of the entire species'.[55] Perhaps he was not modifying Darwin's general presentation so much as observing that the brevity of the life of humanity as a whole would not need, nor perhaps even allow, reference to natural selection as the decisive factor, as it was in natural evolution in general. Firmin was interested in Darwin because he wanted to find a basis for asserting the influence of environment over both the physical features of the human races,[56] as well as their intellectual qualities,[57] in such a way that allowed for their equality.[58]

We saw earlier that monogenists were left with the question of why, given the apparent fixity or permanence of the races, the environmental forces that had led to the development of racial differences were not still operative: if they were still in effect it would seem that Whites in Africa might turn black and that an Englishman who emigrated to the United States might take on the morphological features of a Native American. But within the longer chronology of natural evolution, the idea that racial characteristics were continuing to change could not be discounted. The decisive point was that, if the races were still changing, one could not say definitively that one was naturally superior to another. Further changes could not be ruled out. This was the insight underlying Firmin's vision. It explains why he interpreted Darwin in terms of Lamarck's disavowal of the theory of the fixity of species.[59] This was a fairly widespread tendency at that time, but nobody used it to draw more radical conclusions for the theory of the equality of the races than did Firmin.

The impact of Firmin's application of natural evolution to the human races can be seen in his examination of the argument that the skulls of ancient Egyptians were significantly larger than those of Negroes of his

---

55 *ERH* 401, *EHR* 272.
56 *ERH* 411, *EHR* 278.
57 *ERH* 414, *EHR* 280.
58 *ERH* 403, *EHR* 273.
59 *ERH* 396, *EHR* 269.

own day and therefore evidence that they belonged to different races. One cannot overestimate the importance of this debate for the upholders of Negro inferiority, as they themselves were the first to point out. If the civilization of the ancient Egyptians was a Negro or, more broadly, a black civilization, then some of the more simplistic theories of racial hierarchy would collapse.[60] This explains why the debate over the racial identity of the ancient Egyptians was fought with such virulence.

In his chapter on Egypt, Firmin repeated his suspicions of craniometric studies. In particular he targeted Samuel Morton, who Firmin correctly identified as 'the first to transform into a scientific doctrine the mistaken opinion that the ancient populations of Egypt had belonged to the White race'.[61] However, Firmin also appealed to Darwinism in an effort to reconcile the results of those studies with the thesis that the ancient Egyptians were Negroes. Because the former were more civilized than uneducated Blacks in contemporary Africa, they could be expected to have had larger skulls and, as surviving representations showed, would be more handsome. This was a case of both material and moral 'regressive transformations'.[62] Firmin's argument about ancient Egypt was that that part of the Negro race that had created it had since declined and that this was reflected in their physical appearance. However, this story of decline did not compromise Firmin's belief in progress. He assumed that there was one single path for humanity to follow and that all the races were simply at different stages on the same trajectory.[63] Although he granted to the polygenists their belief that the human species arose in different parts of the world, they were wrong to use that as a basis for denying

60 'I must show that the Caucasian or white, and the Negro races were distinct at a very remote date, and *that the Egyptians were Caucasians*. Unless this point can be established the contest must be abandoned'; Josiah Nott, *Two Lectures on the Natural History of the Caucasian and Negro Races* (Mobile, AL: Dade and Thompson 1844), 8 (emphasis in original).

61 *ERH* 339, *EHR* 229. Firmin twice refers to Morton's *Crania Ethnica* but he almost certainly means *Crania Aegyptica* (Philadelphia: John Pennington 1844); see *ERH*, 25 and *EHR*, 229. See also Robert Bernasconi, 'Black skin, white skulls: the nineteenth-century debate over the racial identity of the ancient Egyptians', *Parallax*, vol. 43, no. 2, April 2007, 6–20.

62 *ERH* 429, *EHR* 288 (translation modified).

63 *ERH* 404–5, *EHR* 274. This might seem to be contradicted by Firmin's claim that 'for our species civilization does not evolve in a linear pattern' (*ERH* 580, *EHR* 390). But this is a mistranslation, perhaps inspired by a desire to make Firmin fit a multicultural agenda. In fact, Firmin is merely stating that the work of civilizing the human species is continuous: 'Ils sont appelés à savoir qu'il n'ya pas de solution de continuité dans l'oeuvre de la civilisation de notre espèce.' This error in translation is perhaps what encourages Gerarde Magloire-Danton to say that Firmin's evolutionary perspective is 'not rigidly linear'. She is also misled when she says, in support of her interpretation, that 'most evolutionists' disregard 'historical and sociological discontinuities'; Gerarde Magloire-Danton, 'Anténor Firmin and Jean Price-Mars: revolution, memory, humanism', *Small Axe*, vol. 9, no. 2, 2005, 160. See, for example, Royer, *Origine de l'homme et des sociétés*, 274.

the unity of the human species.[64] They believed that all races were not endowed with the same evolutionary potential as the other neighbouring groups,[65] but they lacked an explanation of why this might be the case.

Firmin's idea of human evolution was that each racial group developed its potential only under the appropriate circumstances. He picked up on the fact that the monogenists believed that, although the races consisted of unchangeable types, they could undergo some modification under the influence of civilization.[66] Had he had direct acquaintance with the work of James Cowles Prichard, the foremost race theorist of the first half of the nineteenth century, he would have had a powerful precedent for his ideas. Already in 1813, Prichard had argued that civilization transformed both the physical features and the intellectual features of a race. It was on this basis that Prichard defended the view, unusual for its time, that it was probable that 'the fairest races of white people in Europe, are descended from, or have an affinity with Negroes'.[67] Firmin did know Herbert Spencer's *Essais sur le progrès* and he would have read there that, during the course of civilization, there are also changes in appearance.[68] He also appealed to the fact that the polygenist Broca, although initially an opponent of the idea that racial types change as an effect of civilization, had subsequently come round to it.[69] Climate and environment were, for Firmin, neither the only nor the decisive influence. For example, skin colour was a function of climate and living environment, but the shape of the face was a function of the degree or level of civilization.[70] This meant that cranial measurements of the kind employed by Broca did not identify the different races but instead indicated the stage that they had reached on the path of human progress.[71]

64 *ERH* 123, *EHR* 82.
65 *ERH* 408, *EHR* 277.
66 *ERH* 420, *EHR* 283.
67 James Cowles Prichard, *Researches into the Physical History of Man* (London: John and Arthur Arch 1813), 239. Not surprisingly, Prichard's views on the effects of civilization were challenged by Josiah Nott: 'History affords no evidence that cultivation, or any known causes but physical amalgamation, can alter a primitive conformation in the slightest degree'; J. C. Nott, 'Hybridity of animals, viewed in connection with the natural history of mankind', in J. C. Nott and George Gliddon (eds), *Types of Mankind* (Philadelphia: Lippincott, Grambo 1854), 404.
68 Herbert Spencer, 'Personal beauty', in Herbert Spencer, *Essays: Scientific, Political, and Speculative* (London: Longman 1858), 417–24; French translation in Herbert Spencer, 'La Beauté dans la personne humaine', in Herbert Spencer, *Essais de morale de science et d'esthétique. I. Essais sur le progrès*, trans. from the English by M. A. Burdeau (Paris: Germer Baillière 1877), 263–72.
69 *ERH* 420–1, *EHR* 283–4. Firmin cites 'Les selections', Broca's long review of French translations of Darwin's *The Descent of Man* and Alfred Russel Wallace's *Contributions to the Theory of Natural Selection*, which was reprinted in Broca, *Mémoires d'anthropologie*, 244–5.
70 *ERH* 168, *EHR* 115.
71 *ERH* 407–8, *EHR* 276.

Firmin appealed to the theories of evolution and sexual selection formulated by Spencer and Darwin to support his claim that there was a constant correlation between intellectual development and physical beauty.[72] However, at this point in the argument, Firmin's adoption of Comte's belief in progress was decisive: civilization leads men and women to 'become equal and achieve the same qualities'.[73] This applied to beauty of form,[74] as well as to intellectual qualities. Firmin thus insisted on the perfectibility of the whole human species,[75] which was the point that he emphasized in the book when he returned to it twenty years later.[76] This 'unity of plan'[77] directly echoes Comte's belief that the 'entire harmony of the Great Being' would 'call out into intimate cooperation with each other the three great races', the Black (Affective), White (Speculative) and Yellow (Active).[78]

Royer had written at the end of her preface to *The Origin of Species*: 'For me, my choice is made: I believe in progress.'[79] Firmin scoffed at these lines as confirmation that 'women have a natural tendency to embrace current ideas and to perpetuate accepted notions'.[80] However, his real objection must have been that she did not recognize that progress meant full equality for all. Nevertheless, he gave to 'equality' a special meaning. By 'equality' Firmin did not understand moral or legal equality, let alone actual physical or intellectual equality. He meant equal potential. Here is his own explanation of what he meant by the equality of the races: 'they are all capable of rising to the most noble virtues, of reaching the highest intellectual development; they are equally capable of falling into a state of total degeneration.'[81] That Firmin expressed his belief in the equality of races as a belief in human equality alongside his sexist characterizations of Royer as a woman is unfortunately one more instance of a philosopher being unable to put consistency above prejudice.

---

72 *ERH* 287–8, *EHR* 193.
73 *ERH* 291, *EHR* 195.
74 *ERH* 282, *EHR* 190.
75 *ERH* 411, *EHR* 278.
76 Anténor Firmin, *M. Roosevelt Président des États-Unis et la République d'Haïti* (Paris: F. Pichon and Durand-Auzias 1905), 231.
77 *ERH* 116, *EHR* 78.
78 Comte, *Système de politique positive*, ii.462; English translation in Auguste Comte, *System of Positive Polity*, trans. from the French by Richard Congreve, vol. 2 (London: Longmans 1875), 378.
79 Royer, 'Préface de la première édition', lxxi.
80 *ERH* 400, *EHR* 271.
81 *ERH* 462, *EHR* 450.

The influence of Comte

It was this Comtean belief in progress towards human equality that led Firmin to his denial of the dominant views of race in his time. At the beginning of a long chapter on the classification of the races Firmin summarized the definition of 'race' found in zoology and botany: races are 'the varieties of a given species when these varieties have been fixed through reproduction, with particularities which are at first imprecise or idiosyncratic, but which later become constant and transmissible through heredity without violating the general laws of the species.'[82] Firmin challenged that conception, and he insisted that the science of anthropology as practised by the French school would be utterly ruined on the day that it was proved that the human races had no essentially fixed characteristics other than colour, which is a complex result of climate, food and inheritance.[83] This led Firmin to claim in his conclusion: 'There will be no question of race, for the word implies a biological and natural fatality which has no correlation with the degree of ability observable among the different human communities spread around the globe.'[84] Firmin wanted to replace the idea of racial hierarchy with a distinction between superior or civilized and inferior or savage peoples. He had no doubt that there would always be advanced and backward nations and that each nation's level of sociological development could be measured against 'a certain ideal of the civilized state'.[85] Such were the limits of progress and perfectibility. But he insisted: 'Race has nothing to do with it.'[86] Firmin's insistence that race was not as important as widely thought, and his conviction that it would become less so, can also be found already in Comte, who wrote that 'the Progress of mankind in the mass, is gradually undermining the consequences of Race differences'.[87] Firmin was thus entirely justified in identifying his anthropology as philosophically positivist in Comte's sense, but the detailed arguments he brought to bear were for the most part uniquely his own.

On one highly significant point Firmin diverged from Comte. Comte gave the leadership of humanity to Whites and he believed that the study of history should limit itself to their contribution. He was especially critical of the attention given to India and China by historians.[88] By contrast, Firmin took a broader view of history: 'Nations and races interact in the stage of history, exit and return in different roles. In the larger scheme of human

82 *ERH* 126, *EHR* 87.
83 *ERH* 282, *EHR* 190.
84 *ERH* 660–1, *EHR* 449.
85 *ERH* 660, *EHR* 449.
86 *ERH* 424, *EHR* 285.
87 Comte, *Système de politique de positive*, ii.461; English translation in Comte, *System of Positive Polity*, vol. 2, 377.
88 Auguste Comte, *Cours de philosophie positive*, vol. 5 (Paris: Bachelier 1841), 4ff. Quoted in Léon Poliakov, *The Aryan Myth* (New York: Barnes and Noble 1974), 223 and 361.

destiny, none of these roles is insignificant. Equally imbued with dignity, each actor takes a turn at the main role'.[89] This also brought him into conflict with Hegel's racial view of history in his *Vorlesungen über die Philosophie der Weltgeschichte*, even if one can still hear certain echoes of Hegel's conviction that different peoples take the central role at different times. Firmin's expansion of the *dramatis personae* of history so as to include the black race, which Hegel had explicitly excluded, would subsequently be echoed by W. E. B. Du Bois in his 'The Conservation of Races'.[90] Like Du Bois, Firmin posited at the end of this process a transformation: 'So they will continue to be until the day when the actors in the stage can comfortably exchange roles, and support and complement one another, effortlessly and without friction, in the larger enterprise which is to carry the intellectual torch ...'[91] Firmin even asserted a 'right to partake in humanity's common patrimony, that is, to being elevated and to progress'.[92] He believed that backward peoples needed contact with more advanced peoples to progress and that their progress had nothing to do with ethnic characteristics.[93] However, unlike Du Bois, who felt the force of Herder's idea that all cultures contribute to humanity, Firmin took up the idea of 'civilization' as 'common destiny'. For Firmin, 'civilization' was 'the highest level of physical, moral, and intellectual achievement of the species'.[94]

In the end, Firmin believed that all races were equal except for the black race, which was more equal than others insofar as it was more resistant to depression.[95] He also believed that, because the Negro race had suffered so much, it was more prepared to understand and exercise justice. Its generosity would be the main contribution of the black race to progress in striking contrast with the indifferent and heartless races that had arisen in Europe.[96]

Let me close by returning to Firmin's entry into that room in Paris on 11 July 1884 where the meeting of the Société d'Anthropologie de Paris was being held. It seems that Firmin at one and the same time recognized the emptiness and bias of the claims of its most prominent members and decided to confront them on their own terms by studying their works in what must have been a frenzy of activity on his part. Nevertheless, the tone

---

89 *ERH* 653, *EHR* 445.
90 For example, G. W. F. Hegel, *Vorlesungen über die Philosophie der Weltgeschichte. I. Die Vernunft in der Geschichte* (Hamburg: Felix Meiner 1980), 65; English translation in G. W. F. Hegel, *Lectures on the Philosophy of World History* (Cambridge: Cambridge University Press 1975), 56. W. E. B. Du Bois, 'The conservation of races', in W. E. B. Du Bois, *Writings*, ed. Nathan Huggins (New York: Library of America 1986), 819–20.
91 *ERH* 653, *EHR* 445.
92 *ERH* 425, *EHR* 286 (translation modified).
93 *ERH* 437–8, *EHR* 296.
94 *ERH* 124, *EHR* 83.
95 *ERH* 559, *EHR* 377.
96 *ERH* 654–5, *ERH* 446.

he adopted suggests that his aim was not to persuade them to change their minds. It is as if in his eyes they were less a jury to be persuaded than criminals to be convicted. One can juxtapose this scene with another that took place in the same room on 21 April 1892. Firmin had just intervened to point out to a speaker that black Africans lived under difficult conditions and so were largely unable to show their great qualities, at which point Professor Bordier, president of the Société intervened to ask him if he had any white ancestors. The implication of the question was clear: he was being asked whether his intelligence could be explained only in this way. Certainly Firmin answered Bordier as if this was what he was asking, and it showed how in an instant Firmin's colleagues could switch from considering him a participant in their debates to treating him as an object of anthropological study.[97]

But what is Firmin's book to us today? I have shown that Firmin's interpretations of Gobineau and Darwin are sufficiently idiosyncratic to suggest that he did not primarily consider himself to be debating these figures. He used Darwin selectively and strategically in an effort to combat theories of racial inequality and Gobineau was a convenient and relatively easy target. However, what my reading of Firmin also shows is that, whereas it may be a relatively easy task to explore the fallacies of the advocates of racial inequality, it is no easy matter to construct a philosophy of racial equality. As one of only a few such attempts, his theories remain instructive for us, particularly because we must continue to do the same, although without the assistance of a belief in human progress of the kind on which Firmin relied so heavily.

97 *Bulletins de la Société d'Anthropologie de Paris*, 4th Series, vol. 3, April 1892, 329. Carolyn Fluehr-Lobban repeats this story but, according to her, it was Royer who confronted Firmin by asking publicly at one of the meetings of the Société if he did not have some white ancestry; Carolyn Fluehr-Lobban, 'Anténor Firmin and Haiti's contribution to anthropology', *Gradhiva*, no. 1, 2005, 95.

Surviving Maurras: Jacques Maritain's Jewish Question

RICHARD FRANCIS CRANE

In December 1918 the attacks against the Jews revived and soon intensified by the Communist seizure of power in Bavaria and Hungary, and by violent strikes in France itself. The fear of a social upheaval, which for a few weeks seemed imminent, was propitious to variations on the thesis of Jewish Bolshevism, that national tradition more

This article was made possible in part by funds granted to me through a Hoffberger Family Fellowship at the Center for Advanced Holocaust Studies, United States Holocaust Memorial Museum, as well as a Christopher Browning Research Fellowship from the Holocaust Educational Foundation. I am also grateful to the guest editor of *Patterns of Prejudice* and the two anonymous readers of the article, as well as Paul Mazgaj and Oscar Cole-Arnal, for their helpful and insightful comments.

readily than elsewhere described as Judeo-German or even (by Charles Maurras) as
Wilsonian Judeo-German. But France had a strong government ...

—*Léon Poliakov*[1]

Thus a historian of antisemitism narrates a specific historical moment and captures the protean nature of a more-or-less respectable (and manageable) antipathy towards Jews in the western world immediately after the Great War. Not for the first time, the 'spectral Jew' offered a name—or in this case, an inchoate, hyphenated tag—to place on an otherwise nameless fear. Poliakov also might have mentioned that this *grande peur* of late 1918 situates itself at the chronological midway point of two vitally important dates in the history of antisemitism in France. Twenty-four years earlier, in December 1894, the French General Staff charged Captain Alfred Dreyfus with selling military secrets to Germany; almost twenty-four years hence, in July 1942, 12,884 Jewish objects of a French police round-up would be held in the stifling heat of Paris's Vélodrome d'Hiver or brought directly to the transit camp at Drancy, France's 'antechamber to Auschwitz'.[2]

In the five decades separating Dreyfus and Drancy, the so-called Jewish Question remained a fixture in French national discourse. The legacy or legacies of 1789, the omnipresent vagaries of modernization and its discontents, the recurrent conflict with a reborn German *Reich*, the Russian Revolution and consequent rooting of the Communist International in Moscow, and the putative *guerre des deux France*—progressive, secular democratic, cosmopolitan, Dreyfusard France versus traditionalist, clerical, authoritarian, nativist, anti-Dreyfusard France, a myth no less potently divisive for being mythical—all served as present memories for contemplating the national future. And the Jewish Question embraced them all, the question of the place of native-born and immigrant Jews within the French body politic taking as interrelated points of departure both the Jewish emancipation set in motion by the 1789 revolution and a widespread sense of incipient national decline, that is, decadence, which became common currency by 1900.[3] This essay begins to engage the complex, polyvalent nature of the Jewish Question in early twentieth-century France, not by citing the most extreme antisemites of the era, a strategy that tends to sensationalize the subject of anti-Jewish prejudice at the expense of historical understanding, but rather by following closely the evolving ideas of an intellectual who eventually emerged from his association with figures such

---

1 Léon Poliakov, *The History of Anti-Semitism. Volume Four: Suicidal Europe, 1870–1933*, trans. from the French by George Klim (New York: Littman Library of Jewish Civilization 1985), 278–9.

2 Paula E. Hyman, *The Jews of Modern France* (Berkeley: University of California Press 1998), 173–4.

3 See Eugen Weber, *France: fin de siècle* (Cambridge, MA: Harvard University Press 1986), 9–26.

as the aforementioned Maurras to offer a sustained and vehement rejection of antisemitism, a rejection itself almost unheard of in respectable circles.

Jacques Maritain (1882–1973) has been identified as an extraordinarily philosemitic member of the Catholic intelligentsia in interwar France. For Michel Winock, Maritain exemplifies a growing openness to 'the democratic spirit and to tolerance' among French Catholics by the end of the 1930s, 'because this philosopher went from the Action Française to a militant humanism that excluded all forms of totalitarianism and refuted all justifications of antisemitism'.[4] Indeed, Maritain's outspoken and principled opposition to antisemitism provoked attacks by French fascists before the Second World War,[5] complicated his relations with Pope Pius XII when he served as French ambassador to the Vatican after 1945,[6] and merited praise by France's Catholic bishops in their 'statement of repentance' issued at Drancy in 1997.[7]

Maritain's severing of his early ties with the anti-democratic and antisemitic Charles Maurras in 1927 brought recognition as well as notoriety. Employing his pen as the pre-eminent apologist for the papal condemnation of the Action Française,[8] he asserted the 'primacy of the spiritual' against *politique d'abord* and assumed a leading role within what Philippe Chenaux describes as a new category of Catholic intellectual increasingly open to democratic pluralism.[9]

4 Michel Winock, *La France et les juifs de 1789 à nos jours* (Paris: Éditions de Seuil 2004), 214. Translations from the French are by the author unless otherwise stated.
5 'M. Jacques Maritain est marié à une Juive. Il a enjuivé sa vie et sa doctrine. Sa théologie, sa dialectique sont falsifiée comme le passeport d'un espion juif. M. Maritain, corps et âme, représente ce que les Allemandes appellent avec tant de raison un "Rassenschander," un souilleur de la Race'; Lucien Rebatet, 'Juifs et Catholiques', *Je suis partout*, no. 384, 1 April 1938, reprinted in Jacques Maritain et al., *L'Impossible Antisémitisme* (Paris: Desclée de Brouwer 2003), 169–70.
6 Michael Marrus, 'A plea unanswered: Jacques Maritain, Pope Pius XII, and the Holocaust', *Studies in Contemporary Jewry*, vol. 21, 2005, 10.
7 'Why is it, in the debates which we know took place, that the church did not listen to the better claims of its members' voices? Before the war, Jacques Maritain, both in articles and in lectures, tried to open Christians up to different perspectives on the Jewish people. He also warned against the perversity of the anti-Semitism that was developing'; Catholic Bishops of France, 'Declaration of repentance', 30 September 1997, available at www.bc.edu/research/cjl/meta-elements/texts/cjrelations/resources/documents/catholic/french_repentance.htm (viewed 14 June 2008).
8 I refer here specifically to the 29 December 1926 papal ban on Catholics reading the *Action française* newspaper and several of Maurras's own writings, which for all intents and purposes prohibited French Catholics from participation in the Action Française movement.
9 After tracing the gestation of a 'génération intellectuelle' born in the 1880s, coming of age during the church–state conflict of the first decade of the new century, rallying to the *union sacrée* during the Great War and seeing itself as simultaneously Catholic, Thomist and Maurrasian until the moment of the papal condemnation, Philippe Chenaux concludes: 'Avec Maritain, l'intellectuel catholique ... fait son entrée dans la vie publique sous le signe du combat contre le naturalisme maurrassien'; Philippe Chenaux, *Entre Maurras et Maritain: une génération intellectuelle catholique (1920–1930)* (Paris: Éditions du Cerf 1999), 225–8.

But how much and in what ways had Maritain's views on Jews in the modern world changed as a result of his ostensible political realignment? While his writings about the Jewish Question inevitably carried political implications, he always framed the question philosophically and above all theologically. Accordingly, and particularly given Maritain's designation as perhaps the most influential figure in the intellectual world of interwar French Catholicism, the development of his philosemitism from the publication of his first essay specifically devoted to the Jewish Question in 1921 to the appearance of his second one in 1937 merits further attention.

These two essays, written in very different historical contexts, reveal both an increasing opposition to racist antisemitism on Maritain's part and, at the same time, a persistent, even intensified, essentializing of Jews, their author exhibiting not only an undeniable 'anti-antisemitism',[10] but also an ambivalent philosemitism based on Jewish stereotypes both positive and negative. A devout Catholic who had broken with the radical right, Maritain strove to advance a metahistorical understanding of what might be called the Sacred Jew in an era when the racially hygienic construct of the Dirty Jew threatened to prevail in contexts ranging from the gutter to the drawing room to the classroom. But Maritain's recasting of the timely Jewish Question as the timeless Mystery of Israel amounted to just as clear an expression of the political-cultural anxieties of the interwar period as its racist and ever more eliminationist counterpart, articulated as the so-called Jewish Problem. Both removed the Jewish object of the question from the perspective of visible mundane reality and uncovered—or recovered—hidden apocalyptic secrets. Maritain's vision of Jewish identity in the modern world, as it developed in the 1920s and 1930s, thus proved inseparable from his negotiation of the personal and public crises of his time.

Regarding the Jewish Question

In the first essay, 'À propos de la question juive', drawn from a lecture delivered to the Semaine des Écrivains Catholiques (Weekly Meeting of Catholic Writers) and published in *La Vie spirituelle* in July 1921, Maritain scarcely denied the existence of a Jewish Problem, even if he avoided the term. Some Jews, particularly those wounded in the Great War, had demonstrated their assimilation to France or another country but, by and large, European Jewry remained apart 'even as Providence decreed would

---

10 On the use and abuse of antisemitism and associated terminology, see Jonathan Judaken, 'Between philosemitism and antisemitism: the Frankfurt School's anti-antisemitism', in Phyllis Lassner and Lara Trubowitz (eds), *Antisemitism and Philosemitism in the Twentieth and Twenty-first Centuries: Representing Jews, Jewishness and Modern Culture* (Newark: University of Delaware Press forthcoming).

be the case throughout history, as witness to Golgotha'. Therefore 'one should expect from the Jews something other than a real attachment to the common good of western, and Christian, civilization'.[11] Worse, their historical rejection of Christ and the resulting temporalization of eschatological hopes, that is, an earthly corruption of the promise of God's kingdom, made at least some of them agents of revolution:

> It is necessary to add that an essentially messianic people such as the Jews, from the instant when they reject the true Messiah, inevitably will play a subversive role in the world; I do not mean through some premeditated plan, but rather because of a metaphysical necessity, which makes of messianic Hope, and a passion for absolute Justice, when they are brought down from the supernatural to the natural level, and are falsely applied, the most active ferment of revolution. That is why, as Darmsteter and Bernard Lazare[12] have pointed out candidly, Jews, Jewish intrigues and the Jewish spirit can be found at the origin of most major revolutionary movements in the modern era.[13]

In this passage Maritain rejects the kind of antisemitic conspiracy theory ('I do not mean through some premeditated plan') and attendant incitement to violence exemplified by the *Protocols of the Elders of Zion*, in which, as he puts it, '"the Jew" appears in a sort of simplistic mythology as the *unique* cause of the evils from which we suffer'. But he concedes (in a formulation hardly uncommon for the time) 'the evident necessity of a struggle for public safety against secret Jewish-Masonic societies and against cosmopolitan finance'.[14] Exactly what this struggle entailed remained unclear and problematic in a post-Christian political order, and Maritain wished that Jews could be required once and for all 'to opt, some of them, for French, English, Italian etc.... nationality ... others for Palestinian nationality', although unfortunately the latter *patrie* did not (yet) exist. As frustrating as he might have found this practical problem, Christian faith and practice demanded a veneration of the people of Israel for, as Maritain articulated it, updating Saint Paul's Epistle to the Romans: 'However degenerate carnal Jews may

---

11 Jacques Maritain, 'À propos de la question juive', *La Vie spirituelle*, July 1921, reprinted in Maritain *et al.*, *L'Impossible Antisémitisme*, 61–2.

12 Bernard Lazare was an anarchist and maverick Dreyfusard (in fact the very first Jewish Dreyfusard according to Robert Wistrich) who associated closely with Maritain's early mentor Charles Péguy. His 1894 book *L'Antisémitisme, son histoire et ses causes*, cited by Maritain in his essay, is available in English translation, with an informative preface by Wistrich in Bernard Lazare, *Antisemitism: Its History and Causes* (Lincoln, NE: Bison Books 1995). What apparently resonated most with Maritain in Lazare's early work was the latter's idea that 'it would seem that the grievance of the antisemite were well founded; the Jewish spirit is essentially a revolutionary spirit, and consciously or otherwise, the Jew is a revolutionist' (149).

13 Maritain, 'À propos de la question juive', 62.

14 Ibid., 62–3.

be, the race of the prophets, of the Virgin and the apostles, the race of Jesus is the trunk on to which we are grafted. Let us recall chapter eleven of the Epistle to the Romans ...'[15] Maritain's willingness simultaneously to ascribe holiness and degeneracy to the Jewish people—citing Jewish writers such as Lazare and, elsewhere in the essay, the *fin-de-siècle* antisemite René de la Tour du Pin—placed him in an awkward position from which to render judgement on antisemitism; hence he proceeded to render an awkward judgement.

Directly addressing his fellow Catholic writers, Maritain cautioned against, but by no means categorically rejected, antisemitism: 'However antisemitic he might be in other respects, a Catholic writer, it seems evident to me, must in his faith refrain from any hatred and any contempt as regards the Jewish race and the religion of Israel considered in and of themselves.'[16] Not only should one keep in mind 'the number, relatively large, and in any case truly impressive, of Jews who for some time have been converting to Catholicism', but one should recognize also the 'extraordinary *élan* of prayer that manifests itself within the Church for Israel, and of which these conversions are precisely the fruit'.[17] Above all, and in keeping with an Aristotelian-Thomistic understanding of virtue-based ethics,[18] one must prudently distinguish between the theological virtue of *caritas* and the cardinal virtue of justice in one's dealings with Jews in the world:

> Even as they must denounce and combat those depraved Jews who, along with apostate Christians, are leading the anti-Christian Revolution, so too they must guard against closing the door to the Kingdom of Heaven before souls of good will, before those *true Israelites* of whom Our Lord said *in whom there is no guile* [John 1:47]. Charity towards the latter does not invalidate the justice the former deserve, nor the other way around.[19]

15 Ibid., 63–4.
16 Ibid., 64.
17 Ibid., 65–6.
18 A Thomist of a later generation described such virtue ethics as follows: 'With a doctrine of commandments or duties, there is always the danger of arbitrarily drawing up a list of requirements and losing sight of the human person who "ought" to do this or that. The doctrine of virtue, on the other hand, has things to say about this human person; it speaks to both the kind of being which is his when he enters the world, as a consequence of his createdness, and the kind of being he ought to strive toward and attain to—by being prudent, just, brave, and temperate. The doctrine of virtue, that is, is one form of the doctrine of obligation; but one by nature free of regimentation and restriction. On the contrary, its aim is to clear a trail, to open a way'; Josef Pieper, *The Four Cardinal Virtues* (Notre Dame, IN: University of Notre Dame Press 1966), xi–xii. Obviously, such a 'doctrine of virtue ... one by nature free of regimentation and restriction', presupposes an objective moral reality on which to draw, i.e. natural law.
19 Maritain, 'À propos de la question juive', 68.

This injunction at once advocates judging Jews on an individual rather than collective basis, distinguishes between good and bad ones (the parallel between Jewish depravity and Christian apostasy evidently pointing to the perils of secularization), and warns against closing the 'door' of Christian conversion to 'true Israelites'.

At least one historian, John Hellman, has branded the 'early Maritain' an antisemite.[20] But antisemitism—'best defined as unprovoked and irrational hatred toward Jews'[21]—hardly manages to contain Maritain's complex, fluid and even hopeful view of a Jewish Question framed in worldly parameters and pointing to an other-worldly resolution. If nothing else, this construction differs essentially from the ostensibly impersonal and political Maurrasian *antisémitisme d'état*, with its identification of French Jewry as one of the four solid pillars of 'Anti-France' (along with foreigners, Freemasons and Protestants), an antisemitism that, according to Maurras, 'should be defined as the premier organic and positive idea, the premier counterrevolutionary and naturalist idea'.[22] As a reflection of the Action Française chief's overall mindset (the quotation dates from 1901), rather than a singular obsession with the Jews, this viewpoint opposes a reactionary positivism to what a recent study calls Maritain's 'mystic modernism'.[23] Given the prevalence of a Christian supernaturalism in the latter's approach to the Jewish Question, one can more readily perceive the enduring imprint of Maritain's godfather, the Catholic mystic novelist Léon Bloy.

20 'There are good reasons to say simply that Jacques Maritain was—at least for the earlier part of his career—an anti-Semite'; John Hellman, 'The Jews in the "New Middle Ages"; Jacques Maritain's anti-Semitism in its times', in Robert Royal (ed.), *Jacques Maritain and the Jews* (Notre Dame, IN: University of Notre Dame Press 1994), 89. But Hellman's rendering of the term—applied pejoratively and begging clarification—would have to apply as well to the pacifist socialist Jean Jaurès who, during the Dreyfus Affair, could group together 'cosmopolitan Jews without country, conservatives without conscience', not to mention Georges Clemenceau, whose paper *L'Aurore* had published Zola's 'J'accuse' yet who could also write in 1898 about how 'the Semite tried to come back and to fulfill himself by the domination of the earth' (quoted in Poliakov, *The History of Anti-Semitism*, 54, 64). As Poliakov makes abundantly clear throughout his book, this kind of anti-Jewish discourse pervaded western culture to the extent that merely assigning to it the label 'antisemitic' fails to differentiate between this level of unreflective prejudice, fortified by cultural presuppositions, and a pathological hatred of Jews activated by the biological imperative of racial hygiene.
21 Milton Shain, *Antisemitism* (London: Bowerdean 1998), 5.
22 Quoted in Bruno Goyet, *Charles Maurras* (Paris: Presses de Sciences Po 2000), 264.
23 Stephen Schloesser, *Jazz Age Catholicism: Mystic Modernism in Postwar Paris, 1919–1933* (Toronto and London: University of Toronto Press 2005). Maritain figures as a prominent case for Schloesser's thesis that various French Catholic artists and intellectuals advanced a 'catholicity' that engaged rather than rejected modernity.

Anti-modern/ultramodern

The pre-eminence of Bloy's influence over that of Maurras in Maritain's framing of the Jewish Question, if not his confrontation with modernity, drew in part on chronological precedence, as the former association anticipated the latter by several years. The future philosopher had rejected his republican, *libre-penseur* upbringing when he and his Russian Jewish émigrée wife Raïssa sought Catholic baptism in 1906. He had been born the scion of a solidly republican and nominally Protestant family and, for a time, considered himself both an atheist and a socialist, vowing to 'live for the Revolution'.[24] In 1901 he became the 'disciple' of Dreyfusard poet Charles Péguy, inhabiting the latter's bookshop and assisting with the editing of the journal *Cahiers de la quinzaine* while pursuing his university studies. But an intellectual and spiritual crisis led him to reject the positivism and scientism of the Sorbonne and ultimately turn towards the very Catholicism that he had hitherto associated with all things reactionary.[25] As Raïssa, a fellow student who married Jacques in 1904, later recalled, they shared an almost suicidal despair at the prevailing intellectual climate:

> Through some curious *de facto* contradiction, they [their professors] sought to *verify* everything by processes of material learning and of positive verification, and yet they despaired of *truth*, whose very name was unlovely to them and could be used only through the quotation marks of a disillusioned smile.... All in all, the only practical lesson to be had from their conscientious and disinterested instruction was a lesson in intellectual relativism, and—if one was logical—in moral nihilism.[26]

24 'I will be a socialist and live for the revolution.' Maritain made this declaration to the family cook's husband, François Baton; Jacques Maritain, *Notebooks*, trans. from the French by Joseph W. Evans (Albany: Magi Books 1984), 8.

25 Maritain wrote the following in his notebook in early 1906, shortly before his baptism: 'The great obstacle to Christianity is the Christians. This is the thorn which pierces me. The Christians have abandoned the poor—and the poor among the nations: the Jews—and Poverty of the soul: authentic Reason. They horrify me'; Maritain, *Notebooks*, 26. Perhaps it is worth noting that the year 1906, which saw the Maritains convert to Catholicism, also saw both the exoneration of Dreyfus and the implementation of the Combes anti-clerical legislation, no doubt encouraging the image in many people's minds of the Catholic Church as a monstrous, potent force of reaction.

26 Raïssa Maritain, *We Have Been Friends Together*, trans. from the French by Julie Kernan (New York: Longmans 1942), 68. See also Jean-Luc Barré, *Jacques et Raïssa Maritain: les mendiants du ciel* (Paris: Stock 1995), 66–74, which among other things details the desperate suicide pact between the two students; the biography, Judith D. Suther, *Raïssa Maritain: Pilgrim, Poet, Exile* (New York: Fordham University Press 1990); and Phyllis H. Stock, 'Students versus the university in pre-world war Paris', *French Historical Studies*, vol. 7, no. 1, Spring 1971, 93–110.

Péguy advised the couple to attend the lectures of the philosopher of intuition, Henri Bergson, at the Collège de France. Reinvigorated by *élan vital*, but still dissatisfied, they wanted to ascertain the source of being itself, and this finally brought them to Montmarte, and the very doorstep of Bloy, the 'Pilgrim of the Absolute'.

Bloy's 'apocalyptic vision', as Stephen Schloesser writes, 'stirred the passions of a younger elite bitterly contemptuous of the received order in both politics and religion' and 'made suffering not merely a *privileged* path to redemption, but in fact the *exclusive* mode of participation in the super-natural'.[27] Preoccupied with society's outcasts and victims, he particularly focused on Jews, both venerating them as 'the first-born of all peoples', witnesses to eternal truth in a decadent modern bourgeois world,[28] and denouncing them as representative of the worst kinds of anti-human avarice, a 'hostile people' keeping Christ perpetually nailed to the cross.[29] The Maritains, who subsidized the 1906 reprinting of Bloy's book *Le Salut par les juifs*,[30]

27 Schloesser, *Jazz Age Catholicism*, 67, 69–70.
28 'The Jews are the first-born of all peoples, and when all things are in their final place, their proudest masters will think themselves honored to lick the Jewish wanderers' feet. For everything has been promised them, and in the meantime they do penance for the earth. The right of the first-born cannot be annulled by a punishment however rigorous, and God's word of honor is unchangeable, because "His gifts and vocation are without repentance"'; Léon Bloy, *Pilgrim of the Absolute*, ed. Raïssa Maritain, introd. Jacques Maritain, trans. from the French by John Coleman and Harry Lorin Binnse (New York: Pantheon 1947), 263.
29 One of Bloy's most striking passages concerns the Three Jews of Hamburg, depicting a group of merchants, transformed before his eyes into Abraham, Isaac and Jacob (re)incarnate, concluding as follows: 'Je me souviendrai longtemps, néanmoins, de ces trois incomparables crapules que je vois encore dans leurs souquenilles putréfiées, penchées fronts contre fronts, sur l'orifice d'un sac fétide qui eût épouvanté les étoiles, où s'amoncelait, pour l'exportation du typhus, les innomables objets de quelque négoce archisémitique'; Léon Bloy, *Le Salut par les juifs* (Paris: Éditions G. Crès et Cie. 1906), 25. Originally published in 1892, the new edition was dedicated to Raïssa Maritain. These 119 pages of maledictions and benedictions include the following concerning the Jews, Christ and the cross: 'Ils le clouent de façon puissante pour qu'Il ne descende pas sans leur permission' (85). No wonder that, while one scholar can write that Bloy 'venerated the suffering Jew' and offered 'an idiosyncratic vision of the Jewish people radically opposed to that propagated in [Édouard] Drumont's *Libre Parole*', another identifies him as 'one of the most extreme and vociferous anti-Semites of turn-of-the-century France'. See, respectively, Schloesser, *Jazz Age Catholicism*, 68, and Hellman, 'The Jews in the "New Middle Ages"', 91. Without reconciling these perhaps irreconcilable interpretations, Pierre Vidal-Naquet puts it thus: 'Il va sans dire que les Juifs réels, qu'il fussent religieux ou athées, français ou étrangers, ne demeuraient pas indemnes sous les coups de cet instrument de la fureur divine que voulait être Léon Bloy'; Pierre Vidal-Naquet, 'Jacques Maritain et les juifs: réflexions sur un parcours', in Maritain *et al.*, *L'Impossible Antisémitisme*, 24.
30 Philippe Chenaux, 'Léon Bloy et sa postérité', in Annette Becker, Danielle Delmaire and Frédéric Gugelot (eds), *Juifs et Chrétiens: entre ignorance, hostilité et rapprochement (1898–1998)* (Lille: Éditions du Conseil Scientifique de l'Université Charles-de-Gaulle-Lille 3, 2002), 48–52.

found his angriest declamations troubling but tried to explain them away, Jacques insisting that 'it would be unjust to sketch of Bloy a hideous caricature',[31] and Raïssa rather serenely concluding: 'To this man among all others much will be forgiven, because he loved so much … We pardoned him his dross by virtue of the grandeur of his intentions and the magnificence of his language.'[32] Most importantly, Jacques Maritain remained deeply impressed with the theological-historical implications of Léon Bloy's writings, ever returning to the latter's representation of a Jewish people that 'obstructs the history of the human race as a dam blocks a river, to raise its level'.[33] If Péguy had already taught Maritain that 'the whole of Israel's *mystique* demands that Israel should pursue its painful and resounding mission throughout the world',[34] Bloy's tutelage influenced him to envision that mission in predominantly other-worldly, even redemptive, terms.

Maritain, who never repudiated the Dreyfusard convictions of his youth, nonetheless allowed himself to be drawn towards the milieu of the inveterate anti-Dreyfusard Maurras, despite the fact that he never embraced the latter's coldly political *antisémitisme d'état* let alone the more virulently biological *antisémitisme de peau* that still awaited widespread popularity. So, if outright antisemitism had little or nothing to do with Maritain's *rapprochement* with the Action Française, what common ground presented itself?[35] The answer lies in Maritain's philosophical engagement with modernity, which one recent biographer rather dramatically deems a *Kulturkampf*.[36] In 1909 Maritain's new spiritual director, Father Humbert Clérissac, introduced him to Thomas Aquinas and also exhorted him to read the newspaper *Action française*,[37] at a time moreover when writers such as André Gide and Marcel Proust read it as well and when Maurras's literary fame still competed with his political notoriety. Historian Bruno Goyet correctly states that 'classic historiography has run up against the positioning of Maurras between literature and politics'.[38] Reading history backwards

31 Bloy, *Pilgrim of the Absolute*, 8.
32 Raïssa Maritain, *We Have Been Friends Together*, 124.
33 Bloy, *Le Salut par les juifs*, 27.
34 Péguy, quoted in Robert Royal, 'Péguy, Dreyfus, Maritain', in Royal, *Jacques Maritain and the Jews*, 211.
35 I think the term *rapprochement*, used by Vidal-Naquet and Chenaux, best captures the extent of and the intentionality behind Maritain's relationship with the movement. See Vidal-Naquet, 'Jacques Maritain et les juifs', 28; Chenaux, *Entre Maurras et Maritain*, 14, uses the term to describe the relationship between Catholics in general and the Action Française.
36 Ralph M. McInerny, *The Very Rich Hours of Jacques Maritain: A Spiritual Life* (Notre Dame. IN: University of Notre Dame Press 2003), 91.
37 Ibid., 60–5.
38 Goyet, *Charles Maurras*, 208; on Maurras's literary associations more generally, see 147–209.

indeed has its perils: long before the republic convicted Maurras of treason (1945), he succeeded in getting himself elected to the Académie Française (1938).

Maritain, from 1914 a professor at Paris's Institut Catholique, never joined the Action Française in any case, but he did serve as philosophy editor of an affiliated publication called the *Revue universelle*. He spent the rest of his life regretting this association,[39] but his later protestations of a youthful lapse of judgement belie how his antipathy towards what he saw as bourgeois liberal modernity led him to a logical alliance with the royalists who had both protested the Third Republic's disestablishment of the Catholic Church in 1905–6 and supported the papal condemnation of modernism in 1907.[40] This alliance, at least insofar as it was rationally motivated, drew on three motives: a working partnership with and hoped-for Catholicization of Maurras and the Action Française;[41] a shared preoccupation, as evidenced

39 See Maritain's letter many years later to his friend and one-time student Yves Simon in which he insisted that 'la cause de cette erreur est mon obéissance aux conseils du Père Clérissac … Comment distinguer ces choses au lendemain d'une conversion?'; letter from Maritain to Simon, 31 August 1941: Jacques Maritain Center, University of Notre Dame, JM 29/17. Among Maritain biographers, McInerny finds such explanations 'unconvincing', while Bernard Doering is more sympathetic, emphasizing the improbability of the association in the first place. McInerny, *The Very Rich Hours of Jacques Maritain*, 65; Bernard E. Doering, *Jacques Maritain and the French Catholic Intellectuals* (Notre Dame, IN: University of Notre Dame Press 1983), 8. See also Barré, *Jacques et Raïssa Maritain*, 130–97.

40 For Maritain and other Catholics, allying with 'royalists' had little to do with royalism *per se*, and this alliance in turn meant much more to Maurras and his colleagues by the 1920s than did the residual link with French royalism, a consideration supported in a recent essay by Brian Jenkins: 'La relation que l'Action française entretenait avec l'Église catholique était politiquement bien plus significative que son attachement symbolique à la famille royale de France'; Brian Jenkins, 'L'Action française à l'ère du fascisme: une perspective contextuelle', in Michel Dobry (ed.), *Le Mythe de l'allergie française au fascisme* (Paris: Éditions Albin Michel 2003), 130. Nor did this alliance necessarily bespeak a proto-fascist inclination. In the same volume, Maurras biographer Bruno Goyet points out how in the 1920s the Action Française, whatever its formative influence on later French fascism/s, evaluated Mussolini's March on Rome in terms quite congenial to a French Catholic traditionalist understanding of both French and European politics. For example, the *Action française* on 28 October 1922 offered the following appraisal of Italian Fascism: 'Maçonnique, le Facisme est d'essence anticléricale et anticatholique'; quoted in Bruno Goyet, 'La "Marche sur Rome": version originale sous-titrée. La reception du fascisme en France dans les années 20', in Dobry (ed.), *Le Mythe de l'allergie française au fascisme*, 85.

41 Perhaps the very question of the degree of Maritain's adherence to the Action Française's programme distorts the historical picture, i.e. in simply asking how close Maritain approached Maurras's political outlook. We might also ask to what extent, at least from Maritain's perspective, Maurras seemed to be approaching *his* philosophical, if not spiritual outlook. As Oscar Arnal notes: 'In 1917 Charles Maurras wrote a book called *Le Pape, la guerre, et la paix*. Included in its contents were

by their adherence to Henri Massis's 1919 *Pour un parti de l'intelligence* manifesto, with a continued intellectual mobilization against Germanism and a rejection of art-for-art's-sake;[42] and, finally, the practical necessity of disbursing and utilizing the one million francs bequeathed to Maurras and

contrasts of Latin Catholicism and German Lutheranism which paralleled those drawn by Jacques Maritain and others'; Oscar Arnal, *Ambivalent Alliance: The Catholic Church and the Action Française, 1899–1939* (Pittsburgh: University of Pittsburgh Press 1985), 84. One should not forget that the convert Maritain was also the converter Maritain, the celebrated conversion of Jean Cocteau in summer 1925 serving as but one of many such examples. And, even though in retrospect it is clear that Maurras always extolled Roman Catholicism as a functional bulwark of western, i.e. Latin, civilization, Maritain could hope, at least until the end of the Action Française crisis, that the workings of grace might effect a spiritual transformation of the deaf *maître* and his movement. See, for example, Maritain's 11 January 1927 letter to Maurras, in *Non possumus: la crise religieuse de l'Action Française. Actes du Cinquième Colloque Maurras, Palais des Congrès, Institut d'études politiques, 9, 10, 11 et 12 avril 1976*, 2 vols (Aix-en-Provence: Centre Charles Maurras 1986), ii.650–3.

42 Maritain could find common ground with Maurras during the Great War in seeing Germany as an inveterate enemy, even if he did so from a philosophical perspective more than a political one. Maritain's 1914–15 public lecture series rejected the thesis that there were two Germanies, 'one lofty and creative, the other base and destructive. Rather, the modern Germany of 1914, which shelled cathedrals and committed unspeakable atrocities, was the natural and inevitable culmination of an indivisible German culture originating with Luther and including Kant, Goethe, and other "great" Germans'; quoted in Martha Hanna, *The Mobilization of the Intellect: French Scholars and Writers during the Great War* (Cambridge, MA: Harvard University Press 1996), 118. Maritain also opined to Maurras that various peace proposals circulating in autumn 1914 were evidently inspired by Freemasonry; see the letter from Maritain to Maurras, 18 October 1914: Le Centre d'Archives, Cercle d'Études Jacques et Raïssa Maritain, Kolbsheim, France (hereafter 'Maritain Archives, Kolbsheim'). One can see this anti-Germanism in his 1925 book *Trois Reformateurs*, in which he extends his indictment of Luther to account for the subsequent German national character: 'And so in Luther the swollen consciousness of self is essentially a consciousness of will.' Working the vein of national essentialism, Maritain continues: 'Happy the nation whose supreme incarnation of her own genius is not a mere individuality of flesh but a personality radiant with the Spirit of God! If we want to set off against Luther's egocentrism an example of true personality, let us think of that miracle of simplicity and uprightness, of candour and wisdom, of humility and magnanimity, of loss of self in God,—Joan of Arc'; Jacques Maritain, *Three Reformers: Luther, Descartes, Rousseau* (New York: Thomas Y. Crowell Company 1970), 28. This anti-German bias would remain strong into the Second World War, when Maritain wrote the following: 'As long as the unfortunate German people recognizes its temporal sacrament in Thor and Odin, or in Luther and Hitler, it will labour in vain. It can move hell to draw therefrom the most perfect machinery of murder and of death; it will so far remain an ill-starred people'; Jacques Maritain, *Pour la justice: articles et discours (1940–1945)* (New York: Éditions de la Maison Française 1945), 33. Finally, in 1945 Maritain insisted on the collective guilt of the German nation, going so far as to argue that 'the German population as a whole accepted Hitler and the demonic principle that he represented as a convenient tool to be made use of for the grandeur of Germany ...'; Jacques Maritain, report submitted to the foreign ministry, 9 December 1945: Maritain Archives, Kolbsheim.

Maritain jointly by a fallen soldier named Pierre Villard.[43] Rightly or wrongly, and this seems obvious in the case of their differing approaches to the Jewish Question, Maritain thought he could associate with Maurras on an autonomous if not equal footing, preserving a sense of philosophical and spiritual integrity.

After all, in the 1920s, the devout, contemplative Maritain also asserted himself as an ascendant and confident public intellectual who relished the prospect of philosophical confrontation.[44] The very title of his 1922 book *Antimoderne* sounded a battle cry, even if its contents were more nuanced, such as, for example, when it extolled Catholicism as *the* truly ultramodern world-view, for 'Catholicism is as anti-modern in its immutable attachment to tradition as it is ultramodern in how boldly it adapts itself to new conditions arising in the world'.[45] *Trois Reformateurs* (1925) offered a history of the deformation of western thought, that is, a turn to the subjective self as the determiner of all meaning and value, thanks to Luther, Descartes and

43 When Villard died at the front in 1918, he left over a million francs to be spent by Maritain 'conjointly' with Maurras. Maurras apparently directed most of his half to the Action Française, while Maritain purchased the house at Meudon that would serve as the centre for the Thomism study circles and annual retreats of the 1920s and 1930s, and the two legatees decided that each would contribute 50,000 francs to found *La Revue universelle*. For Maritain's recollection of the Villard bequest and reproductions of the letters he and the soldier exchanged during the war, see Maritain, *Notebooks*, 100–32.

44 Maritain deserves his reputation as a humble contemplative, as he and Raïssa lived under a mutual vow of chastity and shared a life as Benedictine oblates with her sister Vera into the 1950s. See René Mougel, 'A propos du mariage des Maritain: leur voeu de 1912 et leurs témoignages', *Cahiers Jacques Maritain*, vol. 22, 1991, 5–44. His ideal philosophical life, personified in Saint Thomas Aquinas, included humble prayer, assiduous study and vigorous debate, all animated by a loving disposition, to be sure, but also an uncompromising, sometimes combative, commitment to truth. For example, in 1945 he waxed rhapsodic to Mortimer Adler about 'the good old tradition of great scholastic controversies, pulverizing adversaries with atomic bombs'; letter from Maritain to Mortimer Adler, 31 August 1945: Maritain Archives, Kolbsheim.

45 Jacques Maritain, *Antimoderne* (Paris: Éditions de la Revue des Jeunes 1922), 14. Stephen Schloesser aptly concludes: 'Like coffee table books that lie unexamined beyond their alluring covers, this book's brazen title has been referred to more often than its contents have been actually explored'; Schloesser, *Jazz Age Catholicism*, 162. Schloesser's book convincingly illustrates Maritain's eager engagement with some of the avatars of modern culture in the 1920s, notably Jean Cocteau, showing the limits of the anti-modernist tag that has been placed on the 'early Maritain'. But Charles Blanchet makes an excellent case for seeing Maritain's interrogation of modernity as a lifelong venture: '... il y aura chez Maritain, d'un bout à l'autre de sa vie un affrontement avec modernité ... [mais] ... ce n'est pas une position figée, statique, établie une fois pour toutes dans un rejet radical'; Charles Blanchet, 'Maritain face à la modernité', in Michel Bressolette and René Mougel (eds), *Jacques Maritain face à la modernité* (Toulouse: Presses Universitaires du Mirail 1995), 11, 14–15.

Rousseau. According to Maritain, Luther banished reason 'to the foulest place in the house', teaching future generations of Germans and others that 'the swollen consciousness of self is essentially a consciousness of will'. Descartes should be held responsible for repudiating reason's reliance on the past and irremediably rupturing the relationship between 'intelligence and Being'. Finally, Rousseau exalted the ego by detaching himself from everything save his own 'exorbitant Individuality'.[46] Having thus slain the fathers of modernism, Maritain could seek a constructive engagement with modernity; but he also named the terms of that engagement, which were to be found in the Catholic tradition. And he further strengthened his hand through his *rapprochement* with the Action Française, a movement popular among French Catholics despite the agnosticism of its leader.

The primacy of the spiritual

But stresses within both Maritain's understanding of the Jewish Question and his overall relationship with the Action Française began to tell even before the papal condemnation forced a wholesale re-evaluation of his temporal application of philosophical and theological positions. In June 1925 Maurras wrote an open letter to Interior Minister Abraham Schrameck, threatening to shoot him 'like a dog' for having taken measures to suppress the Action Française street battalions known as the Camelots de Roi.[47] While Maurras faced criminal charges for incitement to murder, the Camelots found an opportunity to assail Schrameck with antisemitic catcalls. In Maritain's *Réponse à Jean Cocteau*, published in 1926, he found no problem with 'booing an unfit minister', but he objected strongly to 'outraging Heaven by soiling the name of the immense Saint in whose paternity all believers are enveloped. *Abraham begat Isaac, and Isaac begat Jacob* ... The Genealogy of our God [Matthew 1:11–17].'[48]

Maritain proceeded to evoke the emphasis on suffering so typical of Bloy as well as the Jew/Israelite opposition seen for example in the Johannine Gospel:

---

46 Maritain, *Three Reformers*, 35, 79, 111. Maritain concludes his appraisal of the author of *Le Contrat social* as follows: 'A stupendous perverter, Rousseau aims not at our heads but a little below our hearts' (118–19).

47 Barré, *Jacques et Raïssa Maritain*, 449–50; Eugen Weber, *Action Française: Royalism and Reaction in Twentieth-century France* (Stanford, CA: Stanford University Press 1962), 160.

48 Jacques Maritain, 'Abraham, hou, hou', in Jacques Maritain, *Le Mystère d'Israël et autre essais* (Paris: Desclée de Brouwer 1965), 13–14. This excerpt from Maritain's *Réponse à Jean Cocteau* (Paris: Librairie Stock 1926) comprised the first selection in this 1965 anthology in which Maritain collected his writings on the Jews. The otherwise comprehensive anthology did not include his 1921 essay, 'À propos de la question juive', which incidentally has still not been published in English translation.

I have known prideful and corrupt Jews. Above all I have known magnanimous ones, with great and guileless hearts, born poor and dying poorer still, having neither the sense of lucre nor economy, happier to give than receive. If there are always carnal Jews, there are also true Israelites, *in whom there is no guile*.[49]

Nor did Maritain apparently think Maurras possessed any guile, having testified in his defence at a trial that resulted in a suspended two-year sentence. Apparently, as far as Maritain was concerned, Maurras spoke solely as a philosopher, defending the principle of free speech without himself intervening in matters political. But Maritain's biographer Jean-Luc Barré rightly concludes that this culminating event showed how far he had deluded himself:

Maritain thus agreed, without any inordinate concern, to align himself with the most overtly antisemitic intellectual milieu that one could find. He had managed to distance himself so far from comprehension that, in 1925, during a trial initiated by Minister of the Interior Abraham Schrameck, whom Maurras had theatened to 'shoot like a dog', he testified in favour of the offender in the name of 'resisting unjust laws'.[50]

Maritain's disquietude with Action Française Jew-baiting coincided with his failure, in concert with Orientalist Louis Massignon, to enlist papal support for Zionism. For Maritain, it will be remembered, the establishment of a Jewish state promised a resolution to the question of Jewish national identity. His October 1925 report to Pius XI also extolled Catholic collaboration with Zionists as an avenue for evangelization:

Given the great historical importance of the Zionist movement, due above all to the religious vocation of Israel ... it seems desirable that Catholics, in their capacity as private persons, follow closely, and sympathetically, the efforts of the Zionists, and keep in contact with them, so as to allow for the possibility of Catholic penetration (*pénétration catholique*) among the newly reunited Jews, and in order to permit those among them whom grace attracts an easier return to the light of Christ.[51]

---

49 Maritain, 'Abraham, hou, hou'.
50 Barré, *Jacques et Raïssa Maritain*, 449–50.
51 Jacques Maritain, 'Rapport sur le sionisme addressé à Pie XI (1925)', *Cahiers Jacques Maritain*, vol. 23, October 1991, 27–30. Published in the same issue, one finds the note Maritain addressed to Father Édouard Hugon, an intimate of Pius XI, as a preface to the proposal. Maritain's enthusiasm for Zionism appears more than tactical here: 'Il y a là un phénomène historique de la plus haute gravité, où sont mobilisés (dans des fins pour le moment toutes terrestres et nationales) des forces spirituelles, une énergie, parfois même un héroïsme dignes d'admiration. Israël renaît' (28). Nonetheless,

The Pope demurred, inclining instead to 'prudence' and 'reserve'.[52] And, as would prove the case with the Action Française, Maritain reluctantly bowed to the Holy Father's will.

But even before the pontiff forced the issue, Maritain questioned the degree to which Maurras's integral nationalism encroached upon Catholic universalism. His letters to Henri Massis, as the latter worked on the book later published in Maritain's *Le roseau d'or* series as *Défense de l'Occident*, illustrate how, well in advance of the condemnation, he sought to warn his friend away from some of Maurras's fundamental theses. Maritain wrote in October 1925: 'If your Defence of the Christian West is confused with a defence of Latinity in a nationalist or racialist sense, in a strictly Maurrasian sense, then the whole undertaking will have been for nothing.'[53] He would make this critique more explicit in March 1927 shortly after the papal ban took effect, taking a swipe at Maurrasian antisemitism and classicism by invoking 'Christ himself, Jewish and "Oriental"', and concluding that 'Our culture is Greco-Latin, but our religion is not'.[54]

John Hellman concludes simply: 'Like Bloy, then, Maritain saw the good—even world-historical—Jew as the convert'; Hellman, 'The Jews in the "New Middle Ages"', 98. It should be noted that Hellman's restrictive and pejorative use of the word 'good' would be essentially foreign to the Thomist Maritain, and it further bestows a coldness on Maritain that contradicts his basic character and his specific relations with Jews, converts to Christianity or not. This simplification of Maritain's attitude towards Jews—one will remember the driving premise of Hellman's essay is 'Maritain's anti-Semitism'—ignores his relations with Jews such as Absalom Feinberg, an inhabitant of Turkish-ruled Palestine who would die in the Great War. Renée Nehem-Bernheim stresses the consistently open warmth and occasionally muted tensions inherent in such relations: 'Si la compréhension de Maritain pour ce qu'il appellera "le mystère d'Israël" lui vient surtout de son affection pour Raïssa (compréhension qui pour lui, n'a rien de contradictoire avec son désir de convertir les Juifs), sa sympathie pour le Foyer National puis pour l'État d'Israël, il les doit certainement à Avshalom. Bien qu'Avshalom comme sa tante Sonia se soient montrés réfractaires à toute tentative de conversion, Maritain a gardé pour eux une véritable tendresse'; Renée Nehem-Bernheim, 'Rencontre de deux personnalités d'Eretz Israël vers 1900–1920: Aaron Aaronsohn et Absalon Feinberg', *Cahiers Jacques Maritain*, vol. 23, October 1991, 14. Nehem-Bernheim discusses the Maritain–Feinberg friendship at greater length in her *Éclats d'une amitié: Avshalom Feinberg et Jacques Maritain* (Paris: Éditions Parole et Silence 2005).

52   Barré, *Jacques et Raïssa Maritain*, 450. Nor did Vatican officials, according to Sergio I. Minerbi, even agree with Maritain's premises concerning Zionism. Having 'adopted most of the arguments of the Arabs', the Vatican considered Zionism either irreligious or anti-religious, a threat to established Christian interests in the region, unacceptable in that it sought to establish a Jewish government, and a movement aiming at 'radical changes' and an 'accelerated modernization ... damaging to moral values' among the local population; Sergio I. Minerbi, *The Vatican and Zionism: Conflict in the Holy Land, 1895–1925*, trans. from the Hebrew by Arnold Schwarz (New York: Oxford University Press 1990), 198.

53   Letter from Maritain to Henri Massis, 1 October 1925: Maritain Archives, Kolbsheim.

54   Letter from Maritain to Henri Massis, 4 March 1927: Maritain Archives, Kolbsheim.

After a preparatory onslaught begun by the French Cardinal Paulin Andrieu, Pius XI condemned several of Maurras's books and the *Action française* newspaper in December 1926, offering a counter-thrust to the Action Française's political co-opting of French Catholics and forbidding the faithful to retain membership in the movement.[55] Maritain's book *Une Opinion sur Charles Maurras et le devoir des catholiques*, appearing the previous September, had tried to demonstrate the positive aspects of Maurras's fervent patriotism, love of order and invocation of Catholicism as a force behind social cohesion. Indeed, as regards 'spiritual Catholicity … what writer during the war laid greater stress upon it then Maurras?'[56] But a recent study of Maritain's political philosophy deems this book a 'quite naïve brochure',[57] in any event made moot by the climactic papal blow and the *Action française*'s defiant *non possumus*.[58] On 11 January 1927, as the Action Française crisis entered its bitter final phase, Maritain concluded a letter to Maurras as follows:

> I am appealing to something more profound than your reason. No one knows if the faith is dead or simply sleeping in your soul.… In a human sense, you find yourself alone, tragically alone between God who is testing you and your followers who obey you.… Is it possible to serve the common good until the very end … without also recognizing and serving … the Chief of the entire universe,

55 The 29 December 1926 decree promulgated by Pope Pius XI had been formulated as early as 1914 during the pontificate of Pius X, whose hesitancy, along with the coming of war, sufficed to shelve the condemnation. Seven of Maurras's books, together with his newspaper, were now placed on the Index. Doering, *Jacques Maritain and the French Catholic Intellectuals*, 29. Oscar Arnal describes Maritain's defection from the Maurrasian camp as crucial in ensuring the success of the condemnation: 'The shift of his intellectual skills to the Vatican camp constituted a serious blow to the Action Française and marked his emergence as the leading papal theologian in France'; Arnal, *Ambivalent Alliance*, 128. While Arnal makes an important observation about the political episode, another historian analyses the intellectual process: Maritain had begun to move away from what Stephen Schloesser calls the 'deep anxieties and the need to divide the world into absolute oppositions' that prompted the use of such terms as 'charnelle' in his 1920s writings; Schloesser, *Jazz Age Catholicism*, 79.

56 Jacques Maritain, *Une Opinion sur Charles Maurras et le devoir des catholiques* (Paris: Plon 1926), 72. He also remonstrated behind the scenes to convince Maurras to submit to the Pope, and sought the help of a leading theologian in this effort. When Maritain convened the fifth annual Thomist retreat at Meudon, on 24–8 September 1926, he asked Maurras to visit with the retreat chaplain Father Reginald Garrigou-Lagrange: 'Maurras came one morning for an interview with Fr. Garrigou from which I had hoped a great deal, but which produces nothing because of the weakness of Father before the obstinacy of this man'; Maritain, *Notebooks*, 158.

57 Guillaume de Thieulloy, *Le Chevalier de l'absolu: Jacques Maritain entre mystique et politique* (Paris: Éditions Gallimard 2005), 124.

58 'Non possumus!' was the headline in *Action française* on 24 December 1926.

who loves you and who created you? I think that is the big question before you. I too love your soul, and that is why I speak to you thus.[59]

Abandoning further attempts at mediation and mollification in the face of an *Action française* anti-papal press barrage, Maritain undertook to offer a philosophical support for the condemnation. And, in the process, he sought to save Thomism as a viable school of thought, vulnerable as it was to charges by the Catholic philosopher Maurice Blondel and others that in Maritain's hands nature and grace had become separated due to Maurrasian contamination.[60] Maritain's *Le Primauté du spirituel* (May 1927) asserted the imperative of spiritual authority making itself felt in the temporal realm in times of moral crisis, but drew as much on mediaeval precedents as it did on the particulars of the current crisis of the Action Française.[61]

After two private audiences with Pius XI in September 1927 in which the pontiff disabused the philosopher of any continued equivocation regarding Maurras,[62] Maritain led a group of clerics in drafting a more categorical rejection of Catholic collaboration with the Action Française. Even if the papal audiences carried an aftertaste of correction, Maritain could count the commission as a publicly visible honour, for centuries had elapsed since the last time a layperson presided over the drafting of a major doctrinal statement on behalf of the Catholic Church.[63] Maritain introduced and contributed the final chapter of *Pourquoi Rome a parlé*, describing the innocent participation in the movement by Catholics in unmistakably autobiographical terms:

> They nevertheless lent their support to this movement, because they believed the dangers could be remedied, [they could] find a useful support in the zeal for the civic good and in the important partial truths that Maurras re-established in their spirits, and they hoped that grace would one day transfigure this movement of thought by completing it and rectifying it in the light of faith. [But they were]

59 Letter from Maritain to Maurras, 11 January 1927, in *Non possumus*.
60 Chenaux, *Entre Maurras et Maritain*, 147–55. For further details of Blondel's polemic against Catholic collaboration with Maurras, which preceded Maritain's public association with the Action Française, see Michael Sutton, *Nationalism, Positivism, and Catholicism: The Politics of Charles Maurras and French Catholics, 1890–1914* (Cambridge: Cambridge University Press 1982), 123–62; and Jacques Prévotat, *Les Catholiques et l'Action Française: histoire d'une condamnation, 1899–1939* (Paris: Fayard 2001), 218–26.
61 The English translation is titled *The Things That Are Not Caesar's*, trans. from the French by J. F. Scanlan (London: Sheed and Ward 1932). Maritain's profession of the primacy of the expansively spiritual over the merely political did not entail an apolitical stance or a pendulum swing to the extreme left, but as Charles Blanchet describes it, something altogether more ambitious: a metaphysical reawakening and the establishment of a new civilization; Blanchet, 'Maritain face à la modernité', 25.
62 Chenaux, *Entre Maritain et Maurras*, 154–5.
63 Thieulloy, *Chevalier de l'absolu*, 132–3.

ready to denounce, at the first word from their supreme leader, alone competent to appreciate the real gravity of the dangers in question, the alliance thus concluded by them for honest reasons ... Nothing was more loyal and more logical than such a disposition.[64]

The remainder of his intervention argued for the inherently apolitical nature of the papal ban, while offering stinging inversions of the very core aspects of Maurras's self-fashioning. Maritain mocked 'men of order' who 'bring an anarchic agitation into the bosom of the Church of France', indeed calling this 'the very height of liberalism'. He identified the Action Française leadership with the 'prevaricating judges filled with a schismatic spirit' who condemned Joan of Arc (the icon of the Action Française). And, finally, he cited the most dangerous Jew in all history to undercut the Action Française's claim on French Catholic consciences: 'The "Hebrew Christ", the Word made flesh, reminds her [France] that He is her king, reminds her at the same time of what makes her strong, and of the demands of her vocation.'[65] Maritain had burned his bridges.

Maritain's very public break with Maurras and championing of the papal condemnation earned him the enmity of erstwhile friends such as Massis and, at least for a time, the novelist Georges Bernanos, who in 1931 published *La Grande Peur des bien-pensants*, a paean to the turn-of-the-century antisemitic journalist Édouard Drumont. Bernanos scoffed at Maritain's objections to it:

> My dear friend, what a phobia of anti-Semitism! God knows after all the very small place I have given it in my book! But when you write that my book 'wounds Christ from the very beginning,' I find this a very human view, a truly Jewish view of the Mystery of the Incarnation. It is precisely for just such flesh and blood reasons that your friends ended up putting Christ on the cross.[66]

Maritain would reconcile with Bernanos later in the decade but, in the meantime, he also contracted new alliances, such as that with the *Ésprit* founder and spiritual revolutionary Emmanuel Mounier, while solidifying

---

64 Paul Doncoeur, Marie Vincent Bernadot, Jean Étienne Marie Lajeunie, Daniel Lallement, F. X. Marquart and Jacques Maritain, *Pourquoi Rome a parlé* (Paris: Spès 1927), 332–3.

65 Ibid., 358, 361, 378. On Joan of Arc and the Action Française, see Martha Hanna, 'Iconology and ideology: images of Joan of Arc in the idiom of the Action Française, 1908–1931', *French Historical Studies*, vol. 14, no. 2, Autumn 1985, 215–39.

66 Doering, *Jacques Maritain and the French Catholic Intellectuals*, 44–59, 144–6. See also Bernanos's letter of 21 April 1928 to Maritain, in Georges Bernanos, *Correspondance. Tome I: 1904–1934*, ed. Albert Béguin and Jean Murray (Paris: Plon 1971), 321–2.

his reputation as a Catholic philosopher.[67] The early 1930s saw the completion of what has been cited as Maritain's quintessential exposition of Thomism, *Distinguer pour unir, ou les degrés du savoir* (1932) (translated into English as *The Degrees of Knowledge*),[68] as well as the polarization of European politics against the backdrop of the Great Depression, the Nazi seizure of power and France's own 6 February 1934 anti-parliamentary riots in which the Ligue d'Action Française figured prominently. Maritain led a group of five Catholic intellectuals in drafting the 19 April anti-fascist manifesto, *Pour le bien commun*.[69] For Maritain and his friends, and the fifty-two signatories, a sterile separation between the temporal and spiritual violated the vocation of Christians in the earthly city:

> Neither a sulky or fearful prudence nor a lax and opportunistic one have anything to do with Christian prudence. The Jewish people did not understand the depth of what was demanded of them at the moment when Christ brought them a *new* Testament, which was to fulfil and not abolish the old Law. With all due proportion kept, a similar demand is made of men at each visitation of God in their history. The promises made to the Church, and which concern the spiritual and supernatural order, do not dispense its children from vigilance in the temporal order … We have done with the separations and the exclusionism of the preceding age. Religion and politics, while remaining distinct, must be vitally united.[70]

Other manifestos necessarily would follow but dealing with the moral-political dimensions of the burgeoning European crisis rather than with a

67 After they met in 1928, Maritain gave crucial initial support to Emmanuel Mounier, the founder of the journal *Ésprit* who saw a politics of the human person as *imago Dei* as a spiritually revolutionary answer to what Joseph Amato calls 'a soulless world that refused youth's hopes, that denied the poor's needs, and even resisted acknowledging life's mystery'; Joseph Amato, *Mounier and Maritain: A French Catholic Understanding of the Modern World* [1975] (Ypsilanti, MI: Sapientia Press 2002), 129. John Hellman counters Amato's emphasis on the confluence of Maritain's and Mounier's personalist ideas for a Christian renewal of western civilization with a reminder that Maritain's enthusiasm for a journal that began appearing in 1932 had more or less soured by the end of 1933. Maritain objected to Mounier's broad ecumenism, as well as his openness to Third Force and Ordre Nouveau political tendencies within the *Ésprit* group, or, as Maritain put it, 'perfect "Kerenskyist" foolishness'; John Hellman, 'Maritain and Mounier: a secret quarrel over the future of the church', *Review of Politics*, vol. 42, no. 2, April 1980, 160. See also John Hellman, *Emmanuel Mounier and the New Catholic Left, 1930–1950* (Toronto: University of Toronto Press 1981).
68 McInerny, for example, calls *The Degrees of Knowledge* Maritain's 'acknowledged masterpiece'; McInerny, *The Very Rich Hours of Jacques Maritain*, 119.
69 Jacques Maritain, Étienne Borne, Olivier Lacombe, Yves R. Simon and Maurice de Gandhillac, *Pour le bien commun: les responsabilités du chrétien et le moment présent* (Paris: Desclée de Brouwer 1934). For an English translation, see 'For the common good: the Christian's responsibilities in the present crisis', trans. from the French and introd. by Bernard E. Doering, *Notes et Documents*, vol. 5, no. 20, July–August 1980, 1–20.
70 Maritain *et al.*, 'For the common good', 13, 18.

historic Jewish obliviousness to the significance of the Christian message.[71] Nonetheless, maintaining 'all due proportion' when writing about the Jews continued to present a challenge for Maritain.[72]

Impossible antisemitism

Maritain's second essay on the Jewish question, 'L'Impossible Antisé-mitisme' (1937), demonstrates the distance travelled since 1921 and 'Á propos de la question juive'. He now stressed the inanity of approaching the question racially or nationally, arguing instead that 'Race, People, Tribe, all these words used to describe them must be sacralized'.[73] Sacralization entails mystery. Holding to Paul's teaching that the Mystery of Israel can only have an eschatological solution, he averred that 'what is called the *Jewish Problem* is a problem *without a solution*': one must acknowledge the temporal insolubility of the Jewish Problem, the German case proving for example the folly of placing one's faith in assimilation.[74] Continued attempts at worldly solutions could only lead to a 'carnal war directed at the extermination, the deportation, or the enslavement of the Jews, a war of the world and the *animalis homo* against Israel'.[75] Only a *'pluralist and personalist'* willingness to accept Jewish distinctiveness in the framework of a common humanity, the 'opposite of the absurd Hitlerian mediaevalist parody', stood a chance of preventing ongoing tragedy from devolving into total disaster.[76]

Yet, as much as Maritain deplored this 'tragic' predicament of European and world Jewry, seeing in it 'the tragedy of humanity itself … of man in his fight with the world and the world in its fight against God', he still could not separate the travails of modern Jews from the age-old sin of the fathers, 'priests of Israel, bad keepers of the vineyard, killers of the prophets, who for good reasons of political prudence had opted for the world, and to that choice all the people are henceforth bound—until they change of their own accord'.[77] Maritain offered the mystery of a chosen people bound to a fatal choice: 'The Jews chose the world; they have loved it, their suffering comes

---

71 These included À *propos de la repression des troubles de Vienne* (April 1934), *Pour la justice et pour la paix* (October 1935, after Mussolini's invasion of Ethiopia), and *Pour l'honneur* (November 1936, after Interior Minister Roger Salengro was driven to suicide by the slanders of the extreme right).

72 Maritain *et al.*, 'For the common good', 4–8.

73 Jacques Maritan, 'L'Impossible Antisémitisme', in Maritain *et al.*, *L'Impossible Antisémitisme*, 72–3. The essay originally appeared in 1937 in Henri Daniel-Rops (ed.), *Les Juifs* (Paris: Plon 1937).

74 Ibid., 92.

75 Ibid., 74.

76 Ibid., 97, emphasis in original.

77 Ibid., 76–7.

from having been held by their choice. They are prisoners and victims of this world that they love, and of which they are not, will never be, cannot be.'[78]

Here Maritain does not relinquish his old view that Jews have a mission to disturb the world: he sanctifies it. Guillaume de Thieulloy looks back on Maritain's 1921 essay on the Jewish Question and sees it as a *hapax*, that is, an isolated utterance, asserting that its author would never disavow, nor take up again, this early 'critique of revolutionary messianism' in his further meditations on the Mystery of Israel.[79] But this scholarly assessment confuses the point that in 1937 Maritain offered a transcendent update of Jewish 'revolutionary messianism', renegotiating a series of anti-Jewish stereotypes even as he repudiated antisemitism itself. Whereas, in the 1920s, Maritain could see the archetypical insider Jew behind modernity's ills, he now emphasized how Jews were rejected and persecuted in the modern world, for it is 'the vocation of Israel that the world loathes'.[80] Perhaps most importantly, he now saw it as logically impossible to be an antisemite and a Christian for it is only 'in obeying the spirit of the world, not the spirit of Christianity that Christians can be antisemites'. The Christian antisemite betrays Christianity itself, not just in theory, but in practice, for in 'demeaning the race from which God and the Immaculate Mother of God came forth ... the bitter zeal of the antisemite always finally turns into a bitter zeal against Christianity itself'.[81]

Maritain's theology largely remained consistent, but its application reflected a growing emphasis on Christian personalism and democratic pluralism and a degree of empirical perspective not typically associated with the modern revival of mediaeval Thomism. One of his most influential books, *L'Humanisme intégral* (1936), evoked the hope of a new Christendom animated by a humanism that 'does not worship man but really and effectively respects human dignity and does justice to the integral demands

---

78 Ibid., 78. Note that when this essay was published in English as 'The mystery of Israel' in 1941, Maritain changed the first part of this quoted passage: 'The Jews chose the world ... (*Les Juifs ont choisi le monde ...*)' in the 1937 original becomes 'The Jews (I do not mean the Jews individually, but the mystical body of Israel at the moment when it struck against the rock) the Jews at a crucial moment chose the world ...'; Jacques Maritain, 'The mystery of Israel'; in Jacques Maritain, *Ransoming the Time*, trans. from the French by Harry Lorin Binsse (New York: Charles Scribner's Sons 1941), 153. This question of 'choice' also figures prominently in Esther Starobinski-Safran's interpretation of the same essay. She more favourably evaluates Maritain's ability at this point to make a clear distinction between a punishment event and a lasting state of punishment; Esther Starobinski-Safran, 'Judaïsme, peuple juif, et état d'Isräel', in Bressolette and Mougel (eds), *Jacques Maritain face à la modernité*, 225. I argue on the contrary that he still struggled with this problem during the Holocaust itself; Richard Francis Crane, 'Jacques Maritain, the mystery of Israel, and the Holocaust', *Catholic Historical Review*, forthcoming.
79 Thieulloy, *Chevalier de l'absolu*, 106.
80 Maritain, 'L'Impossible Antisémitisme', 91.
81 Ibid., 100–1.

of the person'.[82] Such a 'heroic humanism' would have to overcome 'the extreme partisans of racism in Germany, those who wish to return to a national and racial (Nordic) religion anterior to Christianity', as well as a Soviet Communism that unconsciously aped the Christian mission to redeem a fallen world.[83] Both ideological extremes could be seen as variants of the same anti-human totalitarianism resulting from a centuries-long 'dialectic of anthropocentric humanism', the materialization of man that also characterized a selfish 'bourgeois' humanism. Maritain concludes: 'Let things continue this way and it seems that earth will no longer be habitable, to use a phrase of the venerable Aristotle, except by beasts or gods.'[84]

Maritain's predicating of this new humanism on 'the preliminary liquidation of modern capitalism and of the regime of money-profit',[85] along with his condemnation of the atrocities of Franco's 'crusade' in Spain after 1936, led a number of Catholic critics on the right to call him a 'Marxist Christian', tainted by his association with Jews or, in the revived terminology of the post-war period, Judaeo-Bolshevism. Not only did Maritain become embroiled in a very public quarrel with Paul Claudel in the latter half of the 1930s, but such political tensions managed to disturb the monthly Thomism study circles and annual retreats convened by the Maritains since the early 1920s at their home in Meudon, outside Paris. On 24 September 1937, Jacques confided the following to his notebook concerning the longtime spiritual director at Meudon, Father Reginald Garrigou-Lagrange:

> Father is very worked-up against me; goes so far as to reproach me, a convert, with wanting to give lessons in the Christian spirit to 'us who have been Catholic for three hundred years.' (And why not since the Crusades? He forgets that he also was a convert, through the reading of Ernest Hello.) It seems that Raissa and Vera are being implicated as dragging me along by their influence. (Russian Jewesses, are they not? They who detest these political quarrels, and who would have been so glad if I could have remained isolated from them, if I had not seen there a testimony to be rendered to truth.) This puts me in a black rage, which I do not hide. The retreat begins under a very bad sign. Father Garrigou would like to prohibit me from speaking on the philosophy of history, and from judging events, and from acting on young people in these matters. He is not the only one in Rome to think like this, I know very well, and to be terrified of the 'political Maritain.' Metaphysics only! But he himself does not hesitate to pronounce in favor of Franco and to approve the civil war in Spain.[86]

82 Jacques Maritain, *Integral Humanism: Temporal and Spiritual Problems of a New Christendom*, trans. from the French by Joseph W. Evans (New York: Charles Scribner's Sons 1968), 7.
83 Ibid., 39–40, 51, 145.
84 Ibid., 32, 34.
85 Ibid., 190.
86 Maritain, *Notebooks*, 169.

Lest this seem like oversensitivity on Maritain's part, it should be noted that Franco's interior minister, Ramón Serrano Súñer, would soon devote one of his radio broadcasts to excoriating 'this converted Jew [*sic*] who spreads throughout the world the fable of Franco's massacres and the immense silliness of the legitimacy of the Barcelona government'.[87]

Maritain associated the looming spectre of general war with what he already feared would amount to a 'Passion of Israel' driven by race hatred.[88] Accordingly, he saw it as imperative that Christians oppose the subjection of the human person to racial categorization, drawing on both recent church teachings and his collaboration with other Catholic opponents of racism. Writing in the American Jesuit John LaFarge's *Interracial Review* in May 1937, Maritain insisted that 'racialism to an unimaginable degree degrades and humiliates reason, thought, science, and art, which are henceforth made subservient to flesh and blood and are stripped of their natural "catholicity"'.[89] Both Maritain and LaFarge, the latter an outspoken opponent of racism in his native United States, could cite a papal lead in this regard. The 31 December 1930 papal encyclical *Casti Connubii* had, in upholding the sanctity of the marital bond, condemned the kind of anti-miscegenation legislation that was found in numerous American states and that would be replicated in Nazi Germany in the mid-1930s.[90]

In a personal letter, LaFarge responded to Maritain that inculcating 'the principles of justice toward people of other races' depended vitally on fostering 'a new mentality truly supernatural, in the light of the catholicity of the universal Church'.[91] But how to witness to this 'new mentality', already expounded upon by Maritain in *L'Humanisme intégral*, and broached by LaFarge the following year in a never-to-be-promulgated encyclical commissioned by Pius XI as a denunciation of racist antisemitism?[92] Maritain would lament the fact that this encyclical languished in the subsequent pontificate of Pius XII, sharing with his Swiss friend the future Cardinal Charles Journet

---

87 The 19 June 1938 broadcast is quoted in Vidal-Naquet, 'Jacques Maritain et les juifs', 40.

88 Maritain, 'L'Impossible Antisémitisme', 81.

89 Jacques Maritain, 'The menace of racialism', *Interracial Review*, vol. 10, May 1937, 70.

90 *Casti Connubii*, Encyclical of Pope Pius XI on Christian Marriage, 31 December 1930, available at www.vatican.va/holy_father/pius_xi/encyclicals/documents/hf_p-xi_enc_31121930_casti-connubii_en.html (viewed 24 June 2008).

91 Letter from John LaFarge to Maritain, 26 May 1937: John LaFarge Papers, Georgetown University, Washington, D.C. Maritain himself had long stressed the catholicity of Catholicism, writing in 1922, for example: 'Consider how the thinking elite is focused, more markedly than at any other moment in the past two centuries, on Christianity, and how the Catholic faith appears more demonstrably than ever, amidst the universal failure of human systems, as the only stable light, as the only honest intellectual force, always new and alive in its permanence'; Maritain, *Antimoderne*, 218. For a longer exposition of this usage, see Schloesser, *Jazz Age Catholicism*, 167–70.

92 See Georges Passelecq and Bernard Suchecky, *The Hidden Encyclical of Pius XI*, trans. from the French by Steven Rendall (New York: Harcourt Brace 1997).

his 'sadness and anguish' at Pius XI's death and the indefinite shelving of the letter.[93] This sadness and anguish regarding antisemitism would only increase in the years of atrocity to come.

Surviving Maurras

Restoring the constant of a spiritual supernaturalism in Maritain's Jewish Question complicates an otherwise simple and direct causal linkage between his developing philosemitism and his changing politics. But it reveals much more than the Whig-historical early Maritain/later Maritain schema. A primarily theological framing of the Jewish Question, asserting a reality above and beyond the political, had always allowed Maritain to maintain a measurable, albeit philosophically fluctuating, distance from the antisemitism that formed a tangible component of Maurrasian integral nationalism. One cannot tell whether his discomfort—accentuated by his love for Raïssa—with overtly antisemitic outbursts such as those emitted by the Camelots du Roi would have eventually led him to break with the Action Française, which subsequently became known as much for its quaint monarchism as its radical potential. Indeed, by the mid-1930s, a number of individuals such as the rising fascist writer Robert Brasillach would distance themselves from Maurras for not being *enough* of a right-wing extremist.[94] As it happened, in the 1920s Maritain resisted breaking with Maurras until Pope Pius XI effectively ordered him to do so, until he appreciated the potential discrediting of Thomism due to its association with the extreme right, and until he embraced a clarified vocation of admonishing a new generation of Catholic intellectuals to place their faith above all other considerations.

Yet this very 'primacy of the spiritual' also made some of the anti-Jewish stereotypes he held almost intractable, that is, until the practical consequences of fascism and antisemitism in the 1930s forced him to try to reconcile his theological presuppositions with his burgeoning personalist and pluralist social and political philosophy. As a result, Maritain's ambivalent philosemitism, characterized by a preoccupation with the Mystery of Israel and influenced by his ambiguous engagement with modernity, would remain a work in progress through the 1930s, as well as

93 Letter from Maritain to Journet, 6 February 1939, in Charles Journet, *Journet Maritain Correspondance. II. 1930–1939* (Fribourg: Éditions Universitaires 1997), 787.
94 Paul Mazgaj evokes this disenchantment with Maurras as a quintessential man of inaction, describing how Brasillach 'discovered a circle of young Action française alumni, indebted to Maurras but increasingly impatient with the backward-looking and geographically inward focus of his movement' when he joined the *équipe* at *Je suis partout* and 'found an especially kindred spirit in Lucien Rebatet'; Paul Mazgaj, *Imagining Fascism: The Cultural Politics of the Young Right, 1930–1945* (Newark: University of Delaware Press 2007), 184.

into the Second World War and the Holocaust. Given his acknowledged influence on a 'generation of Catholic intellectuals', what can be said of Maritain might prompt further enquiry into how French Catholics (and Catholics in general) dealt with the antisemitic temptation of their time, which, like other temptations, could present itself in changing forms, according to circumstance if not opportunity.[95]

The Action Française crisis and subsequent estrangement notwithstanding, Maritain's relationship with Maurras did not completely end with the controversies of the interwar era. After the 1940 fall of France to the Wehrmacht, Maurras found himself invoked as the intellectual godfather of Vichy France—the authoritarian regime that finally invoked the series of anti-Jewish laws that served as prelude, however unintentionally, to state co-operation with the Nazi Final Solution—as Maritain condemned the same regime and the same policies from exile in the United States. Condemned to national degradation and life imprisonment after the liberation in 1945, Maurras would famously exclaim: 'This is the revenge of Dreyfus!' But we should not count these as his last words. Before expiring in 1952, the erstwhile *academicien* augmented his lonely narrative of betrayal and vengeance, concluding his last book, a posthumously published tribute to Pope Pius X, with a four-page profession of his hatred for Jacques Maritain. He painted the picture of a consummate opportunist, 'an excellent professor of philosophy lacking the talent to be a philosopher himself', who had dropped Maurras for 'two new masters of sacred sociology', the Abbé Gregoire and Harriet Beecher Stowe, receiving from them 'the revelation of the Rights of Man and *Uncle Tom's Cabin*'. Guilty of simony 'in character and vocation', he could now enjoy a carefree life, this 'happy husband of the

95 A number of French Catholic writers during this time tended to rail at the Jews even as they denounced antisemitism. For example, when Maritain contributed 'L'Impossible Antisémitisme' to Daniel-Rops's volume *Les Juifs*, his essay joined a diverse collection of writings, including contributions by Paul Claudel and lesser known writers such as the Jewish Catholic convert René Schwob. Schwob's essay shocked his friend Maritain: 'Je voudrais que la France se défendît du venin juif, mais par des moyens qui ne soient pas ceux de la démagogie hitlérienne'; René Schwob, 'Être chrétien', in Daniel-Rops (ed.), *Les Juifs*, 326. Another contributor, Jesuit Joseph Bonsirven, an influential biblical scholar, went on to write a 1942 essay on the Mystery of Israel that reinforced, in the very midst of the genocide, the theme of Jewish obliviousness to their divine calling. For Bonsirven this amounted to a renounced, but latent, 'missionary' vocation, whereas Maritain termed it a 'messianic' one. Most importantly, Bonsirven wrote his essay as a contribution to a book intended to counteract antisemitism and persecution in Vichy France, a book prepared clandestinely by Catholic *résistant* clergy also involved in *Témoignage chrétien*, and smuggled to Switzerland for publication; Joseph Bonsirven, 'Le Mystère d'Israël', in Henri de Lubac, Joseph Chaine, Louis Richard and Joseph Bonsirven, *Israël et la foi chrétienne* (Fribourg: Librairie de l'Université 1942).

Jewess'.[96] For Maritain, these words 'literally struck me in the heart (my heart attack, in March 1954)'.[97]

But Maritain had already survived Maurras. Both the scholarly Catholic philosemite on the one hand, and the most violently antisemitic French fascists on the other, had long since left the *vieux maître* behind. They, and the prejudice known as antisemitism, had by the end of the 1930s moved on to a new future.[98] In the 1920s Maritain became embedded in an emergently antisemitic milieu nurtured by a widespread fear of Judaeo-Bolshevism and a distrust of liberal democracy. His significance for the history of antisemitism in modern France lies in how he divested himself of these tendencies as a violently racist prejudice against Jews took hold in interwar Europe. But just as a Catholic rejection of racism—as well as an empirical appreciation of incipient antisemitic violence—helped support this divestment, a fidelity to basic theological presuppositions shackled his philosemitism in fundamentally anti-Judaic stereotypes. Accordingly, Maritain's Jewish Question by no means resolved itself before 1939–45, when the systematic murder of six million Jewish children, women and men reframed the question yet again, this time from interwar anxiety to wartime horror.

96 Charles Maurras, *Le Bienheureux Pie X, Sauveur de la France* (Paris: Plon 1953), 217–20.
97 Quoted in Vidal-Naquet, 'Jacques Maritain et les juifs', 54.
98 Vicki Caron sums up the change in French antisemitism from around 1900 to the outbreak of the Second World War as follows: 'While the animosity aimed at Jews in middle-class professions had begun well before the Dreyfus affair, the tendency to link Jews to the political left, which climaxed in the vitriolic attacks on Blum, together with the theme of Jewish war-mongering, were more specific to the interwar years'; Vicki Caron, '"The Jewish Question" from Dreyfus to Vichy', in Martin S. Alexander (ed.), *French History since Napoleon* (London: Arnold 1999), 198. Caron's assessment, accurate in situating antisemitism socially, politically and economically, might be enhanced by mention of the cultural construction of the Jew-as-vermin, or even bacillus, seen most strikingly in the novels of Céline, for example.

Kenneth B. Clark and the problem of power

DAMON FREEMAN

With increasing attention devoted to the poor and the problem of juvenile delinquency in the United States during the 1960s, a unique opportunity was created for the prominent African American psychologist Kenneth B. Clark to address the needs of Harlem. A professor at City College of New York, Clark is best known for his involvement in the 1954 *Brown v. Board of Education of Topeka, Kansas* decision in which his research helped convince a reluctant US Supreme Court that racial segregation caused psychological damage to African American children.[1] By the early 1960s he had also become a noted authority on the problems of juvenile delinquency. In 1961 President John Kennedy established the Committee on Juvenile Delinquency, headed by his brother, Attorney General Robert Kennedy, to distribute grants to community organizations that worked on reducing crime and expanding economic opportunities among the country's youth. As a member of the board of directors of the Harlem Neighborhoods Association (HANA), a loose affiliation of community groups that had organized in 1958 to confront delinquency and poverty, Clark wrote a planning grant that won $230,000 from the President's Committee; New York City awarded an additional $100,000. By 1962 HANA had created Harlem Youth Opportunities Unlimited, Inc. (HARYOU) to develop a comprehensive programme that would tackle the problems facing teenagers and young adults in Harlem. Clark served as acting chairman of the board of directors and chief project consultant. He wrote most of the 620-page proposal; indeed, many of the ideas and concepts would be re-emphasized in his classic 1965 book *Dark Ghetto*.[2]

However, Clark faced a rival organization. The Associated Community Teams (ACT) had been established the same year as HARYOU at the behest of Congressman Adam Clayton Powell. Representing Harlem in the United States Congress, Powell appears to have been alarmed by the spectre of a new organization over which he did not have control. Due to his efforts, ACT also received funding from the President's Committee to provide jobs for teenagers and young adults in Harlem. Powell also arranged for a merger between the two organizations in the late spring of 1964. Coincidentally, Congress was about to appropriate $118 million to

1 Much has been written about Clark's involvement and testimony during the *Brown* case. See Richard Kluger, *Simple Justice: The History of Brown v. Board of Education and Black America's Struggle for Equality* (New York: Knopf 1976); Ben Keppel, *The Work of Democracy: Ralph Bunche, Kenneth B. Clark, Lorraine Hansberry, and the Cultural Politics of Race* (Cambridge, MA: Harvard University Press 1995); David Rosner and Gerald Markowitz, *Children, Race, and Power: Kenneth and Mamie Clark's Northside Center* (Charlottesville: University Press of Virginia 1996), 90–2; and John P. Jackson, Jr, *Social Scientists for Social Justice: Making the Case against Segregation* (New York: New York University Press 2002). For highly critical analyses of Clark's role and the soundness of his psychological damage theory, see William E. Cross, *Shades of Black: Diversity in African-American Identity* (Philadelphia: Temple University Press 1991) and Daryl Michael Scott, *Contempt and Pity: Social Policy and the Image of the Damaged Black Psyche, 1880–1996* (Chapel Hill: University of North Carolina Press 1997).

2 Kenneth B. Clark, *Youth in the Ghetto: A Study of the Consequences of Powerlessness and a Blueprint for Change* (New York: Harlem Youth Opportunities Unlimited, Inc. 1964), 29; Kenneth B. Clark, *Dark Ghetto: Dilemmas of Social Power* (New York: Harper and Row 1965). See also Woody Klein, 'People vs. politicians: defeat in Harlem', *The Nation*, 27 July 1964, 27–9, and Rosner and Markowitz, *Children, Race, and Power*, 188–9.

HARYOU to implement Clark's recommendations in a new and massive anti-poverty programme.[3]

This article uses the struggle between Clark and Powell over the future and control of HARYOU and ACT as a prism through which to examine the trajectory of the civil rights movement, the politics of race and power, and racial thought more generally by the mid-1960s. It is difficult to situate the conflict historically, for it does not neatly fit within the civil rights or Black Power narratives. Yet the HARYOU–ACT controversy is important for what it tells us about the intra-racial struggle that could and did occur at times over the direction of the movement. The episode also predates many of the conflicts over the control and direction of the War on Poverty programmes that received an unprecedented amount of federal funding during the 1960s in cities such as Philadelphia, Cleveland, St Louis and San Francisco.[4] In what follows I show how the Clark–Powell split symbolized both the promises and the perils of the black freedom struggle. I also explore how the conflict was central to Clark's public life, shaping his thinking regarding the nature of power, the civil rights movement and the prospects for African American leadership. He saw the dilemma of race as being subsumed within what he felt was the larger issue—power—and attempted in writings such as *Dark Ghetto* to explain how Americans thought about and experienced race and, more specifically, the issues of black political power as represented by Powell. In a way, Clark's arguments anticipated many of the salient points articulated by critical race theorists during the 1980s and 1990s.[5] By the end of 1965 he would

3 'HARYOU and ACT: merger problem', *New York Times*, 11 June 1964, 20; Keppel, *The Work of Democracy*, 147–51; Rosner and Markowitz, *Children, Race, and Power*, 197–9; Allen J. Matusow, *The Unraveling of America: A History of Liberalism in the 1960s* (New York: Harper and Row 1984), 258; Charles V. Hamilton, *Adam Clayton Powell, Jr.: The Political Biography of an American Dilemma* (New York: Atheneum 1991), 425–7.

4 For the best historical work on the War on Poverty, see Matusow, *The Unraveling of America*, 243–71; Michael B. Katz, *The Undeserving Poor: From the War on Poverty to the War on Welfare* (New York: Pantheon 1989), 79–123; and Thomas Jackson, 'The state, the movement, and the urban poor: the War on Poverty and political mobilization in the 1960s', in Michael B. Katz (ed.), *The 'Underclass' Debate: Views from History* (Princeton, NJ: Princeton University Press 1993), 403–39. See also Clark's own comprehensive study of anti-poverty and community action programmes in Kenneth B. Clark and Jeannette Hopkins, *A Relevant War against Poverty: A Study of Community Action Programs and Observable Social Change* (New York: Harper and Row 1968).

5 Critical race theory is a body of thought that emerged primarily out of the legal profession during the 1980s and questioned the ideas and assumptions that many civil rights activists took for granted, including the concept that step-by-step racial progress was possible in the American legal system. Today the school of thought has gained influence in other academic fields such as sociology, women's studies and education. For an excellent basic introduction to the field, see Richard Delgado and Jean Stefancic, *Critical Race Theory: An Introduction* (New York: New York University Press 2001). For more extensive analysis from a legal perspective, see Kimberlé Crenshaw, Neil Gotanda, Gary Peller and Kendall Thomas (eds), *Critical Race Theory: The Key Writings That Formed the Movement* (New York: The New Press 1995); Richard Delgado and

forcefully argue that the American dilemma of race that had been articulated so well twenty years earlier by his close friend, the sociologist Gunnar Myrdal,[6] had been replaced by the 'new' American dilemma of power.

Invisible walls

Today it is difficult to find any sign that HARYOU–ACT ever existed in Harlem. Yet, when Clark's proposal was introduced, it created quite a stir due to its sweeping vision and bold agenda. The massive *Youth in the Ghetto* study incorporated a plethora of information: population data, IQ score charts, maps of high crime areas and the proportion of population under twenty years old, high school graduation and drop-out rates, the occupational distribution of males and females, the location of elementary and junior high schools, churches and dilapidated housing units, the number of businesses and types of industries, family income and juvenile delinquency rates, narcotics use and sexually transmitted disease rates, and the number of infant deaths, homicides, suicides, social service organizations and day-care centres. It is no exaggeration to assert that it was the most comprehensive sociological study ever done of Harlem. Yet at the heart of the proposal was

Jean Stefancic (eds), *Critical Race Theory: The Cutting Edge* (Philadelphia: Temple University Press 2000); Francisco Valdes, Jerome M. Culp and Angela P. Harris (eds), *Crossroads, Directions, and a New Critical Race Theory* (Philadelphia: Temple University Press 2002); and Adrien Katherine Wing (ed.), *Critical Race Feminism: A Reader* (New York: New York University Press 2003). For applications of critical race theory to education, see Adrienne D. Dixson and Celia K. Rousseau (eds), *Critical Race Theory in Education* (New York: Routledge 2006).

6 In 1938 the Carnegie Corporation commissioned Swedish sociologist Gunnar Myrdal to conduct a massive study of the so-called 'Negro problem' in the United States. The foundation chose him because it was felt that, as a non-American, Myrdal would bring objectivity to the subject. The project consulted with hundreds of social scientists including Kenneth Clark (who at the time was finishing his Ph.D. in psychology at Columbia University) on the situation of African Americans in the economy, the labour market, education, wealth, health and medicine, and politics. At nearly 1,500 pages, the study became indispensable for social scientists and activists interested in addressing racism in the United States from the late 1940s to the early 1960s. Myrdal concluded that the widening gap between the American principle of equality (which he termed the 'American Creed') and the reality of black life was due less to personal prejudices and discrimination and more to the failure of local authorities to enforce the Constitution, particularly in the South. He predicted, nevertheless, that the American Creed would eventually triumph and racism would disappear, thereby resolving the 'American dilemma'. See Gunnar Myrdal, *An American Dilemma: The Negro Problem and Modern Democracy* (New York: Harper and Brothers 1944). For biographies of Myrdal, see Walter A. Jackson, *Gunnar Myrdal and America's Conscience: Social Engineering and Racial Liberalism, 1938–1987* (Chapel Hill: University of North Carolina Press 1990), and David W. Southern, *Gunnar Myrdal and Black–White Relations: The Use and Abuse of An American Dilemma, 1944–1969* (Baton Rouge: Louisiana State University Press 1987).

Clark's search for a way to empower the Harlem community politically, not only thereby changing the status of the poor but revolutionizing the political and economic relationships that existed between Blacks and Whites. He felt that this was absolutely necessary in order to address the high rate of juvenile delinquency. Only a holistic community-oriented approach that addressed the wider political and economic issues caused by racism would lead to a more prosperous Harlem.

Clark introduced the study by voicing his fears that the civil rights movement was in danger of losing its relevance. He believed that 'emotionally charged issues of this scope' could lead to an over-simplification of the problems facing the black poor. In particular, he felt that the movement at times led to racial posturing and a preoccupation 'with dramatic demonstrations and charismatic ... individuals', confusing these symbolic stances with the need for systematic planning, strategy and social action. When the HARYOU study was first announced, several critics responded publicly by arguing that enough research had already been done on Harlem and that solutions, not more research, were needed.[7] Clark viewed this impatience as a manifestation of the emotion generated by the movement and the failure of the *Brown* decision to produce actual change. For him, the study became an effort aimed at providing the necessary strategy that would be relevant to the needs of Harlem's citizens as well as providing a national blueprint to attack the problems of race and poverty.[8]

Clark's interpretation of black and white culture in a segregated society was evident in the opening pages of *Youth in the Ghetto*. He reiterated his longstanding claim that racism damaged the personalities of black and white children. For Blacks, he argued, it generated feelings of inferiority and self-doubt; for Whites, it generated over-confidence, an exaggerated sense of self-importance and fantasies that represented unrealistic feelings either of racial harmony or of fear bordering on paranoia. Although Clark acknowledged the existence of a resilient African American culture in a nation that upheld white supremacy, he saw problems within that culture. Young black men in particular, he posited, reacted to their powerlessness and outsider status by creating a personality type that in some ways rejected the societal norms and values of the mainstream. At the same time, it also celebrated materialism and a middle-class ethos by embracing the typical business suit and reshaping it to fit their reality. This 'zoot-suit personality', as Clark termed and defined it in the 1940s, was a form of black psychological protection

---

7 James Hicks, 'Another angle', *Amsterdam News*, undated clipping: Library of Congress, Washington, D.C., Kenneth Bancroft Clark Papers, Folder 2, Box 49; 'Uptown rallies to answer sniping at HARYOU and ACT', *New York Courier*, 23 February 1963, 1; 'Publisher's statement', *Amsterdam News*, 9 March 1963, 1. See also Rosner and Markowitz, *Children, Race, and Power*, 192.

8 Clark, *Youth in the Ghetto*, 2–4.

against a racially hostile society. As for how black women specifically coped with their powerlessness, he was markedly silent.[9]

It is significant that Clark had already begun to reject the accepted liberal wisdom of the 1940s and 1950s that American beliefs in equality were incompatible with white supremacy long before the open disenchantment expressed by many black activists with the failures of school desegregation. In a little-known 1950 essay, for example, he argued that the problem of race was much more complex and fundamental than Gunnar Myrdal and others had stated. The 'American Creed', he concluded, was Whites' assertion of *their* belief in equality with other Whites. Therefore, the problem involved more than changing behaviour to conform to beliefs in equality. For him, it meant challenging the core of American beliefs and behaviour, not for the purpose of integrating that society, but for radically and fundamentally altering it.[10]

Nonetheless, in Clark's view, achieving that radical and fundamental alteration of American society from one of injustice to one of social justice

9 During the 1940s and 1950s, Clark raised significant objections to the way that psychology interpreted or lacked the means to interpret the manifestations of living in a segregated society. While many scholars have (mistakenly) pointed to the five articles authored by him and his wife Mamie Phipps Clark that examined and analysed racial identification and preference in young children as evidence that the Clarks saw black culture as damaged, less examined are other articles written by Kenneth Clark that questioned the ability of the social sciences to comprehend the impact of racial socialization or that portrayed a more complicated picture of black identity. For the controversial five articles by Kenneth B. Clark and Mamie P. Clark, see 'The development of consciousness of self and the emergence of racial identification in Negro preschool children', *Journal of Social Psychology*, vol. 10, November 1939, 591–9; 'Segregation as a factor in the racial identification of Negro preschool children: a preliminary report', *Journal of Experimental Education*, vol. 8, December 1939, 161–3; 'Skin color as a factor in racial identification of Negro preschool children', *Journal of Social Psychology*, vol. 11, February 1940, 159–69; 'Racial identification and preference in Negro children', in Ted Newcomb and E. L. Hartley (eds), *Readings in Social Psychology* (New York: Henry Holt 1947), 169–78; and 'Emotional factors in racial identification and preference in Negro children', *Journal of Negro Education*, vol. 19, Summer 1950, 341–50. For criticism of the Clarks and their methods, see Cross, *Shades of Black*, ch. 1, 'Landmark studies of Negro identity', and Scott, *Contempt and Pity*, 82–3, 96–7, 122–4. For other articles by Clark that provide a broader picture of his thinking, especially his 'zoot-suit personality' concept, see Kenneth B. Clark, 'Group violence: a preliminary study of the attitudinal pattern of its acceptance and rejection: a study of the 1943 Harlem riot', *Journal of Social Psychology*, vol. 19, May 1944, 319–37; Kenneth B. Clark, 'A brown girl in a speckled world', *Journal of Social Issues*, vol. 1, May 1945, 10–15; Kenneth B. Clark and James Barker, 'The zoot effect in personality: a race riot participant', *Journal of Abnormal and Social Psychology*, vol. 40, April 1945, 143–8; Kenneth B. Clark, Stella Chess and Alexander Thomas, 'The importance of cultural evaluation in psychiatric diagnosis and treatment', *Psychiatric Quarterly*, vol. 27, 1953, 102–14; and Kenneth B. Clark, 'Color, class, personality and juvenile delinquency', *Journal of Negro Education*, vol. 28, Summer 1959, 240–51.

10 Kenneth Clark, 'Racial prejudice among American minorities', *International Social Science Bulletin*, vol. 2, Winter 1950, 506–13.

would not occur without personal and social trauma. The problem involved more than changing the beliefs and behaviour of Whites, for the American system of racial segregation had created a peculiar society that was 'not only damaging but protective in a debilitating way'.[11] Interestingly, Clark saw the 'ghetto' as America's ultimate symbol of a segregated society, unlike the millions of Americans who viewed the South as that symbol due to the daily images of racial violence televised from Albany, Georgia and Birmingham, Alabama at the time of the HARYOU study:

> The dark ghetto's invisible walls have been erected by the white society, by those who have power, both to confine those who have *no* power and to perpetuate their powerlessness. The dark ghettos are social, political, educational, and —above all—economic colonies. Their inhabitants are subject peoples, victims of the greed, cruelty, insensitivity, guilt, and fear of their masters.[12]

Despite this bleak and desolate description, Clark acknowledged in the same paragraph the complexities and contradictions of black life within a segregated urban space:

> Yet within its pervasive pathology exists a surprising human resilience. The ghetto is hope, it is despair, it is churches and bars. It is aspiration for change, and it is apathy. It is vibrancy, it is stagnation. It is courage, and it is defeatism. It is cooperation and concern, and it is suspicion, competitiveness, and rejection. It is the surge toward assimilation, and it is alienation and withdrawal within the protective walls of the ghetto.[13]

In an interesting way, Clark's interpretation of the ghetto mirrored his 'zoot-suit personality' theory that he had formulated twenty years earlier to help explain what he thought was really happening to young black men. This overall philosophy of the ghetto as an internal American colonial institution, damaging while protecting its inhabitants, rejecting while embracing mainstream middle-class values, shaped his thought as he conceived the HARYOU programme.

A blueprint for social change

The HARYOU proposal called for the creation of pre-school academies (a precursor of the federal government's Head Start programme), the establishment of after-school remedial centres that would focus on teaching

---

11 Clark, *Youth in the Ghetto*, 5–6.
12 Ibid., 10–11.
13 Ibid. These lines would be prominently featured again in the opening pages of his classic work *Dark Ghetto* (11–12).

basic academic skills to elementary and junior high school children, the creation of a Reading Mobilization Year that would replace the curriculum in all grades for one year, and the reorganization of teacher training and promotion.[14] Beyond education the proposal appealed for the establishment of junior academies that would serve children between the ages of eight and seventeen who were returning to the community from treatment centres or juvenile facilities. Personnel for the programmes would come from the community and include seventeen- to twenty-one-year-olds who would be hired as group counsellors and teacher aides.[15] Clark also proposed the establishment of a community-run Institute for Narcotics Research. The institute would emphasize treatment, education and rehabilitation over punishment, and even organize protests against Harlem drug dealers.[16] Another component of the HARYOU agenda was the creation of arts and cultural centres to complement the educational and juvenile programmes. The centres would provide opportunities for young children to participate in arts and performing arts classes; establish studios in film, sound, industrial arts and interior design; and employ artists, craftspersons and technicians as consultants, designers and teachers for all of HARYOU's programmes, such as the pre-school academies. Clark emphasized that teenage members of HARYOU had already taken the initiative on this by forming the HARYOU Company.[17] Finally, the proposal called for an Employment and Occupational Training Program that would not only provide marketable job skills for those youths who had been left out of traditional educational and training institutions (such as drop-outs), but also those youths and young adults who had received an education but lacked the basic skills to get a job. Teenagers and young adults would receive these skills by training for community service occupations and would also be trained for the setting up and operation of local co-operative enterprises, which would then be linked with downtown businesses to help ensure their success.[18]

Although all of these programmes primarily addressed the needs of Harlem's youth, Clark believed this approach would work only if the HARYOU philosophy stressed an 'insistence upon social action rather than dependence upon mere social services'.[19] 'Vehicles for social action', he explained, had to be developed within the community in order to resolve social problems satisfactorily. In other words, new political organizations and institutions would have to be established if the community were to solve its problems. This was to be implemented primarily in two ways. The first was to establish Local Neighborhood Boards and a Community Action

14 Clark, *Youth in the Ghetto*, 408–45.
15 Ibid., 471–9.
16 Ibid., 479–90.
17 Ibid., 491–504.
18 Ibid., 449–64.
19 Ibid., 388.

Institute. The Local Neighborhood Boards would be used to channel HARYOU programmes and services and would consist of adults and youth. While conducting different types of activities, the boards would generally develop social action, education and social welfare programmes; conduct systematic community research; and inform local residents about available community resources. The boards would be led by an indigenous leadership partly identified by already existing organizations and the HARYOU staff. The Community Action Institute would be responsible for training community residents for professional positions in HARYOU programmes. Although mainly intended for professional staff, members of the Local Neighborhood Boards would also attend the Institute as a condition of their membership. In addition, any community resident who expressed an interest in the Institute's educational programmes would have the opportunity to attend.[20]

A second vehicle for change was the almost accidental creation of the HARYOU Associates. While conducting the research for the proposal, Clark pointed out that over 200 teenagers and young adults volunteered their time to get involved in the process.[21] They organized themselves into the HARYOU Associates. Comprised mostly of lower-middle-class youth who were set on attending college—very few of them had criminal or anti-social backgrounds—they were not only a valuable source of information for the staff, but they also provided ideas for designing the HARYOU proposal. Indeed, at times they became so excited at the prospect of creating a programme for change that other staff members complained that the Associates were 'taking over' the programme. Many of the Associates went out into the community and conducted interviews for the HARYOU study, while others organized workshops and brainstorming sessions to develop solutions to Harlem's problems. Some took skills and knowledge they had learned from the HARYOU staff (such as African American history or mathematics) and began teaching younger children in classes they organized on their own.[22]

The HARYOU study in fact contributed to an indigenous black student movement in New York City, with its southern counterpart, the Student Nonviolent Coordinating Committee (SNCC), already active in social change efforts in Georgia, Tennessee and Mississippi. The principal goal of the HARYOU Associates would be 'the creation of a youth movement intent upon changing the culture and face of Harlem'. Indeed, by the spring of 1964 when the proposal was announced, the Associates were already helping to organize rent strikes in Harlem, had participated in the 1963 March on Washington, picketed Harlem leaders who had criticized the HARYOU operation, lobbied New York City Council members to support the 1964 Civil Rights Act symbolically, and were helping to organize voter registration campaigns.[23]

20 Ibid., 388–406.
21 Ibid., 88, 565.
22 Ibid., 88–93, 568.
23 Ibid., 567–8, 81.

In constructing the HARYOU project, Clark in fact promoted the democratization and decentralization of political power in Harlem. The millions of dollars that he envisioned being appropriated for HARYOU would be effectively controlled by the Local Neighborhood Boards with HARYOU as a partner, and not by the traditional centres of power such as the Mayor's Office, the City Council, the New York City Department of Welfare or the office of Congressman Adam Clayton Powell. That money would be leveraged into creating independent political and economic bases of power in Harlem. But, more importantly, Clark and the HARYOU staff rejected the traditional social service approach to Harlem and other African American communities that saw them as not only pathological but dependent on outside help for survival. Most social welfare agencies that operated in Harlem did so reluctantly and independently of both financial support and co-operation from the local community they purportedly served. In other words, social welfare agencies were primarily seen as 'colonial' agents instead of as community organizations that worked on behalf of the community.[24] As an alternative to the traditional social service approach that highlighted juvenile delinquency as the central problem to be addressed, thereby starting with a deficiency-oriented model to addressing crime among black youth, HARYOU would begin with a positive approach that envisioned the kind of world Harlem wanted its youth to grow up in. Instead of seeking solutions from *outside* the community that would create further dependency, HARYOU sought solutions from *inside* the community that would lead to independence.

To be sure, many of Clark's ideas for HARYOU were not new. For example, researchers from the University of Chicago created the Chicago Area Project during the Great Depression, which hired community activists to create youth programmes for the poor.[25] In 1960 Columbia University social work professors Richard Cloward and Lloyd Ohlin published *Delinquency and Opportunity: A Theory of Delinquent Gangs*, which argued for the creation of new economic opportunities for the poor that would reorganize their slum areas. Cloward and Ohlin had the chance to put their ideas into practice when Mobilization for Youth (MFY) was created in 1959 and received a significant funding boost from President Kennedy's Committee on Juvenile Delinquency.[26] Clark later admitted the similarities between HARYOU and MFY.

---

24 See, generally, ibid., 64–80.
25 Clifford R. Shaw and Henry D. McKay, *Juvenile Delinquency and Urban Areas: A Study of Rates of Delinquents in Relation to Differential Characteristics of Local Communities in American Cities* (Chicago: University of Chicago Press 1942), 322–6.
26 Matusow, *The Unraveling of America*, 109–10; Richard A. Cloward and Lloyd E. Ohlin, *Delinquency and Opportunity: A Theory of Delinquent Gangs* (Glencoe, IL: Free Press 1960). See also Harold H. Weissman (ed.), *Community Development in the Mobilization for Youth Experience* (New York: Association Press 1969), and Joseph H. Helfgot, *Professional Reforming: Mobilization for Youth and the Failure of Social Science* (Lexington, MA: Lexington Books 1981).

Concentrated on New York's Lower East Side, MFY stressed an approach like HARYOU's that would diagnose and treat the pervasive conditions in the community in order to end juvenile delinquency. By emphasizing a community-oriented approach, HARYOU and MFY departed from traditional efforts to treat the problem of juvenile delinquency as a failure of individuals. The novelty of HARYOU's approach was that it called community action the 'indispensable factor' in social change. 'Just as the Mobilization Program expanded the view of juvenile delinquency to include the framework of community', Clark stated, 'the HARYOU program added the idea of social action and social change as fundamental requisites for dealing with the problems of disadvantaged youth'.[27] HARYOU was also significant because it had been able to secure $118 million in federal funds. Soon other news magazines such as *Time* and *Newsweek* came to the same conclusion and, in the wake of the 1964 Harlem riot, stated that HARYOU represented something new.[28] By the end of April 1964, HARYOU received an initial $5 million to begin the job training portion of the project.[29] However, Clark's hope that HARYOU would be a novel demonstration project for national anti-poverty efforts ran into opposition from Harlem's most powerful elected official.

The political education of Kenneth Clark

Adam Clayton Powell, Jr had become one of the most visible opponents of racial segregation in Harlem, even before he was elected to Congress in 1944. During the 1930s, as an assistant minister in his father's church, Abyssinian Baptist, Powell had picketed Harlem Hospital for firing five black doctors, administered a relief programme sponsored by his church for the unemployed, and helped initiate a boycott of Harlem businesses that refused to employ African Americans. Powell established himself as a Harlem leader during the Depression years. Upon succeeding his father as Abyssinian Baptist's pastor, he increasingly moved towards electoral politics. He won election as a New York City councilman in 1941 and used that as a springboard to become the first African American congressman from the northeastern United States. In 1947 he was appointed to the House Education and Labor Committee and, through seniority rules, became chairman of that committee in 1961, the first African American to gain such a position. Powell used his status and notoriety to clash with segregationist representatives from the South, and sponsored anti-lynching legislation, a bill to outlaw poll

---

27 Clark and Hopkins, *A Relevant War against Poverty*, 5; Kenneth B. Clark, 'HARYOU–ACT in Harlem—The dream that went astray', in John Henrik Clarke (ed.), *Harlem U.S.A.*, revd edn (New York: Collier Books 1971), 80–1.
28 Keppel, *Work of Democracy*, 140–1.
29 Clark, *Dark Ghetto*, xxvii–xxviii.

taxes and other laws to ban discrimination in employment, housing, transportation and the armed forces. By the early 1960s, he was the most well-known political figure in black America.[30]

As the House Education and Labor Committee chairman, Powell held a crucial position. Following the assassination of President Kennedy, Lyndon Johnson became president, determined to expand on his civil rights and anti-poverty initiatives. Nearly all of Johnson's programmes had to be approved by Powell's committee, and Powell could count on the loyal support of most committee members. Theoretically and practically, he could complicate any attempt by the White House or the ruling Democratic congressional majority to pass legislation. Neither the Johnson administration nor other elected officials in New York wished to cross Powell and lose backing for their own campaigns and pet projects.

In a 1976 interview, Clark discussed the moment in the spring of 1964 when Powell began pressuring him to merge HARYOU and ACT into one organization with Powell as the 'power' and Clark as the 'brains'. Because of the project's implications both for Harlem and the nation, Clark felt that he had to keep control of it. He believed that Powell would dilute the project's effectiveness and turn it into a wing of his political machine, thereby transforming HARYOU into a conventional social welfare organization and watering down its effectiveness as a social change agent. Furthermore, Powell explicitly stated that HARYOU was a threat to his career because of its potential to develop as an alternative power base. 'It was clear to Adam', Clark said, 'the people had to be dependent upon him, to have him fight for their destiny, so that he would be re-elected over and over again'.[31]

Frustrated by Clark's resistance, Powell upped the pressure. 'Look, Kenneth, in a public fight with me, there's no way you can win', he stated. He pointed out his chairmanship and the dependency of the Johnson White House on the Education and Labor Committee for its War on Poverty. 'You see that telephone?' Powell pointed. 'I was in Lyndon's office a month ago, and he gave me that phone which was sitting in his office. Now, do you think you could get Lyndon Johnson to be on your side?' he asked. Powell turned his attention to Robert Kennedy, then US Attorney General and a potential candidate for the US Senate. Clark thought he knew Kennedy well, but apparently not as well as he believed. 'Bobby Kennedy wants to run for Senator in New York', Powell stated. 'He needs me.' At that moment, David Hackett, a top aide to Kennedy, called Powell. Clark also thought he knew Hackett well. Powell put him on the speakerphone so that Clark could hear

---

30 For more on the life and career of Powell, see Hamilton, *Adam Clayton Powell, Jr.*, and Wil Haygood, *King of the Cats: The Life and Times of Adam Clayton Powell, Jr.* (Boston: Houghton Mifflin 1993).

31 Kenneth Clark, transcript of interview by Ed Edwin, 10 May 1976: Library of Congress, Washington, D.C., Kenneth Bancroft Clark Papers, interview no. 5, Folder 6, Box 199.

the conversation. Hackett said: 'Adam, we've got Puerto Rican support, and they're prepared to come out with a statement backing you and condemning Kenneth Clark (over HARYOU).' Hackett and Powell continued to talk while the congressman winked at Clark. After the call, Powell stated: 'See what I told you? Now, you thought they were on your side. You thought you could depend on them. Kenneth, you can't depend on anybody in this business. You gotta make it while you can. Don't be stupid.'[32]

By August 1964, HARYOU had merged with ACT, and Clark had been forced out as chairperson of the board of directors (he officially resigned). His feud with Powell presented a new opportunity to think about the issues of power and the problems facing black leadership within the context of the civil rights movement. Clark argued that Powell's victory blocked any serious effort to end poverty in Harlem. 'The poor were fought *about* [emphasis in the original] but not for', he declared. But HARYOU was not the only anti-poverty programme that was on the defensive. Prior to the publication of *Youth in the Ghetto*, from 1962 to 1964, the Mobilization for Youth (MFY) programme operated without constraints. After the report's publication, and especially after the Harlem riot in June 1964, MFY staff persons were charged by school principals, the press and City Hall with employing 'full-time paid agitators', 'organizers for extremist groups' and 'communists from top to bottom', charges that prompted an FBI investigation. Clark pointed out how devastating these attacks were to MFY; eventually, several top administrators resigned and the agency was reorganized under new leadership that emphasized accommodation over confrontation.[33]

In HARYOU's case, however, the project was undermined even before it began. Clark underscored Powell's demand that 'if HARYOU were going to operate in his district, it would have to be under his control'. He also hinted at the larger implications of Powell's intervention in other War on Poverty programmes. 'It is quite probable', Clark said, that the congressman 'alerted other officials in New York and other cities to the built-in threat in community-action programs'. He criticized the HARYOU board of directors, the White House, the Congress and the city government for refusing to resist

---

32 Ibid. For a sample of public sources on the controversy, see Klein, 'People vs. politicians'; 'HARYOU and ACT: merger problem'; 'Threat on fund laid to Powell men', *New York Times*, 15 June 1964, 32; and 'Clark quits HARYOU, deploring politics', *New York Times*, 30 July 1964, 1.

33 Clark, 'HARYOU-ACT in Harlem', 82. See also Alfred Fried, 'The attack on Mobilization', in Weissman (ed.), *Community Development in the Mobilization for Youth Experience*, 139–42. HARYOU and MFY were not the only programmes that faced this type of political struggle for power and control. In Philadelphia, for example, the Philadelphia Antipoverty Action Committee, established in 1965 to co-ordinate community action programmes, essentially became an arm of the Democratic Party political machine; see Matthew J. Countryman, *Up South: Civil Rights and Black Power in Philadelphia* (Philadelphia: University of Pennsylvania Press 2006), 296–300.

'the power and persuasiveness of the Powell forces' because of the 1964 elections.[34] Rather than representing a source of power for Harlem, he argued that Powell actually symbolized the powerlessness of Harlem's residents.

Racial heroism and black politics

Clark used Powell as a prism through which he would examine the role that all black elected officials played as representatives of the 'dark ghetto'. In his opinion, Powell took on a larger-than-life role as a symbol that taunted white power and control. Powell represented 'a concrete hero' who fought the battles ghetto inhabitants could not fight due to their powerlessness: 'Here is the gratifying joy of vicarious revenge without the attendant penalties of a real encounter.' More importantly, Clark thought that Powell embodied all that was denied to African Americans during the era of *de jure* segregation. On the one hand, black readers could fantasize about journeying with Powell to 'enjoy a home in Puerto Rico, have beautiful girls at his beck and call, change wives "like rich white folks"'. On the other hand, he fulfilled the need of most African Americans to speak publicly against racism, something many felt they could not safely do in their individual lives.[35]

As a result, whenever federal investigations were undertaken or were threatened in response to Powell's alleged abuses of political power, the black community interpreted these as an attack on *them*. Many Blacks, Clark maintained, did not see Powell as amoral 'but as defiantly honest in his protest against the myths and hypocrisies of racism'. Since most Blacks had seen or heard of abuses by white officials that went unpunished (indeed, one could argue that the settlement of North America and the imposition of slavery was one huge crime that went unpunished), individuals' judgements were suspended when the press and others, perceived to be a part of the 'white power structure', attacked Powell.[36]

In criticizing Powell's role and motivations, Clark cautiously highlighted Powell's accomplishments as a Harlem community leader and politician since the 1930s. As one of only a handful of black congresspersons during the first two-thirds of the twentieth century, Powell was by far the most visible, thrusting himself forward as a national and global freedom fighter on behalf of the 'race'. Nonetheless, he noted that, despite a record of activism, Clark felt that Powell was not a prime mover in the civil rights movement on the scale of a Martin Luther King, Ralph Abernathy or A. Philip Randolph. Instead, Powell was 'a successful fellow traveler with the ability to act as if he is directing a movement he is merely following'. Yet, even though he believed

34 Clark, 'HARYOU–ACT in Harlem', 83.
35 Clark, *Dark Ghetto*, 163.
36 Ibid., 163–4.

Powell less than central to the civil rights movement, Clark argued that the illusion of power motivated Whites to act as if he had something to deliver (which in most cases was black votes). Referencing the HARYOU–ACT struggle, he stated: 'The fear among whites compensates for Powell's actual loss of power in the civil rights movement. If people believe one has power it is almost as good as having it—particularly if one's needs require not the substance but only the illusion of power.'[37]

As chairman of the House Committee on Education and Labor, Powell however did have the power to prevent HARYOU's implementation. Indeed, under congressional rules that vested quite a bit of power in committee chairpersons, Powell knew and boasted that he could stop the War on Poverty. Once again, Clark argued that this 'substance of power' had less to do with the political strength of African Americans, although he was not clear on what Powell's power was actually built: he likely referred to Powell's committee chairmanship and his ability to win that position. Nonetheless, he contended that Powell's position as the only black committee chairperson gave him an opportunity to claim that any effort to oppose him was an effort to oppose the needs of all African Americans. The Whites' fear of this, he reasoned, actually helped to grant Powell a power that he did not in fact have within the civil rights movement.

According to Clark, the future of black political heroes like Powell was necessarily limited. The problem was not only whether the civil rights movement was relevant to the needs of poor black folk, which worried Clark in the opening pages of *Youth in the Ghetto*; it was also what black politics should be in an era in which *de jure* segregation was rapidly disappearing. As black demand for political power increased, would black politicians seek to replicate past white political machines in both the North and the South in the desire to win election and re-election, or would they create a new form of democratic and revolutionary politics that empowered poor and marginal black neighbourhoods? By the mid-1960s, many barriers to African American voting were being swept away by the Voting Rights Act and, in predominately black areas in the South and the North, the energy generated by the movement was naturally leading to campaigns for public office. Candidates that emphasized a politics of Booker T. Washington-like accommodation or racial moderation were increasingly viewed with impatience and exasperation by many African Americans.[38] Clark was concerned that the new black politicians who would emerge in the post-civil-rights years would look to

37 Ibid., 165–6.
38 For more on the rapid rise and spread of black electoral politics during the 1960s, see, generally, Countryman, *Up South*; David R. Colburn and Jeffrey S. Adler (eds), *African American Mayors: Race, Politics, and the American City* (Urbana: University of Illinois Press 2001); and Leonard N. Moore, *Carl B. Stokes and the Rise of Black Political Power* (Urbana: University of Illinois Press 2002). For a more specific case study of the rural South, see Hassan Kwame Jeffries, 'Freedom Politics: Transcending Civil Rights in Lowndes County, Alabama, 1965–2000', Ph.D. dissertation, Duke University, 2002.

Powell as a model for their own cities and communities. Yet, without significant social and economic changes to the status of poor black communities, he feared that Powell would serve as an inspiration to many who would seek public office as to how to organize successfully a winning political machine using the issues of the black poor. In his view, Powell was a living symbol both of the lack of power in the black community and the misuse of power, a symbol of the ghetto as both a prison and a cocoon:

> As long as the predicament of Negroes in American cities endures, just so long will Powell. The amorality of the larger society makes the amorality of the ghetto possible. Those who oppose Powell must oppose the ghetto first, for Powell is a creature of the ghetto; and for Powell to survive, the ghetto itself must survive. To transform the ghetto would lead to Powell's political destruction.[39]

Power, interest-convergence and the problem of social change

How to move from mere verbal assertions of power to actual power came to dominate Clark's thinking throughout the rest of the 1960s and into the 1970s. He thought that it was essential to define both what power actually meant and to devise appropriate and rational strategies to obtain it if the civil rights movement were to succeed. 'The problem of change in the ghetto is essentially a problem of power', he stated, 'a confrontation and conflict between the power required for change and the power resistant to change'. More specifically, he defined power as 'the force required to bring about—or to prevent—social, political, or economic changes'.[40] Clearly approaching the question of power with his HARYOU experiences fresh in his mind, he attempted to articulate a theory of power and social change that sought to redefine what the goals of the civil rights movement should be and ultimately to rethink the concept of racial integration.

Clark differentiated what he called 'pseudopower' from 'actual power'. Pseudopower was 'restricted to a verbal or posturing level of reality', while actual power was demonstrated by 'social action' and 'social change'. Forces resistant to change could use social action as a diversion that would allow the release of social tensions—a sort of safety valve—without actually leading to meaningful changes. Those who were cunning in their opposition would not resist social action overtly, but would 'identify with the goals, techniques, and demonstrations as to obscure for the protesters the real goals of the protest'.[41]

To illustrate his point, Clark focused on the 1963 March on Washington. Consisting of 250,000 peaceful demonstrators, the march showed, on the one hand, the possibilities of interracial unity. Many church groups, labour

---

39 Clark, *Dark Ghetto*, 167–8.
40 Ibid., 199.
41 Ibid., 200–1.

unions, community associations, politicians, business leaders, academics and others joined civil rights activists. Broadcast around the world, the march testified to the possibilities of American democracy for Blacks and seemed to show the country capable of rejecting racial segregation. Indeed, many credited the march with indirectly making possible the 1964 Civil Rights Act. However, the march did not stop the racial violence taking place in the South or the resistance by Whites nationally to integration. Within a year, four black girls were killed in a Birmingham church bombing, scores of other black churches were bombed or set ablaze, and civil rights activists were beaten and shot at. When three SNCC workers investigated a church bombing in Mississippi in June of 1964, they were murdered and the killers got off lightly. Meanwhile, in the North and the South, ghetto conditions worsened as white flight accelerated, leading to a withdrawal of the resources that would prevent poor housing, inferior schools and increasing poverty from developing. For example, at Washington, D.C.'s McKinley High School, located barely two miles north of the US Capitol building—which had peacefully desegregated after the *Brown* decision—the student body included 404 Blacks and 562 Whites when it opened for the school year in September 1954. Within a decade, there were over 1,400 black students and only nine Whites and the poverty level among the students had increased rapidly.[42]

Clark argued that this was the central issue with social action demonstrations. Whenever a boycott or demonstration had been successfully organized, a counter-boycott or demonstration or some type of social force arose to preserve the *status quo*. The problem then for black activists and their white allies was how to identify and mobilize those forces that would not only lead to legislative changes, but would actually lead to changes in the daily lives of people. As Clark put it:

> This problem of power is one of the more difficult ones to resolve positively because masses of whites believe that they stand to gain by maintaining the Negro in his present predicament, because some whites and a few Negroes actually do gain economically and politically by maintaining the status quo, and because energy must always be mobilized to counteract social inertia.[43]

Identifying the economic concerns of Whites as the key to understanding the problem, he argued that moral or ethical appeals alone could not work for movement activists. 'Social change that appears on the surface to benefit a minority—as in the case of civil rights—rarely engages the commitment of the majority.' But at the same time he seemed to contradict himself, ultimately arguing that morality was the only weapon that Blacks had on their side. Instead, he surmised that activists would have to 'convince the majority, who are white, that continued oppression of the Negro minority

42 Ibid., 201–2; Eric L. Wee, 'Shades of gray', *Washington Post*, 4 April 2004, W32.
43 Clark, *Dark Ghetto*, 203–4.

hurts the white majority too. ... Ethical and moral appeal can be used to give theoretical support for a program of action.'[44]

By arguing that real social change for Blacks only occurred when it benefitted the white majority, Clark's analysis anticipated one of the central arguments made by critical race theorists two and three decades later. In an influential and controversial 1980 *Harvard Law Review* article, former National Association for the Advancement of Colored People (NAACP) attorney Derrick Bell, an experienced litigator with more than 300 school desegregation cases under his belt, argued that the 1954 *Brown* decision only occurred because of what he called the 'interest-convergence' principle. Sympathy, morality and even legal precedent had little to do with the Supreme Court's decision in *Brown*, he reasoned; instead, it was due to the pressures caused by the possibility of massive domestic racial unrest following the Second World War on the one hand, and the growing conflict between the United States and the Soviet Union for control of Africa, Asia and Latin America on the other. Bell argued that it would not serve American interests to maintain racial segregation—particularly the most vicious symbols existing in the South—while seeking to influence much of the non-white world.[45] Historian and law professor Mary Dudziak agreed with much of Bell's analysis in her study of the role that *Brown* played in American foreign policy, showing how both the US State and Justice Departments intervened together on the NAACP's side in the landmark case for entirely self-serving reasons.[46]

Although Clark had been what Bell called a 'racial idealist' during his involvement with *Brown*—he believed like his friend Gunnar Myrdal that desegregation could occur quickly and peacefully if southern authorities took a firm stance to follow the Supreme Court's ruling—he also saw at the same time the complications inherent in that approach.[47] As I stated earlier,

---

44 Ibid.
45 Derrick A. Bell, '*Brown v. Board of Education* and the interest-convergence dilemma', *Harvard Law Review*, vol. 93, no. 3, January 1980, 518–33. See also Derrick A. Bell, *Silent Covenants: Brown v. Board of Education and the Unfulfilled Hopes for Racial Reform* (Oxford and New York: Oxford University Press 2004), 49.
46 Mary L. Dudziak, *Cold War Civil Rights: Race and the Image of American Democracy* (Princeton, NJ: Princeton University Press 2000).
47 Clark was the first social scientist to record as fully as possible every known instance of desegregation during the 1943–53 period. The examples included churches, the armed forces, housing, transportation, hospitals, public accommodations, sports, labour unions and employment, politics and government, higher education and elementary and secondary education. These findings were summarized by him and presented as evidence to the Supreme Court in determining whether and how immediate desegregation could occur. The paper was simultaneously published as 'Desegregation: an appraisal of the evidence', *Journal of Social Issues*, vol. 9, no. 4, 1953, 1–76. For a condensed version of this article, see Kenneth B. Clark, 'Some principles related to the problem of desegregation', *Journal of Negro Education*, vol. 23, Summer 1954, 339–47.

Clark had argued as early as 1950 that the 'American Creed' and American racism could and did coexist without tension or contradiction. Changing beliefs or behaviour was not enough, in his mind, for American racism was fundamentally rooted in the historical experience of European immigration and settlement of a previously occupied land inhabited by Native Americans. According to Clark, racism developed as a rationalization for the taking of both land and labour—African slave labour—for the purpose of economic exploitation and enrichment. A social hierarchical system developed that institutionalized that history, and subsequent waves of immigrants became 'Americanized' through the adoption of these prevailing American values and beliefs. This helped to provide many white Americans with a complex psychological security by denying humanity to non-white human beings.[48]

In this sense, Clark was arguably what many critical race theorists would call a 'racial realist'; that is, he believed that American racism developed in order to redistribute material wealth and status in the New World settled by Europeans. Yet this does not explain his involvement in *Brown* or his optimism that desegregation could be achieved through the legal system during the early 1950s, political acts that would clearly land him in the camp of racial idealists. Clark resolved this contradiction the way that many black activists and intellectuals before and after him resolved their ambivalence about the larger issues of racial integration versus black nationalism. Recently, civil rights and Black Power scholars have begun resisting the simple dichotomy that existed in past scholarship between the two historical periods (1954–65 and 1966–75). Scholars such as Peniel Joseph, Richard King, Barbara Ransby and Timothy Tyson have synthesized the two movements, arguing that many activists and intellectuals worked for both civil rights and Black Power; in other words, many did not see one as precluding the other.[49] Although Clark later rejected many of the ideas of Black Power advocates as too simplistic and vacuous, he never fully rejected associating and working with those who clearly identified themselves in the Black Power camp. Indeed, he was close friends with the Nation of Islam leader Malcolm X, and his book *Dark Ghetto* showed his familiarity with the community activism of the Muslims and other black nationalists in Harlem.[50] Clark was firmly

48 Clark, 'Racial prejudice among American minorities', 506–7.
49 For examples of this scholarship, see Richard H. King, *Civil Rights and the Idea of Freedom* (Athens: University of Georgia Press 1996); Timothy B. Tyson, *Radio Free Dixie: Robert F. Williams and the Roots of Black Power* (Chapel Hill: University of North Carolina Press 1999); Barbara Ransby, *Ella Baker and the Black Freedom Movement: A Radical Democratic Vision* (Chapel Hill: University of North Carolina Press 2003); and Peniel E. Joseph, *Waiting 'til the Midnight Hour: A Narrative History of Black Power in America* (New York: Henry Holt 2006).
50 See Clark, *Dark Ghetto*, ch. 7, 'The power structure of the ghetto', and ch. 8, 'Strategy for change'; and Kenneth B. Clark, *The Negro Protest: James Baldwin, Malcolm X, and Martin Luther King Talk with Kenneth B. Clark* (Boston: Beacon Press 1963).

committed to the overall ideal of racial integration, but he also firmly believed that something had to be done for those black children who by no fault of their own were consigned to living in increasingly segregated and deteriorating conditions. The HARYOU proposal can be seen as an example of Clark's pragmatism and willingness to abandon the goals of racial integration, if only for the short term. On the other hand, at a time when many African Americans could expect little or no justice from a legal system that virtually sanctioned voting restrictions, economic exploitation, acts of racial violence and even murder, *Brown* presented Clark and others with a rare opportunity to win at last a major victory.

In any event, Clark believed that civil rights activists and leaders should engage in careful and rational planning for any programme of social action. The *Youth in the Ghetto* study stands as a testament to that desire. While he was no radical destabilizer, he did believe in pursuing wise and judicious methods that in the end would produce controlled social change. He implored activists not to fall into the trap of orthodoxy and militancy for their own sakes, and urged them instead to re-evaluate constantly their methods and goals to see whether they were actually achieving change in the lives of people. His approach was reflected in how he viewed two of the most obvious manifestations of black social movements in the early 1960s, the non-violent struggle embodied by Martin Luther King and the separatist project emphasized by the Nation of Islam (NOI).

Clark insisted that the approaches of King and the NOI actually had more similarities than differences, for both reflected Blacks' impatience with the slow pace of change. This indicates that he believed the non-violent struggle waged by King and his followers in the South was a radical shift from civil rights protests in the past, recognition by him of the grassroots nature of the fight.[51] Although the NOI appealed to more working- and lower-class African Americans, it had a message that many Blacks agreed with. Begun in a small storefront Detroit church in 1930, the NOI argued that black economic self-sufficiency, racial self-love and separation from Whites were critical to a politics of liberation.[52] The NOI's honest defiance of integration reflected, according to Clark, the feeling among many African Americans that American society placed skin colour above justice and humanity. Although many Blacks sympathized with the NOI's perspective, Clark contended that black and white Americans had evolved together over 300 years and shared in some ways a common culture and destiny. He thought

---

51 Clark, *Dark Ghetto*, 214–15.

52 For more on the NOI's history and influence, see Clifton E. Marsh, *From Black Muslims to Muslims: The Resurrection, Transformation, and Change of the Lost-Found Nation of Islam in America, 1930–1995*, revd edn (Lanham, MD: Scarecrow Press 1996); Claude A. Clegg, *An Original Man: The Life and Times of Elijah Muhammad* (New York: St Martin's Press 1997); and Jeffrey O. G. Ogbar, *Black Power: Radical Politics and African American Identity* (Baltimore: Johns Hopkins University Press 2004).

that King's approach of 'preaching love' represented in some ways a historical truth that existed between Blacks and Whites, and wryly noted that the wide 'variations in skin color' among Blacks indicated a long history of interracial sexual intimacy that belied some of the beliefs of white supremacy. The two approaches therefore represented the 'basic dilemma and ambivalence' that constituted black life.[53] Nevertheless, the 'love the oppressor' approach, as Clark put it, had less appeal among northern Blacks than those in the South due to the nature of *de facto* racial segregation. But Clark argued that the non-violent approach involved a deeper problem from a psychological perspective. While King's approach seemed reasonable, healthy and stable on the surface, Clark maintained that King asked his followers to carry a heavier psychological burden than Whites.[54]

Clark endorsed the 'Gandhian method of passive resistance' that he argued was limited to social action; King's Christian interpretation, he felt, called for both action and feelings of love 'for the oppressor'. He surmised that the majority of Blacks would be unable to cope with the psychological burdens of adopting King's approach while daily facing the concrete injustices of living in a racist society, and feared that they were being asked to do work that was humanly impossible. Yet, he also concluded that the approaches of the NOI were not satisfactory. While the NOI's method satisfied many Blacks' immediate psychological needs and, in some cases, effected the direct rehabilitation of individuals such as ex-prisoners, it also represented wishful thinking with its calls for a separate black homeland and its beliefs in white racial inferiority. Even its goal of creating self-sufficient business enterprises in the black community was problematic because of the NOI's desire to use these institutions to recruit more members, not necessarily for the sole reason of community empowerment. King's tactics of direct non-violent action such as the massive demonstrations in Albany and Birmingham had arguably done more to empower southern Blacks politically, but Clark ruled out as unrealistic his idea of transforming white oppressors through Christian love. Moreover, the effectiveness of his tactics and ideas was questionable in the North, as evidenced by the failed 1967 campaign in Chicago.[55] And, in the South, residential patterns during the 1960s increasingly resembled northern cities, particularly in urban areas where a strong black middle class existed or was growing, such as Atlanta, Birmingham and Little Rock. As the civil rights movement changed the political status of Blacks, geographic segregation based on race and class increased in the urban South, replacing the more intimate form of racial segregation that had existed between Whites and

53 Clark, *Dark Ghetto*, 215–17.
54 Ibid., 217–18.
55 Ibid, 218. For more on the Chicago campaign, see James Ralph, *Northern Protest: Martin Luther King, Jr., Chicago, and the Civil Rights Movement* (Cambridge, MA: Harvard University Press 1993).

Blacks since the Civil War.[56] This fact alone threw into doubt the efficacy of King's non-violent approach to social change and black empowerment.

It must be understood that Clark's thinking and criticism had a long lineage in his work. Since the early 1940s, when he first articulated the idea of the 'zoot-suit personality' as a way to explain how African Americans developed psychological protection in a racially hostile society, he was sensitive to what he saw as the manifestations of that personality in everyday black life and activism. Although he did not directly say so, his interpretation of King and the NOI clearly followed this intellectual trajectory. The 'zoot-suit personality', while providing some immediate protection, was ineffective as a general liberating strategy both politically and psychologically; it merely ameliorated some of racism's effects while protecting the individual's ego needs. Both the strategies of King and the Muslims, one could say, reflected in some measure an adaptation of the 'zoot-suit personality'. King's approach brought about the end of 'Whites only' signs and other forms of overt racism, while the NOI's approach created small black-run businesses in cities such as New York, Philadelphia, Chicago and Detroit. In the long term, however, it was debatable whether either strategy could actually lead to the social change envisioned by Clark because of powerful structural changes that were already underway by the 1950s and 1960s that led to deindustrialization in both the North and the South. He wanted powerless communities living under *de facto* racial segregation to develop the necessary skills and strength to create actual change within this context, and neither King nor the NOI explained satisfactorily to him how this could come to pass.

Undoubtedly, by 1965, Clark had arrived at a point at which he had begun to think about and articulate new ways of conceptualizing race, power and social change, although his philosophy had been evolving for some time. Part of this emphasis emerged from his struggles with Adam Clayton Powell, but Clark was also increasingly concerned with the overall liberal orientation of the movement. As I already stated, he long had reservations about the Myrdalian concept of the 'American dilemma'. By 1966 he had rejected that ideal:

> The new American Dilemma is one of power. The dilemma is a confrontation between those forces which impel a society to change and those which seek to maintain the past. ... The fact is that man has never effectively resolved the issue of power versus ideals, or power as an instrument of the maintenance of ideals, or of ideals themselves as a form of power, or of fundamental emotions, such as love and hatred, as primary sources of power. The American racial dilemma is merely one of the more recent manifestations of this prolonged confusion of man.[57]

56 Clark, *Dark Ghetto*, 22–3.
57 Kenneth B. Clark, 'Introduction: the dilemma of power', in Talcott Parsons and Kenneth B. Clark (eds), *The Negro American* (Boston: Houghton Mifflin 1966), xi–xii.

Overall, the foundation for much of Clark's work was based on this conception. In his view, the civil rights struggle was not a moral struggle, but was fundamentally about deep unmet psychological needs within human beings that led to a desire for security and status. These desires for security and status manifested themselves in inequitable struggles for power over land, resources and even human beings, of which racism was one outcome. This is not to say that race could be easily dismissed in favour of a power analysis; Clark recognized that race had been central, since the early days of European settlement, to articulating a vision of what it meant to be an American. However, black progress could only be made if and when activists and leaders began to grapple seriously with the fundamental issues of power and not merely the symbols or tools of power. While Powell, King and the NOI might serve a useful purpose in some ways, the black freedom struggle ironically would eventually have to move beyond symbols of progress created by a segregated black world if it was to maintain its relevance.

Clearly, the conflict with Powell influenced Clark to think about the politics of race and power and the problem of social change differently than he had at the time of the *Brown* decision. Clark wrote in 1953 and 1954 that the most important factor in determining whether desegregation was successful was the ability and willingness of white-dominated governments to implement desegregation without delay; gradual implementation, he found, increased the likelihood of violence and disorder.[58] Nonetheless, by 1964 Clark had rejected the Myrdalian conception of the 'American dilemma' and sought to construct a new theory of American racism based on practical experience, contending that human beings had never learned how to handle power humanely squarely at the centre. With this theory, he hoped to encourage new research and practice among all intellectuals and activists that would move beyond simplistic attacks on the most visible symbols of white racial oppression (such as segregation in public accommodation) to focus on the dilemma of power. As important as traditional civil rights work was, Clark rightly feared that the political and economic problems of the black community would not be addressed.

Central to Clark's fear most of all was the lack of attention to the problems of the black poor. The HARYOU–ACT controversy was not only about black politics, but also about the failures of the War on Poverty. To be sure, the programme became embroiled in a political struggle for control before it even started. Although HARYOU–ACT was implemented, it quickly abandoned many of its goals and became essentially a jobs placement programme for Harlem youth. For instance, the community action component—the Local Neighborhood Boards and the Community Action Institute—was delayed and never fully implemented.[59] Indeed, the

---

58 Clark, 'Desegregation', 45–7; Clark, 'Some principles related to the problem of desegregation', 343.
59 Clark and Hopkins, *A Relevant War against Poverty*, 220–1.

original HARYOU design actually had a longer life in Paterson and Newark, New Jersey, where two of Clark's associates attempted to implement similar programmes in both cities.[60] For, if HARYOU had actually been implemented as planned, it is possible that not only Powell but the city and state governments of New York would have faced a political confrontation and demands by Harlem's residents for more resources and power. To put it another way, the needs of the black poor were sidelined during the political struggle for control between a black congressman and a black academic. It is not too farfetched to accuse Powell of providing a model for other black politicians to emulate in the future, in terms of how to gain control of potential threats to their power from within their communities. In the case of HARYOU, federal funding was the key, and Powell could heavily influence its distribution. On the other hand, Powell and his allies could argue that, with the strong possibility of a $118 million appropriation to an anti-poverty programme, only a politically savvy, astute and experienced leader should be in control in order to maximize the programme's effectiveness. Powell had after all successfully navigated a hostile Congress dominated by southerners to become one of its most powerful leaders. Clark, they could say, lacked the political skills and capital to ensure the programme's continued success each year. One only need look at how Clark withered in the face of Powell's ability to outmanoeuvre him to realize how powerless he was in the face of political pressure.

It is difficult to say without further research how the Clark–Powell dispute influenced the direction and intersection of community action programmes —particularly for youth—and black politics in New York City.[61] Nevertheless, Powell's actions and the subsequent events of the dispute were troubling to say the least. In an odd way, the Clark–Powell conflict epitomized Derrick Bell's 'interest-convergence' principle, namely that Whites never support black progress unless they benefit in some way. Political figures such as Lyndon Johnson, Robert Kennedy and New York City Mayor Robert Wagner either endorsed Powell's side or remained silent once they concluded that nothing could be gained politically by supporting Clark. Simultaneously, Powell remained in power and controlled much of

---

60 Ibid., 215–16. An examination of the successes and failures of the Newark and Paterson programmes is beyond the scope of this essay but, for a firsthand account of the Newark programme, see Cyril DeGrasse Tyson, *2 Years before the Riot! Newark, New Jersey and the United Community Corporation, 1964–1966* (New York: Jay Street Publishers 2000).

61 Surprisingly, few scholars have examined the history of community action programmes designed to combat juvenile delinquency or in New York City more generally. And, apart from Noel Cazenave's recent book, no studies known to the author exist that examine the connection between the development of black politics and anti-poverty programmes; see Noel A. Cazenave, *Impossible Democracy: The Unlikely Success of the War on Poverty Community Action Programs* (Albany: State University of New York Press 2007).

Harlem community politics for at least the remainder of the 1960s. Stricken by cancer and contemptuous of his political opponents, he finally lost an election for the first time in 1970; he died two years later.[62] A disillusioned Clark returned to his academic work, but within two years, in 1967, he had created a new think tank called the Metropolitan Applied Research Center (MARC). One of the centre's goals would be to organize the first national conferences of black elected officials in order to provide training and educational opportunities. With these conferences, Clark hoped to provide black politicians with practical skills that would be useful in serving their communities free from ideological or self-serving concerns.[63] Even so, as the country's most visible black politician during the 1950s and 1960s, Powell undeniably provided a model for future black mayors, congresspersons, state legislators and city council members to emulate within the context of polarizing racial politics and steadily deteriorating local economies in the African American community.

---

62 Hamilton, *Adam Clayton Powell, Jr.*, 445–78.
63 Brochure, 'The MARC Experiment: Goals and Assumptions': Library of Congress, Washington, D.C., Kenneth Bancroft Clark Papers, Folder 6, Box 316. See also, among the Clark Papers, 'Proposal for the Establishment of an Institute on Urban Problems': Folder 6, Box 316, 2; brochure, 'Institute for Black Elected Officials', 11–14 September 1969: Folder 1, Box 329; and the memorandum, 'Status Report on MARC Projects', 2 August 1971: Folder 2, Box 295.

Listening to melancholia: Alice Walker's *Meridian*

LEIGH ANNE DUCK

Though the political objectives of Alice Walker's womanist fiction—in her words, 'commit[ment] to survival and wholeness of entire people, male *and* female'[1]—might seem laudable, they have elicited almost non-stop criticism. Initially and subsequently labelled 'racial infidelity' for their feminism, her novels have more recently been described as 'postpolitical'.[2] In confronting such charges, of course, Walker has accompanied several African American women writing during the 1970s—including Gayl Jones, Toni Morrison and Ntozake Shange—whose work explored how a patriarchal and capitalist culture might affect individual psychology and intimate relationships among African Americans. As Toni Cade Bambara argued in 1969, black feminists faced the formidable task of averring that African Americans had 'not been immune' to the 'honky horseshit' of 'oppressive socially contrived' gender roles.[3] Novelists who explored such problems

---

1 Alice Walker, *In Search of Our Mothers' Gardens: Womanist Prose* [1983] (New York: Harvest Books 2003), xi.
2 Ann DuCille, 'Phallus(ies) of interpretation: toward engendering the black critical "I"', *Callaloo*, vol. 16, no. 3, Summer 1993, 559; Robert E. Washington, *The Ideologies of African American Literature: From the Harlem Renaissance to the Black Nationalist Revolt* (Lanham, MD and Oxford: Rowman and Littlefield 2001), 336.
3 Toni Cade, 'On the issue of roles', in Toni Cade Bambara (ed.), *The Black Woman: An Anthology* [1970] (New York: Washington Square Press 2005), 125.

violated not only the gender norms but also the ideological tenets—including an emphasis on representing a unified racial community—of the Black Aesthetic movement.[4] Such critical norms no longer dominate readings of contemporary African American fiction, and much of that literature now focuses, in Keith Byerman's words, on 'the psychological and social effects of suffering', but critics still question whether such representations displace more productive political debates.[5] Observing representational politics more generally, for example, Lauren Berlant warns that 'the public recognition by the dominant culture of certain sites of publicized subaltern suffering is frequently (mis)taken as a big step toward the amelioration of that suffering'.[6]

Walker's second novel *Meridian* (1976) is prominently attuned to such questions of political significance, as it examines from its first chapter to its last the meanings, methods and goals of 'revolutionary' action.[7] Still, it can hardly be described as a typical protest novel, given that so much of the text concerns intimate relationships and internal pain; as Madhu Dubey notes, there are even moments when 'Meridian's body ... fades off into a mystical haze that blurs the novel's political focus'.[8] That focus is itself indirect and chiefly internal, as the novel seems less concerned with the question of how to transform society than that of how to transform social actors. In this way, it explores Bambara's argument that 'the individual, the basic revolutionary unit, must be purged of poison and lies that assault the ego and threaten the heart'.[9] Written after the civil rights movement—which Walker credits elsewhere for awakening her political consciousness—the novel describes that period of rapid social change in which the former activist community is divided by both emotional conflicts and the lure of commodity culture.[10] As Meridian's activist network dissolves, painful incidents from the character's past threaten to engulf her, isolating her and occasionally even paralysing her. The novel's project, however, is both psychological—in the effort to explore her suffering—and political as her efforts to promote a new social formation force her to confront her own beliefs and feelings that have developed amid existing injustice.

4 Madhu Dubey, *Black Women Novelists and the Nationalist Aesthetic* (Bloomington: Indiana University Press 1994), 16–32.

5 Keith Byerman, *Remembering the Past in Contemporary African American Fiction* (Chapel Hill: University of North Carolina Press 2005), 3.

6 Lauren Berlant, 'The subject of true feeling: pain, privacy, and politics', in Jodi Dean (ed.), *Cultural Studies and Political Theory* (Ithaca, NY: Cornell University Press 2000), 62.

7 Alice Walker, *Meridian* [1976] (New York: Pocket Books 1986), 14. Subsequent references to this edition are cited parenthetically in the text.

8 Dubey, *Black Women Novelists and the Nationalist Aesthetic*, 142.

9 Cade, 'On the issue of roles', 133.

10 Alice Walker, 'The civil rights movement: what good was it?' [1967], in Walker, *In Search of Our Mothers' Gardens*, 119–29.

In her efforts to overcome these difficult dynamics, Meridian suggests that 'revolution', while primarily a social struggle, must include explicit attention to cultural and psychological change; in a society in which so many of the forms of judgement exercised even in daily life prove to be deeply compromised by racism and sexism, those seeking to create external change may also need to generate new internal patterns of thought and emotion. In Berlant's words, 'the feelings we acknowledge having are unreliable measures of justice and fairness ... new vocabularies of pleasure, recognition, *and* equity must be developed and debated'.[11] Accordingly, *Meridian* proves an exemplary text through which to explore contemporary critical debates regarding the political significance of psychoanalytic theory, particularly regarding melancholia, a condition in which individuals internalize lost relationships in ways that affix the self to the past. Rather than a condition to be embraced or denigrated—a choice so often debated in scholarly writing on the topic—melancholia constitutes, in Walker's novel, a source of insight into problems that are simultaneously social and psychological.

'Race', literature and psychoanalysis: fixation or transformation?

In recent years, scholars have begun to highlight psychoanalytic theory as a possible resource for understanding how people can fortify themselves for further struggle against racial oppression. This enquiry acquires substantial urgency in a world shaped by both a 'crisis of raciology'—that is, the delegitimation (despite repeated recurrence) of ideas that once secured 'race' as a category of biological and cultural difference—and proliferating practices that politically and economically disenfranchise groups so demarcated.[12] As activists seek to battle discrimination in purportedly 'raceless' institutions, the strategies and even the terminology of past movements become questionable.[13] Anti-racists have always been in pursuit of a condition in which the issues and vocabularies central to their struggle would be of only historical interest, but this objective can create ambivalence, as Paul Gilroy notes, for 'those groups whose oppositional, legal, and even democratic claims have come to rest on identities and solidarities forged at great cost from the categories given to them by their oppressors'.[14]

11 Berlant, 'The subject of true feeling', 61–2.
12 Paul Gilroy, *Against Race: Imagining Political Culture beyond the Color Line* [2000] (Cambridge, MA: Belknap Press of Harvard University Press 2001), 28. Bill Lawson noted this sense of urgency in 'Hope, Derrick Bell, and the permanence of racism', a paper given at the Scholars in Critical Race Studies workshop, University of Memphis, 20 November 2006.
13 On the discriminatory practices of 'raceless states', see David Theo Goldberg, *The Racial State* (Oxford and Malden, MA: Blackwell 2002), 227–37.
14 Gilroy, *Against Race*, 52.

Accordingly, current accounts of anti-racist work often manifest retrospective or even nostalgic tendencies: Kenneth Warren notes, for example, that several scholars in African American Studies respond to contemporary disappointment by regretting the loss of supposedly unified communities from the segregated past.[15] This tendency appears also in novels from other contexts now said to be 'post-racial': thus, for example, a character in Achmat Dangor's *Bitter Fruit* (2001), set in post-apartheid South Africa, contemplates 'the "grand" days in the old townships' when 'people [could] understand each other and empathize' because 'everyone recognized that the need to survive was paramount'.[16]

Opinions concerning how psychoanalytic theory may function in such a context are divided. On the one hand, psychoanalysis has always sought to understand how individuals can work through painful and internalized experience in order to transform their psyches and, ultimately, their lives. Accordingly, it could have the potential, in Hortense Spillers's words, to elucidate 'how "race," as a poisonous idea, insinuates itself not only across and between ethnicities but within', and thus to produce 'discernment of the nicest sort', the kind of understanding and alertness necessary to combat racism's social and psychological effects.[17] Other critics warn, however, that psychoanalytic thinking could produce 'a prescription for a politics of quietism, fatalism and defeat'.[18] Their concern is not restricted to the fact that psychoanalysis has in the past tended either to privilege colonialist hierarchies or to ignore how race functions as a vector for oppression; scholars working at the intersections of anti-racist and psychoanalytic theory are, after all, committed to disrupting those historical patterns.[19] Rather, critics fear that psychoanalytic accounts of identity may discourage engagement with contemporary political problems precisely because of their focus on the past, exacerbating the nostalgia described above and producing, in Slavoj Žižek's argument, a 'melancholic attachment to ... lost roots'.[20]

These debates often emerge in discussions of contemporary African American literature, in which 'historical narrative' has become 'the dominant mode'.[21] Such novels challenge triumphalist accounts of United

---

15 Kenneth W. Warren, 'The end(s) of African American Studies', *American Literary History*, vol. 12, no. 3, Autumn 2000, 639.

16 Achmat Dangor, *Bitter Fruit* [2001] (New York: Black Cat 2005), 85.

17 Hortense Spillers, '"All the things you could be by now, if Sigmund Freud's wife was your mother": psychoanalysis and race', *boundary 2*, vol. 23, no. 3, Autumn 1996, 88, 83.

18 Paul Gordon, 'Psychoanalysis and racism: the politics of defeat', *Race & Class*, vol. 42, no. 4, April 2001, 31.

19 See, for example, Spillers, '"All the things you could be by now, if Sigmund Freud's wife was your mother"', 75–141.

20 Slavoj Žižek, 'Mourning, melancholy and the act', *Critical Inquiry*, vol. 26, no. 4, Summer 2000, 659.

21 Byerman, *Remembering the Past in Contemporary African American Fiction*, 1.

States history by describing the oppression central to the nation's experience, and may, in that process, provide catharsis: in Byerman's words, they enable readers 'to go through the shame and disruption of remembering in order to begin to forge relationships that can become communities that can make a difference'.[22] But, while psychoanalysis holds that such 'working through' is necessary for individuals who seek to create new patterns for their lives, it also warns that subjects may resist such change, clinging instead to the very dynamics that cause them pain. This destructive potential is encapsulated especially by theories of melancholia, in which identity is not only haunted but actually constituted by 'attachment to a certain strain of its own dead past', with a 'structure of desire [that] is backward looking and punishing'.[23]

At stake in these arguments is not simply the plot or concerns of any individual novel but rather the way in which literature informs contemporary cultural and potentially political thought. As Warren explains, 'discussion and analysis of literature and culture has been central to ventriloquizing a black collective state of mind'; in such arguments, these texts are said to reflect a shared and determinate experience of marginalization.[24] Given this history, literary scholars interested in melancholia are duly wary that their commentary could be taken to classify such mental states as fixed racial attributes, a particular danger in a national context that so vigorously circulates accounts of African American 'pathology'.[25] Meanwhile, Dubey notes that some of this literature truly does seem melancholic, as it 'recoil[s] from ideals of political modernity' while 'affirm[ing] ... cultural traditions ... inextricably embedded in the deeply inequitable conditions of racial segregation'.[26]

Accordingly, though analysis of such literature might provide frameworks through which to explore, in Patricia Williams's words, the 'psychic obliteration' produced by racist and other forms of oppression, it could also risk suggesting that persons subjected to 'spirit-murder' are unable to recover, an account that would support racist stereotypes while simultaneously promoting a pained and passive criterion for racial belonging.[27] Such a process already occurs in some uses of trauma theory, another

22 Ibid., 10.
23 Wendy Brown, 'Resisting left melancholy', *boundary 2*, vol. 26, no. 3, Fall 1999, 26.
24 Warren, 'The end(s) of African American Studies', 644; Kenneth W. Warren, *So Black and Blue: Ralph Ellison and the Occasion of Criticism* (Chicago: University of Chicago Press 2003), 90–9.
25 Jermaine Singleton, 'Cryptic Conversations: Melancholy, Ritual, and the (African American) Literary Imagination', Ph.D. dissertation, University of Minnesota, 10 July 2005.
26 Madhu Dubey, 'Postmodern geographies of the U.S. South', *Nepantla: Views from South*, vol. 3, no. 2, Summer 2002, 362, 364, 365.
27 Patricia Williams, 'Spirit-murdering the messenger: the discourse of fingerpointing as the law's response to racism', *University of Miami Law Review*, vol. 42, September 1987, 139.

psychoanalytic paradigm often applied in African American Studies. While some such analyses explore how subsequent generations represent the historical experience of slavery in order to construe an understanding of the past that may be useful in their contemporary political milieu, others produce the essentializing, ahistorical and even pathologizing argument that contemporary African American identities are unconsciously determined by 'the real of slavery's trauma'.[28]

Nor are such dangers posed solely by the pressures surrounding production and reception of African American literature; they emerge also from beliefs concerning the treatments and causes of melancholia. Even if this condition is described as a contingent response to interpersonal dynamics, as it is in psychoanalytic theory, it might still be considered a fixed attribute once initiated: melancholics are, in Freud's account, notable for the intensity with which they defy healing. While discussions of trauma play a problematic role in discourses of collective identity, scholars concerned with that phenomenon are at least focused on transformation though efforts to situate traumatic events in 'the past (rather than the obsessively present)' and even to 'recontextualize them within a meaningful narrative of heroism, collective identity, or resistance'.[29] In psychoanalytic treatment, experiences that destabilize the psyche must be 'transformed into narrative language' through the shared work of the traumatized subject and an empathetic listener, a therapy that has become a kind of model for psychoanalytic 'working through'.[30] In contrast, melancholia—though equally influential in Freud's thought—was less responsive to his treatment: some cases ended in suicide while others simply 'pass[ed] off ... without leaving any traces', or, in other words, without producing new understandings.[31]

Today, when even the committed psychoanalyst Julia Kristeva acknowledges that melancholia is often considered an 'illness ... that responds only to the administration of anti-depressants', it may be particularly difficult to imagine that discussion of this ailment could prove politically instructive.[32]

28 For an example of the former, see Ron Eyerman, 'Cultural trauma: slavery and the formation of African American identity', in Jeffrey C. Alexander, Ron Eyerman, Bernhard Giesen, Neil J. Smelser and Piotr Sztompka, *Cultural Trauma and Collective Identity* (Berkeley: University of California Press 2004), 60–111; for the latter, see Sheldon George, 'Trauma and the conservation of African-American racial identity', *Journal for the Psychoanalysis of Culture and Society*, vol. 6, no. 1, Spring 2001, 58–72.

29 Rebecca Saunders and Kamran Scot Aghaie, 'Introduction: mourning and memory', *Comparative Studies of South Asia, Africa and the Middle East*, vol. 25, no. 1, 2005, 21.

30 Bessel A. Van der Kolk and Onno Van der Hart, 'The intrusive past: the flexibility of memory and the engraving of trauma', in Cathy Caruth (ed.), *Trauma: Explorations in Memory* (Baltimore: Johns Hopkins University Press 1995), 176.

31 Sigmund Freud, 'Mourning and melancholia' [1917], in Sigmund Freud, *The Standard Edition of the Complete Psychological Works*, vol. 14, trans. from the German and ed. by James Strachey (London: Hogarth Press 1957), 253, 252.

32 Julia Kristeva, *Black Sun: Depression and Melancholia* [1987], trans. from the French by Leon S. Roudiez (New York: Columbia University Press 1989), 10.

And yet contemporary scientific discourse suggests that it may now be especially important to engage multiple frameworks for thinking about psychological dynamics in order to challenge accounts that settle prematurely on biology. As Ian Hacking argues, though 'changes in biological and chemical psychiatry' are leading researchers to alter their conceptions of 'real illnesses', dynamic and interpersonal therapy 'still seems relevant to many clinicians'.[33] But, while Hacking seems right to suggest a broad 'confusion' concerning the sources and classes of psychological distress, other philosophers of science note that studies in biochemistry are serving to 'remap ... psychiatric categories' such that they are delineated not by symptom or cause but by the drug that best alleviates them.[34] This trend leads observers to emphasize the role of genetics over environment in shaping mental life: Peter Kramer's popular *Listening to Prozac*, for example, accepts a biologically oriented view of depression even while acknowledging the dangers of such a view in a culture 'that prefers to ignore [social] victimization'.[35]

Such perspectives, focused on biology and pharmacology, are antithetical to that presented in *Meridian*, which insists that oppressive societies initiate and exacerbate psychological pain. In this way, of course, Walker was exploring a concern central to the black feminist movement of the 1970s that held, in the words of the Combahee River Collective, that 'the psychological toll of being a black woman and the difficulties this presents in reaching political consciousness and doing political work can never be underestimated'.[36] The purpose of such discussions was not to delineate the psychological contours of a shared identity formation but rather to examine how political, economic and social structures generate psychological difficulties and especially to share these insights in ways that could imbue multiple women with greater understanding and agency in regard to the relationship between psyche and society. Though this movement was hardly restricted to 'consciousness-raising', that did constitute one of the 'resources' it sought to provide its members: to combat 'the nearly classic isolation most of us face', members exchanged accounts of how they recognized and confronted the effects of racism, sexism, classism and heterosexism in their mental lives.[37] This project directly opposes the ideas that psychological knowledge can be restricted to the scientific community or that individuals' experiences of psychological distress can be addressed

33 Ian Hacking, *Mad Travelers: Reflections on the Reality of Transient Mental Illnesses* (Charlottesville: University of Virginia Press 1998), 95.
34 Jennifer Radden, 'Is this Dame Melancholy? Equating today's depression and past melancholia', *Philosophy, Psychiatry, & Psychology*, vol. 10, no. 1, March 2003, 37.
35 Peter D. Kramer, *Listening to Prozac* (New York: Viking 1993), 298, 17.
36 Combahee River Collective, 'A black feminist statement' [1977], in Beverly Guy-Sheftall (ed.), *Words of Fire: An Anthology of African-American Feminist Thought* (New York: New Press 1995), 236.
37 Ibid., 236–8.

solely by pharmaceutical prescription; rather, this movement insists that psychological discomfort can become a source of political insight.

Accordingly, Alice Walker, like many African American women writing in this period, presented literature as a venue in which to begin understanding and untangling the relationships between political culture and diverse forms of psychological pain. Given this mission, Walker seems particularly careful to underscore that her protagonist's condition is neither an essential racial attribute nor immutable within the character: Meridian pronounces herself 'a woman in the process of changing her mind' (25). Sharply differentiated from others, from the novel's very first paragraphs, she is figured as both something of a local celebrity and a mystic.[38] Nor is Meridian situated within a solely black community: rather, the novel often focuses on interracial interactions, including collaboration, violence, intimacy and commercial enterprise. Finally, the novel overtly stages the danger of treating narratives as models for fixed, predetermined identities: Meridian is plagued by a 'recurring dream' that 'she was a character in a novel and that her existence presented an insoluble problem, one that would be solved only by her death at the end' (117). The novel seeks to understand how individuals can overcome such monolithic narratives, particularly when they have been vital in establishing one's sense of self.

In this way, Walker's novel engages with concerns that have become increasingly prominent in several interdisciplinary fields of social enquiry. Because of its setting in a period of explicit uncertainty concerning what forms and goals of political activism might be most trenchant to the moment, *Meridian* explores a form of confusion similar to that which Wendy Brown finds characteristic of contemporary leftists, for example, in a neo-liberal era that manifests, amid an array of more palpable losses, also the abrogation of 'the promise that left analysis and left commitment would supply its adherents a clear and certain path toward the good, the right, and the true'.[39] At such a moment, the challenge is not simply to resist capitulation and cherish the lost object, but rather to find productive ways of transforming precisely what one might prefer to preserve. In Walker's example, Meridian meets the first challenge in that she avoids the common fate of 's[elling] out, sh[ooting] it out, or ... simply drift[ing] with the current of the time', but her attachment to the past is overdetermined and overwhelming; she imagines herself 'not to belong to the future' (189, 221).

In imagining a solution for Meridian's dilemma, this novel diverges sharply from the tenets that activists must learn to narrate historical oppression and the collective suffering it caused or to develop a sense of group identity, two goals so often articulated in trauma studies that Saidiya Hartman has questioned whether 'remembering has become the only

38 Joseph A. Brown, S.J., '"All saints should walk away": the mystical pilgrimage of *Meridian*', *Callaloo*, vol. 12, Spring 1989, 310–20.
39 Brown, 'Resisting left melancholy', 22.

conceivable or viable form of political agency'.[40] Though Walker argued elsewhere the need to 'stud[y] our ancestors',[41] *Meridian* has less interest in narrating scenes from history than in finding a way for the protagonist to function more freely in the present. Walker does not describe Meridian's condition in psychoanalytic terms; rather, in commentary on the novel, she links her experimental method of representing Meridian's psyche to folk cultural forms that model, in Dubey's words, 'a multilayered vision of time as a synthesis of past and present'.[42] Further, in keeping with its goals and historical moment, the novel is more attuned to cultural and individual approaches to psychology than to clinical practice. But both its stylistic innovation and the thematic centrality of time point directly to the question of how individuals might overcome painful or restrictive attachments to the past, a problem now explored, in scholarly discourse concerning social movements, through reference to melancholia.

Melancholic subjects: psyche and ideology

In 'Mourning and Melancholia' (1917), Freud differentiates between 'normal' and 'pathological' approaches to 'the real loss of a loved object': where mourning facilitates the eventual 'withdrawal of the libido from this object and a displacement of it on to a new one', melancholia 'establishes an *identification* of the ego with the abandoned object'.[43] Rather than accepting—however slowly and painfully—that the loved object is no longer accessible, melancholic subjects refuse to accept separation: instead, they identify so closely with the lost object that their feelings towards it are transferred back on to themselves. This refusal of loss should not be mistaken for a refusal of pain, however, for the feelings newly directed towards the ego are deeply ambivalent. Freud notes that the loss of a relationship is initiated not solely by death but more typically by insurmountable conflict; thus, when 'the shadow of the object f[alls] upon the ego', both previous idealization of the object and anger or frustration with it are reflected inward. Experiencing the 'trends of sadism and hate' established in the disrupted relationship as a structural element in their identities, melancholics are unable to escape these dynamics of blame and reproach even for a moment.[44]

40 Saidiya Hartman, 'The time of slavery', *South Atlantic Quarterly*, vol. 101, no. 4, Fall 2002, 774.
41 Alice Walker, 'A letter to the editor of *Ms.*' [1974], in Walker, *In Search of Our Mothers' Gardens*, 274.
42 Dubey, *Black Women Novelists and the Nationalist Aesthetic*, 136–7.
43 Freud, 'Mourning and melancholia', 249–50.
44 Ibid., 245–51.

The protagonist of *Meridian* exemplifies precisely the symptoms Freud ascribed to melancholia: self-vilification, expectation of rejection and abuse, and neglect of her health to the point of collapse. She views herself, for much of this novel, as uniquely debased, and the central source of her self-reproach is her relationship with her mother. Mrs Hill, who finds that motherhood 'shatter[s] her emerging self', subtly communicates her anger to her daughter: 'When her mother asked, without glancing at her, "Have you stolen anything?" a stillness fell over Meridian and for seconds she could not move' (51). This paralysis is affective as well as physical: Meridian never responds to her mother's rage, but rather idolizes her, viewing her as a 'giant', and immediately dismissing any reproaches she might feel towards her parent as 'petty and ridiculous', asserting that 'it is death not to love one's mother' (122, 30). Instead, Meridian turns any potential criticism towards herself, incessantly contemplating her own 'inadequacy and guilt' (122). These self-effacing dynamics shape all of Meridian's subsequent relationships: silent in the face of disagreement, she feels the satisfaction of neither embrace nor rebellion, but rather guilt for her refusal either to satisfy others or to articulate her own position.[45]

Importantly, Mrs Hill is for her daughter both a loved and effectively lost person, and the symbol of an abstraction. As Barbara Christian argues, Meridian identifies her mother with 'the monumental myth of black motherhood', an image based on a real history of sacrifice by enslaved and oppressed women but often presented as an essentializing stereotype; emerging from an oppressive history, this icon displaces the possibility of choice in changed circumstances.[46] Mrs Hill seems also to have succumbed to this ideal: though she values the 'independence' and 'respect' she experiences as a young adult and a teacher, she marries and has children because she believes such a path necessary for a normative gendered existence (49, 50). When she later feels 'buried alive', she never complains because doing so would defy all the authorities in her life (51). Rather than acknowledging the real interpersonal conflict between herself and her mother—and between her own goals and values and those she incorrectly believes are embodied by her mother—Meridian feels shame for not adhering to her mother's painful path. Observing Mrs Hill's visible 'sacrifice', Meridian determines that this aspect of motherhood might somehow atone for the sacrifice of mothers in slavery whose children were forcibly taken from them. When she later gives up her own child in order to go to college—a decision stimulated by her participation in the civil rights movement—she determines that 'her mother [was] worthy of [African American] maternal history, and [Meridian belonged] to an unworthy

45 Lynn Pifer, 'Coming to voice in Alice Walker's *Meridian*: speaking out for the revolution', *African American Review*, vol. 26, no. 1, Spring 1992, 77–8.
46 Barbara Christian, 'The black woman artist as wayward' [1983], in Harold Bloom (ed.), *Alice Walker: Modern Critical Views* (New York: Chelsea House 1989), 47.

minority, for which there was no precedent and of which she was, as far as she knew, the only member' (91).

This pattern further aligns Meridian's characterization with psycho-analytic theories of melancholia, which describe how social relations—between persons, but also between persons and ideological norms—are transformed into internal object-relations. In Freud's account, the melancholic's lost 'object' may not be a person at all but 'some abstraction which has taken the place of [a loved person], such as one's country, liberty, an ideal, and so on'.[47] Freud eventually drew his understanding of both identity and conscience from his observation of these dynamics: much as melancholics internalize lost objects, young children, in 'The Ego and the Id' (1922), introject early authority figures, or the parents whom the child wishes to possess and, in jealousy, destroy. These early introjections derive particular importance as the ego-ideal, 'the heir of the Oedipus complex', which functions, in another sense, as the super-ego. Granted the libidinal power to manage both desire and aggression towards parents, the ego-ideal becomes the locus of social authority: 'Social feelings rest on identifications with other people, on the basis of having the same ego ideal.'[48] Meridian and her mother, for example, identify with destructive norms and, because that attachment constitutes their very sense of self, they cannot attain a critical distance from it; instead, their anger is redirected—towards family members in the elder's case and, in the child's case, the self.

Because melancholia marks a crisis in identification with dominant ideals, it has become an important model for scholars seeking to understand how cultural hierarchies influence mental life. As Judith Butler argues, 'melancholy offers potential insight into how the boundaries of the social are instituted and maintained'.[49] Though Freud's individual and familial analysis is notoriously inattentive to the exclusions that attend such social identifications, contemporary work in postcolonial, feminist, queer and critical race theories has expanded his model to consider how this same process of introjection may affect people who live, as Anne Anlin Cheng explains, 'within a ruling episteme that privileges that which they can never be'. Though the marginalized subject does not necessarily internalize exclusive racial, gendered or heterosexual models of identity—in Cheng's words, 'This does *not* at all mean that the minority subject does not develop other relations to that injunctive ideal which can be self-affirming or

---

47 Freud, 'Mourning and melancholia', 243.

48 Sigmund Freud, 'The ego and the id' [1922], in Sigmund Freud, *The Freud Reader*, ed. Peter Gay (New York: W. W. Norton 1989), 638–43. In 'Mourning and melancholia' Freud also noted that the self-reproach of the melancholic psyche resembled 'conscience' (247).

49 Judith Butler, *The Psychic Life of Power: Theories in Subjection* (Stanford, CA: Stanford University Press 1997), 167.

sustaining'—such subjects are still forced to find a place in a society that devalues some aspect of their being.[50]

And subjects who do introject these hostile identity-formations incorporate idealizations of selfhood that are already melancholic, or based on disavowed intra-psychic conflict. Certain formations of whiteness, for example, depend on and even introject 'blackness' as an object that stimulates waves of both idealization and resentment; experiencing an intra-psychic racial drama, the racist white subject is unable consciously to acknowledge its depth and difficulty, let alone its social and political dimensions.[51] Rather, as David Eng and Shinhee Han argue in the context of the United States, 'discourses of American exceptionalism and democratic myths of liberty, individuals, and inclusion force a misremembering of [racial] exclusions, an enforced psychic amnesia'.[52] For a minoritized subject, then, to identify with such a norm would be to sacrifice a critical counter-perspective while also internalizing multiple forms of social conflict.

Walker's exploration of this problem demonstrates why aspects of Freud's individualized study remain useful in politically oriented theories of melancholia. The novel observes a host of media outlets that encourage damaging identifications: magazines, for example, inform Meridian that 'Woman was a mindless body, a sex creature, something to hang false hair and nails on', and her peers assume they are living 'the lives of their movie idols' that pit 'blondes against brunettes and cowboys against Indians, good men against bad, darker men' (71, 75). The danger of such ambient sexism and racism is compounded when they become embedded—whether through direct embrace or passive acceptance—into an existing melancholic identification that, in Freud's argument, 'behaves like an open wound, drawing to itself cathectic energies ... from all directions, and emptying the ego until it is totally impoverished'.[53]

Meridian's melancholic identification with her mother, for example, leads her to surrender critical insight. Reciting a speech assigned by her high school 'that extolled the virtues of the Constitution and praised the

---

50 Anne Anlin Cheng, *The Melancholy of Race* (Oxford and New York: Oxford University Press 2000), 7.

51 Ibid., 10–12; see also Paul Gilroy, *Postcolonial Melancholia* (New York: Columbia University Press 2006), 101. For an account of colonial desire and hostility in the intra-psychic encounter with racist stereotypes, see, for example, Homi Bhabha, 'The other question: stereotype, discrimination, and the discourse of colonialism', in Homi Bhabha, *The Location of Culture* (London: Routledge 1994), 66–84. For an example concerning the United States, one might look to the 'racial masquerade' Michael North elucidates in the writing of white modernists; see Michael North, *The Dialect of Modernism: Race, Language, and Twentieth-century Literature* (New York: Oxford University Press 1994).

52 David L. Eng and Shinhee Han, 'A dialogue on racial melancholia', in David L. Eng and David Kazanjian (eds), *Loss: The Politics of Mourning* (Berkeley: University of California Press 2003), 347.

53 Freud, 'Mourning and melancholia', 253.

superiority of The American Way of Life', she suddenly stops, realizing the speciousness of what she is saying. But, when her mother, who rejects political thought, criticizes Meridian's failure to 'trust in God, hold up her head, [and] never look back', Meridian is confronted with two socially sanctioned and politically passive identifications: the disavowing nationalist and the unquestioning sufferer. Though she recognizes the former as false and destructive, she respects the latter and further believes that, by refusing quietly to accept the marginalization and abuse inflicted on previous generations, she has failed to honour their experience. Thus she chastises herself for her activist spirit: 'doubled over, as if she might shrink into a ball and disappear' (121–2). This transgenerational exchange of loss and prohibition constitutes what Jermaine Singleton describes as a 'cryptic conversation', a moment when unconscious beliefs about or even attachments to an oppressive past constrain action in the present.[54]

The centrality of this passivity in Meridian's life—even when she perceives feelings of desire or rage—cannot be overstated; among her many psychological symptoms, the novel presents her early paralysis in the face of her mother's rage—itself a response to overwhelming social pressure—as a prototype for later responses. This immobility returns, for example, after she confronts local elites over injustice, and becomes for a time her standard physical state, overcome each morning through slow and careful stretching exercises. It also marks her sexual responses, in which her legs 'are like somebody starched them shut' (64). In one sense, this physical reflex might be read as a kind of hysteria or post-traumatic response, since Meridian learns about sex from being exploited by the director of a funeral home and later his assistant. Though Meridian insists that she 'use[d] them' to learn about sex, the reader recognizes that the gropings, chases and grinds forced upon an early adolescent who finds the men 'distasteful' and 'hate[ful]' would constitute precisely the kind of 'traumatic ... experience' that might, in Freud's words, be expressed as a 'mnemic symbol', in this case, a corpse-like pose that quite aptly reflects her experiences 'around the embalming table' (66–7).[55] Reasonable and meaningful insofar as it goes, such an interpretation focuses too narrowly on one series of experiences in one small set of relationships; in that way, it replicates literary critic Claudia Tate's charge against 'mainstream psychoanalysis', that it 'effaces racism and recasts its effects as a personality disorder caused by familial rather than social pathology'.[56] In contrast, Meridian repeatedly returns to the social difficulties facing black families and individuals: the funeral director, for example, was discarded as an infant when his white grandparents discovered that their daughter—immediately 'shut ... up in the cellar'—'was pregnant by the black man who worked for

54 Singleton, 'Cryptic Conversations', 11–12.
55 Sigmund Freud, 'The aetiology of hysteria' [1896], in Freud, The Freud Reader, 98.
56 Claudia Tate, Psychoanalysis and Black Novels: Desire and the Protocols of Race (New York: Oxford University Press 1998), 16.

them' (65). Assaulted by a man who has himself been abandoned, Meridian bodily responds in a way that is also shaped by her melancholic identification with her mother, who feels 'dead[ened]' by her efforts to comply with gender norms and expresses all her emotion 'in the ironing of her children's clothes', producing 'stiff, almost inflexible garments for them to wear' (51, 79).

The point of this analysis—and, one gathers, of Walker's narrative—is not to criticize either Meridian or Mrs Hill, each of whom seeks to create as honourable and productive a life as she can in a world shaped by hostile norms, powerful injunctions against critical speech and nonconformist behaviour, and systematic political and economic disfranchisement. The goal, rather, is to explore, in Cheng's words, how 'political domination is reproduced at the level of personal experience' in a variety of ways (including attachments to loved ones), through diverse institutions (including the family) and with a range of effects (a stimulus to resistance or passivity).[57] To be clear, Meridian represents anything but a typical character, given her out-of-body experiences, occasional catalepsy and final definitive claim that her 'value' is to be 'always alone' (220). Still, her quest is in many ways paradigmatic: though her friends and acquaintances differ in class background, racial identification and gender, they all experience psychological effects from their time spent in a toxic political culture and are, as described in Meridian's poetry, 'cast out alone/ to heal/ and re-create/ ourselves' (213).

Melancholic politics: movements in time

These characters' restorative efforts—or lack thereof—are differentiated by chronological orientation: the focus on past suffering or a potentially transformable present. Too great a focus on the past, as in the case of Meridian's identification with her mother's suffering, can be paralysing. Worse, it can even be seductive: like her father and grandmother, Meridian experiences moments of intense spiritual and physical ecstasy when lying next to a Cherokee burial mound, from which she develops a sense of 'so tangible a connection to the past' that she feels closer to the dead than to the living. Though these brief experiences are psychologically free-ing—Meridian 'become[s] a speck in the grand movement of time'—the text vigorously dissociates them from productive political action (59). Mr Hill's 'compassion for people dead centuries before he was born' leads to a 'withdrawal from the world', a problem exacerbated by the continuing colonization of the state (58, 29). Feeling personal guilt over Native American removal, Mr Hill gives part of his land to the Cherokee Walter Longknife, but the government later appropriates the land for a tourist attraction from which African Americans are barred.

57 Cheng, *The Melancholy of Race*, 19.

On the other hand, a refusal to acknowledge the past can lead to a reductive understanding of social life or even cruel behaviour. Where Mr Hill's melancholic attachment to the Cherokee past proves politically ineffectual, Mrs Hill's sweeping and synchronic analysis—'The answer to everything ... is we live in America and we're not rich'—is no more productive, suggesting, in fact, that her husband should abandon his concerns for social justice in the pursuit of personal wealth (56). Similarly, where Meridian is often so mired in grief that her friend Anne-Marion suspects she 'might never be ready for the future', Anne-Marion is incapable of tolerating any connection to a painful past and therefore chooses to 'kick' the backward-looking Meridian away rather than to acknowledge her own ambivalence. Anne-Marion explains: 'I can not afford to love you. Like the idea of suffering itself, you are obsolete' (125).

Such conflicts between grief-stricken contemplation of the past and impatient dismissals thereof have, in recent decades, been noted in many activist approaches to loss; they are influenced by and also reflect a national context that pathologizes subjects who do not 'get over' past injustice. For example, Douglas Crimp observed in 1989 that some AIDS activists described mourning as an 'indulgent, sentimental, defeatist' attachment to lost loved ones. Arguing that 'misery comes from within as well as without', Crimp suggested that responses to this suffering might shape political action in unconscious and destructive ways. Those experiencing 'deadening numbness or constant depression' may need to confront internalized hostility or disavowed ambivalence in order to restore their ability for militancy in the present. On the other hand, those who respond to grief with reflexive social protest may be unable to recognize how their needs and emotions continue to be shaped by past experience.[58]

Where Crimp argued that activists must acknowledge and attend to melancholic attachments, other critics suggest that they must be strictly maintained. By this logic, if dominant identifications chastise subjects for diverging from a certain norm, the productive response must be to identify all the more strongly with the position of those who have been similarly beset in the past.[59] Such an effort not only serves to resist racist and heterosexist normalization, but also to challenge triumphalist accounts of unceasing progress, such as the blithe optimism that enables Meridian's friend Truman to tell her, even with some irony, 'Revolution was the theme of the sixties ... We're here to stay: the black and the poor, the Indian, and now all those illegal immigrants from the West Indies who adore America just the way it is' (188–9).

58 Douglas Crimp, 'Mourning and militancy', *October*, vol. 51, Winter 1989, 5, 16–17.
59 Eng and Han, 'A dialogue on racial melancholia', 363–6; Phillip Novak, '"Circles and circles of sorrow": in the wake of Morrison's *Sula*', *Publications of the Modern Language Association*, vol. 114, no. 2, March 1999, 191.

Still, as Žižek argues, critical endorsement of the 'conceptual *and* ethical primacy of melancholia' flies in the face of Freudian theory, which deems melancholia 'pathological' not so much because it is non-normative (especially since some degree of ambivalent introjected attachment seems inevitable) but because it is psychologically deadening.[60] In psychoanalytic models, after all, melancholia includes all the suffering caused by mourning—'profoundly painful dejection, cessation of interest in the outside world, loss of the capacity to love, inhibition of all activity'—and, further, 'an extraordinary diminution in ... self-regard, an impoverishment of ... ego on a grand scale'.[61] Given these affective dynamics, it is hard to imagine how the lived experience of melancholia could facilitate an activist stance regarding social hierarchies.[62] Where Truman abandons activism, Meridian is left not just psychically but even physically overwhelmed by her occasional valiant efforts. Just as she experiences momentary paralysis and desperate weeping as a child when she witnesses her mother's displeasure, her later activism is followed by episodes of fever, hair and weight loss, and catalepsy.

From a political perspective, the dangers in celebrating melancholia emerge also from the lack of awareness it imparts regarding the conflicts that sufferers internalize. Freudian melancholics cannot even name what they have lost (and, indeed, such objects are 'usually to be found in [the melancholic's] immediate environment').[63] In Judith Butler's explanation, they experience 'ungrievable' losses: these forms of hierarchy, restriction and oppression are so simultaneously integral to and disavowed within their society that distraught subjects cannot find the language or even psychological space from which to articulate the divisions they instead incorporate into their identities.[64] Those who celebrate the 'aggressive and militant preservation of the lost and loved object' describe it as a form of racial, gendered or sexual identity, but these formulations are politically problematic.[65] They risk not only essentialism but also the suggestion that a

---

60 Žižek, 'Mourning, melancholy and the act', 658. This distinction is a slim one: Freud does not deem melancholia 'pathological' because it is non-normative, but he does accept mourning as 'normal' only because it is so familiar. In his words: 'It is really only because we know so well how to explain it that [mourning] does not seem to us pathological' ('Mourning and melancholia', 244). In other words, here—as in much of his work—he insists that 'normal' describes the assessment of onlookers, or their relative comfort and familiarity with a form of behaviour.

61 Freud, 'Mourning and melancholia', 246, 248.

62 See also Greg Forter, 'Against melancholia: contemporary mourning theory, Fitzgerald's *The Great Gatsby*, and the politics of unfinished grief', *differences: A Journal of Feminist Cultural Studies*, vol. 14, no. 2, Summer 2003, 139.

63 Freud, 'Mourning and melancholia', 245, 251. See also Forter, 'Against melancholia', 138–9.

64 Vikki Bell, 'On speech, race and melancholia: an interview with Judith Butler', *Theory Culture & Society*, vol. 16, no. 2, April 1999, 169–71.

65 Eng and Han, 'A dialogue on racial melancholia', 364.

politically and psychologically 'whole' existence can be found in an inevitably fabricated past rather than in a more obviously hypothetical future towards which the subject might strive.[66] It is for this reason that the positive stance towards melancholia is accused of political quietism: in Žižek's words: 'The melancholic link to the lost ethnic Object allows us to claim that we remain faithful to our ethnic roots while fully participating in the global capitalist game.'[67] Walker's novel represents this possibility as Truman, following his participation in the civil rights movement, moves to New York to create 'the century's definitive African-American masterpieces', which depict African American women as 'magnificent giants, breeding forth the warriors of the new universe', precisely the identity formation that has devastated Meridian (167, 168).

Even outside psychoanalytic criticism, scholarly commentary concerning contemporary social and political movements expresses concern that centring activist efforts on fixed ideas of identity or culture can have deleterious effects. Questions about how to situate social movements in time—whether to emphasize themes associated with the past, present or future—are aggravated by the fact that, in many locales, current experiences of time may resist sustaining forms of political affiliation. Where movements for social justice once opposed efforts to preserve oppressive traditions, they now often battle neo-liberal formations whose incessant change often militates against the maintenance of enduring activist networks.[68] Further, critiques of the narrative of linear progress, while usefully revealing modernity's dynamics of oppression, have also disrupted hope for beneficial political transformation.[69] Observing a social field characterized by hostility, abstraction and fragmentation, many theorists suggest that the embrace of monolithic, stable and nostalgic identity-formations may be immediately satisfying to subjects even if they are ineffective for political movements.

As Stuart Hall explains, identification with a narrative of coherent cultural history can be a sustaining force—'restor[ing] an imaginary fullness or plenitude, to set against the broken rubric of our past'—but this narrative

---

66 Judith Butler suggests such a concern about essentialism in 'Subjection, resistance, resignification: between Freud and Foucault', in John Rajchman (ed.), *The Identity in Question* (New York: Routledge 1995), 233, 243–6.

67 Žižek, 'Mourning, melancholy and the act', 659; Freud, 'Mourning and melancholia', 245, 251.

68 Spillers, '"All the things you could be by now, if Sigmund Freud's wife was your mother"', 85–6; David Harvey, 'Militant particularism and global ambition: the conceptual politics of place, space, and environment in the work of Raymond Williams' [1995], in David Harvey, *Spaces of Captial: Towards a Critical Geography* (New York: Routledge 2001), 169, 173–82.

69 Dubey, 'Postmodern geographies of the U.S. South', 363–8; Anne McClintock, 'The angel of progress: pitfalls of the term "postcolonialism"', *Social Text*, nos 31/32, Spring 1992, 96–7; Wendy Brown, *Politics out of History* (Princeton, NJ: Princeton University Press 2001), 3–17.

must be balanced with an awareness of diversity and discontinuity in the present: 'Cultural identities come from somewhere, have histories. But ... [f]ar from being eternally fixed in some essentialised past, they are subject to the continuous "play" of history, culture, and power.' Nonetheless, the prospect that identity must continually be built and revised amid destructive economic, political and social dynamics is, as Hall acknowledges, 'unsettling'.[70] Under such psychologically strenuous circumstances, an individual could prefer nostalgic contemplation to contemporary confrontation, or might imaginatively displace the relatively abstract and diverse political collective of the present with an idealized lost and homogeneous community.[71]

Meridian both thematizes and resists such nostalgia. Though Walker has famously asserted that 'what the black Southern writer inherits as a natural right is a sense of *community*', her second novel presents any possibility of a stable and homogeneous social whole as untenable.[72] Meridian is perpetually isolated from others and regularly subjected to sexual assault as well as racist and classist harassment; even the social networks of the civil rights movement manifest these divisive hierarchies. Though activism provides occasional '*ecsta[tic]*' experiences of togetherness, participants are dispersed in much of their daily life, mourning losses while also experiencing a form of alienation attributed to technological change: '*But now the television became the repository of memory, and each onlooker grieved alone*' (33).

Further, the novel suggests that too great an attachment to ideas of a socially cohesive past may be inherently restrictive, even when held by proponents of social justice. Because the civil rights movement initiates and participates in an 'age of choice', it requires that previous conceptions of 'the people', based on a segregated Jim Crow context, give way to new realities that can prove as perplexing as they are freeing (124). When Meridian attends Martin Luther King's funeral, for example, she listens to families telling 'their children stories about the old days before black people marched, before black people voted, before they could allow their anger or even their exhaustion to show'. By the end of the day, however, 'people began to engage each other in loud, even ringing, conversation', and to 'call for Coca-Colas, for food'. Meridian—who still harbours a melancholic attachment to that avowedly oppressive past—finds this 'feeling of relief in the air' to be 'repulsive' (185). In contrast, the narrative presents the funeral not only as a commemoration of loss but also as a celebration of accomplishment. The chapter opens with an account of a once relentlessly

70 Stuart Hall, 'Cultural identity and diaspora', in Jonathan Rutherford (ed.), *Identity: Community, Culture, Difference* (London: Lawrence & Wishart 1990), 225, 226.

71 Žižek, 'Mourning, melancholy and the act', 676; Dubey, 'Postmodern geographies of the U.S. South', 367.

72 Alice Walker, 'The black writer and the southern experience' [1970], in Walker, *In Search of Our Mothers' Gardens*, 17.

suppressed African American populace but closes with the image of 'a black woman ... laughing, laughing, as if all her cares, at last, had flown away' (186). Where Meridian focuses on the loss of Dr King, the novel observes how possibilities for black publicity have been profoundly and beneficially opened.

Part of Meridian's task, then, is to learn to negotiate and appreciate new opportunities. The novel clearly values her persistence in forms of activism that have been abandoned by her erstwhile friends in the face of spurious claims that the problems addressed by the civil rights movement have been solved. It begins, for example, with her confrontation of an army tank that seeks to prevent the poor children of Chicokema from seeing a travelling freak show except on 'their' segregated 'day': no longer isolating race as a strategy for social hierarchy, the town now segregates 'po' folks' who work in a guano factory (19). But Meridian's psychological and even physical rigidity threatens to overwhelm her activism, as she is unable to exercise her political voice without suffering painful illness and also only in sacrifice to others, as one critic argues, 'as if in expiation'.[73] The narrative states explicitly that she must learn to imagine some liveable future for herself as opposed to martyrdom: 'All saints should ... do their bit, then—just walk away' (151). Otherwise, her identity is based on a kind of reflexive and self-punishing repetition: 'Why not go all out', asks Truman, 'and put rocks in your shoes?' (192).

Psyche and polity: working through

In its distinct non-linearity, Walker's narrative suggests the temporality of psychoanalytic treatment, as analyst and analysand probe associated thoughts, memories and feelings in order, in Freud's words, to find the 'conflicts ... which give rise to the symptoms' and to 'lift ... internal resistances'.[74] Meridian begins near the end of its plot's chronology and moves backward and forward in time, indicating that the ordering of events is less relevant than their impression on the protagonist's development. Further, the chapters have no requisite relationship to the novel's plot; instead, they suggest thematic contiguities. For example, a chapter narrating the destruction of the tree Sojourner, which commemorated the life of a slave tortured for telling white children a story that literally frightened one to death, directly precedes a chapter describing Meridian's continuous feelings of guilt at having deprived her mother of independence. Many of these narrative moments, such as the chapter 'Gold', seem unassimilable to

73 Karen F. Stein, 'Meridian: Alice Walker's critique of revolution', Black American Literature Forum, vol. 20, nos 1–2, Spring–Summer 1986, 139.
74 Sigmund Freud, Introductory Lectures on Psycho-Analysis, trans. from the German by James Strachey [1920] (New York: Norton/Liveright 1966), 560–1.

biographical chronology, despite the fact that they occur during a fictional life clearly situated in calendrical time. As these narratives repeat and in other ways emerge out of chronological order, readers realize that, for Meridian, events such as the denunciations of her mother and the pain of her abortion and sterilization do not recede into the past or into the even flow of time. Instead, they are felt, inconsistently, as monads in the present: condensations of experience, understanding and feeling.

The narrative even seems to manifest a kind of repetition compulsion, as Walker's lyrical prose is frequently punctured by shocking images. From the 'mummified' woman in the Chicokema freak show who is displayed by the husband who killed her, to the slave who buries her tongue after her owner cuts it from her mouth, to the homeless and pregnant 'Wile Chile' covered in garbage from her survivalist scavenging, to the corpse of a child who was drowned in the sewer system after an unofficial swimming hole—used as a substitute for racially restricted public pools—flooded, to the young girl who bit her baby's face before strangling it with a curtain ruffle, the novel continually returns to images of bodies distorted almost beyond recognition from their experiences of abuse and neglect. In psychoanalytic theory, subjects may unconsciously seek to repeat 'distressing situation[s]' in order to 'master the stimulus' of a previous conflict.[75] Similarly, these images of egregiously damaged female and infantile bodies echo the experiences and beliefs that haunt Meridian, who not only observed how Mrs Hill viewed motherhood as a kind of violent disruption but also experienced violent fantasies while holding her own child.

By reading these images in this way, I do not mean to suggest that they reflect only Meridian's psychological state, for they unquestionably evoke pervasive social injustice. They also suggest, however, that Meridian's attention is compulsively drawn to images and stories that align with her feelings of marginalization and debasement. Because the narrative does not discursively thematize the connections among these images, they seem simultaneously incongruous and steeped in emotional significance. Isolated in time but clearly resonating with the whole of the novel, they create, for the reader, a sense of *déjà vu*, a kind of alienating and estranged familiarity that, in psychoanalytic theory, suggests repressed knowledge. Crucially, what is excluded from language in these scenes is not a traumatic experience that Meridian could not consciously process as it occurred; this character is remarkable for her ability to confront and comprehend dehumanizing violence. Rather, Meridian resists awareness of how her psyche reproduces such dynamics within and against itself.

The cognitive and political consequences of such non-linear and impressionistic narrative have long been debated, as critics argue that it belies the

---

75 Jean Laplanche and Jean-Bertrand Pontalis, *The Language of Psycho-Analysis*, trans. from the French by Donald Nicholson-Smith (New York: W. W. Norton 1973), 78; Sigmund Freud, *Beyond the Pleasure Principle*, in Freud, *The Freud Reader*, 609.

significance of historical time, capitulates to perceptions that contemporary society lacks coherence, and obscures the possibility of political action.[76] But Walker's novel explores a problem that such criticism merely cites as a source of anxiety, and that is how people in fragmented societies attempt to understand each other as they struggle to create 'new forms of collective living'.[77] Though *Meridian* employs progressive linear time in the sense that it lends itself to representing processes of change, it also suggests that such a temporality can be alienating, particularly for those who recognize the ways in which public time—the temporality established and narrated by a society's dominant institutions—seeks to encode marginalized persons and scenes of oppression as exceptions that must be 'left behind'.[78]

Through Meridian's melancholic perspective, the novel constructs a fissured and 'four-dimensional' view of space, one in which locales have been palpably constructed by 'social interrelations and interactions' that have occurred through time and that have been experienced differently depending on residents' race, gender and class.[79] In such a context, Meridian achieves success as a community activist because she is able to recognize and address diverse histories and circumstances before asserting her own paradigms for progress. From her own experiences and from her father, she is cognizant of the multiple ways in which history has positioned individuals and social groups, differences emerging from cultural affiliations, political orientations and psychological or spiritual traits that must be taken seriously. But while Meridian repeatedly forces dominant groups in a given locale to confront their exclusivity—bringing 'Wile Chile' into her honours dorm, for example, and carrying the corpse of the drowned child into a town meeting—she simultaneously accepts her own marginalization, and the novel serves to elucidate and challenge that pattern.

Beginning with her demonstration in Chicokema, which is followed by an episode of literal paralysis, the narrative unpacks her conviction that 'something's *missing*' in her character (14); in Kristeva's terms, she perceives 'a primitive self—wounded, incomplete, empty'.[80] She recalls that this belief struck her with particular intensity when she was chastised by an activist group for her inability to swear that she would 'kill for the Revolution' (14). She imagines, at the time, that she is too deeply moved by the music she has heard in African American churches, which condemned even 'revolutionary

76 See, for example, Fredric Jameson, 'Beyond the cave: demystifying the ideology of modernism' [1975], in Fredric Jameson, *The Ideologies of Theory: Essays 1971–1986*, 2 vols (Minneapolis: University of Minnesota Press 1988), II.131.

77 Ibid., II.132.

78 On linear time, see Thomas Luckmann, 'The constitution of human life in time', in John Bender and David E. Wellbery (eds), *Chronotypes: The Construction of Time* (Stanford, CA: Stanford University Press 1991), 157.

79 Doreen Massey, 'Politics and space/time', *New Left Review*, Series I, no. 196, November–December 1992, 79–80.

80 Kristeva, *Black Sun*, 12.

murder': she describes herself, accordingly, as being '*held* by something in the past'. As the novel proceeds in its non-linear fashion to explore this memory, however—describing her relationships with others in the church, for example, and revealing her scepticism concerning the social norms she associates with churches—it also suggests that she misunderstands her own past. Her reflections on the music and the continued pressure from her friends carry her thoughts to 'the day she lost her mother', that is, when her mother insisted that she go to the altar to 'accept ... Christ', an injunction that makes 'her heart flutter ... like that of a small bird about to be stoned'. The emotion she associates with this day—the feeling that precludes her from revolutionary violence—appears to have emerged less from the music, which she describes as 'the purity that lifted [choirs'] songs like a flight of doves above her music-drunken head', than from her desire to escape—like the doves or small, frightened birds—from the experience of a deep love for her mother that is nonetheless intertwined with fear and repressed rage (27–8).

This confusion does not merely illustrate another aspect of Meridian's psychological difficulties; rather, it suggests her early, unarticulated and perhaps even unconscious insight concerning a central philosophical problem in social movements. Engaging with others who believe, with Frantz Fanon, that violence—or at least the willingness to kill—is a 'cleansing force ... making [the oppressed] fearless and restoring ... self-respect', Meridian's experience leads her to be wary: she is deeply aware that hostility may be inadvertently turned against loved ones or even oneself.[81] Her revolutionary friends intuit—better than Meridian herself—her concerns about the difficulties of controlling emotion in the service of revolutionary violence, suggesting that she suffers from internalized racism: 'You hate yourself instead of hating them' (28). But they are not willing to work through Meridian's feelings to the conclusion she reaches near the end of the novel, which suggests that activism must coexist with ethical discernment and critical insight: 'even the contemplation of murder required incredible delicacy as it required incredible spiritual work, and the historical background and present setting must be right' (200).

Depicting the debate between Meridian and her 'cadre', the novel links the individual's psychological health with the cumulative wisdom of social movements but, rather than suggesting that activism will heal those who have been hurt, it implies that the voices of people in pain provide wisdom crucial for the process of transformation. Meridian's friends are uninterested in discussing the relationships between past experiences and present actions or feelings; instead, they make her 'ashamed' of the 'decidedly unrevolutionary past' that they nonetheless shared and even consign her to that past, calling her a 'drag' (30–1). Exclusive and cruel in the moment, they go on to

81 Frantz Fanon, *The Wretched of the Earth*, trans. from the French by Constance Farrington (New York: Grove 1963), 94.

'unrevolutionary' lives: Anne-Marion, their leader, writes poems 'about her two children, and the quality of light that fell across a lake she owned' (201). In contrast, the novel suggests that Meridian's willingness to explore and work through these internal conflicts renders her both a model and a resource: 'that is my value', she asserts, confidently, in the conclusion (220). Representing, in Kristeva's words, a 'subject's battle with symbolic collapse', the novel ultimately suggests that its protagonist's 'skewed time sense' enhances perception.[82]

But neither can the individual find healing without a movement: Meridian finally recognizes that she needs 'a place ... to congregate, where the problems of life were not discussed fraudulently and the approach to the future was considered communally, and moral questions were taken seriously'. This new social network cannot be one that requires her immediate and unquestioning conformity, as that would stimulate precisely the kind of deflected rebellious energy that she routinely turns against herself, such as the internalized condemnation that she derives, for example, from her erstwhile cadre. Further, in order to find models for working through her own resistances, she must witness others who openly acknowledge how their current state of being is shaped by previous experience. Accordingly, her epiphany occurs at a black church service among a community that, though she had previously considered it 'a reactionary power', is transforming itself to be sustaining in a changing world.[83] The potency of this moment in the narrative suggests how badly Meridian has needed to interact with others, to find new ways of framing the emotions that emerge from her intra-psychic battle or new possibilities for expressing dissent. Suddenly, the previously isolated and often suicidal Meridian experiences a new and reviving sense of worth and connection: 'She understood, finally, that the respect she owed her life was to continue against whatever obstacles, to live it, and not to give up any particle of it without a fight to the death, preferably *not* her own' (199–200).

The fact that this revelation occurs within a specifically African American institution, however, raises problems for any theory of melancholia that seeks to resist racially restrictive or backward-looking paradigms. Insuperably, Meridian's transformation occurs through interaction with social categories rooted in the past, a segregated institution shaped by gender hierarchy. Though the narrative refuses to delimit this community according to dogma—'Meridian knew they did not mean simply "church," as in

---

82 Kristeva, *Black Sun*, 10, 24.

83 The text's insistence on these multiple changes suggests that, though Byerman persuasively describes Meridian's feelings of isolation from rural southern black communities, his representation of those communities as a static folk 'outside of history' is overstated; see Keith Byerman, 'Gender and justice: Alice Walker and the sexual politics of civil rights', in Jeffrey J. Folks and Nancy Summers Folks (eds), *The World Is Our Home: Society and Culture in Contemporary Southern Writing* (Lexington: University Press of Kentucky 2000), 102.

Baptist, Methodist or whatnot, but rather communal spirit, togetherness, righteous convergence'—its members have shared experiences with racist oppression 'which had', in the novel's words, 'created them One Life' (200). Further, the aesthetic environment created for church members to mourn losses—as this service explicitly mourns the murder of an activist—is vigorously patriarchal, presided over by the image of 'a tall, broad-shouldered black man ... in one hand he held a guitar ... the other arm was raised above his head and it held a long shiny object the end of which was dripping with blood' (198). Walker's extended description of 'B.B., With Sword' suggests the kind of substitution for the melancholic's lost object implicitly prescribed by Julia Kristeva, particularly when depression manifests a 'matricidal drive' redirected towards the self: in such cases, she argues, melancholics must discover 'a third party—father, form, schema', a 'phallic or symbolic' identification 'capable of playing his part as oedipal father in symbolic Law'.[84]

Contrasting this moment with the scenes that lead Meridian to feel a closer connection with the dead than with the living, however, the novel suggests that, by participating in a practice compromised by an oppressive past (as, it would seem, human collectives inevitably are) but changing in the present, Meridian is able to suture her psychological difficulties into the social and political realm to which they properly belong. Observing the father of the slain activist, whose 'throat ... seem[s] stoppered with anxiety, memory, grief and dope', she recognizes that melancholia may be pervasive in influence but variable in form, neither her unique failing nor a manifestation that must necessarily resemble her own symptoms (197). (This multiplicity among sufferers and responses is demonstrated also by the chapter's title, 'Camara', which refers to the murdered child of the atheist Truman and his Jewish ex-wife Lynne; referenced nowhere within the chapter, the name 'Camara' thus comes to signify one particular tragedy among a plethora of losses, one distinct source of unfinished grieving among many that may be expressed very differently.) Further, the significance of this scene for Meridian seems to reside less in the experience of a binding community—as the grieving father himself 'did not allow closeness' and was ultimately 'left alone with his ghosts'—than in her realization that the worshippers gather political motivation from interacting with him: his willingness to 'share' ritual and story constitute 'the ways to transformation that [they] know' (200). Finally, despite this church's embrace of phallic imagery—itself a revolutionary displacement of the previous 'pale Christ'—neither Meridian nor those around her seeks to create a fixed schema, an array of newly empowered but nonetheless

---

84 Kristeva, *Black Sun*, 23. Juliana Schiesari argues that *Black Sun* reflects the author's 'ambivalence, if not hatred, toward women'; see Juliana Schiesari, *The Gendering of Melancholia: Feminism, Psychoanalysis, and the Symbolics of Loss in Renaissance Literature* (Ithaca, NY: Cornell University Press 1992), 91.

restrictive identity formations. On the contrary, the narrative insists that church members seek to 'weave' new stories—particularly of resistance to oppression—'into what [they] already know—into the songs, the sermons, the "brother and sister"' in order to facilitate political transformation (198).

Ultimately, then, Meridian learns to view personal pain as neither fixed nor solely internal; rather, it becomes a fact that facilitates interpersonal dialogue and desire for social change. Her epiphany is not presented as a final revelation, but rather as a model for how she may continue to grow: it begins in 'puzzle[ment]', suddenly 'allow[s] her to breathe freely', and ultimately leads her to walk away 'as if hurrying to catch up with someone' (198, 199, 220). Depicting the protagonist's departure to sites unknown, as well as her continuing affection for multiracial friends, the novel suggests that this project of seeking to comprehend the past and shape the future must eventually extend outward into more heterogeneous spaces. Consistent with Walker's later claim that African Americans constitute 'the mestizos of North America' and thus cannot 'function as only one', this ending nonetheless reflects needed stages of recovery for the melancholic Meridian, who must relinquish a direct, unconscious and singular identification for an identity that lacks any fixed model, an unending process of self-formation.[85]

Though it concerns a profoundly committed activist, Walker's experimental novel seems, in many ways, inconsistent with the literature of social movements, not least because the politically vexing theme of melancholia informs every aspect of Meridian's narrative: style, images, plotting and tone. But Walker insists that politically oppressive societies induce psychological pain in numerous and inexorable ways and, further, that an activist community must seek to understand these dynamics in order to find what wisdom may be produced by these perspectives and also to restore the persons and eventually the polity that has been hurt. Though both psychologically inflected literature and psychoanalysis have been criticized for focusing too much attention on the past rather than on a present in which change can occur, Meridian suggests that reorienting one's relationship to the past may facilitate engagement in the present. The advent of melancholia attests, after all, that justice and wholeness must be sought in a changed world: there is no unalienated, unbroken past relationship to which the melancholic can return. But pursuit of a more just society can only benefit from efforts to understand how our experiences in this world have shaped or limited our ability to imagine such a future.

---

85 Alice Walker, 'In the closet of the soul' [1988], in Guy-Sheftall (ed.), *Words of Fire*, 540.

Riots, disasters and racism: impending racial cataclysm and the extreme right in the United States

GEORGE MICHAEL AND D. J. MULLOY

Over the past few decades, the extreme right in the United States has taken on an increasingly revolutionary orientation. Extrapolating trends, such as demographics, immigration and crime, the movement's prognosticators have frequently warned of an impending societal implosion. In late 2005 representatives of the movement cited three events in particular as further proof of this sombre future: Hurricane Katrina and its aftermath in New Orleans; the riots that convulsed the suburbs of Paris; and an inter-ethnic mêlée that occurred on a beach in Sydney, Australia between native Whites and Middle Eastern immigrants. This article critically examines these three events from the perspective of the American far right. Analysing the contemporary discourse of this milieu can provide an indication of where the movement is likely to be headed in the near future but, more than this, it can also help to provide important insights as to how issues of race, immigration and multiculturalism may play out in the wider American society. As Jeffrey Kaplan and Leonard Weinberg, two noted observers of political extremism, have correctly argued, 'the study of this esoteric subculture can foretell national controversies yet to take place'.[1]

---

1 Jeffrey Kaplan and Leonard Weinberg, *The Emergence of a Euro-American Radical Right* (New Brunswick, NJ: Rutgers University Press 1998), 109–10. Likewise Wilcox and

Hurricane Katrina, Jared Taylor and *American Renaissance*

The October 2005 issue of *American Renaissance*, arguably the most intellectually sophisticated organ of the American far right, contained an article written by Jared Taylor about the impact of Hurricane Katrina on New Orleans. Entitled 'Africa in Our Midst: The Media Suppresses Katrina's Lessons', it was one of the most widely discussed articles the monthly *American Renaissance* (*AR*) had published in its fifteen-year history.[2] Endorsed and reproduced by numerous other far rightists, it led to a symposium appearing in David Horowitz's conservative political online journal *FrontPageMagazine.com* (which was denounced, in turn, in a blog by the liberal journalist Max Blumenthal), and was also the subject of a highly critical editorial by Mark Potok in the Autumn 2005 issue of the Southern Poverty Law Center's *Intelligence Report*.[3] Regular readers of *American Renaissance*, however, were more than fulsome in their praise of Taylor's work, with the article being variously described as 'wonderful', 'masterful', 'essential reading', 'a tour-de-force', 'powerful and penetrating' and 'an incredible eye opener'. 'It should be 'required reading at every high school around the country', said Robert Binion, while 'OZBoy' hoped it would be 'spread to every end of the earth'. Taylor had provided a 'grim insight into the future of the United States', contended 'JR', one that he hoped would 'swell the ranks of race conscious Caucasians at long last'.[4]

That the article garnered such lavish praise from the *AR* readership was a reflection, in part, of the fact that it seemed to provide compelling evidence of everything Taylor and *American Renaissance* had been arguing since its formation in 1990: the innate inferiority of Blacks in relation to

George argued that extremist groups sometimes fulfil a 'watchdog' function in society insofar as they are especially sensitive to issues concerning their particular interests; John George and Laird Wilcox, *Nazis, Communists, Klansmen, and Others on the Fringe: Political Extremism in America* (Buffalo, NY: Prometheus Books 1992), 61.

2 Jared Taylor, 'Africa in our midst: the media suppresses Katrina's lessons', *American Renaissance*, vol. 16, no. 10, October 2005, 1–8. The article first appeared on the *American Renaissance* website on 5 September 2005, under a slightly different title, 'Africa in our midst: lessons from Katrina', www.amren.com/mtnews/archives/2005/09/africa_in_our_m.php (viewed 10 July 2008).

3 'Symposium: Katrina, race and silence', *FrontPageMagazine.com*, 30 September 2005, www.frontpagemag.com/Articles/ReadArticle.asp?ID=19676 (viewed 10 July 2008); Max Blumenthal, 'The demons of David Horowitz', 26 April 2006, http://maxblumenthal.com/2006_04_01_maxblumenthal_archive.html (viewed 10 July 2008); Mark Potok, 'The blame game', *Intelligence Report*, no. 119, Fall 2005, 1.

4 These responses are all taken from the comments section of the *AR* website, all posted in 2005: Arthur Pendleton, posted 7 September; Robert Kelly, posted 6 September; Glenn, posted 8 September; AngloSaxon1965, posted 5 September; Bethany, posted 6 September; Tawny, posted 29 September; Robert Binion, posted 6 September; OZBoy, posted 6 September; and JR, posted 5 September. Taylor's article provoked 151 pages of comments before postings were closed in March 2006.

Whites; African Americans' greater propensity to commit crimes, especially violent crimes; the threat black Americans pose to white Americans and to the very future of the United States; and, no less importantly, the mendacity of mainstream media sources when it comes to the reporting of racial issues. And it did so in the context of a major news story of national and international significance, one that was very difficult to ignore.

Katrina's 'lessons'

In the respectable, journalistic-cum-academic style preferred by *American Renaissance*, Taylor set out to elucidate the 'lessons' to be learned from the disaster. Hurricane Katrina, he said, had demonstrated that the world's 'sole remaining superpower can be reduced to squalor and chaos nearly as gruesome as anything found in the Third World'. But the 'most serious damage', he contended, was 'done not by nature but by man'.[5] The focus of Taylor's analysis, though, was not on any inadequacy in the local, state and federal response to the disaster, not on what Katrina might have to say about the social and economic realities of life in America's inner cities, and not indeed on what it revealed, if anything, about the US government's underlying racism.[6] What Taylor wanted to focus on was what he called the 'barbaric behavior of the people of New Orleans'.[7]

More specifically, of course, it was the 'barbaric behavior' of the black residents of New Orleans that Taylor was interested in discussing. As a result, most of the article was taken up with accounts of black looting and violence—including rape and murder—the shooting of rescue workers, attacks on ambulances and the ransacking of hospitals. Particular attention was paid to the horrific conditions that existed inside the Superdome and the Convention Center, which had become rescue centres of last resort for those approximately 50,000 people who had been unable to get out of the city before the hurricane hit, and which resembled, Taylor said, with the racist connotations fully intended, a 'jungle'. Instead of being safe havens,

---

5 Taylor, 'Africa in our midst', 1.
6 The charge of racism was most famously expressed by the rapper Kanye West during a concert to raise money for the hurricane's victims when he declared that the federal response to Katrina demonstrated that 'George Bush doesn't care about black people!'; see Lisa de Moraes, 'Kanye West's torrent of criticism, live on NBC', *Washington Post*, 3 September 2005. For an account of the more widely expressed criticisms of the various authorities' handling of the Katrina disaster and its lessons for the nation, see Douglas Brinkley, *The Great Deluge: Hurricane Katrina, New Orleans, and the Mississippi Gulf Coast* (New York: HarperCollins 2006). Brinkley was particularly critical of Ray Nagin, the mayor of New Orleans. An unflattering account of the Bush administration's role in the disaster can also be found in Frank Rich, *The Greatest Story Ever Sold: The Decline and Fall of Truth from 9/11 to Katrina* (New York: Penguin Press 2006), 197–205.
7 Taylor, 'Africa in our midst', 1.

both sites, he contended, had became places of degeneracy where young black men 'robbed and raped with impunity', and emblematically stranded groups of white British and Australian tourists, who huddled together to protect themselves before being ushered to safety 'past seething crowds of blacks' by sympathetic National Guardsmen. Although Taylor acknowledged that, of the 'blacks who stayed [in New Orleans], probably only a minority committed crimes', they were 'enough to turn the city into a hell hole'.[8] And it was this that offered the real 'lesson' of the whole tragedy:

> Our rulers and media executives will try to turn the story of Hurricane Katrina into yet another morality tale of downtrodden blacks and heartless whites, but pandering of this kind fools fewer and fewer people. Many whites will realize—some for the first time—that we have Africa in our midst, that utterly alien Africa of road-side corpses, cruelty, and anarchy that they thought could never wash up on our shores.
>
> To be sure, the story of Hurricane Katrina does have a moral for anyone not deliberately blind. The races are different. Blacks and whites are different. When blacks are left entirely to their own devices, Western Civilization—any kind of civilization—disappears. And in a crisis, civilization disappears over-night.[9]

That the 'races are different', and that Blacks—and Hispanics—are predisposed to be more violent and commit more crimes than Whites, had been a staple of Taylor's discourse for the previous fifteen years. In issue after issue of *American Renaissance*, in interviews and media appearances, and in publications like *The Color of Crime* and *Paved with Good Intentions*, the same argument was made, with endless statistics, charts, tables and graphs deployed to confirm its purported basis in fact.[10]

8 Ibid., 4.
9 Ibid., 7–8. According to Taylor, the situation would have been markedly different had '50,000 whites' been similarly stranded: 'They [Whites] would have established rules, organized supplies, cared for the sick and dying. They would have organized games for children. The papers would be full of stories of selflessness and community spirit.' For an interesting discussion of how people respond to disaster situations, see Rebecca Solnit, 'The uses of disaster: notes on bad weather and good government', *Harper's*, vol. 311, no. 1865, October 2005, 31–7.
10 New Century Foundation, *The Color of Crime: Race, Crime and Justice in America*, 2nd edn (Oakton, VA: New Century Foundation 2005); Jared Taylor, *Paved with Good Intentions: The Failure of Race Relations in Contemporary America* (New York: Carroll & Graf 1992). For a discussion and critique of these arguments, see the Southern Poverty Law Center, 'Coloring crime', *Intelligence Report*, no. 99, Summer 2000, 37–9; Carol Swain, *The New White Nationalism in America: Its Challenge to Integration* (Cambridge and New York: Cambridge University Press 2002), 113–16; and George Michael, *Confronting Right-wing Extremism and Terrorism in the USA* (New York and London: Routledge 2003), 55–8.

What was different about the Hurricane Katrina situation in the eyes of Taylor and his sympathizers was only the sheer scale of the disaster, and the national and international media attention it received. Indeed, it was precisely because of this media attention that it was hoped (as the response by 'JR' cited above indicates) that Katrina would provide the long-wished-for 'wake-up call' that would alert the silent, uncomprehending majority of somnolent white Americans to what was 'really' going on around them. This, after all, was why *AR* had been founded: to put an end to what the inaugural issue of the journal had described as the 'dispossession' of white America's European cultural heritage by African Americans, Hispanics and other immigrant groups.[11] Taylor, it must be said, was under no illusion that this was an easy task, but he was nonetheless certain that it would eventually take place. As he reflected on the occasion of *AR*'s twelfth anniversary:

> we do not pretend that AR has had any but the slightest role in changing the way Americans think. It is the constant racial double standards, the destruction of neighborhoods, the demonizing of whites, and the alien and unpleasant behavior of the newcomers that are waking up more and more people. The truth can be denied for only so long. Whites can run away only so many times. Eyes are constantly being opened.[12]

For Taylor, when it came to the raising of white racial consciousness, actions and events would always speak louder than words—whether proximate local events like Blacks moving into white neighbourhoods or increasing immigration, or more distant national and international events such as particularly newsworthy crimes involving African Americans or 'racially relevant' civil unrest in cities as far apart as Paris, France and Sydney, Australia.[13] Indeed, in the view of *AR*, the bigger the 'event' the better. The greater the disaster, the more publicity would be generated, and the more eyes would be 'opened' as a result. Crises of the kind Katrina was taken to represent were exactly what the organization had been predicting from its inception. The very first article in the very first issue of *American Renaissance*, for example, was called 'Who Speaks For Us?', and it contained the following warning:

11 [Jared Taylor?], 'Who speaks for us?', *American Renaissance*, vol. 1, no. 1, November 1990, 1.
12 Jared Taylor, 'Twelve years of American Renaissance: an editor's reflections', *American Renaissance*, vol. 13, no. 11, November 2002, 4.
13 For example, the story of the so-called 'Wichita Massacre'—in which two African American brothers, Reginald and Jonathan Carr, killed five and left two others injured in a 'week long crime spree'—was followed closely by *American Renaissance* from 2000 until the brothers' convictions in 2002, as were the 'immigration riots' in Paris and Sydney in 2005, which are discussed more fully below.

> If we continue to permit the erosion of the essential conditions of nationhood, and indeed, of any healthy sense of neighborhood or community, the frictions that torment us today will be as nothing compared to the chaos that will come. The squalor of Detroit, the violence of Washington (DC), and the savagery of New York City must not mark the way to the future.[14]

Post-Katrina New Orleans, a major 'black city' with a prominent black mayor, Ray Nagin, and predominantly black government and police force, seemed to offer a particularly resonant example of the squalor, violence and savagery *AR* had been warning about.[15] Indeed, for all *AR*'s protestations about being a reasonable, intellectually inclined magazine, with 'malice towards none' and 'no wish to trample the rights of others',[16] Taylor seemed to take a special delight in the city's chaos and misery, an implicit recognition on his part perhaps that only complete societal breakdown—the 'disappearance of civilization'—would ever provide *American Renaissance* with the opportunity to realize its goals. For all its 'reasoned' articles, 'evidence' and statistics, 'starting over' on the ashes of a ruined society offered the best way to achieve its aims: a belief, ironically, that would ultimately make *AR* little different from the more explicitly apocalyptically minded 'racial warriors' of White Aryan Resistance or the William Pierce-inspired 'lone wolves'.[17]

Heroic dissent?

While Taylor may provide a realistic assessment of the 'slight' impact *AR* has had in 'improving' white Americans' self-conception—a point his

14 [Taylor?], 'Who speaks for us?', 2.
15 African Americans constituted 67 per cent of the population of New Orleans in 2005. See Brinkley, *The Great Deluge*, 33. An important subtheme of Taylor's article concerned the failings of the New Orleans Police Department during the disaster: the desertions, suicides and general inability to protect and aid citizens in peril. This was important to Taylor because it allowed him to address another recurring *AR* issue: the failings of affirmative action programmes in the United States. New Orleans, Taylor noted, had 'spent decades making the police force as black as possible' ('Africa in our midst', 3). The article following 'Africa in our midst' also addressed the issue of policing in New Orleans; see 'Voodoo, violence, and victimology: New Orleans was ailing long before Katrina', *American Renaissance*, vol. 16, no. 10, October 2005, 8–9. On the complicated issues surrounding the policing of the city both before and after Hurricane Katrina, see Dan Baum, 'Deluged: when Katrina hit, where were the police?', *New Yorker*, 9 January 2006, 50–63, and Brinkley, *The Great Deluge*, esp. 49–50, 201–3, 509–13.
16 [Taylor?], 'Who speaks for us?', 2.
17 A similar point was made by Mark Potok in his editorial 'The blame game'. For an interesting take on the wider appeal of apocalyptic thinking within the extreme right, see Roger Griffin, 'Shattering crystals: the role of "dream time" in extreme right-wing political violence', *Terrorism and Political Violence*, vol. 15, no. 1, Spring 2003, 57–95.

colleague and fellow *AR* founder Samuel Francis was also forced to admit when reviewing the first twelve years of the journal[18]—this has not prevented *AR*'s writers from constantly congratulating themselves for their willingness to speak out against what they regard as America's misguided racial orthodoxy. On the contrary, breaking the silence surrounding the underlying 'racial realities' of the United States is key to what *American Renaissance* sees as its task. 'The racial ideas that circulate in this country are unnatural and destructive', Taylor has written, 'but they are in the ascendancy, and only the most remarkable people can single-handedly face down the zeitgeist'.[19] Indeed, this sense of being heroic dissenters within the mainstream culture—a few 'most remarkable people'—is one that is especially prized, not just by *AR* but also by the wider far-right milieu. Taylor's 'Africa in Our Midst' article provides a telling example of its articulation: the answer to the question posed in *American Renaissance*'s first issue, 'Who Speaks for Us?', being, of course, no one within the political or cultural mainstream.

Like so many other far rightists, Taylor and his colleagues are convinced they have access to The Truth. (The masthead of every issue of *American Renaissance* announces this, with its quotation from Thomas Jefferson: 'There is not a truth existing which I fear or would wish unknown to the whole world.') Hence the importance attached to the neutral, fact-based tone of *AR*'s reportage, complete, in the specific case of its coverage of Katrina, with photographs and verifiable quotations from eye-witnesses and participants in the disaster, including Louisiana State Police Chief Henry Whitehorn, Lieutenant General Steven Blum of the National Guard, and the then head of the Federal Emergency Management Agency, Michael Brown. As noted earlier, for Taylor and the readers of *American Renaissance*, it was the overwhelming nature of the 'evidence' of New Orleans—its apparently undeniable factuality—that gave it such 'eye-opening' potential. All the more galling then that the central allegations made by Taylor to support his assessment of African Americans as innately barbaric inferiors—the attacks on rescuers, the hijacked ambulances, the shots fired at helicopters, the looted hospitals—turned out to be false.

As Taylor admitted in a 'Postscript on Katrina', initially posted on the *American Renaissance* website and later published as 'Katrina and the US Media' in the December 2005 issue: 'It now appears that some of the reports of mayhem in the Convention Center and at the Superdome were

18 Francis noted that 'the racial consciousness' of Whites in the United States had 'not grown appreciably' between 1990 and 2002, while the 'political and cultural threats to them and their nation and civilization are as powerful today as they were twelve years ago'; Samuel Francis, 'Twelve years after: AR's contributions to our movement', *American Renaissance*, vol. 13, no. 12, December 2002, 1.

19 Taylor, 'Twelve years of American Renaissance', 4.

exaggerated.' Yet, in an amazing display of inverted logic, it didn't really matter that the evidence Taylor had relied on to make his case didn't exist. On the contrary, what 'is more important' than whether the rapes, shootings and hospital attacks had actually occurred was the fact that 'virtually everyone—even reporters from the most liberal papers—passed on gruesome accounts as entirely plausible'. These reporters would not have done so had Katrina hit somewhere like New Hampshire or Iowa, Taylor contended; they only reported these events in New Orleans 'because everyone knew the Superdome and the Convention Center were filled with blacks'. Which is to say that, as Taylor saw it, 'by accepting reports about blacks they would have rejected about whites', the mainstream media were actually subconsciously agreeing with his own assessment about the racial inferiority of African Americans and their propensity to commit crimes and acts of violence, thus making 'a mockery of the official view that race does not matter, and that all groups are equal'. And hence the 'lessons to be learned from Katrina' remained unchanged.[20]

Taylor could have ignored these later reports of course, and simply let 'Africa in Our Midst' stand as *American Renaissance*'s account of the disaster. That he didn't, that he felt the need to correct the mistakes in his original article, is in keeping with his sense of himself as an embattled truth-dealing intellectual, as well as with the journalistic-academic tone the journal tries so hard to maintain. Yet the convolutions involved in maintaining the original 'lessons' of the article speak, in the end, not to intellectual integrity but to intellectual dishonesty, to *AR*'s desire for its own brand of the truth to prevail over the facts of the situation. Indeed, having issued his partial correction in the December issue of *American Renaissance*, Taylor couldn't quite let the matter go. Three months later the journal returned again to Katrina, this time publishing a 'first-hand account from someone who saw it all' in the form of diary entries by James Hendrickson, a thirty-five-year-old cook who claimed to have spent five days inside the Superdome. With its detailed descriptions of drunken looting, violence, murder and frenzied 'black folks', the publication of Hendrickson's diary seemed intended only to confirm the accuracy of Taylor's original 'Africa in our Midst' article.[21]

20 Jared Taylor, 'Katrina and the US media', *American Renaissance*, vol. 16, no. 12, December 2005, 7–8. The only media commentator that Taylor could find who agreed with his assessment of Katrina was Leighton Levy, a black journalist, who wrote a piece called 'The dark side of black people' for the *Jamaica Star*; Leighton Levy, 'The dark side of black people', *Jamaica Star Online*, 2 September 2005, www.jamaica-star.com/thestar/20050902/cleisure/cleisure1.html (viewed 12 July 2008). Levy's article can also be found on David Duke's website at www.davidduke.com/?p = 383 (viewed 12 July 2008).

21 James Hendrickson, 'Katrina diary: a first-hand account from someone who saw it all', *American Renaissance*, vol. 17, no. 3, March 2006, 1–7.

Hurricane Katrina, David Duke and EURO

David Duke, that other prominent purveyor of 'respectable' white power politics, also paid close attention to the Katrina disaster and what he thought it had to say about race relations in the United States. Indeed, given his family home in New Orleans and his infamous membership of the Louisiana legislature, he had a very personal interest in doing so.[22] Duke's analysis of the Katrina situation, while ostensibly in the same 'intellectual' vein as *AR*'s—and despite claims that he is 'always careful not to overstate things'—was much more hyperbolic than Taylor's, a point clearly reflected in the titles of some of the articles that appeared on Duke's websites in the aftermath of the tragedy: 'White Genocide in New Orleans', 'Now Its [*sic*] Rape', 'Did New Orleans Blacks Resort to Cannibalism?' and 'Welcome—To the America of the Future!'[23] However, if the tone was different, the underlying message was the same, and the arguments and evidence deployed in these articles closely mirrored *AR*'s. (It is interesting to note, then, that, although it failed to generate the same amount of attention as 'Africa in our Midst', Duke's first substantive discussion of the Katrina disaster, 'White Genocide in New Orleans', which described how the city had 'turned into Somalia' after the hurricane struck, actually appeared the day before Taylor's.[24]) Operating in full heroic dissent mode, Duke also saw

22 Having won his seat in the Louisiana state legislature in 1989, Duke went on (between 1990 and 1998) to make unsuccessful bids for the US Senate, House of Representatives, the Louisiana governorship and even the presidency. His failure to win the presidency seems to have left him with some delusions of grandeur, as his website contains a State of the Union address he 'would have made to Congress as the President', as well as an account of what he would 'say to the nation' on the occasion of his inauguration. See 'David Duke's State of the Union address', 23 October 2004, and 'My first day in the White House', 21 January 2005, www.davidduke.com/general/david-dukes-state-of-the-union-address_5.html and www.davidduke.com/general/david-duke-live-on-internet-radio-today_213.html, respectively (viewed 12 July 2008).

23 David Duke, 'White genocide in New Orleans: mass racial attacks against Whites in New Orleans', 4 September 2005, www.davidduke.com/general/the-crisis-worsens_379.html; David Duke, 'Now its [*sic*] rape!', 1 September 2005, www.davidduke.com/general/now-its-rape-right-in-the-superdome-housing-the-refugees_378.html; Jeff Davis, 'Did New Orleans Blacks resort to cannibalism?', 5 September 2005, www.whitecivilrights.com/did-new-orleans-blacks-resort-to-cannibalism_150.html; 'Welcome—To the America of the future', 7 September 2005, www.davidduke.com/general/welcome-to-the-america-of-the-future_392 (all viewed 12 July 2008).

24 Duke, 'White genocide'. Duke's very first posting on Katrina appeared the week before. It described a recent 'attempted bombing' against him, as well as his concerns about the threat the approaching storm posed to his home and office in New Orleans; David Duke, 'Bombs and hurricanes: our struggle', 29 August 2005, www.davidduke.com/general/bombs-and-hurricanes-our-struggle_371.html (viewed 12 July 2008). Two days later he posted another article describing the 'arduous task' he faced after the hurricane had struck; David Duke, 'My home and

himself offering painful truths and 'I-told-you-sos' against the weight of misinformation handed down by the nation's political and cultural elites:

> And the media is [*sic*] silent. And the political leaders are silent. I and the other belittled leaders of our people are almost the only honest voices on this crisis.
>
> If our words would have been heeded, this incomparable human suffering would not be happening ... Hurricane Katrina has blown away with her fierce winds and raging floods the lies of multiculturalism, the lies of egalitarianism. She has exposed the underlying danger to our people that is growing like a slow moving Tsunami across the European-American world.
>
> My God, may our people understand the warnings we have been given. May we awaken in time![25]

In another article on Katrina of 12 September 2005, Duke argued that what had happened in New Orleans was exactly what he had been 'writing and speaking and warning about' since he was a teenager in the 1960s, when 'America was still a 90 percent White nation'. 'I find no joy, no pleasure in saying that I was right, that my predictions are coming true for New Orleans and America', Duke unconvincingly protested. 'My heart breaks to see what is happening to our people, our once great city, and our fast-fading nation.'[26] But, if he shared Taylor's sublimated delight in the destruction Katrina had wrought on New Orleans, Duke did not share his colleague's willingness to revise—however convolutedly—his analysis in the face of the evidence that contradicted the rape and murder stories he had been so gleefully repeating. Indeed, in a report on the rebuilding of New Orleans of 1 January 2006, long after Taylor had issued his 'retraction' about the reliability of the evidence on which he had based his original Katrina article, Duke was still recounting how 'gangs of Blacks' had ravaged old-age care centres and children's hospitals, and shot at rescue workers.[27] In fact, the only concession by Duke's

---

EURO office damaged severely: we face an incredible challenge', 31 August 2005, www.davidduke.com/general/my-home-and-euro-office-damaged-severely_372. html (viewed 12 July 2008).

25 Duke, 'White genocide'.

26 David Duke, 'Racial realities exposed in New Orleans', 12 September 2005, www.whitecivilrights.com/racial-realities-exposed-in-new-orleans_166.html (viewed 12 July 2008). Like Jared Taylor, Duke also thought things would have been different had Katrina struck a 'white city'. He unfavourably contrasted Katrina's impact on New Orleans with that of Hurricane Betsy in 1965. Back then, he recalled, 'when we had a White mayor and almost entirely White police force and a safe and excellent school system, there was no mass rape, murder and mayhem against the White people.'

27 David Duke, 'African-American Mayor of New Orleans says New Orleans must be chocolate again', 1 January 2006, www.davidduke.com/general/african-american-mayor-of-new-orleans-says-new-orleans-must-be-chocolate-again_492.html (viewed 12 July 2008). It was all like those 'seemingly far-fetched scenes in Johnny Weissmuller

organization, the European-American Unity and Rights Organization (EURO),[28] to the erroneous nature of many of these reports was an article by James Buchanan of 29 September 2005 that alleged that neo-conservatives within the Bush administration were engaged in a 'snow job' to downplay the extent of the mayhem unleashed in New Orleans because of their 'HUGE failures' in handling the crisis. 'Bush needs to minimize all the bad news, including stories about little White girls getting gang raped and murdered by Blacks', Buchanan argued, while the mainstream media had its own 'liberal motivation to censor stories about Black murderers and rapists running loose during a disaster'. The 'truth', however, was still out there, and Buchanan urged his readers to 'search the Internet and use their common sense' to find it.[29]

Riots, immigrants and 'the future of the white race'

As befits the global aspirations of EURO, Duke's New Year's Day article in 2006 sought to draw out the connections between the Katrina disaster and the fate of Whites elsewhere in the world. 'It is not just Whites in America that are under siege', he contended, 'it is true in Canada, throughout Europe, in Australia, New Zealand, wherever our people dwell upon the Earth'. To support the argument—a longstanding one that in many respects provides EURO with its *raison d'être*—Duke urged his readers to consider the 'widespread riots' that had rocked France in October 2005.[30] The riots began on 27 October after the death of two teenagers of African descent, Zyed Benna and Bouna Traore, who were electrocuted in an electrical substation in Clichy-sous-Bois, northeast of Paris, where they were allegedly hiding from the police. The resulting nationwide civil unrest lasted for twenty-one nights, during which time pitched battles were fought between rioters and police, 9,193 cars were

---

Tarzan movies depicting White folks pursued by bloodthirsty African natives', Duke noted.

28 Founded in January 2000, the organization was originally called the National Organization for European-American Rights, or NOFEAR, but was renamed EURO shortly thereafter. Its aim, according to Duke, is to protect 'the rights and heritage of people of European descent in America and around the world'; 'David Duke biography', www.duke.org/biography.html (viewed 12 July 2008).

29 James Buchanan, 'Neocons claim: New Orleans looting and rapes exaggerated', 29 September 2005, www.whitecivilrights.com/neocons-claim-new-orleans-looting-and-rapes-exaggerated_194.html#%20more-194 (viewed 12 July 2008). Duke and the other EURO writers routinely criticize the Bush administration and the neo-conservatives presumed to control it, both for their handling of the Iraq war and their unstinting support for Israel.

30 Duke, 'African-American Mayor of New Orleans says New Orleans must be chocolate again'.

burned, 2,921 arrests were made, and curfews and bans on public meetings were imposed before order was restored.[31]

Duke first addressed the riots in a typically understated article entitled 'Europe Faces Apocalypse' of 7 November 2005. Commentating on an Associated Press (AP) report that had appeared on the Fox News website three days earlier about a fifty-year-old woman on crutches who had been set alight by African immigrants as she tried to get off a bus in the Parisian suburb of Sevran, Duke argued that the rioters were 'driven by racial hatred for all things European'. The AP article amply demonstrated this, said Duke: 'it shows the brutality of the savages who are turning centers of European refinement, culture and civilization into examples of the darkest horrors of Africa.'[32]

That Duke was relying on mainstream media sources to make this point might seem a little odd given his hostility to the 'controlled media', but it is a strategy he and his colleagues regularly employ. This is understandable since it allows EURO's writers to appear both up-to-date and well informed about current events while relieving the organization of the need to send their own reporters to cover them. Significantly, though, the articles also implicitly rely on their readers having confidence in the accuracy of the mainstream newspaper report being referred to. Duke tried to address the seeming contradiction by arguing: 'Once in a while a little truth ekes out in the controlled media.' Nonetheless, the frequency with which the mainstream media are employed on both his and the EURO website suggests that they are actually a very reliable source of news. Yet, for Duke, that there had been no widespread reporting of the burning of the fifty-year-old woman smacked of the racial hypocrisies and double standards that he and his followers had long denounced.[33] 'Now you tell me how the mainstream press would treat this if White attackers doused a crippled, middle-aged Black woman with gasoline and set her on fire', he asked. 'Tell me please would not every newspaper from Paris to New York to Sydney be screaming about this horrible racist crime?' It was Katrina all over again, Duke argued, and what he said it revealed was that 'New Orleans and Paris and London

31 Statistics from the French police, cited in Harry Astier, 'Suburban gangs defy French police', *BBC News*, 31 October 2006, http://news.bbc.co.uk/1/hi/world/europe/6096706.stm (viewed 12 July 2008). For discussions of the origins and significance of the riots, see James Graff, 'Why Paris is burning', *Time*, 14 November 2005, 36–9; Christopher Dickey, 'Europe's time bomb', *Newsweek*, 21 November 2005, 42–3; and Oliver Guitta, 'Paris when it sizzles: the intifada comes to France', *Weekly Standard*, 14 November 2005.

32 David Duke, 'Europe faces apocalypse', 7 November 2005, www.davidduke.com/general/europe-faces-apocalypse_449.html. The original article, 'Paris rioters set woman afire as violence spreads', *Associated Press*, 4 November 2005, is available on the Fox News website at www.foxnews.com/story/0,2933,174533,00.html (both viewed 12 July 2008).

33 See Swain, *The New White Nationalism in America*, 318–19.

and a host of other European cities' were 'rushing headlong toward becoming Mogadishu'.[34]

The central problem, of course, was immigration, exactly as Duke had been suggesting for the previous thirty years. 'Only the brain dead in Europe and America cannot help but realize that opening our borders to millions of non-Europeans is the most insane, traitorous action in perhaps all of European history', Duke stated. The very existence of the white race was at stake, it seemed. Employing one of his favourite metaphors, Duke argued that, unless the 'dark tsunami' of non-European immigration was brought to a halt, Whites would be 'driven to extinction under the attack' of the 'ruthless hatred' felt towards them, a hatred epitomized in Duke's eyes by 'setting a poor handicapped woman on fire!'. Although the 'media tells us that multiracialism only blesses us', the 'real blessings' of immigration were actually 'rising crime, gang rape, teeming ghettos of hatred and these barbaric riots'.[35] It was a lesson seemingly confirmed when riots broke out in Sydney in December 2005 following the alleged assault of two Cronulla beach lifeguards by a gang of youths of Middle Eastern descent. According to EURO's Charles Coughlin, the riots were a 'fantastic development'. Australia, he contended, 'has been a model of peace and prosperity in the south Pacific thanks to its White population'. And it was a 'crime against humanity for Australian politicians to allow in swarms of Asians, Indians and Lebanese' because a 'once beautiful paradise' was being 'rapidly turned into a sickening, over-crowded, crime-plagued Babylon'.[36]

Closer to home, the issue of Mexican immigration in the United States has also provided EURO writers with the opportunity to re-emphasize their longstanding warnings about the threat posed by immigrants to the heritage, values and traditions of 'European-Americans'.[37] Indeed, President Bush's

---

34 Duke, 'Europe faces apocalypse'.

35 Ibid. Other articles by EURO writers on the riots included Jeff Davis, 'Gibbering neocon lets agenda out of bag', 23 November 2005, www.whitecivilrights.com/gibbering-neocon-lets-agenda-out-of-bag_277.html#more-277; and James Buchanan, 'Muslim riots in Paris: time to decide who can be French', 4 November 2005, www.whitecivilrights.com/muslim-riots-in-paris-time-to-decide-who-can-be-french_256.html#more-256 (both viewed 12 July 2008). According to Buchanan: 'The evidence of the failure of [America and Europe's] multi-racial experiment can be seen in the clouds of smoke rising from the Paris riot.' Duke repeated his analysis of both the Katrina situation and the Paris riots in a speech he gave at a conference on 'The white world's future' in Moscow in June 2006; see David Duke, 'The future of the white race', 17 June 2006, www.davidduke.com/general/international-conference-in-moscow-on-the-future-of-european-mankind_554.html (viewed 12 July 2008).

36 Charles Coughlin, 'Massive race riot in Australia', 14 December 2005, www.whitecivilrights.com/massive-race-riot-in-australia_298.html (viewed 12 July 2008).

37 Preserving this heritage from the 'threat' posed by the supposed massive increase in non-European immigrants was one of the principal reasons for the formation of

recent proposals on immigration reform, including expanding the Border Patrol, deploying the National Guard and building 700 miles of new fencing along the Mexican border, together with the privatized activities of so-called Minutemen vigilantes and more generalized concerns about border security in the wake of 9/11, have combined to create an environment that Duke and his colleagues have worked very hard to exploit.[38] Numerous articles and 'commentaries' with titles such as 'Waiting for the Floodgates to Open', 'Immigration Reform: Bush's Latest Load of Fertilizer', 'Will Amnesty Lead to Rebellion', 'Nat. Guard on the Border: Another Bush Deception' and 'Do We Want Latinos to Get Citizenship?' have appeared online over the past eighteen months.[39] The arguments of these articles have been both consistent and familiar: continuing Mexican immigration threatens to 'destroy the

---

EURO. As Duke said in an interview in February 2000: 'The reality is that unless the immigration policies in this country change and unless the government ceases to pursue policies which will make the minority elements of our society dramatically grow in number from higher birthrates and immigration rates, and unless our government begins enforcing our border laws, whites will become a minority in America'; quoted in Carol M. Swain and Russ Nieli (eds), *Contemporary Voices of White Nationalism in America* (Cambridge and New York: Cambridge University Press 2003), 170. See also the 'No More Immigration' section of EURO's 'Statement of Principles', 29 August 2005, www.whitecivilrights.com/?p = 63 (viewed 12 July 2008). As Roger Daniels has pointed out, however, the 'commonly held perception that America is receiving an unprecedented proportion of immigrants [since the 1970s] is false'. He contends that what has changed in recent years has been 'American attitudes toward immigration and immigrants', with many 'reveling in the nation's immigrant past' on the one hand, while 'rejecting much of its immigrant present' on the other; Roger Daniels, *Guarding the Golden Door: American Immigration Policy and Immigrants since 1882* (New York: Hill and Wang 2004), 4–5.

38 On Bush's proposals for immigration reform, see 'Bush's speech on immigration', *New York Times*, 15 May 2006; and David Stout, 'Bush, signing bill for border fence, urges wider overhaul', 27 October 2006. For a discussion of the activities of the Minutemen and other 'private' border patrol organizations, see the Anti-Defamation League, *Border Disputes: Armed Vigilantes in Arizona* (New York: ADL 2003); and the Winter 2005 issue (no. 120) of the Southern Poverty Law Center's *Intelligence Report*, especially Susy Buchanan and David Holthouse, 'Minuteman leader has troubled past', 21–4; and Susy Buchanan and Tom Kim, 'The nativists', 26–42. For an overview of some of the problems in policing the US–Mexican border, see Peter Andreas, *Border Games: Policing the US-Mexico Divide* (Ithaca, NY: Cornell University Press 2000). On arguments about the economic costs and benefits of immigration, see Tamar Jacoby, 'Immigration nation', *Foreign Affairs*, vol. 85, no. 6, November/December 2006, 50–65. For an evocative account of the experience of both illegal immigrants trying to cross the border and the Border Patrol officers charged with stopping them, see Cecilia Ballí, 'The border is wide: guarding the southern flank of the American dream', *Harper's*, vol. 313, no. 1877, October 2006, 63–70. This issue is also interestingly addressed in Tommy Lee Jones's recent film *The Three Burials of Melquiades Estrada* (2005).

39 Jeff Davis, 'Waiting for the floodgates to open', 18 August 2005, www. whitecivilrights.com/waiting-for-the-floogates-to-open_114.html; Charles Coughlin, 'Immigration reform: Bush's latest load of fertilizer', 29 November 2005, www.

social fabric of Western civilization' and turn the United States into 'a Third World Nation'; mainstream politicians are 'stabbing' the people 'in the back' by failing to deal effectively with the problem; the floodgates have to be closed and 'the border sealed'; and the time has come for 'patriotic Americans' to stand up and put the whole calamitous situation to rights.[40]

Indeed, just as *American Renaissance* believed that Hurricane Katrina was going to be the much-vaunted 'wake-up call' that would finally rouse Americans from their racial unconsciousness, so EURO's writers argued that the 'Mexican illegal alien problem ... is the five alarm fire that is waking up America'.[41] For the American far right, it seems, such an epoch-making event is always tantalizingly around the next corner, just one more crisis—the right crisis—away, a time when all their predictions of societal apocalypse will finally, they hope, come true.

The view from the National Alliance and National Vanguard

Arguably the leading neo-Nazi style organization on the American extreme right, the National Alliance was founded in 1974 by the late William L. Pierce, best known for his authorship of *The Turner Diaries*, a fictional story described by the FBI as the 'bible' of the racialist right and a 'blueprint for revolution'.[42] Written as the futuristic narrative of a revolutionary

whitecivilrights.com/immigration-reform-bush%e2%80%99s-latest-load-of-fertilizer_283.html#more-283; James Buchanan, 'Will amnesty lead to rebellion', 31 March 2006, www.whitecivilrights.com/will-amnesty-lead-to-rebellion_404.html#more-404; James Buchanan, 'Nat. Guard on the border: another Bush deception', 16 May 2005, www.whitecivilrights.com/nat-guard-on-the-border-another-bush-deception_451.html#more-451; Jeff Davis, 'Do we want Latinos to get citizenship?', 31 May 2005, www.whitecivilrights.com/do-we-want-latinos-to-get-citizenship_466.html#more-466. Duke's own views on the issue are best captured in his radio address, 'The disaster of illegal immigration', 7 June 2006, available at www.davidduke.com/mp3/dukeradio060607.mp3 (all viewed 12 July 2008).

40 Jeff Davis, 'Can we talk about immigration now?', 8 January 2006, www.whitecivilrights.com/can-we-talk-about-immigration-now_320.html#more-320; Jeff Davis, 'Will Congress get tough on illegals', 30 March 2006, www.whitecivilrights.com/will-congress-get-tough-on-illegals_403.html#more-403; Buchanan, 'Will amnesty lead to rebellion?'; Davis, 'Waiting for the floodgates'; James Buchanan, 'Will 6,000 troops ever be sent to the border', 2 June 2006, www.whitecivilrights.com/will-6000-guard-troops-ever-be-sent-to-the-border_468.html#more-468 (all viewed 12 July 2008).

41 James Buchanan, 'Illegal alien rallies will backfire', 1 May 2006, www.whitecivilrights.com/illegal-alien-rallies-will-backfire_436.html. See also Jeff Davis, 'May 1, 2006—The Aztlan revolution begins', 2 May 2006, www.whitecivilrights.com/may-1-2006-the-aztlan-revolution-begins_437.html (both viewed 12 July 2008).

42 See FBI Internal Memorandum, File Number 100-487473-50, 23 January 1987 and FBI Internal Memorandum, File Number 100-487473-67, 10 September 1987: Federal

fighter—Earl Turner—the book depicts a sombre future in which American society implodes under the weight of racial strife. The novel gained Pierce considerable notoriety and was even thought to have inspired several episodes of right-wing violence, including the campaigns of The Order and the Aryan Republican Army, the Oklahoma City bombing and the London bombing spree of David Copeland.[43] Since Pierce's death in July 2002, the National Alliance has survived despite leadership struggles and disaffection among some members. Currently, the organization is led by Eric Gliebe. The National Alliance website carries a weekly Internet radio programme —*American Dissident Voices*—which attracts, by far-right standards, a large number of listeners.[44] A typical broadcast begins with some current event as a launching point and then gets 'behind the scenes' of the news to uncover alleged machinations of Jewish power. Racial themes figure prominently in broadcasts as well. Unsurprisingly, several programmes were devoted to Katrina, and the riots in France and Australia.

As host of *American Dissident Voices* at the time of the disaster, Shaun Walker saw Hurricane Katrina and its aftermath as highlighting the race problem in the United States. Moreover, its effects could not be confined to New Orleans, as he predicted that the displacement of tens of thousands of African Americans from the city would engender a crime wave in those areas in which they resettled. The response by the largely black New Orleans Police Department was criticized as corrupt and incompetent, and Walker noted that roughly 200 officers quit during the chaos that ensued after the

---

Bureau of Investigation Library, FBI Academy, Quantico, VA. During an interview by David Neiwert of MSNBC, Robert Burnham, the FBI's section chief for domestic terrorism, remarked on the connection of the book to acts and potential acts of terrorism. According to him, FBI field offices had received numerous calls from local police departments reporting that they had found terrorist materials such as guns and bomb-making materials together with copies of *The Turner Diaries*; David Neiwert, 'Domestic terrorism: the FBI view', *MSNBC News*, 5 July 1999, available in the Ross Institute Internet Archives for the Study of Destructive Cults, Controversial Cults and Movements at www.rickross.com/reference/hate_groups/hategroups44.html (viewed 12 July 2008).

43 Statements by Timothy McVeigh seem to indicate that *The Turner Diaries* may have played a crucial part in his choice of target and his decision to carry out the attack; see Lou Michel and Dan Herbeck, *American Terrorist: Timothy McVeigh and the Oklahoma City Bombing* (New York: ReganBooks 2001), 304. For more on The Order, see Kevin Flynn and Gary Gerhardt, *The Silent Brotherhood: Inside America's Racist Underground* (New York: Signet 1990). For more on the Aryan Republican Army, see Mark S. Hamm, *In Bad Company: America's Terrorist Underground* (Boston: Northeastern University Press 2001). For more on David Copeland, see Graeme McLagan and Nick Lowles, *Mr Evil: The Secret Life of Pub Bomber and Killer David Copeland* (London: John Blake Publishing 2000).

44 According to a statement made by Pierce in 1999, his website received on average 8,500 hits per day; quoted in Greg Barrett, 'National Alliance grows quickly', *Detroit News*, 16 July 1999. Not long after the 9/11 attacks, Pierce claimed that downloads of *American Dissident Voices* broadcasts doubled.

hurricane. He was quick to point out the seemingly stark contrast between how locals responded to being hit by the category five hurricane in the largely white small towns of Mississippi and how those in the city of New Orleans responded. While residents in the former were commended for their altruism and civic-mindedness, residents in the latter were characterized as savages who took advantage of the chaos to embark on a campaign of rape, pillage and lawlessness:

> The Negro race does not have the temperament and compassion to rise to the occasion of the crisis and work tirelessly for days on end, for free. They don't even feel a sense of pride to maintain their homes. Instead, Negroes have the temperament to shoot at White fireman [*sic*] that try to put out fires, they have the compassion to shoot at White cops that are trying to rescue Negroes from rooftops and they have the organizational skills to allow White Red Cross workers to place them on a bus, or a plane, and ship them to another region of the country, so that Whites can solve their problems in the newly declining cities that they arrive in.[45]

Presciently, Walker predicted that some mainstream commentators would cite white racism as principally responsible for the lack of an adequate government response to the hurricane, a situation he attributed to the Jewish 'ownership' of the American media. Supposedly, Jews were in the forefront of the effort to 'misdirect' the innate sense of altruism Whites felt during a crisis:

> The liberals, the Jews, the Negroes, are working today on creating a different spin on this story. They want to generate sympathy towards these Negroes, which is another way of saying they want Whites to misdirect our White nurturing energy away from Whites. The healthy, nurturing energy that the White race possesses must remain entirely within the White race or the White race falters. During this present time of racial antagonism, the White people are more focused on helping their own kind. This leaves the Negroes out in the open, stark without their previous White providers. This only highlights the racial differences that much more.[46]

As Walker explained, it was become increasingly difficult for both the public and the government to ignore the consequences of multicultural-ism, immigration and the notion of racial equality. Recent events in

---

45 Shaun Walker, 'Katrina knocks off the blindfold', *American Dissident Voices*, broadcast 10 September 2005, transcript at www.natall.com/adv/2005/09-10-05.html (viewed 12 July 2008).

46 Shaun Walker, 'The tooth fairy and interracial harmony', *American Dissident Voices*, broadcast 17 September 2005, transcript at www.natvan.com/pub/2005/091705.txt (viewed 12 July 2008).

Europe, including the subway bombings in London and the murder of
Theo van Gogh in the Netherlands by an enraged Muslim, together with
the aftermath of Hurricane Katrina in New Orleans indicated a serious
'break in the system's levee'. A rising tide of greater awareness among
Whites was evident in the fact that the issue of immigration had finally
attained salience. As he commented, echoing the views of both *American
Renaissance* and EURO on the matter, more people were waking up 'to the
truth about race'. Still, many Whites in both the United States and Europe
remained befuddled due to the 'poison coming out of MTV and other
Jew-owned brainwashing media'.[47]

Walker, like Duke, was also quick to draw parallels between New
Orleans and the Parisian riots. As he saw it, the results were similar: the
non-white population in both areas seized the opportunity to 'loot, rob,
and rape'. Furthermore, he saw the governmental responses in both
nations as paralysed by political correctness in the sense that authorities
were supposedly reluctant to react forcefully against the non-white rioters
and looters. He took issue with mainstream interpretations that the rioters
in France had understandable grievances and that French society should be
criticized for its failure to assimilate the immigrants. According to Walker,
it was not poor living conditions and racism that contributed to the riots.
Rather, France burned because the country lacked racism. Consequently,
immigrants were merely 'exploit[ing] the stupid mistakes of White
nations'. At the 'forefront' of this 'bad policymaking', once again, was
'the powerful Jewish media'.[48] Looking for some hope in the seemingly
dismal situation, Walker predicted that the riots would enhance the
electoral fortunes of Jean-Marie Le Pen and his radical-right party, the
Front National.

If Walker was despondent over events in New Orleans and Paris, he was
jubilant over the mêlée that occurred at the Australian beach town of
Cronulla in December 2005. While the white populations of North America
and Western Europe were derided for their torpidity and timidity in the
face of racial antagonism by non-Whites, white Australians were lauded
for their near spontaneous revolt against mostly Lebanese Middle Eastern
immigrants. Before reporting on the incident, Walker first lamented the
state of white nationalist politics in the West, a condition that extended to
Australia, where the far-right One Nation Party, led by Pauline Hanson,
faced considerable opposition from the government, the media and anti-

---

47 Shaun Walker, 'Cracks in the power structure's levee', *American Dissident Voices*,
broadcast 24 September 2005, transcript at www.natvan.com/adv/2005/09-24-
05.html (viewed 12 July 2008).
48 Shaun Walker, 'France burns . . . let them eat cake', *American Dissident Voices*,
broadcast 12 November 2005, transcript at www.natvan.com/adv/2005/11-12-
05.html (viewed 27 July 2008).

racist organizations. Furthermore, that nation's White Australia Policy, which strictly limited non-white immigration, had been dismantled in 1966, just one year after the US Congress passed the 1965 Immigration Act that marked a sea change in American immigration policy. Despite being 'sold out' by their government, Walker argued that white Australians still retained a sense of racial identity and took matters into their own hands after corrupted and timid police refused to protect white Australian beachgoers. Reportedly, a string of gang rapes of white women had been perpetrated by Lebanese immigrants. After two white lifeguards were severely beaten by such a gang, a crowd of roughly 5,000 outraged Whites embarked on a spree of violence in which they drove the Lebanese immigrants off the beaches and out of the surrounding towns. In marked contrast to the situations in New Orleans and Paris, the episode in Australia was heralded as gallant display of white solidarity and spontaneous activism.[49]

The Vanguard weighs in

In April 2005 long-time National Alliance member, and Pierce's successor as host of the organization's *American Dissident Voices* radio programme, Kevin Alfred Strom was expelled for attempting to organize a coup against the leadership. Not long thereafter, Gliebe resigned as chairman and Shaun Walker assumed that position. Strom then created a new organization called National Vanguard, which he claimed was the legitimate successor to the National Alliance organization.[50] After the split, he continued to release Internet radio broadcasts under the title 'American Dissident Voices'. Commenting on Hurricane Katrina and its aftermath, Strom highlighted the stark contrast between news reports coming from New Orleans and those emanating from Mississippi and Alabama. While early accounts from the former included tales of barbarism, stories from the latter included examples of heroism and selflessness, he said. The reason for the difference, Strom maintained, was the preponderance of Blacks in New Orleans, which accounted for the 'animalistic evil' that ensued after the hurricane. And, in a familiar comparison, the city was likened to Mogadishu, the Somali capital that was ravaged by warlords in the early 1990s. The less than competent response by authorities—such as the failure to evacuate residents as hundreds of school buses remained idle—was attributed to the largely

---

49 Shaun Walker, 'Australia fights back', *American Dissident Voices*, broadcast 24 December 2005, transcript at www.natall.com/adv/2005/12-24-05.html (viewed 12 July 2008).

50 National Vanguard subsequently dissolved in March 2007.

black city administration in which corruption had become endemic. Numerous accounts of hapless Whites trapped in the Superdome told of skirmishes with black 'savages'. Strom claimed that, if so many National Guard troops and helicopters were not in Iraq, more people in New Orleans could have been rescued. By tying in the crisis in New Orleans to his critique of the Iraq war, Strom was implicating Jews in the tragedy, since, as far as he was concerned, Jewish neo-conservatives had been the principal force clamouring for US military intervention in the Middle East as a means of safeguarding the interests of Israel. Despite the damage, though, Strom found a silver lining in the events surrounding Hurricane Katrina because, like Jared Taylor and David Duke, he thought they would undermine the essential fiction of the 'equality of races' idea.[51]

The now defunct National Vanguard website featured a 'new service' that included numerous articles and postings of interest to white racialists. Several persons contributed letters and stories. In an article entitled 'Whites Will Survive', Dan Osterton contended that the civil breakdown after Katrina presaged a societal collapse of the United States that would include 'chaos, famine, diseases, and open warfare'. To prepare for this situation, Osterton exhorted Whites to organize and begin stockpiling the necessities of survival.[52] Towards that end, the National Vanguard announced that it had established a 'staging area' in Mobile, Alabama where supplies were being sent to assist white families affected by Katrina.[53]

Instructive of the cross-fertilization between the more radical and respectable segments of the far right, David Duke appeared as a guest on an interview programme hosted by Kevin Alfred Strom. Not surprisingly, Duke repeated his argument that Katrina would be a wake-up call for American Whites, bringing home to them the potential danger they faced as a decreasing segment of the population. In addition, he decried the double standard he said he faced when he was attacked as a 'racist' and 'hater' for merely pointing out that some Whites were victimized in the aftermath of

---

51 Kevin Alfred Strom, 'Katrina and the black tsunami', *American Dissident Voices* (National Vanguard), broadcast 4 September 2005. Interestingly, in a not dissimilar analysis, the British newspaper, the *Independent*, described a confidential report commissioned by the US Secretary of Defense that concluded that endemic corruption, divisions within the US military and troop shortages caused by the war in Iraq resulted in the catastrophic failure to respond adequately to Katrina and its aftermath; Kim Sengupta, 'Iraq war delayed Katrina relief effort, inquiry finds', *Independent*, 3 October 2005.

52 Dan Osterton, 'Whites will survive', June 5, 2006, now available on the Stormfront website at www.stormfront.org/forum/showthread.php?t = 300936 (viewed 14 July 2008).

53 Anti-Defamation League, 'Racists blame Jews, seek to help Whites only in hurricane's aftermath', 9 September 2005, www.adl.org/main_Extremism/Hurricane_katrina.htm (viewed 14 July 2008).

Katrina. According to the current 'racial protocol', Duke felt that he was meant to remain silent on the issue of white victimization by non-Whites.[54]

The riots in France understandably also drew much attention from National Vanguard. Frank Roman, who hosted the radio programme *Frankly Speaking* on the National Vanguard website, warned that the riots were a harbinger of a larger racial calamity that would afflict all of the nations of the West. The root cause for the strife, he claimed, was the fact that 'multiracial societies don't work'. Rueful about having been right, Roman commented that he and like-minded activists had warned Whites for decades of the impending calamity that would occur once the white nations 'opened the immigration floodgates to the Third World'.[55] Roman predicted that soon Hispanics would wreak similar havoc in the United States, egged on by powerful elements of the establishment, including the US government, the Ford Foundation, the Carnegie Corporation and the Rockefeller Foundation. He claimed that openly chauvinistic groups such as 'La Raza' (meaning 'The Race' in Spanish) drew support and succour from all these bodies.[56]

Not unlike the National Alliance, the reportage on Australia was upbeat on the National Vanguard website. Roman, for example, was exultant that white Australians had taken matters into their own hands, describing the riot as a 'spontaneous uprising' against the 'general debasement of their country ... caused by Arab immigrants ...' Indeed, like other fellow travellers on the American far right, Roman believed that the events of late 2005 vindicated the dire warnings that white racialists had been making for years.[57]

Several bloggers weighed in on the so-called 'Cronulla uprising'. 'J.J.S., Ph.D.' from Seattle decried the fact that the mainstream media, in their coverage of the riots, focused on the perfidy of white Australians, who were characterized as 'neo-Nazis', and the undeserved victimization of Lebanese immigrants. On the contrary, 'J.J.S.' lauded the Australians who 'retook' Cronulla Beach, claiming that such action was justified in retaliation for assaults and rapes carried out by armed Lebanese gangs.[58]

A National Vanguard contributor from New South Wales reported that the 'average guys' in Australia were supportive of the Whites who took action at

---

54 David Duke interviewed by Kevin Alfred Strom, 'Our heritage, our freedom, and our future, part 1', *American Dissident Voices* (National Vanguard), broadcast 5 March 2006, now available at www.amfirstbooks.com/IntroPages/ToolBarTopics/ Articles/Featured_Authors/strom,_kevin/kevin_strom_works/Kevin_Strom_2005- 2006/Kevin_A._Strom_20060305_Our_Heritage,_Our_Freedom,_and_Our_Future,_ Part_1.html (viewed 14 July 2008).

55 Frank Roman, 'We were warned', *Frankly Speaking*, broadcast 7 November 2005.

56 Frank Roman, 'It's coming to America, too', *Frankly Speaking*, broadcast 14 November 2005.

57 Frank Roman, 'The Cronulla rising', *Frankly Speaking*, broadcast 24 December 2005.

58 'J.J.S., Ph.D.', 'Australia: rape gangs and multiculturalism', posted on the (now defunct) National Vanguard website, 14 December 2005.

Cronulla, and commended them for defending their women. Australian policemen were described as steeped in political correctness and thus paralysed from effectively handling crime associated with the Lebanese immigrants. Instead, they chose to harass white Australians for petty offences, including drinking and playing music too loudly on the beach.[59] Another Australian correspondent drew comparisons between the riot at Cronulla and other episodes of violence in the West. However, he suggested that, unlike the more effete Whites elsewhere, 'Aussies ... eventually get to the point where [they] won't take any more garbage from people [they] have reached out to and let live [there]'.[60] Similarly, another Australian blogger derided the response from public officials who had characterized the riots as 'un-Australian'. After all, as the correspondent pointed out, the white population of that country was largely descended from rebellious white slaves and convicts 'that combined fierce racial nationalism with militant labor organizing, beating the ruling class into a "White Australia" policy, which kept Australia as a White continent for generations'. Consequently, the Cronulla violence was the 'inevitable outcome of a multiracial society'.[61] Still another blogger reported that the far-right Australia First Party planned on capitalizing on the riot to increase its political presence. At the riots, the Australia First Party had activists who sought to channel popular frustration with immigrant crime into more constructive political organizing.[62]

Waiting for the apocalypse

Since the early 1980s the American extreme right has evolved from a movement characterized by ultra-patriotism to one increasingly character- ized by a revolutionary outlook. This can be explained in large part by the fact that various social trends over the past several decades have signifi- cantly changed the texture of the United States. For those on the extreme right, the United States is not the same country they once knew. What's more, many in the movement consider the 'damage' too great to be repaired by conventional methods. Only radical solutions, it seems, can save the

59 'The truth about the Oz riots', posted on the (now defunct) National Vanguard website, 13 December 2005.
60 'Australia—multiculturalism, Sydney and an Aussie point of view', posted on the (now defunct) National Vanguard website, 12 December 2005, now available at www.opennntp.com/Education/australia—multiculturalism-sydney-and-an-aussie- point-of-view-62065711.html (viewed 14 July 2008).
61 'Australia: anti-Muslim violence erupts', posted on the (now defunct) National Vanguard website, 11 December 2005, now available at www.network54.com/Forum/ 398831/message/1144008502/%22%3BAustralia-+Anti-Muslim+Violence+ Erupts%22%3B (viewed 14 July 2008).
62 'Australia: nationalists to capitalize on Cronulla uprising', posted on the (now defunct) National Vanguard website, 4 January 2006.

nation and race. From their perspective, this increasingly desperate predicament demands that the old order be torn asunder and a new order be built on the ruins. Out of this destruction it is believed that the remnants of western civilization will create a new golden age characterized by creativity and racial solidarity.[63] However, in order to arrive at this much-heralded new revolutionary era, some trigger event or catalyst is necessary to usher it in, a transition that would include great tribulation and sacrifice. Although the extreme right is certain that Whites as a group are intellectually, morally, organizationally and creatively superior to other races, it is feared that, if their numbers diminish below a certain critical mass, then they will share a fate not unlike the French settlers in San Domingo in the early nineteenth century.[64]

Over the past two decades, several multinational countries including Yugoslavia, Somalia and Rwanda have imploded due to centrifugal ethnic rivalries. The American extreme right is fearful that such a fate may also befall the United States and, as this article has illustrated, the events of late 2005 only served to amplify these fears. What's more, as this article has also shown, some of the key prognosticators of the American far right are increasingly moving from a narrowly nationalist world-view to one that is more global in outlook. And as they look around this globalized world— from New Orleans to Paris to Sydney—they find a great deal to confirm their analysis of impending racial cataclysm.

63 This is consistent with Roger Griffin's notion of the palingenetic myth that permeates fascist ideology; see Roger Griffin, *The Nature of Fascism* (New York and London: Routledge 1993).

64 A popular book that has been reprinted and is still sold by far-right publishers is T. Lothrop Stoddard, *The French Revolution in San Domingo* [1914] (Torrance, CA: Noontide Press 1986). The black uprising against the French that led to the virtual extermination of the latter is invoked as a paradigm of what awaits Whites if they do not organize quickly to stem Stoddard's 'rising tide of color' in their home countries.

Assia Djebar's *qalam*: the poetics of the trace in postcolonial Algeria

BRIGITTE WELTMAN-ARON

The colonized and language

Postcolonial francophone writers unanimously agree that the imposition of the French language was not merely one example among others of colonial oppression, but its very instrument, a fundamental vector whose impact still has enduring effects. The frequency of that charge and of that critical turn in the analysis of both French colonialism and racism is evident in the writings of *Négritude* authors such as Aimé Césaire and Léopold Sédar Senghor, and in the essays of Frantz Fanon. Lately, this critique has been stated by postcolonial novelists and essayists as disparate as the Caribbean authors of *Eloge de la créolité* (*In Praise of Creoleness*) or Édouard Glissant, and the Maghrebian writers Rachid Boudjedra and Abdelkebir Khatibi, to mention only a few. All have in common the recognition that the French politics of assimilation was pre-eminently enforced through the compulsory use of the French language.

Since this shared position, however, comes from various geopolitical contexts, it gives rise to different processes of disalienation specific to the location and time of the diagnosed acculturation. Furthermore, although the emphasis on discrimination and domination through the French language recurs in postcolonial writings, individual reactions show that the evaluation of the extent and the impact of acculturation is remarkably diverse. I will first recall a few paradigmatic positions among French postcolonial theorists, ranging from the claim of an irreversible alienation to the embrace of 'the construction of hybrid identities'[1] or 'cultural *metissage*'.[2] My general purpose in this paper is to delineate the Algerian writer Assia Djebar's interrogation of the possibility of idiomaticity in a postcolonial context, specifically in Algeria. As in all former French colonies, perhaps more so than in others since Algeria was claimed 'to be France', the French colonial administration in Algeria repressed until a late date (1947) the official use of any language but French, including in school instruction.[3] Djebar, who was schooled in French Algeria, was discouraged or prevented from studying written Arabic, which in turn had an impact on the 'choice' of the language in which she could write, a condition on which she has often reflected. Fanon's discussion, which was not restricted to black Antilleans but aimed to include 'every colonized people ... face to face with the language of the civilizing nation',[4] sheds light on Djebar's predicament and, conversely, Djebar's position is indebted to Fanon's (and other thinkers') insight into the process of the racialization and biologization of difference.

In the wake of the *Négritude* movement, what Fanon called in the first chapter of *Black Skin, White Masks* the issue of 'the Negro and language' was particularly emphasized. Fanon demonstrated the extent to which, in the Caribbean, the relation to the French language constituted a modality

---

1 Leonard R. Roos, 'Colonial culture as francophone? The case of late nineteenth-century Algeria', in Kamal Salhi (ed.), *Francophone Post-Colonial Cultures* (Lanham, MD: Lexington Books 2003), 17.

2 See Léopold Sédar Senghor, *Le Dialogue des cultures* (Paris: Seuil 1993), esp. the chapter 'Du métissage biologique au métissage culturel'.

3 Jonathan K. Gosnell, *The Politics of Frenchness in Colonial Algeria, 1930–1954* (Rochester, NY: University of Rochester Press 2002), 48.

4 Frantz Fanon, *Black Skin, White Masks*, trans. from the French by Charles Lam Markmann (New York: Grove Press 1967), 18.

of alienation and domination that commanded all others: 'The Negro of the Antilles will be proportionately whiter—that is, he will come closer to being a real human being—in direct ratio to his mastery of the French language.'[5] In Fanon's formulation, then, speaking French became racialized, and Fanon went on to describe a process of alienation that got reinforced through what he repeatedly called 'a lack of judgment',[6] perversely supporting the myth of French assimilation even though it remained an unfulfilled promise to the majority. In effect, Fanon consistently argued that Europeans promoted assimilation as long as the colonized remained short of it, that is, as long as he 'keep[s] [his] place'.[7]

Aimé Césaire made a related point when he declared that 'the Antilleans live in a fiction of assimilation, and the language was an excellent carapace'.[8] But, whereas Fanon tactically underscored the rigidity of the givens of the colonial situation and argued that the pre-eminence of French was not about to be overthrown, for instance, by the literary use of Creole,[9] Césaire relied on the possibilities of racializing writing positively. He famously claimed, for instance, to have used French as a 'tool' in order to create a 'black French'.[10] In 'Black Orpheus', originally written as an introduction to an anthology of *Négritude* poetry, Jean-Paul Sartre precisely remarked that racializing writing was a way out of the predicament of the colonized. But Sartre detected an inevitable ambivalence in the process. On the one hand, he emphasized the difficulty of avoiding alienation:

> Blacks can meet only on that trap-covered ground that the white has prepared for them: the colonist has arranged to be the eternal mediator between the colonized … And since words are ideas, when the negro declares in French

---

5 Ibid.

6 Ibid., 38.

7 Ibid., 34. Likewise, in his assessment of French colonization in Algeria, Mohammed Harbi says that 'colonization opened doors, only to close them straight away'; Mohammed Harbi, 'L'Algérie en perspectives', in Mohammed Harbi and Benjamin Stora (eds), *La Guerre d'Algérie 1954–2004: la fin de l'amnésie* (Paris: Editions Robert Laffont 2004), 37. Fanon's irony culminates whenever he evokes the hollowness of the colonizer's purported assimilation. He recalls in that respect the reactions to Césaire's poetry in France: 'for example, Charles-André Julien introducing Aimé Césaire as "a Negro poet with a university degree", or again, quite simply, the expression, "a great black poet"'; Fanon, *Black Skin, White Masks*, 39. Why marvel at educated Martinicans, in other words, if assimilation through the French school system is the declared intention of colonization? Fanon's ultimate point is that the French perception of their racial and cultural dominance is endangered when 'the mastery of the French language' is thrown back at them with a vengeance by a non-white writer.

8 Quoted in Thomas A. Hale, 'Bibliographie commentée', *Études françaises*, vol. 14, no. 3–4 (a special issue, 'Ecrits d'Aimé Césaire: Bibliographie commentée'), 1978, 407. All translations from the French, unless otherwise stated, are by the author.

9 Fanon, *Black Skin, White Masks*, 27.

10 Aimé Césaire, *Discourse on Colonialism*, trans. from the French by Joan Pinkham (New York: Monthly Review Press 1972), 67.

that he rejects the French culture, he takes in one hand what he rejects with the other; he sets up the enemy's thinking-apparatus in himself, like a crusher.[11]

On the other hand, Sartre also concurred with Césaire that 'since the oppressor is present in the very language that they speak, they will speak this language in order to destroy it'.[12]

The legacy of these positions cannot be overestimated. Working in and on the French language, and thereby inscribing a poetic as well as a political response to the issues that Fanon, Césaire, Senghor, Sartre and others framed—from lament to affirmation—are crucial to francophone writers today. The authors of *Eloge de la créolité*, for instance, while distancing themselves from the objectives of *Négritude*, still asserted that 'Creoleness left its indelible mark on the French language. ... In it we built our own language.'[13] The ability to make a productive mark on the French language could also be viewed from a different perspective. Instead of concentrating on the issue of the creolization of the French language, for instance, Édouard Glissant foregrounded a less discussed effect of *Négritude*, namely, to 'put into question the normative unity of [the French] language'.[14] By focusing on the difference from itself already at work within the French language, Glissant redirects otherwise the process of disalienation (although he does not contest that some normative effects may still be operative). Indeed, Césaire had remarked that Surrealism, the poetic form he powerfully enriched, was a mode of liberation from the French language *for the French themselves*. It was its constitutive hybridity that made that form paradoxically foreign to the French in their own language, and therefore irresistible to a practitioner of *Négritude*: 'What scandalized the French in this form of art which is so little French was precisely what pleased us.'[15]

The *Négritude* project strove to resist the alienating effects of French assimilation through the authentication in and revalorization of the black race. Césaire wanted to encompass a '"Negro situation" that existed in different geographical areas',[16] a situation that Senghor defined as 'the whole complex of civilised values—cultural, economic, social and political—which characterize the black peoples'.[17] In their argument in favour of

11 Jean-Paul Sartre, 'Black Orpheus', trans. from the French by John MacCombie, in Robert Bernasconi (ed.), *Race* (Oxford: Blackwell 2001), 121.
12 Ibid., 122.
13 Jean Bernabé, Patrick Chamoiseau and Raphaël Confiant, *Eloge de la créolité/In Praise of Creoleness*, trans. from the French by Mohamed B. Taleb-Khyar (Paris: Gallimard 1993), 107.
14 Édouard Glissant, *Introduction à une poétique du divers* (Paris: Gallimard 1996), 55.
15 Quoted in Hale, 'Bibliographie commentée', 406.
16 Césaire, *Discourse on Colonialism*, 77.
17 Leopold Senghor, 'What is "Negritude"?', in Robert Bernasconi and Tommy L. Lott (eds), *The Idea of Race* (Indianapolis, IN: Hackett 2000), 137.

'creolization', Jean Bernabé, Patrick Chamoiseau and Raphaël Confiant slightly shifted the emphasis that Césaire and Senghor put on the singular situation of Blacks by insisting that the issue of race was not primary. Yet they retained the notion of a 'complex of values' by suggesting that race was one factor in a 'mosaic' of others, in which questions of language and geopolitics were equally significant.[18] But those who questioned *Négritude* were critical of what in that discourse articulated race and universality, failing to account for the heterogeneity of Blacks' historical, social and economic conditions. Césaire and Senghor defined 'the values of Negritude'[19] as 'universalizing, living values that had not been exhausted. ... We thought that Africa could make a contribution to Europe':[20] 'they must flow towards the meeting point of all Humanity; they must be our contribution to the Civilization of the Universal.'[21] Some critics of *Négritude* felt that these

---

18 Bernabé, Chamoiseau and Confiant, *Eloge de la créolité*, 89, 94. About the ways in which the inclusion of a 'common region' as a factor in determining racial belonging has affected the discourse on race, Anthony Appiah writes: '[for Du Bois] people are members of the same race if they share features in virtue of being descended largely from people of the same region. Those features may be physical ... or cultural'; Anthony Appiah, 'The uncompleted argument: Du Bois and the illusion of race', in Henry Louis Gates (ed.), *'Race', Writing, and Difference* (Chicago: University of Chicago Press 1986), 29. Yet Appiah worries about a discourse of 'race' that would work as 'a metonym for culture ... it does so only at the price of biologizing what *is* culture, or ideology' (36). Fanon, who, like Appiah, put into question the reality of race conceived in biological terms (Fanon, *Black Skin, White Masks*, 119), thought that problematizing the biological notion of race in that fashion would not end racism since, by means of what he called 'the racial epidermal schema' (112), the Negro was 'overdetermined from without' (116) through a historical and mythical process that became naturalized as essential to blackness; see Jeremy Weate's excellent remarks in 'Fanon, Merleau-Ponty and the difference of phenomenology', in Robert Bernasconi (ed.), *Race*, 174–5. In *French Hospitality*, Tahar Ben Jelloun, who deals with the issue of racism in France, seems close to Appiah in his concern over a perceived tendency to essentialize culture in a way that would merely displace (from so-called 'nature' to 'culture') the attributes that racism previously conferred on racialized Others. He first quotes Philippe Rouger, who was then director-general of the National Blood Transfusion Institute: 'During the colonial era, the notion of race was used to justify the economic and political enslavement of the peoples colonized.' Ben Jelloun agrees with Rouger that nowadays this view does not prevail among scientists, who find more evidence of socio-cultural than of genetic differences. However, Ben Jelloun does not seem to think that 'cultural identity' is more promising. 'The attempt to preserve identity goes with a silent and unnatural urge that produces ... a turning in on a cleansed and purified version of one's heritage'; Tahar Ben Jelloun, *French Hospitality: Racism and North African Immigrants*, trans. from the French by Barbara Bray (New York: Columbia University Press 1999), 30.
19 Senghor, 'What is "Negritude"?', 137.
20 Césaire, *Discourse on Colonialism*, 76.
21 Senghor, 'What is "Negritude"?', 137. Senghor often stressed that the enforced French policy of assimilation 'was a failure' and 'deepened our despair' in terms that were

positions could also lead to the repetition of problematic western philo-sophemes that were not thought through. Glissant, for instance, takes such statements to represent marks of what he calls a 'system thought' or 'a thinking of Being',[22] a project that he substitutes with another that he names the 'thinking of the trace'.[23] Glissant associates a poetics of the trace with the possibility of 'conceiving the unutterable of a totality'.[24] Although he does not explicitly name Jacques Derrida and his reflection on the trace—for example in *Writing and Difference*, *Of Grammatology* and *Margins of Philosophy*—Glissant preserves from that reflection an emphasis on a trace that *is not*, that challenges a presentation and a presencing.[25] He calls for what he remarkably names 'a prophetic vision of the past',[26] where the past (for instance, slavery in the Antilles) cannot be reconstructed ('the trace does not repeat'),[27] but is legible through heterogeneous elements that are not identical to it but effect an 'unpredictable realization'.[28] Thus the past, of which the colonized were dispossessed, cannot be recollected but may be constructed through fragments or poetically imagined. It is not rooted in memory but, paradoxically, can be arrived at only in the future in a prophetic mode. Assia Djebar provides remarkable instances of this odd spatio-temporality, for instance, in *Fantasia: An Algerian Cavalcade* or *So Vast the Prison*. Djebar—who became in 2005 the first Algerian woman writer ever to have been elected to join the Académie Française, an institution founded in 1635 with the mandate of defining the French language by writing its dictionary—is also one of several Maghrebian writers who have minutely

---

close to Fanon's: 'we could assimilate . . . the French language, but we could never strip off our black skins nor root out our black souls' (136). Whether Senghor argued that there were irreducible cultural specificities, as when he wrote about Negro art as opposed to Greek art (Senghor, *Le Dialogue des cultures*, 22) or, more radically, that any culture involved an opening to the Other and was both a rooting in a soil *and* an uprooting (25), he endorsed a notion of cultural complementarity. Thus he gives the French language a chance in post-independence Africa, but only when appropriated and instrumentalized in new ways: 'Cartesian clarity must enlighten, but essentially our riches' (26).

22 Glissant, *Introduction à une poétique du divers*, 17, 69.
23 Ibid., 17.
24 Ibid., 69.
25 For instance: 'What the thought of the trace has already taught us is that it could not be simply submitted to the onto-phenomenological question of essence. The trace *is nothing*, it is not an entity (*étant*), it exceeds the question *What is?* and contingently makes it possible'; Jacques Derrida, *Of Grammatology*, trans. from the French by Gayatri Chakravorty Spivak (Baltimore: Johns Hopkins University Press 1976), 75; 'the play of the trace . . . which is not. Which does not belong'; Jacques Derrida, 'Différance', in Jacques Derrida, *Margins of Philosophy*, trans. from the French by Alan Bass (Chicago: University of Chicago Press 1982), 22.
26 Glissant, *Introduction à une poétique du divers*, 86.
27 Ibid., 70.
28 Ibid., 29.

analysed the condition of writing in what she calls 'the adverse language'.[29] While generally agreeing with Fanon's insight that the ascription of race occurs through language, she also focuses on the chance afforded by a thought of the trace, which would be neither a restitution of the forbidden nor a reconstitution of the forgotten in Algeria before and during French colonization but, not unlike Glissant's poetics, would attempt to delimit what does remain unutterable. Promoting a 'writing for the trace', for instance by paying attention to scenes of vanishing inscriptions or an alphabet under erasure, is, for Djebar, a way of resisting colonial expropriation, as well as of avoiding well-intentioned assurances of authentic recovery that would sidestep enduring political and cultural dispossession. In that respect, Djebar aligns her work with the textual strategies elaborated by other Maghrebian writers, Abdelkebir Khatibi in particular, while inscribing a difference. Likewise, Djebar's position converges with the thought of Jean-François Lyotard and Jacques Derrida in their assessment of the racialized Other's exclusion from the property of language. For Lyotard and Derrida, though each inflects it differently, the issue is then both to deconstruct the appropriation of language by the master or the oppressor, and to point to the conditions of possibility of justice not only against that fantasized totalizing language but also through and in spite of it.

Djebar's *qalam*

The reader familiar with Assia Djebar's work and that of her critics is aware that *qalam*, the Arabic word transliterated in a Latin alphabet, appears frequently in her idiom.[30] It is found most memorably at the end of *Fantasia*, in which Djebar examines French colonial narratives written at the time of the conquest of Algeria. Drawing on the painter Eugène Fromentin's memoir of his stay in Algeria, she recalls his witnessing of the aftermath of the battles mounted by the resisting Algerians against the invading French army:

> In June 1853 . . . he visits Laghouat, which has been occupied after a terrible siege. He describes one sinister detail: as he is leaving the oasis . . . Fromentin picks up out of the dust the severed hand of an anonymous Algerian woman. He throws it

29 Assia Djebar, *L'Amour, la fantasia* (Paris: Albin Michel 1995), 243 (my translation). Dorothy S. Blair's translation reads 'the enemy's language'; Assia Djebar, *Fantasia: An Algerian Cavalcade* (London and New York: Quartet Books 1989), 216.

30 Among the monographs wholly or partly devoted to Assia Djebar, I shall mention in particular Jeanne-Marie Clerc, *Assia Djebar: ecrire, transgresser, résister* (Paris: L'Harmattan 1997); Marta Segarra, *Leur pesant de poudre: romancières francophones du Maghreb* (Paris: L'Harmattan 1997); Mireille Calle-Gruber, *Assia Djebar ou la résistance de l'écriture* (Paris: Maisonneuve et Larose 2001); and Anne Donadey, *Recasting Postcolonialism: Women Writing between Worlds* (Portsmouth, NH: Heinemann 2001).

down again in his path. Later, I seize on this living hand, hand of mutilation and of memory, and I attempt to make it take the *qalam*.[31]

The word 'qalam' is written in Djebar's French text with a Latin alphabet and in quotation marks,[32] but without any additional translation or explanation.

Much has been written on this passage, which is often taken to allegorize Djebar's position: first, the Algerian woman's mutilation is attested in the 'colonizer's' text and in his language, perhaps unbeknownst to him. A sort of *lapsus calami*, perhaps, a slip of the pen like the one Jacques Derrida mentions near the end of his reading of another scene of writing.[33] Therefore, the detour through the French corpus describing the violently severed Algerian body is necessary, at least in a first gesture, as much as it is indispensable to assert women's active involvement in all Algerian wars—for there have been more than one—a condition that explains why their bodies become privileged sites of reinscription for Djebar.[34] The narrator's 'attempt' to make the hand, which is now said to be 'living', 'take the *qalam*' and write has also been interpreted as a gesture of testimony and defiance displacing both French documents and the official Algerian history of the conquest and the war of independence. Another writing seems to be promised at the end of *Fantasia*, and the attempt to make the hand take the *qalam* is often understood as a recapitulation of the entire thrust of Djebar's project.[35]

But what are we to make of the promise of this other inscription through the Arabic word, thrown into her French text, not unlike the way Fromentin throws the Algerian woman's mutilated hand into his path? That *qalam* stands for difference thrown in the way, or interrupting the patterns, of the 'adverse language' and discourse seems obvious. By using an Arabic word

---

31 Djebar, *Fantasia*, 226.
32 Djebar, *L'Amour, la fantasia*, 255.
33 Jacques Derrida, 'Freud and the scene of writing', in Jacques Derrida, *Writing and Difference*, trans. from the French by Alan Bass (Chicago: University of Chicago Press 1978), 230.
34 Katherine Gracki, 'Writing violence and the violence of writing in Assia Djebar's *Algerian Quartet*', *World Literature Today*, vol. 70, no. 4, Autumn 1996, 835–43 (836).
35 For a discussion of this specific passage in *Fantasia*, see Katherine Gracki, 'Assia Djebar et l'écriture de l'autobiographie au pluriel', *Women in French Studies*, vol. 2, 1994, 55–66; Patricia Geesey, 'Collective autobiography: Algerian women and history in Assia Djebar's *L'amour, la fantasia*', *Dalhousie French Studies*, vol. 35, 1996, 153–67; Anne Donadey, 'Assia Djebar's poetics of subversion', *L'Esprit Créateur*, vol. 33, no. 2, Summer 1993, 107–17 (in which Donadey refers to her unpublished paper, 'Writing the trace: Assia Djebar's *L'Amour, la fantasia* as a bilingual palimpsest'); Nada Turk, '"*L'Amour, la fantasia*" d'Assia Djebar: chronique de guerre, voix des femmes', *Celfan Review*, vol. 7, no. 1–2, 1987–8, 25–9; and H. Adlai Murdoch, 'Rewriting writing: identity, exile and renewal in Assia Djebar's *L'Amour, la fantasia*', *Yale French Studies*, no. 83, 1993, 71–92.

in her French text, is Djebar suggesting a resisting idiomaticity that can be read or heard but not quite understood by a francophone reader? We have already mentioned that in post-independence Algeria, the issue of idiomaticity was not only linked to the 'expression' of discourses that had been silenced under French rule. Equally crucially, the question was to determine in what language that idiomaticity would speak or could be written. No simple answer to that question has been formulated, and no mere equation can be made between the 'choice' of a language for writing and publishing and a specific political affiliation as far as language is concerned.[36] This is a singular situation for this particular generation of writers, one that is neither exactly that of other Maghrebian writers who, as Abdelkebir Khatibi wrote in *Love in Two Languages*, could also write 'in [their] mother tongue with great enjoyment',[37] nor that described by Jacques Derrida in *The Monolingualism of the Other*, and summed up in that difficult sentence: 'I have only one language, yet it is not mine.'[38]

Unlike Khatibi, Derrida—and Djebar to a great extent—cannot rely or simply fall back on bilingualism, that is, 'a single mother tongue *plus* another language'.[39] In this essay, Derrida explains what deprived him of an 'authorized mother tongue',[40] the French language being the 'language of the master'.[41] This is, to be sure, the story of the colonized in general: the colonized have monolingualism imposed on them by the master, but are denied its property. But, for Derrida, there is never a relation of belonging, property and mastery to language; language is 'ex-appropriation',[42] and this is the case even for the master or the colonizer. With the thought of a general ex-appropriation from and in language, the notion of alienation shows its limitations, for no property, no self is, properly speaking, 'alienated' in

36 In *Ces Voix qui m'assiègent*, Djebar recalls that the Algerian intellectuals who were murdered in Algeria in the 1980s and 1990s were not necessarily killed because of their 'francophonie', mentioning the counter-example of the arabophone poet Youssef Sebti, who was killed in 1993; Assia Djebar, *Ces Voix qui m'assiègent* (Paris: Albin Michel 1999), 216. For the critic Hafid Gafaïti, colonization in Algeria did not happen to a homogeneous group that had never been colonized; Hafid Gafaïti, 'The monotheism of the Other', in Anne-Emmanuelle Berger (ed.), *Algeria in Others' Languages* (Ithaca, NY: Cornell University Press 2002), 37. This reminder may be linked to Abdelkebir Khatibi's consideration of what he calls the 'idiomatic discontinuities' within Algeria irrespective of French colonization; Abdelkebir Khatibi, 'Diglossia', in Berger (ed.), *Algeria in Others' Languages*, 157.
37 Abdelkebir Khatibi, *Love in Two Languages*, trans. from the French by Richard Howard (Minneapolis: University of Minnesota Press 1990), 66. This passage is quoted in Jacques Derrida, *Monolingualism of the Other*, trans. from the French by Patrick Mensah (Stanford, CA: Stanford University Press 1998), 36.
38 Derrida, *Monolingualism of the Other*, 2.
39 Ibid., 36.
40 Ibid., 31.
41 Ibid., 42.
42 Ibid., 24.

relation to language. However, to say that there is nothing but appropriations of a language, to some extent and never entirely, is not to deny the
impact of the racialization of the Other through language. On the contrary,
since the master is such inasmuch as he 'can give substance to and articulate
this appropriation ... in the course of an unnatural process of politico-
phantasmatic constructions',[43] it becomes possible to contest naturalized
appropriations. Derrida's essay also emphasizes that stating that monolingualism is *of* or comes from the Other is not only a threat, but also an
opening, including the possibility for something to happen in and to
language.[44] Hence, Derrida's 'desire to make it arrive *here*, by making
something happen to it. ... forcing the language then to speak itself, in
another way, in its language'.[45]

Djebar's work resonates with this last statement. Like the Algerian
francophone writer Kateb Yacine, Djebar could not easily write in Arabic,
even though she might have liked to.[46] For her, the question of 'turning to
Arabic' could not be a matter of 'return',[47] a return to the comfort of a
mother tongue for instance. Conversely, the 'adverse language' is never
simply that, but also the very element of Djebar's writing. Rather, her
interrogation involved the (political, artistic) decision whether to continue or
to stop writing. The dilemma that these writers inherited from (post)coloniz-
ization was not the deprivation of a mother tongue, but the fact that neither
the 'language of writing' they had acquired at school nor their national
language after independence (modern standard Arabic) was their mother
tongue.

The time of the differend

Another way of addressing the issue of idiomaticity and the possibility of
justice in a colonial or postcolonial context is afforded by Jean-François
Lyotard's thought of the 'differend'. In *The Differend* and elsewhere, Lyotard
has recourse to the term with two particular examples in mind: one is the
case of a Holocaust survivor seeking justice, and the other is that of a worker

43 Ibid., 23.
44 Ibid., 68.
45 Ibid., 51.
46 Lucette Valensi shows, for example, that Kateb Yacine turned to theatre for the rest of
his career, and Assia Djebar to television and cinema for a while, because these forms
allowed them to use vernacular Arabic rather than the modern standard Arabic they
had trouble 'mastering'; Lucette Valensi, 'The Scheherazade syndrome: literature and
politics in postcolonial Algeria', in Berger (ed.), *Algeria in Others' Languages*, 142–3.
47 Mildred Mortimer, 'Entretien avec Assia Djebar, écrivain algérien', *Research in African
Literatures*, vol. 19, no. 2, Summer 1998, 197–205 (199).

seeking redress from his employer in a social conflict.[48] In the preface to *La Guerre des Algériens*, he applies the term to the Algerian/French conflict in a way that shows that his idea of the differend was profoundly informed by his encounter with the injustice of colonialism and of racialized Others:

> I owed and I owe my awakening, *tout court*, to Constantine [where he taught in a secondary school]. The differend showed itself with such a sharpness that the consolations then common among my peers (vague reformism, pious Stalinism, futile leftism) were denied to me.[49]

The differend is a conceptual tool for comprehending the racialization of Europe in the wake of the Holocaust and in the grip of decolonization (in Africa and Indochina). In *The Differend*, each example involves a scene in which a tribunal cannot give justice to what Lyotard calls the victim (as opposed to the plaintiff who may receive justice). The injustice is first and foremost due to the lack of a common idiom between the victim on the one hand and the tribunal and the second party on the other hand.[50] Importantly for Lyotard, injustice is not merely (though it may be that as well) a question of ill will or bad faith on the part of the tribunal: 'there is a differend between two parties when the "settlement" of the conflict that opposes them appears in the idiom of one of them while the tort from which the other suffers cannot signify itself in this idiom.'[51] *The Differend* shows that, unlike the damage, the tort cannot be heard because it cannot be said or, more precisely, is not receivable in the idiom of the tribunal, which it shares with the party against whom the victim is pleading. Lyotard goes on to show that the criteria of receivability rely—silently or not—on the concept of evidence as a demonstrable proof that can be presented. This anchors the understanding of the opposition between true and false, or of the connection made between what takes place and what is real. In that respect, Lyotard examines some of Plato's dialogues, which establish rules 'proper to ... a consensus' between the protagonists before the dialogue can be instituted.[52] The terms of the agreement stipulate that an idiom must be shared, but also that there should be a preliminary accord as to the objectives of the dialogue: what is at stake

---

48 Jean-François Lyotard, *The Differend: Phrases in Dispute*, trans. from the French by Georges Van Den Abbeele (Minneapolis: University of Minnesota Press 1988). In her study of acts of racialization, Colette Guillaumin points out that, in the nineteenth century, 'it was held that factory workers were from a different race'; quoted in Dominique Schnapper, 'Racism and the radical condemnation of modernity', in Christina Howells (ed.), *French Women Philosophers: A Contemporary Reader* (London: Routledge 2000), 377.

49 Jean-François Lyotard, *Political Writings*, trans. from the French by Bill Readings and Kevin Paul Geiman (Minneapolis: University of Minnesota Press 1993), 170.

50 Lyotard, *The Differend*, 49.

51 Ibid., 9.

52 Ibid., 43.

in the dialogue is the search for an agreement.[53] This passage complicates any hasty reliance on the possibility of resolving differends through a common idiom, if there is such an idiom. For the preliminary agreement regarding agreement, which seems commonsensical, is also a process of elimination, of exclusion of the Other, that is to say, the occasion of a potential or actual differend:

> For instance, one can dialogue with the friends of forms, they are better 'domesticated' (tamed, *hèmérôteroi*) than the materialists. ... The latter would have to be 'civilized' (*nômimôteron*) before they could be admitted to dialogue. But in fact (*ergô*), there is no question of this. One will act as if (*logô*) they were civilized: one speaks in their place, one reinterprets (*aphermèneué*) their theses, one makes them presentable for dialogue.[54]

The differend describes two phrases that are heterogeneous and untranslatable. But, as Lyotard also says, although or because they are heterogeneous, the two phrases can be 'linked'.[55] Rather than being only a sign of homogeneity or continuity, this link also marks rupture and heterogeneity. Likewise, Lyotard says that the differend is 'the unstable state and instant of language wherein something which must be put into phrases cannot yet be'.[56] It is the space of excess of the 'not yet' that constitutes both the injustice and the call for justice in another idiom. Lyotard's point is that the marks of the differend must also be upheld in order to promote its opposite, namely, justice.

Lyotard shows that the search for, and reliance on, a common idiom actually rests on the exclusion of some Other. Yet, instead of urging the demise of the idiomatic in his delineation of a way out of the differend, Lyotard calls, on the contrary, for new idioms, new phrases to link ('This requires new rules for the formation and linking of phrases'; 'bear witness to differends by finding idioms for them').[57] The answer is not fewer idioms, but more idioms; not more homogeneity, but more heterogeneity. What constitutes the differend or injustice itself is also what, slightly displaced or 'new', is the condition of a call for justice and will, if possible, make justice happen. Or, in other words, the conflicting phrasing in the differend is what can also put an end to it. With another phrase. Regarding the idiomaticity of the idiom, Lyotard does not decide once and for all between what it makes possible: both the differend and its contrary. The idiom is the problem and its solution. Yet it seems that the question of justice does not only depend on

53 Ibid., 24.
54 Ibid.
55 Ibid., xii.
56 Ibid., 29.
57 Ibid., 13.

'institut[ing] new addressees',[58] which would assume that, once the idiom reaches its destination, justice happens or may happen. If *The Differend* cautions time and again against the reductiveness of understanding language as 'communication', it may also be because it wants to leave untouched something from the time of the differend, the time of the not-yet: this something would be silence, the inexpressible, the unheard-of, what resists formulation or prevents it (as Lyotard shows in the case of the Holocaust survivor). 'To give the differend its due (*faire droit*)'[59] should also include paying attention to that silence or that resistance, in order for the as yet unheard-of idiom to be just, and not to reiterate the tort in the old terms (which always know what to say), a state of affairs that allowed for the differend in the first place. Giving utterance to this difficult formulation is what is at stake.

Diglossia or dissemination

When Djebar uses the word 'qalam' in her French text, she makes a gesture that may recall what Abdelkebir Khatibi performed in *Love in Two Languages*: 'He calmed down (*se calma*) instantly when an Arabic word, Kalma, appeared.'[60] Réda Bensmaïa has pointed out that the object of such a writing is not to '"dialect-ize" or "Maghreb-ize" French',[61] which, as we mentioned earlier, has been a common strategy adopted by francophone postcolonial writers to mark in French their difference to the French language and discourse. It could be said that Khatibi's sentence is not opposed to the kind of dislocation of the French idiom in which the foreign word would abruptly interrupt the other language; more precisely, it increases the impact of the dislocation by making it less locatable. What is most defeating for logic, which can accommodate the exotic disruption of an occasional Arabic word, however opaque, within a French text, is that the apparent diglossia (French and Arabic) of this example ('calma/Kalma') is nevertheless not merely a bringing together, nor is it simply about the 'two' that the very notion of 'diglossia' would seem to imply. On the one hand, the homophony of Arabic and French terms is paradoxically endowed with, and entrusted to, difference *through* the recognizable harmonious similarity. It remains unassimilable in its very proximity. On the other hand, as Bensmaïa writes about Khatibi, 'the task is to found a mode of thinking of the *milieu*',[62] this rather unrepresentable site being for Khatibi 'a (thought) riddled by its

---

58 Ibid.
59 Ibid.
60 Khatibi, *Love in Two Languages*, 4.
61 Réda Bensmaïa, 'Multilingualism and national "character": on Abdelkebir Khatibi's "bilanguage"', in Berger (ed.), *Algeria in Others' Languages*, 167.
62 Ibid., 181.

marginality, displaced, and full of silent questions'.[63] Rather than a process of consolidating abundance (in which diglossia would imply one language + another language), this new space for writing and thought inscribes a tangential semantic recognition that implicates, and perhaps risks confusing, one language with another, while forbidding stable (re)appropriations.

Djebar's use of the Arabic word 'qalam' resembles that process, but it takes it in another direction. To a French ear hearing 'qalam' as 'calame' (meaning 'calamus' in English), the term designates a writing instrument, one used by the ancients, a reed pen, a stylus or a quill.[64] The word may also refer to a manuscript that was written with a reed pen. Khatibi relies on homophony to point to difference, or to dissemination rather than diglossia, where 'calma' and 'Kalma' unpredictably affect each other's meaning and, by association, evoke other terms that almost sound like them, such as the Arabic 'kalima' or 'klima'. But, in this instance, Djebar seems to promote on the contrary the premises of the receivability, to mention Lyotard's term again, of such a term as 'qalam'. Unlike 'Kalma', which makes the very bilingual speaker speechless at this undecipherable scene in which two words 'observe each other',[65] 'qalam' can be heard and relatively under- stood by a non-arabophone francophone reader. Yet, at this juncture, receivability, the very *milieu* or meeting ground for comprehension and understanding, is now turned around and francophones find themselves in a position in which that possibility or that site occurs not in French but in Arabic. At the moment of the flash of recognition of convergences, one is already on other grounds. If Djebar's move when using 'qalam' is not an attempt to undermine or implode French from within, but to bring the language or the speaker to recognize itself at the moment when the foreign is heard or read, what are the implications? What is the point of bringing the French to the Algerian site? Again?

Critics have argued that Djebar intersperses the paternal language or 'adverse language' with the orality of the 'mother', and that she exposes Algerian women's bodies in a French and Algerian masculine space before and after independence. Yet, she has consistently questioned the interests vested in rigid oppositions that she represents as actually untenable, an untenability that does not prevent them, however, from having real and enduring effects. For example, her remarkable analysis of the veil in *Women of Algiers in Their Apartment* shows that, far from univocally relegating the feminine to seclusion and the private sphere, the veil functions as the very

---

63 Quoted from Khatibi's *Maghreb pluriel* in ibid.
64 See *Ces Voix qui m'assiègent*, in which Djebar writes 'le calame à la main' (184), or 'le *kalam* à la main' in *Le Blanc de l'Algérie* (Paris: Albin Michel 1995), 261. David Kelley and Marjolijn de Jager translate the latter as 'writing brush in hand'; Assia Djebar, *Algerian White* (New York: Seven Stories Press 2000), 219.
65 Khatibi, *Love in Two Languages*, 4.

borderline between public and private, outside and inside, a location that is not one, or a position at which all sorts of roles or alibis can find an uneasy accommodation with their opposites.[66]

Redoubling this first movement of deconstitution, like Rachid Boudjedra, who talks in *Lettres algériennes* of 'amnesia' and of 'aphasia' in the relation of France to Algeria,[67] Djebar diagnoses a forgetting involved in the occupation of the Algerian site. But, in the same way that, in *The Differend*, Lyotard arguably strives to keep in the formulation of a new idiom a mark of reticence or silence, the trace of what could not as yet find a language in the victim's tort, so Djebar does not rush to transcribe the contents of a lost memory, but records the very absence of memory. How is it possible to tell the 'memory blank' ('trou de mémoire') or the 'hidden transmission'?[68] A section of Djebar's *So Vast the Prison* entitled 'Erased in Stone' ('L'Effacement sur la pierre') can shed light on the dual gesture developed in her work.

Erasure, or writing for the trace

In *So Vast the Prison*, Djebar reconstitutes and imagines what happens when Europeans 'discover' archaeological treasures of antiquity in the Maghreb.[69] Edward Said's *Orientalism* examined the complicities of the academic discourse about that region with 'European-Atlantic power over the Orient',[70] whether such complicities are actually intended or not, whether they are acknowledged or unconscious. Likewise, Djebar recalls that military invasions of the Maghreb have been accompanied by scholars, from the time of Scipio's Roman army marching on to Carthage to the invasion of the French army after 1830. Not far from the former site of Carthage can be found the archaeological ruins of Dougga. Djebar rehearses the repeated finding and forgetting of a monolithic monument, a cenotaph bearing a stone with a bilingual inscription. Happening on to this ancient monument was at first accidental and, for a long time, in spite of several attempts, no information on the site managed to be successfully passed on. Hardly found,

---

66 Assia Djebar, *Women of Algiers in Their Apartment*, trans. from the French by Marjolijn de Jager (Charlottesville: University Press of Virginia 1992). Homa Hoodfar makes a related point in her discussion of the veil in 'The veil in their minds and on our heads', in Elizabeth Castelli (ed.), *Women, Gender, Religion* (New York and Basingstoke: Palgrave 2001): for women, the veil can play a 'role of mediation and adaptation' (439), it is strategic. In her discussion of the veil in Iran, she points out for instance that 'both rejection of the shah's Eurocentric vision and the resistance to the compulsory veil represent women's active resistance to the imposed gender role envisaged for women by the state' (434).

67 Rachid Boudjedra, *Lettres algériennes* (Paris: Grasset 1995), 57.

68 Djebar, *Ces Voix qui m'assiègent*, 140.

69 Assia Djebar, *So Vast the Prison*, trans. from the French by Betsy Wing (New York: Seven Stories Press 1999).

70 Edward Said, *Orientalism* (New York: Vintage Books 1994), 6.

it was already about to be forgotten, first in 1631, then in 1815, 1833 and 1842. Like another Rosetta stone,[71] the bilingual inscription seems to call for deciphering, for only one of the languages has been found to be unknown. That language is presumably a translation of the first understandable language (Punic); furthermore, its alphabet has, in Djebar's words, 'vanished', which makes it a 'lost language'.[72] Djebar presents a hieroglyphic, opaque language, which turns out in time to be the most familiar one, in fact the indigenous language of the region, Berber. For a long time, it had been thought that Berber was only an oral language, and therefore it was transcribed with Arabic signs. It follows that it was not the language of the inscription that was 'lost' since it was still spoken, but the possibility of linking it to a different alphabet. As Djebar also shows, while apparently no longer used in scholarly circles, the alphabet had in fact become nomadic, kept by Tuaregs who left behind them inscriptions engraved on rocks in the desert, while transporting it with them written on the palms of women's hands.[73] The effect of such statements is to refute the immediate association of orality with the feminine. The latter should not be simply aligned either with the mother's tongue or with the native who is, as opposed to the colonizer, supposedly 'without writing'.[74]

In a second move, Djebar contests the hierarchical structure that might be afforded by the bilingualism of the stone: the autochthonous language that goes temporarily unrecognized by scholarly discourses, as opposed to Punic signs, the dominant language, that endure. In order to complicate the notion of bilingualism, she frames the time of the erection of the stone as following the destruction of Carthage by the Romans. At that moment, though defeated, the military and cultural metropolis Carthage is shown to live on through its language and the scattered books of its libraries among the Berbers it had formerly 'colonized'. The stone commemorates the death of a Berber king whose people still speak the language and contribute to the culture of Carthage, against Carthage and, indeed, after it.[75] But to the bilingualism of the stone ('the language of our ancestors and the others' language'), she adds Latin, the 'language of the future' in the region.[76] While not scripted, that future language of domination is represented: Djebar stages a scene in which the commemoration in two languages is prolonged by an improvised oral translation into Latin of the bilingual inscription. It would be possible to interpret that scene as writing in advance the politically

71 Calle-Gruber, *Assia Djebar*, 80.
72 Djebar, *So Vast the Prison*, 146–7.
73 Ibid., 148.
74 Hafid Gafaïti also points out 'the central importance of women in the production, transmission and safeguarding of the original cultural "patrimony"' in Djebar's work'; Hafid Gafaïti, 'The blood of writing: Assia Djebar's unveiling of women and history', *World Literature Today*, vol. 70, no. 4, Autumn 1996, 813–22 (816).
75 Djebar, *So Vast the Prison*, 159.
76 Ibid., 156.

charged current linguistic triangle in Algeria (Arabic/Berber/French) if she did not add another twist to her Babelian plot by evoking Polybe, the Greek master of the Roman general Scipio, in exile from his already defeated homeland and witnessing in Greek the destruction of Carthage. These interpolated oral and written passages testify to the need to consider the Maghrebian or Algerian site as a multilingual space.[77] At stake in this reconfiguration is the liberation of the speakers and that site, or liberation in that site from an 'illusory duality' and 'false bilingualism',[78] not only because such a duality has codetermined a hierarchy among, indeed a racialization of, language speakers. For if she shows that there is more than one and even more than two languages in the region, this also happens from a position of dispossession, and the gains (more than one) do not quite add up. In the vein of Derrida's 'ex-appropriation', Djebar explores on what terrain to inscribe this condition.

In the episode of the Dougga ruins, Djebar does not break the silence dissimulating the 'message' of the inscription, even though the reader is able to understand its commemorative purpose and some of its effects. She emphasizes the greater relevance of examining the very condition of multilingualism. Even when depicting the scholarly work on the inscription, she focuses on the investigation conducted into the name and functions of the unknown language. At the same time, she stresses that the end of unreadability happens through the intervention of an Other reading the inscription.[79] Furthermore, when she relates the fate of the stone over time, we witness a doubling of the stone as well as a division from itself. In 1833 the stone was cut off from the monument and the inscribed part was sent to the British Museum. In 1910, 'with the exception of the bilingual inscription, which is still in London, the mausoleum is once again standing, almost intact, but stripped of its double writing'.[80] But fifty years later, further archaeological research will demonstrate that 'at Dougga there were, in fact, two steles, and that the second—probably the most important—of these had been partially erased'.[81] The stone doubles itself but, this time, writing (in which languages and which alphabets?) cannot in any simple sense lend itself to the hermeneutic achievements previously accomplished when interpreting the bilingual inscription. On the one hand, Djebar is less interested in the decoding of the message than in the exposure of a linguistic condition that goes beyond bilingualism. But the second instance of a

77 In that respect, see Anne Donadey's analysis of what she calls Djebar's 'subterranean languages' and of Djebar's 'multilingual French'; Anne Donadey, 'The multilingual strategies of postcolonial literature: Assia Djebar's Algerian palimpsest', *World Literature Today*, vol. 74, no. 1, Winter 2000, 27–36 (29).
78 Djebar, *Ces Voix qui m'assiègent*, 56.
79 Ibid., 148.
80 Djebar, *So Vast the Prison*, 145.
81 Ibid.

lapidary writing that has 'almost entirely vanished'[82] serves to accentuate the first point, that is to say, the disappearance or lack of content, a content that might itself be felt to be a metonym for cultural plenitude or self-coincidence, must be the main focus of analysis. Djebar delves into this spectrality, and denounces the poetic as well as political temptation to fill in the blanks, to provide keys that would unlock the past and answer for the present.[83] Instead, paying attention to vanishing inscriptions epitomizes for her the task of the Algerian writer, which entails 'being a writer for the trace'.[84] 'Trace' means for Djebar the transmission of something that remains elusive and radically defies presentation. 'How to testify through writing? The terrain has slipped under your steps.'[85] 'It is your dispossession that you transmit. Inherit my non-inheritance.'[86] Such injunctions show that Djebar has addressed differently in her fiction the anguished question posed by the formerly colonized, namely, how to say or to think the Other *of* the former colonizer in his language, one that has already comprehended the racialized Other? Withdrawing or emptying out the content does not amount to an absence of thematization, but the reluctance or inability to present that this gesture testifies to becomes what is the most urgent to tell.

The very word 'trace' used by Djebar may productively be put in conjunction with Jacques Derrida's work on the trace. Djebar's claim that she is 'writing for the trace' or her attention to inscriptions in a process of 'erasure' can be related to that thinking. When Derrida writes about the trace, he is first inheriting other scenes of writing (in Freud, Levinas and Heidegger, for example). In 'Freud and the Scene of Writing', Derrida recalls Freud's attempts, before his invention of the 'Mystic Writing-Pad', to account for the ways in which memory functions, that is, simultaneously for 'the permanence of the trace and for the virginity of the receiving substance'.[87] Derrida radicalizes Freud's gesture by showing that the very structure of the trace is its own erasure, the erasure of its own presence. 'It is constituted by the threat or anguish of its irremediable disappearance. ... An unerasable trace is not a trace',[88] for if that were not the case, as Derrida writes in another essay, 'it would not be a trace but an indestructible and monumental substance'.[89] With the trace, Derrida undoes the opposition between the effective presence of ontology and its Other, a logic that he later called 'hauntology'.[90] The trace is what arrives through erasure, was never

---

82 Ibid.
83 Djebar, *Ces Voix qui m'assiègent*, 215.
84 Ibid., 216.
85 Ibid., 215.
86 Ibid., 261.
87 Derrida, 'Freud and the scene of writing', 200.
88 Ibid., 230.
89 Derrida, 'Différance', 24.
90 See Jacques Derrida, *Specters of Marx*, trans. from the French by Peggy Kamuf (New York and London: Routledge 1994), 10, 40.

experienced or perceived in its meaning in the present,[91] what therefore does not present itself as such:

> Traces thus produce the space of their inscription only by acceding to the period of their erasure. From the beginning, in the "present" of their first impression, they are constituted by the double force of repetition and erasure, legibility and illegibility.[92]

In an economy of traces, what seems to remain or to be retained keeps in itself, or is haunted by, the mark of an Other (the past, but also the future, and the double movement of repetition and erasure); what is called the present or presence is constituted by this relation to the Other. This makes the location of the trace untenable if one takes into account the relation of, and the relation within, the trace to something other than itself, hence the mention of 'erasure': 'Since the trace is not a presence but the simulacrum of a presence that dislocates itself, displaces itself, refers itself, it properly has no site (*n'a pas lieu*)—erasure belongs to its structure.'[93] 'Writing for the trace', in Djebar's words, would then be writing in view of that dislocation, *for* it, because it can bring about another relation to (a de-limited) proximity that cannot be simply either opposed or opened to alterity, one that challenges appropriations or haunts what it contests.

---

91 Derrida, 'Freud and the scene of writing', 214.
92 Ibid., 226.
93 Derrida, 'Différance', 24.

'Everybody else just living their lives': 9/11, race and the new postglobal literature

ALFRED J. LÓPEZ

> *Questo progetto di economia mondiale integrate, regolata pressoché esclusivamente dai meccanismi dello scambio, all'insegna del mutuo vantaggio di ogni singolo partecipante ma con ricadute positive per tutta la società, appare oggi come un sogno infranto: la crescita potrà riprendere, le illusioni che solo o prevalentemente con la crescita si possano, in un clima di mercato, risolvere le contraddizioni delle società uname sono del tutto svanite.*
> —Mario Deaglio, *Postglobal*[1]

I wish to thank Eva Cherniavsky, Deborah Cohn and Masao Miyoshi for their very helpful comments on an earlier version of this essay.

1 Mario Deaglio, *Postglobal* (Roma: Editori Laterza 2004), vii: 'This project of an integrated worldwide economy, regulated almost exclusively by the mechanisms of exchange, to the mutual advantage of every individual participant but also with positive consequences for all society, appears today like a shattered dream: although growth will resume, the illusions that it is only or mostly growth that can, in a market climate, resolve the contradictions of human societies have vanished.' Translations, unless otherwise stated, are by the author.

The rise of the postglobal

The *illusioni* of the epigraph—the 'illusions', as Mario Deaglio puts it, of global economic growth as a panacea for the world's social ills—were of course never a universally held *sogno* or dream.[2] The idea that globalization was ever intended to transform the lives of migrant labourers and other subalterns in any meaningful way remains at best questionable, just as the 'civilizing mission' rhetoric of colonization proved hollow in its day. The hegemony of the neoliberal paradigm known as globalization over the past two decades—the idea, in short, that globalization is good for everyone, from London CEOs to Chinese rice farmers—has thus not gone uncontested. And for good reason. As the aftermath of each of the global cataclysms of the last decade have amply illustrated, it is the poor, the disenfranchised and marginalized who are most vulnerable to the vicissitudes of increasingly volatile global markets and bear the brunt of the suffering when things inevitably go wrong.

As Saskia Sassen points out, in our global cities these 'disadvantaged workers' are disproportionately 'women, immigrants, and people of color, whose political sense of self and whose identities are not necessarily embedded in the "nation" or the "national community"'.[3] Similarly, Mohammed Bamyeh explains that the much-trumpeted denationalization of national territory, while portrayed as a positive, even utopian development by states and global economic organizations and their neoliberal exponents, is not experienced as such by immigrants, visible minorities and other marginalized subjects.[4] This is because it is these latter who experience the anxieties set in motion by the economic, political and cultural changes unleashed by globalization at the level of neighbourhoods and communities. As David Harvey demonstrates, the turn in the 1980s and 1990s towards neoliberal economic policies friendly to globalization has almost without exception resulted in lower wages, increased unemployment, decreased job security and reduced social services for the working poor, a group disproportionately composed of immigrants and minorities.[5] These developments are consistent with Harvey's overarching view of globalization as part of a larger neoliberal project to diminish the power of middle- and working-class groups, and protect that of political and economic elites.[6]

The study of such political, economic and cultural tensions has long been a staple of postcolonial and colonial discourse studies. What I will call the

2 Ibid.
3 Saskia Sassen, *Globalization and Its Discontents* (New York: New Press 1998), xxi.
4 See Mohammed A. Bamyeh, *The Ends of Globalization* (Minneapolis: University of Minnesota Press 2000), esp. 20–1 and 34–45.
5 David Harvey, *A Brief History of Neoliberalism* (Oxford: Oxford University Press 2005), 75–6 and 96–8.
6 Ibid., 19, 29–38.

'postglobal', however, diverges from the postcolonial in that it is glimpsed precisely at those moments when globalization as a hegemonic discourse stumbles, when it experiences a crisis or setback. Since the rise of globalization during the 1980s and 1990s, its forces and proponents have suffered a series of such setbacks that have postponed, if not entirely derailed, the neoliberal dream of an integrated world regulated only by the global market and global capital, which, as Harvey explains,

> should then deliver higher living standards to everyone. Under the assumption that 'a rising tide lifts all boats', or of 'trickle down', neoliberal theory holds that the elimination of poverty (both domestically and worldwide) can best be secured through free markets and free trade.[7]

These setbacks include the Asian, Russian and Brazilian economic crises of 1997–8; the end of the US market boom in 2000; the attack on the World Trade Center on 11 September 2001; the exposed multibillion-dollar scams of Enron and other major corporations, culminating in their collapse; the Argentine fiscal crisis; and the recent and current crises and infrastructural meltdowns in Iraq and New Orleans.[8] With the possible exception of pictures and video images associated with the occupation of Iraq, the most indelible single image from the above list is arguably that of an airplane slamming into one or other of the Twin Towers on 9/11. Of all these events, then, 9/11 provides the most concise, visceral signifier to date of the failures of neoliberalism and globalization.

What is extraordinary, yet perhaps not surprising, about the recent outpouring of literary responses to 9/11 is the utter lack of attention to precisely those groups Sassen identifies as having most to lose under globalization: women, immigrants, visible minorities, the poor generally. Recently published fictions by Joyce Carol Oates, Ian McEwan, Reynolds Price and others present 9/11-related stories in which the protagonists are invariably white and affluent; in Frédéric Beigbeder's widely celebrated *Windows on the World*, a divorced father is having breakfast with his sons in that famed restaurant, located on the 107th floor of the World Trade Center, on the fateful morning, hardly the face of proletarian struggle.[9] Yet most of the immediate victims of 9/11, in arguably the most multicultural city in the

7 Ibid., 64–5 and, for a fuller exposition of the neoliberal model, 64–7.
8 See Deaglio, *Postglobal*, viii.
9 See, respectively, Joyce Carol Oates, 'The Mutants', in Joyce Carol Oates, *I Am No One You Know: Stories* (New York: Ecco 2004), 281–8; Ian McEwan, *Saturday* (New York: Nan A. Talese 2005); Reynolds Price, *The Good Priest's Son: A Novel* (New York: Scribner 2005); and Frédéric Beigbeder, *Windows on the World: A Novel*, trans. from the French by Frank Wynne (New York: Miramax 2005). For reviews of these texts, placing them in the specific context of post-9/11 literature, see James Wood, 'On A darkling plain' (review of McEwan's *Saturday*), *New Republic*, 14 April 2005; and Edward Wyatt, 'After a long wait, literary novelists address 9/11', *New York Times*, 7 March 2005, E1.

world, would much more closely resemble Sassen's discontents than Beigbeder's dining dad.

In this essay I will focus on a novel that I believe heralds the emergence of a new postglobal literature, one that captures the experience of globalization not from the rarefied heights of Windows on the World but from the streets of London's Banglatown: Monica Ali's *Brick Lane*. It is too soon yet to attempt any critical project as vainglorious as a definition or poetics of these nascent literatures that I will collectively call 'postglobal'. The future of postglobal literature remains to be written, as does the future of this uncertain time of the crisis of globalization. We can, however, begin to identify texts that stand in a different relationship to globalization and its aftermath, texts that begin to capture something of the anxieties and fears of this time. Let us then provisionally agree to label as 'postglobal literature' those writings that 1) are produced in the aftermath of 9/11, 2) contain either manifest or latent material informed by 9/11 and other globally felt crises, or that directly or indirectly refer to these and, most importantly, 3) *focus on the lives and struggles of those most exposed to the vicissitudes of globalization and its impact on the world's subalterns, especially those living in global urban centres.*

Of the three parameters I propose, the first is both the most self-explanatory and the most arbitrary. As with postcolonial and globalization studies, critics differ widely on the starting-point for these 'periods', and indeed on whether to consider them as historical categories or periods at all.[10] Also, such a reliance on 9/11 as a central trope of the postglobal might rightly be criticized as yet another recentring of the West and/or the United States, along the lines of earlier critiques of postcolonial studies. Yet, just as Columbus's first arrival in the so-called New World arguably embodies an entire myth of origin for the cultural logic of colonization, an epistemic break that we can retroactively read as the beginning of a new era, so can 9/11 serve as globalization's mythic before-after moment: The Day When Everything Changed. As we have already seen, the second requirement above has already been fulfilled in an obvious way by recent fiction specifically and directly addressing 9/11. Such references, however, need not be thematic or obvious, and to some degree even post-9/11 writings that are otherwise utterly disconnected from current events cannot escape some latent relation to that event, no matter how circuitous or repressed. To cite possibly the most absurd example, even the latest Harry Potter novel has been found by

---

10 Regarding postcolonialism's 'start date', see, for example, Alfred J. López, *Posts and Pasts: A Theory of Postcolonialism* (Albany: State University of New York Press 2001), 17 and 40–1; Robert J. C. Young, *Postcolonialism: An Historical Introduction* (Oxford: Blackwell 2001), 182–92; and Ella Shohat, 'Notes on the "post-colonial"', *Social Text*, no. 31/2, Spring 1992, 99–113 (103). For a representative range of historical frames for globalization, see Anthony Giddens, *Runaway World: How Globalisation Is Reshaping Our Lives* (New York: Routledge 2000), 28; Malcolm Waters, *Globalization*, 2nd edn (London: Routledge 2001), 1–3; and Deaglio, *Postglobal*, 17–32.

reviewers, among them Michiko Kakutani, to contain a 'dark' and 'unsettling' quality attributable to a post-9/11 sensibility:

> [The] terrible things that Ms. Rowling describes as being abroad in the green and pleasant land of England read like a grim echo of events in our own post-9/11, post-7/7 world and an uncanny reminder that the Hogwarts Express, which Harry and his friends all take to school, leaves from King's Cross station—the very station where the suspected London bombers gathered minutes before the explosions that rocked the city nine days ago.[11]

Thus one could no doubt argue for a latent post-9/11 'sensibility' in practically any fiction published after the fall of the Twin Towers, although the demonstration of such an argument would be both time-consuming and not terribly relevant for my own interests here.

What *is* central to my understanding of a nascent postglobal literature, however, is the third of my proposed characteristics: the representation of an emergent global urban subaltern, and narratives that offer a glimpse into the marginalized subjectivity and agency of—in the terms of Mariano Azuela's classic novel of the Mexican revolution, *Los de abajo*, the underdogs—those who have experienced globalization from the bottom.[12] Reading the events of 9/11 in this context also serves to shift our understanding of it away from the increasingly apocalyptic arguments that have mobilized 9/11 as the centrepiece of a 'war on terror' serving to advance and consolidate the dominance of the United States around the world, and towards its lingering political and cultural impact on global subalterns.[13] Postglobal literature, in

---

11 Michiko Kakutani, 'Harry Potter works his magic again in a far darker tale', *New York Times*, 16 July 2005, 1. See also Mary Newsom, 'Review: "Half-Blood Prince" delights, frightens', *Charlotte Observer*, 21 July 2005.

12 Mariano Azuela, *Los de abajo: novela de la revolución mexicana* [1916] (Mexico City: Fondo de Cultura Económica 1992).

13 As an example of the kind of heated apocalyptic rhetoric that has abounded in the aftermath of 9/11, and which the political right has trotted out at every opportunity to justify its invasion of Iraq, note US Vice President Dick Cheney's response, before a national television audience two years after the events of 9/11, to the question of whether Americans have 'recovered' from 9/11: 'And in a sense, sort of the theme that comes through repeatedly for me is that 9/11 changed everything. It changed the way we think about threats to the United States. It changed about our recognition of our vulnerabilities. It changed in terms of the kind of national security strategy we need to pursue, in terms of guaranteeing the safety and security of the American people. And I'm not sure everybody has made that transition yet. I think there are a number of people out there who hope we can go back to pre-9/11 days and that somehow 9/11 was an aberration. It happened one time; it'll never happen again. But the president and I don't have that luxury.' Such language has become typical of the ways in which the events of 9/11 have been used in its aftermath to justify US military aggression in the Middle East, and the so-called war on terror more generally; NBC News, 'Transcript for Sept. 14: Sunday, September 14, 2003 GUEST: Dick Cheney, vice president Tim Russert, moderator', 7 September 2003, www.msnbc.msn.com/id/3080244/ (viewed 14 July 2008).

short, is about those who live under what Joseph Stiglitz correctly calls 'global governance without global government': people far removed from the machinations of power and wealth, people whose lives are shaped by the policies of world organizations but have no chance at all to respond and be heard.[14] As Sassen suggests, these groups form informal 'unofficial' economies and subcultures based on ethnic or religious or national identification, and they go about their lives *without* many of the advertised wonders and benefits of globalization even as they bear the brunt of its costs in real human (economic, political) terms. The new postglobal paradigm does not at all resemble Anthony Giddens's master opposition of 'fundamentalism against cosmopolitan tolerance', a view that exposes Giddens's own neoliberal allegiances (to the 'cosmopolitans' as the unquestioned good guys) and oversimplifies matters by ignoring how each of his master terms exists in both the pro- and anti-globalization camps.[15] The novel I offer as an avatar of the new postglobal literature, *Brick Lane*, does not allow for such a simple analysis of the world.

Brick Lane fits the above criteria quite well, portraying a process of globalization that, according to Teresa Brennan, '*substitutes speed and space for time*'.[16] Brennan's argument that global capital transcends time with speed and space in order to overcome the limitations of local resources—and undermine the demands of labour—are strongly pertinent to Ali's novel, particularly in the latter's portrayal of the characters' relations to globalization. As Brennan explains:

> A multinational corporation can, after all, pay less in taxes somewhere else, and get labor and raw materials there as well. It does not have to wait for them to regrow (in the case of many natural raw materials) or simply grow up (in the case of people). Nor does it have to wait for them to rest and repair themselves. Waiting takes time. Crossing the globe to get labor and raw materials cuts that time. If it saves money, there is even less reason to wait. Reversing the course of globalization ... means focusing on how *globalizing capital substitutes speed and space for time*.[17]

Of course the process by which the 'speed and space' of global capital displaces time also works the other way around, in the form of immigrant

---

14 Joseph E. Stiglitz, *Globalization and Its Discontents* (New York: W. W. Norton 2002), 21.

15 Giddens, *Runaway World*, 22.

16 Teresa Brennan, *Globalization and Its Terrors: Daily Life in the West* (London: Routledge 2003), 11. Brennan's argument leans heavily on both Fredric Jameson's and David Harvey's descriptions of postmodernism in precisely these terms. See Fredric Jameson, *Postmodernism, or, the Cultural Logic of Late Capitalism* (Durham, NC: Duke University Press 1991), 1–54, and David Harvey, *The Condition of Postmodernity: An Enquiry into the Origins of Cultural Change* (Oxford and Cambridge, MA: Blackwell 1990), 201–307.

17 Brennan, *Globalization and Its Terrors*, 11.

labour that comes to the global city in search of the better life it cannot afford to wait for in their own countries: places that often have had their own economies undermined by precisely the same logics of neoliberal capital that rule the global cities to which they migrate. Ali's *Brick Lane* chronicles the impact of globalization in terms of the ongoing struggle between speed/ space and time in the lives of its characters. The novel's depiction of the way that faraway political and economic events have an impact on the lives of its immigrant characters—culminating in its protagonists' responses to and lives after the attacks of 9/11—provide arguably the best fictional presentation yet of how that cataclysmic event, and the onset of the postglobal generally, is having an impact on the lives of those on the bottom.

Further, Ali's novel crosses over into the postglobal where those of Beigbeder *et al.* do not precisely because it demonstrates that the most tangible evidence on the ground of Brennan's process unfolding in the post-9/11 West is not only how immigrants and other vulnerable inhabitants of the nation confront the perils of globalization in their own lives, but their rapidly growing presence among the native populace. The transformation of society in global cities such as London and New York does not follow a logical *temporal* sequence, that is, as part of a generational process. Instead, the rapidity with which immigrant populations have exploded in these and other cities across North America and Europe defies time and collapses space and distance in a manner that echoes Brennan's description of global capital, a perhaps unforeseen (but not unforeseeable) counter-development. Novels such as *Brick Lane,* and more recently Kiran Desai's *The Inheritance of Loss* and Gary Shteyngart's *Absurdistan,*[18] succeed in portraying the polyglot dystopia of the postglobal world because they foreground those subjects most immediately impacted by it.

Still, even if we can provisionally identify *who* is postglobal, there remains the question of producing and/or discovering postglobal *cultures* that would enable or generate a postglobal politics and economics of inclusion and enfranchisement for those left out of the globalization rush. What will define the postglobal, in other words, is less a particular method or thesis than a *condition*: if not a common history of living under globalization then a shared state or condition of having to live under its rule (and rules) and survive. *Brick Lane*, I believe, provides an important glimpse into that future, or at least one possibility for reading and writing it.

In postglobal fictions such as *Brick Lane* a colonial legacy and history of conquest, with all its racial and cultural stratifications, undeniably plays a major role in the narrative. Such novels function as a sort of ironic *Bildungsroman*, one that paradoxically measures the subaltern protagonist's progress in terms of the chasm that remains between their aspirations and the ways in which they remain marginalized as subjects. The *Bildungsroman* captures the

---

18 Kiran Desai, *The Inheritance of Loss* (New York: Atlantic Monthly Press 2005); Gary Shteyngart, *Absurdistan* (New York: Random House 2006).

struggles of the young protagonist as she or he comes of age and into self-knowledge within a society that mediates, and often hinders, their progress.[19] It also depicts the growth of not only the protagonist's social and economic success but also their personal agency, of empowerment over, or at least coexistence with, the larger forces that have acted upon them over the course of the text. The *Bildungsroman* thus functions as a narrative of subject formation and struggle, both processes immanent to the immigrant and subaltern experience. What renders the immigrant *Bildungsroman* ironic is the impossibility in most cases of its protagonists achieving their personal *Bildung*, as they strive for reconciliation with a society that for myriad reasons (the immigrant's status as 'unwanted' surplus labour, as political scapegoat, as racial and cultural Other) always denies them full integration into the national corpus.

The crucial difference in *Brick Lane*, and what distinguishes it as a *postglobal Bildungsroman*, lies in the subject also reckoning with the *additional* impact of globalization as an economic, political and cultural force upon her life and the imperative of continuing to live and struggle in its aftermath. The extent to which the protagonist of this new postglobal *Bildungsroman* succeeds in this reckoning with globalization largely determines their burgeoning sense of self-empowerment as a subject, that is, of their individual *agency* in the face of the larger forces that would suppress and manage (if not completely destroy) them.

Brick Lane and postglobal agency

Brick Lane's defining postglobal characteristics are its sense of subaltern agency, and the quiet way in which its protagonist and those around her doggedly carry on in the face of their reluctant host nation's hostility or, at best, malignant neglect. In this essay I am thus less interested in offering a comprehensive reading of the novel than in examining how the narrative becomes the sort of ironic postglobal *Bildungsroman* I describe in the previous section. Crucial to the narrative structure of a *Bildungsroman* is its depiction of the lifelong relation and interaction between the protagonist's personal history and the economic, political and cultural context in which that history unfolds. That context acts as an impersonal mediating force on the individual, constantly subjecting her to the influence and power of the larger forces that shape her life. By tracing the protagonist's development and growth in her struggles with her adopted society, the narrative parodies the conventions of the *Bildungsroman* while paradoxically revealing only the

---

19 For fuller discussions of the *Bildungsroman*'s efficacy as an ethnic or immigrant narrative, see Annie O. Eysturoy, *Daughters of Self-Creation: The Contemporary Chicana Novel* (Albuquerque: University of New Mexico Press 1996), 3–28, and Martin Japtok, *Growing Up Ethnic: Nationalism and the Bildungsroman in African American and Jewish American Fiction* (Iowa City: University of Iowa Press 2005), 2–28.

protagonist's failure to reach a sense of full empowerment or at least reconciliation with that society.[20] As several critics of ethnic and immigrant *Bildungsromane* have observed, it is paradoxically the *impossibility* of the protagonist's complete reconciliation with the racist or otherwise oppressive society that defines subaltern variations on the traditional *Bildungsroman*.[21]

Appropriately for a postglobal *Bildungsroman*, then, *Brick Lane* is largely a narrative of *agency*: indeed, a depiction of subaltern agency and determination. What distinguishes *Brick Lane* from any number of other such explorations in postcolonial narratives is the horizon towards which that agency sets itself. The diverging directions in which the novel's characters ultimately decide to move exemplify the choice facing so many of globalization's discontents today: to strive towards an incomplete *rapprochement* with an at best ambivalent adopted nation, or to enter into a struggle to the death against it. This terrorist struggle to the death is not explicable through either Hegel's 'Lordship and Bondage' dialectic or later revisions of it by Sartre, Fanon and others, all of which are more or less reducible to the combatants' battle for recognition (*Anerkennen*) as the ground of subjectivity.[22] Rather, it represents a move for the disenfranchised *away* from the desire for recognition entirely, as they engage the Other in the name of an Imaginary (in the Lacanian sense) relation and desire for union with God. This opting out of the dialectic, I believe, means that the terrorist and insurgent are fighting for completely different stakes than the western subject. Given the radical way in which this otherwise conventionally structured *Bildungsroman* presents agency in terms of the choices faced by its characters, the recent flap over the novel's representation of Bangladeshis as well as some prominent scholars' questioning of its author's ethnic and feminist credentials—controversies exacerbated during the filming and screening of an adaptation in 2006 and 2007, respectively—seems to miss the point entirely. Whether, as Germaine Greer avers, Ali has created characters that would 'appear odd but plausible to a British audience' yet actually constitute 'a defining caricature' of the communities the novel portrays,[23] or, as Salman Rushdie asserts in his pointed rebuke of Greer, the

20 See López, *Posts and Pasts*, 97–101.
21 See, for example, James Holte, 'The representative voice: autobiography and ethnic experience', *MELUS*, vol. 9, no. 2, Summer 1982, 25–46; and Sondra O'Neale, 'Race, sex, and self: aspects of Bildung in select novels by black American women', *MELUS*, vol. 9, no. 4, Winter 1982, 25–37.
22 See G. W. F. Hegel, *Phenomenology of Spirit* [1807], trans. from the German by A. V. Miller (Oxford: Clarendon Press 1977), 111–18; Jean-Paul Sartre, *Being and Nothingness: An Essay on Phenomenological Ontology* [1947], trans. from the French by Hazel E. Barnes (New York: Philosophical Library 1956), 233–51; Frantz Fanon, *Black Skin, White Masks* [1952], trans. from the French by Charles Lam Markmann (New York: Grove Press 1967), 216–22; and Francis Fukuyama, *The End of History and the Last Man* (New York: Free Press 1992), 13–38 and 59–69.
23 Germaine Greer, 'Reality bites', *Guardian*, 24 July 2006.

'ad-feminam sneers' about Ali and Greer's support of them represents 'a kind of double racism [by which] the British-Bangladeshi Ali is denied her heritage and belittled for her Britishness',[24] what is at stake for *Brick Lane*'s characters is neither a monocultural (or acultural) feminist agency grounded in sexual liberation nor one framed within orthodox postcolonial notions of hybridity or of 'speaking for' the subaltern.[25] What positions *Brick Lane* beyond such formulations of agency is its unerring focus on individuals living in the long shadow of globalization, and making daily choices in the aftermath of the failures of neoliberalism

Brick Lane's careful, intimate documentation of a single Bangladeshi immigrant's life runs the entire length of the narrative, beginning with Nazneen's birth in what was then East Pakistan and culminating in her decision to stay in London with her children rather than return to Dhaka with her husband.[26] For present purposes I will focus on two crucial moments in Nazneen's trajectory towards agency. I also want to demonstrate the ways in which the events of 9/11 act quietly on the narrative long before they explicitly appear in the plot. Once the events of 9/11 do explicitly enter the plot, however, they act as a sort of narrative fulcrum on which Nazneen's and the lives of the other characters precariously hang.

The narrative itself employs the word 'agency', to both introduce Nazneen's transformation and qualify it:

> What could not be changed must be borne. And since nothing could be changed, everything must be borne. This principle ruled her life. It was mantra, fettle, and challenge. So that, at the age of thirty-four, after she had been given three children and had one taken away, when she had a futile husband and been fated a young and demanding lover, when for the first time she could not wait for the future to

24 Salman Rushdie, 'Brickbats fly over Brick lane' (letter to the editor), *Guardian*, 29 July 2006.

25 The cited passages do not accurately represent either the heat of the rhetoric surrounding the film adaptation of *Brick Lane* nor the level of invective traded by Greer and Rushdie. In her commentary in the *Guardian*, Greer reproaches Ali for forgetting 'her Bengali, which she would not have done if she had wanted to remember it'; and belittles her Bangladeshi background by reducing it to the night her mother 'met a Bangladeshi man at a dance' and her later decision to '[follow] him when he returned to his job at Dhaka University and [marry] him there'. In his letter to the editor responding to Greer, Rushdie calls her support for the attacks on Ali 'philistine, sanctimonious and disgraceful', comparing it to her refusal to support him during the *fatwa* declared after publication of *The Satanic Verses*. Not to be outdone, Nick Cohen accused Greer of being 'on the side of the book burners' and called Prince Charles 'spineless' for canceling the Royal Film Performance of *Brick Lane* in 2007. Greer, 'Reality bites'; Rushdie, 'Brickbats fly over Brick lane'; and Nick Cohen, 'Prince Charles vs Monica Ali' (blog), 26 September 2007, www.nickcohen.net/?p = 251 (viewed 15 July 2008).

26 See Monica Ali, *Brick Lane: A Novel* (New York: Scribner 2003), 1–4 and 400–2. Further references to this edition will appear parenthetically in the text.

be revealed but had to make it for herself, *she was as startled by her own agency as an infant who waves a clenched fist and strikes itself upon the eye* (5, emphasis added).

The infant metaphor's poignancy (and perhaps patronizing tone) notwith-standing, Nazneen's transformation does not hang on a single moment of agency, but rather on a slow, incremental march towards it. As Paul de Man once observed in his reading of Proust, the text's declaration of itself in and as metaphor conceals the metonymic movement of the actual narrative.[27] In true de Manian fashion, then, the above paragraph's operative metaphor, the child's 'clenched fist', belies the stages of the child's growth and develop-ment of its motor skills that culminate in its ability to clench and wave a fist in the first place. This is the true, if latent, logic of the narrative, which its own metaphor conceals: the climactic moment of agency that so surprises the character will perhaps surprise us as well, *despite* its having been there all along. This point is especially important for understanding the impact of 9/11 in the novel: on the characters on a manifest level, at the point two-thirds of the way through the novel when it arises in the plot, *and* throughout, in a more latent manner, retroactively having an impact on Nazneen's entire progression towards empowerment and agency.

One could plausibly argue that Nazneen's movement towards agency begins with the narrative's first indications of a desire in her for such an agency, perhaps the point at which Nazneen, laying in bed with her sleeping husband, catches herself wishing for a different life: 'Was it not the same as making the wish? If she knew what the wish would be, then somewhere in her heart she had already made it' (7). One could reasonably argue that this is the narrative's first indication of a departure, however slight, from Nazneen's initial belief that 'everything must be borne' (5). Alternately, if we were to privilege the desire for and acquisition of language as the index of agency, we could begin with Nazneen's declaration to her husband Chanu that she wishes to learn English (23); or the moment when she first speaks aloud to Chanu and their dinner guest, joining the conversation and momentarily stunning both men (19). For present purposes, however, I will focus on Nazneen's first venture into the city, an experience that brings her into direct contact for the first time with the world outside her flat, an experience that incorporates both Nazneen's burgeoning, albeit as yet objectless and generalized, desire *and* the manifestation of that desire in her first successful wielding of language. More to the point, it is a scene that stands intimately intertwined with 9/11 and our retroactive knowledge of it, even if that day's events remain safely in the future for Nazneen.

The opening pages of Chapter Three follow Nazneen one weekday morning, as she ventures alone for the first time to the East London beyond her council estate, an impulsive act partly triggered by her growing

27 See Paul de Man, 'Semiology and rhetoric', *Diacritics*, vol. 3, no. 3, Fall 1973, 27–33 (30–1).

desperation over her sister's troubles back in Bangladesh.[28] Nazneen finds herself disoriented, we could say defamiliarized, in this new world of skyscrapers that 'crushed the clouds' and people 'who brushed past her on the pavement ... on a private, urgent mission to execute a precise and demanding plan' (39). One characteristic of the narrative technique known as 'defamiliarization'—*ostranenie* for the Russian Formalists—a staple of magical realism, is that the character's lack of familiarity with her surroundings forces her to describe the unknown in terms of the known; objects familiar to readers may be narrated in such a way as actually to obscure them, thus compelling readers to reconsider things and places that may have been rendered invisible by familiarity. Readers more familiar with urban/metropolitan locations may smile at the idea of comparing a car horn to a muezzin, but their familiarity with the sound of the former (and perhaps latter) does not, I would argue, pre-empt their recognition of the comparison. Defamiliarization thus functions as a kind of metaphoric dissonance, if not precisely metonymy; in this case it is the narrator's or character's culturally alien perception of otherwise perfectly banal objects that forces the reader's reconsideration of them.[29]

Nazneen is initially defamiliarized by almost everything she encounters during her first journey through East London, and the narrative's description of these new objects in terms of images more akin to Nazneen's old Bangladeshi village serves to emphasize how little removed she is from that world. A car horn blares 'like an ancient muezzin ululating painfully, stretching his vocal cords to the limit' (38); a revolving glass door in front of an office building is 'like a glass fan, rotating slowly, sucking people in, wafting others out'; the building itself is so tall as to be 'without end ... Above, somewhere, it crushed the clouds' (39); a man speaks to something inside his jacket 'and it appeared to speak back' (42). All of this narrative defamiliarization serves to emphasize the degree of Nazneen's accomplishment when she is able to adjust to the bewildering new environment enough to interact with others and find her way home, a moment of agency undercut only slightly by her inability to tell her husband about the adventure:

> *Anything is possible.* She wanted to shout it. *Do you know what I did today? I went inside a pub. To use the toilet. Did you think I could do that? I walked mile upon mile, probably around the whole of London, although I did not see the edge of it. And to get home again I went to a restaurant. I found a Bangladeshi restaurant and asked directions. See what I can do!* (45, emphasis in the original).

28 Nazneen undertakes the journey after reading a disturbing letter in which her sister, Hasina, writes that she will leave her abusive husband and 'go away to Dhaka' (41–2).

29 For a more thorough discussion of how defamiliarization works in magical realist fiction, see López, *Posts and Pasts*, 155–64. For an English translation of the Russian Formalist text that coined the term, see Viktor Shklovsky, 'Art as technique' [1917], trans. from the Russian by Lee T. Lemon and Marion J. Reis [1965], in David Lodge (ed.), *Modern Criticism and Theory: A Reader* (London: Longmans 1988), 16–30.

If we return to the narrative's initial description of the skyscraper, however, something more ominous emerges, something that indelibly marks *Brick Lane* as a postglobal text. The description of the skyscraper is thus worth citing in its entirety:

> She looked up at a building as she passed. It was constructed almost entirely of glass, *with a few thin rivets of steel holding it together.* The entrance was like a glass fan, rotating slowly, sucking people in, wafting others out. Inside, on a raised dais, a woman behind a glass desk crossed and uncrossed her thin legs. She wedged a telephone receiver between her ear and shoulder and chewed on a fingernail. Nazneen craned her head back and saw that the glass became as dark as a night pond. The building was without end. Above, somewhere, it crushed the clouds (39, emphasis added).

The defamiliarization that elsewhere functions as a reminder of the character's ignorance here confronts us with our own: we thought those towers were indestructible. The automata of perception had blinded us to the knowledge that really there was so little preventing these buildings from crashing to the ground. And there are so many just like them, ambitious, even vainglorious monuments to global capital, 'constructed almost entirely of glass, with a few thin rivets of steel holding [them] together'. After 9/11 it is difficult not to think of such buildings in precisely the way that Nazneen, the naive, defamiliarized immigrant, sees that skyscraper. Other details correspond vaguely yet disturbingly to the indelible images many of us retain from the events of that day: the stark contrast between the glass door 'rotating slowly, sucking people in, wafting others out' with widely circulated scenes of New Yorkers—far from wafting, far from slowly—leaping or falling to their deaths from tall windows; the woman working calmly behind her desk in the (she believes, as we once did) safety of the building. That the scene in question is set in 1985 lends it an even greater poignancy, as modern globalization was then only beginning its triumphant ascendancy.[30]

My immediate point is that only in a post-9/11 text is such a moment of defamiliarization—even vertigo—possible. Arguably such a post-9/11 sensibility will play an irreducible role in the rise and development of a new postglobal literature. But what casts the entire novel as an important avatar of the new postglobal literature is that this and other such moments of critique strewn throughout the text come to us through the consciousness of a relative *outsider* to globalization. Nazneen is positioned both within, in the sense that she inhabits a global capital city, and without,

---

30 Most commentators agree that globalization as we know it today began its ascendancy during the mid- to late 1980s. See, for example, Giddens, *Runaway World*, 24–37; Deaglio, *Postgobal*, 59–101; and Stiglitz, *Globalization and Its Discontents*, 13–22.

in that she is a marginalized worker and non-citizen within that city; we can truly say of Nazneen's relation to globalization that she is *in* it but not *of* it.

Although *Brick Lane* gains much of its narrative force from the almost imperceptible yet steady driving force of Nazneen's nascent sense of agency, the implications of 9/11 are present from the novel's first pages. For the characters, however, the events of 9/11 come as a profound, even visceral shock, disrupting not only their present situations but also the very horizon of their expectations. Much of the novel's success at building narrative tension, I would argue, stems precisely from the disjunction between our knowledge of the disastrous event that will so irrevocably alter the characters' lives, and our experience of seeing them carrying on in the days leading up to 9/11, each acting out their individual grievances and worries and aspirations in complete ignorance of the utterly transformed world that will so soon be upon them.

In the chapters leading up to 9/11 the narrative focuses on the furious exchange of increasingly incendiary leaflets between the Bengal Tigers, a Muslim activist group led by Nazneen's young lover Karim, and their white reactionary counterparts, the Lion Hearts. Leaflets bearing titles such as 'Multicultural Murder' and 'March against the Mullahs' appear regularly in the estate where the novel's characters live, with the Bengal Tigers responding with pamphlets of their own (204–5, 212, 224–5); and the textual confrontation escalates into mutual announcements of simultaneously planned demonstrations (235–7). The nature of these collective demonstrations, and practically all of the individual characters' plans and projections, are transformed in the wake of the events of 9/11. But one leaflet in particular will resonate most strongly with 9/11 and beyond, even though no one in the book ever mentions it again. Its text contains this:

> A reminder to give thanks to Allah for our brothers who gave up their lives shaheed to defend their brothers ... We give thanks for Farook Zaman who died in the Duba Yurt operations in Chechnya, February 2000. He lived most of his life an unbeliever until he repented and devoted himself to jihad (225).

Chanu's immediate and indignant, but also frightened, response to the leaflet is rooted firmly in the narrative's post-9/11, postglobal sensibility. His visceral reaction to the Arabic word 'shaheed' (martyr) functions in the text as both prophecy and apocalyptic warning of both the looming events of 9/11—unknown, obviously, to the characters—and the fear of the nightmare scenario that such an event would create for Muslims living in a white world: 'Are they mad? Poking these mad letters through white people's doors. Do they want to set flame to the whole place? Do they want us all to die shaheed?' (225). It is precisely that final question, and its implied choice for every Muslim living in the post-9/11 West, that haunts the collective imaginary of its Muslim characters for the rest of the novel: to die *shaheed*, or live among the ruins.

As for so many of us, for the characters of *Brick Lane* 9/11 happens on television. Nazneen's husband Chanu bursts suddenly through the front door:

> He rages around the room looking for the remote control, passing the television several times. Eventually, he switches it on by pressing the button below the screen. 'Oh God', he says. 'The world has gone mad.'
>
> Nazneen glances over at the screen. The television shows a tall building against a blue sky. She looks at her husband.
>
> 'This is the start of the madness', says Chanu. He holds on to his stomach as if he is afraid that someone may snatch it away (304).

So begins Nazneen's dawning awareness that something ominous has happened. As Nazneen continues to watch the incessant replay of the planes flying into the towers, 'straining to comprehend', the sense of defamiliarization that she had largely shed by now returns with a vengeance. She and Chanu stare at the television and its images of death and destruction so long that they 'fall under its spell'. Like the many wondrous yet mysterious objects she encounters on her long-ago first sojourn into London, Nazneen finds the video image of plane and tower 'at once mesmerizing and impenetrable; the more it plays, the more obscure it becomes until Nazneen feels she must shake herself out of a trance' (305). Later, when the entire family watches the images together, Nazneen feels 'as though they have survived something together, as a family' (306).

Yet the question that hangs over this entire scene had already emerged from Chanu's mouth as he raged fearfully against the Bengal Tigers' incendiary newsletter: 'Do they want us all to die shaheed?' (225). As the pace of narrative events accelerates from this point forward, we can see retroactively how Chanu's despairing question anticipates the sudden eruption on 9/11 of a demand on the collective imaginary of *Brick Lane*'s Muslim characters: which possibilities for survival and coexistence might remain for a Muslim in the globalized West and which lay broken in the smoke and rubble of the towers? In short: how to be a Muslim and live in the postglobal North after 9/11?

The narrative offers only the briefest of glimpses of how that life reveals itself to the characters, the most substantial of which is perhaps this passage:

> A pinch of New York dust blew across the ocean and settled on the Dogwood Estate. Sorupa's daughter was the first, but not the only one. Walking in the street, on her way to college, she had her hijab pulled off. Razia wore her Union Jack sweatshirt and it was spat on. 'Now you see what will happen', said Chanu. 'Backlash' (306).

Responses to the post-9/11 backlash against Muslims vary among individuals, but the two most pertinent (because most directly relevant to the novel's protagonist) are those formulated by the two men in Nazneen's life. Chanu revives with some alacrity his family's plan to return to Bangladesh: "'It's time to go'', he told no one in particular and hitched up his stomach, girding himself for action. "Any day, any moment, life can end'" (307). Conversely, Karim embraces confrontation, planning a demonstration to counter one planned by the now-resurgent Lion Hearts: 'Let them come. We'll be ready' (323). Nazneen thus finds herself compelled to choose between two insufficient options: flight or jihad. The choices that Nazneen finally makes, which side with neither of the options that these men have attempted to impose on her, form the crux of the remainder of the narrative, culminating in the emergence of Nazneen's nascent agency and the postglobal feminist consciousness that informs *Brick Lane.* The moment in question offers an advance glimpse of Nazneen's growing dissatisfaction with the respective paths that the two men in her life would have her take. As Nazneen is being lectured (if not hectored) about 9/11 by a strident Karim, she admonishes herself for drifting off into daydreams of *'barbers and pipal trees, as if there is nothing important to think about'* (319). Almost immediately, however, with a quickness and force that presages her more overt acts of agency later on, Nazneen reverses her verdict against herself and redirects her judgment: *'Only my husband and this boy are thinking all the time about New York and terrorists and bombs. Everybody else just living their lives'* (319). From this point forward, the narrative moves inexorably towards a resolution that finally embraces neither jihad nor return, but a quiet, unshakeable resolve to live, remain and prevail.

Appropriately, then, Nazneen's most powerful articulations of her new-found agency emerge as acts of negation: moments when she denies the hegemony of the two men who have sought in different ways to define and reduce her choices and her very subjectivity. Nazneen's final rejection of Karim's proposal of marriage, and her last-minute refusal to follow Chanu back to Bangladesh, influence the course of her life and agency more profoundly than the more overt acts of confronting the usurers from whom Chanu has unwisely borrowed, and braving Brick Lane during the riot in search of her daughter, despite the fact that the latter take up significantly more space in the narrative.[31] While all represent definitive and irrevocable steps towards the agency that the novel presages from its first pages, Nazneen's calm, intimate, firm denial of the hold that Karim and Chanu claimed over her life, and her resolve to stay and live as a single immigrant mother in London rather than submit to a fate without agency, more fully (if

---

31 In terms of page lengths, Nazneen's heroic search for Shahana takes up nearly nine pages (392–400); the showdown with Mrs Islam and her enforcer sons covers over six (369–75); her farewell to Karim takes up a little over four pages (378–82); and the final scene with Chanu barely two (400–2).

less dramatically) portray both Nazneen's precarious sense of agency and all it has had to overcome to come even this far.

Nazneen's choice

By the end of *Brick Lane*, Nazneen has become a fictional exemplar of a process that Sassen describes as 'the incorporation of Third World women into wage employment on a scale that can be seen as representing a new phase in the history of women'.[32] However, much of what is new in characters such as Nazneen, and in novels such as *Brick Lane* generally, could not have been foreseen by Sassen or anyone else writing during globalization's ascendance as a planetary hegemon. By the end of the novel, which spans roughly the rise and fall of globalization as a market utopia (from 1985 to the aftermath of 9/11), Nazneen has survived the surrender and withdrawal of her husband after fifteen years of striving and failing to partake of globalization's promised bounties. She is now part of a small group of self-employed women, all abandoned in some form or another by their men; she exists at the margins of the postglobal urban economy, making a living with her hands. By the novel's end Nazneen has joined what Sassen calls 'a broad range of ... types of workers, types of work cultures, types of residential milieu, never marked, recognized, or represented as being part of globalization processes'.[33]

In working with her friend Razia and the other displaced or abandoned worker women, Nazneen in effect becomes part of a postglobal version of Sassen's 'informal economy', living and working essentially outside of globalization's regulatory framework albeit within its cultural and political grasp.[34] Rather than retreat into a kind of neocolonial bourgeois fantasy life in Bangladesh with her husband, or to 'a mountain cave, surrounded by men in turbans wielding machine guns', as she envisions Karim after his disappearance (409), Nazneen chooses neither jihad nor *shaheed*, not Islam (in the sense of the word's literal meaning of 'submission') or withdrawal. Instead she chooses to remain and prevail in the very belly of the urban global capital, participating in the informal or, as Roger Burbach has called it, the 'postmodern economy' inhabited by those industries and people that global processes have cast off or found superfluous.[35]

Nazneen's final choice to remain as an informal but no less real worker in the postglobal city—and indeed all of her key decisions throughout the

---

32 Sassen, *Globalization and Its Discontents*, 111.
33 Ibid., xxiv.
34 Ibid., 153–72.
35 See Roger Burbach, Orlando Núñez and Boris Kagarlitsky, *Globalization and Its Discontents: The Rise of Postmodern Socialisms* (London: Pluto 1997), 5–7 and 154–6.

novel—stands in instructive contrast with the choices and life trajectory of her sister Hasina, who stayed behind in Bangladesh. Hasina elopes in a love match soon after Nazneen's arranged marriage and departure to London and, after leaving her husband, her life—revealed to both Nazneen and the novel's readers in the form of a sporadic correspondence between the sisters (see, for example, 12–13, 116–41 and 275–80)—becomes a meandering succession of husbands and other men, low-paying jobs and dangerous living arrangements (including a landlord who regularly rapes her). Hasina eventually finds safe but increasingly unstable refuge as a servant in the home of a prominent couple in Dhaka, but continues to lament where her life has led her (for example, 179–85). Although the novel does not comment directly on this implicit comparison, it is through Hasina's letters that readers encounter globalization's impact on the country Nazneen has left, and to which Chanu seeks to return: Hasina's Bangladesh is wracked by environmental degradation, violence (especially domestic violence), abusive labour practices for women and children, even child trafficking. Through Hasina's letters, Chanu's dream of return is exposed as an illusory escape from the now-global wreckage of globalization and its aftermath. Likewise, Nazneen's mental image of Karim as an insurgent 'in a mountain cave' succinctly captures her view of her erstwhile lover as naive to the daily struggles she knows only too well.

With two children to support and an absent husband, Nazneen's only real option for survival is to join the swelling ranks of those in the informal or postmodern economy 'who lurk on the sidelines, seizing those activities that the transnational world decides to dispose of'.[36] The presence of such workers further exemplifies Deaglio's description of the failure of globalization as a utopian master narrative and the arrival of the postglobal era: not merely the fact that globalization has generated discontents at all, but the reality that 'for millions of people globalization has not worked' and has instead '[created] poverty and instability'.[37] By the end of *Brick Lane* Nazneen has has become one of the millions of marginalized urban workers who function outside the global economy, or at least at some remove from it. One could argue that practically the novel's entire cast (with the possible exception of Dr Azad) lives within an ethnic micro-economy within globalized London, whose development we can plot over the course of the narrative. This condition, I would argue, illustrates that much of the informal or postmodern economy that Sassen and Burbach have, respectively, recently celebrated is merely what ethnic and immigrant peoples have always done in order to survive outside of a dominant economy that has excluded and alienated them. What is different this time is the imperative to improvise in the aftermath

36 Ibid., 5.
37 Stiglitz, *Globalization and Its Discontents*, 248; see also Deaglio, *Postglobal*, 11–16.

of a failed globalization that has spit out that which it has proven unable to integrate.

Finally, then, the recognition of the postglobal as a new subaltern literary paradigm leaves us closer to Sassen's description of 'those who lack power but now have "presence"' than to Stiglitz's rosier picture of 'global governance without global government'.[38] The world of *Brick Lane* is populated by those far removed from the machinations of power and wealth, people whose lives are shaped by the policies of world organizations but who have little or no chance to respond and be heard outside of a riot—or the spectacle of a terrorist attack. Some such people go home if they can; others end up in mountain caves wielding rifles, or in a public place with explosives strapped to them. Everybody else—the vast majority—form their informal economies and political and cultural bodies based on ethnic or religious or national identification, and go about their lives without the promised wonders and benefits of globalization even as they bear the brunt of its costs in real human terms every day.

Although *Brick Lane* was published well before the bombings that shook London on 7 July 2005, it proves to have been prescient in its exploration of the challenges that immigrants and people of colour encounter every day in the post-9/11 West. The question is not whether they, especially Muslims, living in global cities such as London, bear any responsibility for the onslaught of globalization and its failures, or even whether the bombers and their ilk see them that way. More to the point, rather, is the novel's eloquent exposition of how much of the multicultural, multi-ethnic face of today's global cities is as irreducibly a part of globalization as the multinational corporations and global treaties more often associated with it. It is my hope that the emergent postglobal literature, by giving prominence to the world's Nazneens, might help in combatting the 'politics of exclusion' that Sassen and others criticize, in which 'political systems and rhetorics ... can only represent and valorize corporate actors as participants' in globalization.[39]

The emergence of the postglobal and its literature of discontents may also contribute to the rethinking of the meaning and constitution of citizenship in the globalized West. The then Mayor of London Ken Livingstone's grand statements in 2005 about London being 'the most multicultural city in the world' where 'everybody lives side by side in harmony'—a line that proved equally useful for pursuing the 2012 Olympic Games and for standing up to terrorists after the 7/7 bombings—belie the fact that immigrants and people of colour have found it increasingly difficult to live as just some of the '7 m1llion

---

38 Sassen, *Globalization and Its Discontents*, xxi; Stiglitz, *Globalization and Its Discontents*, 21.

39 Sassen, *Globalization and Its Discontents*, xx.

LONDONers' cited in the posters that were prominently displayed in London's underground stations in the aftermath of the bombings.[40] In the days following the 7/7 bombings that took the lives of 56 people and injured over 700, Muslims and other minorities expressed fear of reprisals and experienced greater levels of post-traumatic stress.[41] Hundreds of attacks on Muslims were reported in the aftermath of the bombings, ranging from schoolyard beatings to the attempted arson of Muslim homes.[42] That these minorities nevertheless carry on is yet another sign of the emerging postglobal: the realization that although, as Deaglio puts it, the *tempi facili* (easy times) of ascendant globalization may be behind us and *tempi difficili* (difficult times) may be on the way, the struggle for a better life goes on no matter how many skies—or towers—have fallen.[43]

40 Ken Livingstone, 'Why London won its Olympic bid', *The Londoner*, August 2005, 4; see also the website of the (former) Mayor of London's 'We Are London, We Are One' campaign at www.london.gov.uk/onelondon/index.jsp (viewed 15 July 2008). From the beginning of their successful bid to host the 2012 Summer Olympics, London officials worked to characterize London's status as a global multicultural capital as a strength. Statements such as this one from Sally Hamwee, Chair of the London Assembly, are typical of this effort: 'London's greatest asset is its people. Their diversity will be reflected in the Games, which offers a unique opportunity for partnerships to be forged and communities to come together'; quoted in 'We're ready to host the 2012 Olympics', Greater London Authority press release, 6 November 2003, www.london.gov.uk/view_press_release.jsp?releaseid=2086 (viewed 15 July 2008). For images of the London underground poster ('7 million Londoners, 1 London'), see Annie Mole, 'One London ad—seen at Bank Station', 9 August 2005, www.flickr.com/photos/anniemole/32702240; and Tired Fool, 'Here, Harry, isn't that Cat Stevens?' (blog), 2 August 2005, http://rustle.blogsome.com/2005/08/02 (both viewed 30 July 2008).
41 A *British Medical Journal* study found that 32 per cent of Muslims planned to reduce their reliance on public transportation, out of fear not of another bombing but of reprisals by angry white Londoners; 'Bombings "severely stressed" 31%', *BBC News*, 26 August 2005, http://news.bbc.co.uk/1/hi/health/4183712.stm (viewed 12 July 2008).
42 See Mike Ingram, 'British Muslims face increased racist attacks and state harassment', *World Socialist Web Site*, 12 August 2005, www.wsws.org/articles/2005/aug2005/race-a12.shtml (viewed 15 July 2008); and Mike Cole and Alpesh Maisuria, '"Shut the **** up", "you have no rights here": critical race theory and racialisation in post-7/7 racist Britain', *Journal for Critical Education Policy Studies* (online), vol. 5, no. 1, May 2007, www.jceps.com/index.php?pageID=article&articleID=85 (viewed 30 July 2008).
43 Although the terms appear throughout Deaglio's book *Postglobal*, the chapters that feature them most prominently begin on pp. vii and 131.

So what's new? Rethinking the 'new antisemitism' in a global age

JONATHAN JUDAKEN

In February 2006 a young French Jew, Ilan Halimi, was kidnapped and tortured to death by 'les barbares' (the Barbarians), a gang of West-African Muslim racketeers operating in Paris. They believed that because he was Jewish he had to be rich and that, by abducting and tormenting him, they would get paid off. In August that year, a twelve-year-old girl on a bus in

Part of this paper was first presented at the conference 'Global anti-Semitism post 9/11', Maison des science de l'homme, Paris, 8–9 June 2007. I am grateful to the organizers Eric Mielants, Ramon Grosfoguel and especially Lewis Gordon for the invitation to participate. I also want to thank Étienne Balibar, whose very thoughtful comments helped to reshape some of my thoughts. The paper was sharpened by presenting it at Arizona State University, where I was grateful for the comments of, among others, Norbert Samuelson, Hava Tirosh-Samuelson and Arieh Saposnik, and at the University of Virginia, where I was especially grateful to Jennifer Geddes, Alon Confino and Asher Biemann. I also want to thank Törbjorn Wandel, Anne Reef and Kent Schull for their input.

London was kicked unconscious and robbed after her attackers asked if she was Jewish or English. In December, the so-called 'International Conference to Review the Global Vision of the Holocaust' was convened in Teheran, where President Mahmoud Ahmadinejad predicted that 'the Zionist regime will be wiped out soon'. In May 2007 arsonists heavily damaged Hekhal Haness, Geneva's largest synagogue. These incidents illustrate what the statistics make plain: the troubling rise of global antisemitism in the new millennium.[1]

In this essay, which has two parts, our task is to assess critically the phenomenon dubbed by many the 'new antisemitism'. There are seven main points that I will develop. First, I insist that the so-called 'new antisemitism' is not new in two senses. Notably, following every crisis that has marked the Arab-Israeli conflict since the Six Day War, there have been books or articles by activists or scholars with similar titles and basically the same arguments, insisting on what Abraham Foxman called in the subtitle of his 2003 work 'The Threat of the New Anti-Semitism'. Indeed, not only Foxman's title but also his assessment drew heavily on work by the former heads of the Anti-Defamation League, Arnold Forster and Benjamin Epstein, published in 1973 and called simply *The New Anti-Semitism*. Foster and Epstein's book itself rested on scholarship that was already being published in 1968.[2] Moreover,

---

1 There are many problems with data collection on incidents of antisemitism, not least being how 'antisemitism' is defined. This very definition is at the heart of the clashes about the significance of antisemitism today. Related to this issue is how to characterize different types of occurrences and the matter of reporting or lack of reporting as well as how to gauge this against the rise of other 'hate crimes'. There is no universally followed methodology in this area, although international watchdog organizations, like the European Union Monitoring Committee on Antisemitism (now the European Union Agency for Fundamental Rights, FRA), are working to establish more uniform criteria. The Stephen Roth Institute for the Study of Contemporary Antisemitism and Racism is one monitoring institution that publishes current comparative data. In *Antisemitism Worldwide 2006* they reported that antisemitic incidents that year reached the highest level of physical, verbal and visual manifestations since 2000, with Australia, Canada, the United Kingdom, France and South Africa among others all witnessing new highs. On the whole, antisemitic violence has seen a sevenfold increase from 1989 to the present and there has been a disturbing increase in the number of attacks on individuals as opposed to earlier incidents that targeted Jewish institutions. For the most up to date statistics, see the online report, Dina Porat and Esther Webman (eds), *Antisemitism Worldwide 2007: General Analysis*, www.tau.ac.il/Anti-Semitism/asw2007/gen-analysis-07.pdf (viewed 17 July 2008). It concludes: 'The year 2007 witnessed mixed tendencies: on the one hand, a decrease in antisemitic activity of all kinds in several countries and, on the other, a rise in violent incidents, and especially major attacks. Sometimes both trends were evident in the same country. A decline in overall numbers was monitored in France, Belgium, Germany, South Africa, the UK and the US; however, in France, Germany, the UK and the US antisemitic violence rose, in some cases substantially.'
2 Abraham Foxman, *Never Again? The Threat of the New Anti-Semitism* (San Francisco: HarperSanFrancisco 2003); Arnold Forster and Benjamin R. Epstein, *The New Anti-Semitism* (New York: McGraw-Hill 1974).

none of the strands said to characterize the new antisemitism—Holocaust denial, the antisemitism of the extreme left, antisemitism in the Islamic world, anti-Zionism as antisemitism, even anti-racism as antisemitism—are new. Each goes back at least as far as June 1967, if not to the Holocaust itself, and several of these vectors of transmission have much deeper roots.

Second, this article is animated by a frustration at the fact that both critics and defenders of the state of Israel are so infused by their respective partisan divisions that every intellectual resource is mobilized to suffocate the voices of their enemies with the result that the truths of each side cannot be heard. With that said, the paper does not seek to take a middle ground. Rather, as Senator Patrick Daniel Moynihan is supposed to have said, while everyone is entitled to their own opinions, they are not entitled to their own facts. In this spirit, I draw on the analysis of a wide variety of scholars and interlocutors in the discussion across the political spectrum in order that the positions on all sides are articulated even as my own authorial stamp will clearly demarcate where I stand in the various sub-debates within the clamour on the new antisemitism.

Third, the paper is a reaction against the homogenizing, hyperbolic, sometimes paranoid construction of what discussants of the new antisemitism have described as a new set of *coalitions* that are said to be emerging. Roger Cukierman, the former president of the Conseil représentatif des institutions juives de France (CRIF), put this most famously when he indicated that a new 'red-green-brown alliance' was now animating anti-Jewish hostility. The suggestion of many commentators is that a political alignment is coalescing made up of leftists, greens and jihadists all working in tandem, for which there is little evidence. As part of this homogenizing discourse, an undifferentiated 'left' or an undifferentiated 'Europe' as monolithically antisemitic or anti-Israel is often invoked. To the extent that such constructs emerge in the fight against antisemitism, they are phantasms. As such, we need to assess the political agenda behind their construction. We also need to evaluate the extent to which this helps to feed the new Judaeophobia rather than serve the fight against it. Since, without properly describing and evaluating what we seek to curtail, we cannot satisfactorily hope to oppose it.

Fourth, I maintain that while there is no direct causal correlation between the social facts producing antisemites and the social acts of antisemitism, they cannot be separated wholesale. There is a relation between the Arab-Israeli conflict and the experience of Muslims in Europe and a relationship between the history of western incursions into the Middle East and the rise of antisemitism in the Arab and Islamic world. To analyse antisemitic acts, we must take the social conditions that give rise to them into account and do so within a global optic. Today this entails comprehending how what happens in Palestine becomes a symbolic filter through which the concrete experience of Muslims in Europe and elsewhere is given meaning and internalized, and also how the Palestinian intifada has become a globalized symbol for the throwing off of the shackles of oppression elsewhere.

Fifth, the formula that 'anti-Zionism is antisemitism' is too simplistic. It is an analytically blunt tool that often only serves the political ends of those who sympathize with the canard that 'Zionism is racism'. These charges are mirror-images of each other. As we will see, one motor of the new Judaeophobia is the rhetorical polemics that reduce the contemporary situation to sound-bites and symbols. It is not only those who disseminate Judaeophobic notions, but also the warriors combatting them, who engage in such reduction. Polemics (etymologically from *polemikos*) are the discourse of war: they are about defining enemies. Those interested in dampening down antisemitism have got to consider the ways in which rhetorical warfare feeds the very phenomenon it seeks to 'combat'.

Sixth, definitional approaches like those pursued by Natan Sharansky or analytic assessments like the one undertaken by Bernard Harrison in *The Resurgence of Anti-Semitism* prove facile in their effort to interpret a phenomenon that requires more nuanced interpretations.[3] I find more penetrating resources in the dialectical approaches of Jean-Paul Sartre and the Frankfurt School or in the historical investigations of Léon Poliakov.

Finally, I want in this essay to contribute to a better delineation of what is truly new. To this end, Pierre-André Taguieff's notion of a 'new Judaeophobia' makes more sense because anti-Jewish sentiments and actions are no longer based on racialized arguments akin to those deployed during the Dreyfus Affair or by the Nazis. They are based on cultural and religious and political claims, often articulated in a specifically anti-racist idiom.

So we begin by interrogating what's new in '*la nouvelle judéophobie*', as Taguieff has most fittingly called it. In the first part of the paper, 'Old news', I maintain that the often-homogenizing account of the new Judaeophobia needs to be understood in terms of the varied traditions that animate it, and that none of these traditions are new. Here, I dissect the five key vectors in the transmission of the new Judaeophobia and provide a brief historical overview of their origins and development. My point in outlining them is not to provide a comprehensive overview of each, but to make clear that none of these vectors are new. At the same time, I highlight what is novel in each area. In the second part, 'Reflections on the new Judaeophobia', I draw on the work of Judith Butler, Jean-Paul Sartre, and the Frankfurt School to reflect on antisemitism in the age of globalization. With Butler, I wrestle with the necessity and difficulty of distinguishing between anti-Zionism and antisemitism. If we can conceptually pull these terms apart, I show, following Sartre, how anti-racist anti-Zionism can nonetheless reinscribe

---

3 I discuss Natan Sharansky below. See Bernard Harrison, *The Resurgence of Anti-Semitism: Jews, Israel, and Liberal Opinion* (Lanham, MD: Rowman and Littlefield 2006). For a full exposition of Harrison's work, see Jonathan Judaken, '*Homo antisemiticus*: lessons and legacies', *Holocaust and Genocide Studies* (forthcoming).

the logic of racism. I conclude on a dissonant note from the Frankfurt School, explaining why antisemitism might be on the rise in an era when there are supposedly no more antisemites.

Old news

As has been the case throughout the life of what Robert Wistrich has dubbed 'the longest hatred',[4] there are continuities and breaks over the course of the history of antisemitism. When scholars and analysts discuss the new antisemitism, they often point to a burgeoning *alliance* that is said to cohere in producing the new wave of rhetorical outbursts, violent acts and vicious incidents that make the period from September 2000 (the beginning of the Second Intifada) to the present unprecedented in terms of post-Holocaust hostility towards Jews and Judaism. A 'frightening coalition of anti-Jewish sentiment is forming on a global scale', writes Abraham Foxman.[5] 'The new anti-Semitism', warns Phyllis Chesler, 'is being waged on many fronts—mili-military, propaganda, political, and economic—throughout the world'.[6]

The troops amassed in this war against the Jews come from very different armies, however. As Leon Wieseltier puts it:

> The taxonomy of present-day anti-Semitism is ominously large. There are religious varieties and secular varieties; theological varieties; political varieties and cultural varieties; old varieties and new varieties. There is the anti-Semitism of Christians, which comes in many forms, and the anti-Semitism of Muslims, which comes in many forms. There is the anti-Semitism of the Right, in Europe and in the United States, still stubbornly blaming the Jews for modernity ... and there is the anti-Semitism of the Left, most recently seeking shelter (and finding it) in the antiglobalization movement, which has presided over a revival of the New Left's dogmas about capitalism and liberalism and Americanism. And there is the anti-Semitism that manifests itself as anti-Zionism.[7]

Omer Bartov adds to this long list by suggesting that there are antisemitic voices among a diversity of social groups, including 'the rabble and the leaders ... terrorists and intellectuals, students and peasants, pacifists and militants, expansionists and antiglobalization activists'.[8] Indeed, the claim

---

4 Robert S. Wistrich, *Antisemitism: The Longest Hatred* (New York: Schocken Books 1991).
5 Foxman, *Never Again*, 274.
6 Phyllis Chesler, *The New Anti-Semitism: The Current Crisis and What We Must Do about It* (San Francisco: Jossey-Bass 2003), 245.
7 Leon Wieseltier, 'Old demons, new debates', in David I. Kertzer (ed.), *Old Demons, New Debates: Anti-Semitism in the West* (Teaneck, NJ: Holmes and Meier 2005), 1–8 (1).
8 Omer Bartov, 'The new anti-Semitism: genealogy and implications', in Kertzer (ed.), *Old Demons, New Debates*, 9–26 (11).

that there is a new modality of anti-Jewish hatred—a new epoch in the long history of antisemitism—depends on the notion that these very different groups are coalescing around antisemitism, and that this is what is causing the undeniable rise in antisemitic violence and attacks globally.

But, to begin with, as a label, the term the 'new antisemitism' is flawed in several ways. Even if one grants some shared discourse among these very different actors,[9] Taguieff is right to insist on calling this a new 'Judaeopho-bia' as opposed to 'antisemitism' for several reasons. In the first place, as he says:

> Post-Nazi Judeophobia is grounded not upon the vulgar racialist theories of the late nineteenth century, with their myth of a 'race war' between two imaginary constructs, 'Semites' and 'Aryans,' but upon a set of cultural and political elements quite different from those characterizing the anti-Semitism of the Dreyfus Affair or the state racism of the National Socialists.[10]

The new Judaeophobia, unlike antisemitism, is not premised on the Aryan myth or biological racism, white supremacy or ultra-populist ethno-nationalism. Indeed, it is often explicitly articulated in terms of an anti-racist agenda. Secondarily, there are some Muslims who sometimes defend their hostile defamation of Jews, their denigration of Judaism or their demonization of Israel with a standard sophism that claims that they cannot be antisemites since Arabs are 'Semites' too. This is patently nonsense since, of course, while there are Semitic languages, there is no such entity as a Semitic people and 'Semitism' is itself the illusory construct on which racial antisemitism was established. So to make the assertion that there are 'Semites' or a Semitic people is to buy into the racism on which antisemitism was grounded.[11]

---

9 As I argue in detail below, Brian Klug is justified in questioning the extent to which 'there is a single unified phenomenon, a "new anti-Semitism"'; Brian Klug, 'The myth of the new anti-Semitism', *The Nation*, 2 February 2004. Steven Beller puts it more forcefully: 'it is my view that the hyperbolic rhetoric and paranoia that produces such a Manichaean world-view on the part of so many Americans and Jews is not only wildly inaccurate and unhelpful. It is actively working, intentionally or not, to destroy the great promise of that moment after 1967'; Steven Beller, 'In Zion's hall of mirrors: a comment on *Neuer Antisemitismus*', *Patterns of Prejudice*, vol. 41, no. 2, May 2007, 215–38 (217).

10 Pierre-André Taguieff, *Rising from the Muck: The New Anti-Semitism in Europe*, trans. from the French by Patrick Camiller (Chicago: Ivan R. Dee 2004), 11.

11 It is for this reason that it really makes no sense to hyphenate antisemitism as is often done in English. On this point, see Shmuel Almog, 'What's in a hyphen', *SICSA Report: The Newsletter of the Vidal Sassoon International Center for the Study of Antisemitism*, Summer 1989, 1–2n2. There is only one sound motive for continuing the practice of hyphenation and that is if the hyphen were a sign of the vestige of the shared

As Paul Iganski and Barry Kosmin point out, therefore, there is a 'semantic flaw' within in the very notion of antisemitism.[12] Consequently, in our discussion of antisemitism, we cannot afford to be anti-semantic.[13] This flaw is compounded by the ways in which 'antisemitism' is currently used as a term to cover everything from prejudices, biases or stereotypes about Jews and Judaism to a causal factor in the genocide of European Jewry. 'Antisemitism' also occludes the distinctions between different epistemic configurations and the differing social forces that were and are at work in ancient Judaeophobia, what Zygmunt Bauman calls the 'contestant enmity' of the *adversos Judaeos* tradition of the early Christian church,[14] the diabolical anti-Judaism of the mediaeval church, the secularization of Jew-hatred that created antisemitism *per se* and the current neo-Judaeophobia.[15] The use of the single term 'antisemitism', therefore, often stifles discussion, skews conversations and leads to misunderstandings of the issue.

The new Judaeophobia is racialist, but not racist, rooted in cultural and religious arguments that are nonetheless sometimes as dogmatically essentialist as their racist predecessors and that often characterize Jews

opprobrium cast upon Jews and Muslims in the discourse of Orientalism and as a signifier of the overlaps between Orientalist and antisemitic constructions. On these links, see Ivan Davidson Kalmar and Derek J. Pensler (eds), *Orientalism and the Jews* (Waltham, MA: Brandeis University Press/ Hanover, NH: University Press of New England 2005). See also Gil Anidjar, *The Jew, the Arab: A History of the Enemy* (Stanford, CA: Stanford University Press 2003) and Gil Anidjar, *Semites: Race, Religion, Literature* (Stanford, CA: Stanford University Press 2008). Nonetheless, the hyphen and (mis) spelling will stand as printed in all citations and quotations of the work of others.

12 Paul Iganski and Barry Kosmin (eds), *A New Antisemitism? Debating Judeophobia in 21st-Century Britain* (London: Profile Books 2003), 7.

13 Ron Rosenbaum suggests that sometimes this issue of whether something is or is not antisemitic becomes a red herring and therefore he takes an 'anti-semantic' stance on John J. Mearsheimer and Stephen M. Walt's *The Israel Lobby and U.S. Foreign Policy* (Cambridge, MA: Harvard University Press 2006); Ron Rosenbaum, 'The Israel Lobby and the second Holocaust debate: an emblematic error in a controversial book', *Slate* (online), 19 September 2007, www.slate.com/id/2173908/ (viewed 17 July 2008).

14 Zygmunt Bauman, *Modernity and the Holocaust* (Ithaca, NY: Cornell University Press 2000), 64.

15 Wolfgang Benz makes this point unapologetically in 'Antisemitism research', in Martin Goodman (ed.), *The Oxford Handbook of Jewish Studies* (Oxford and New York: Oxford University Press 2002), 943–55 (944). It is also important to realize that there are gradations to what Taguieff calls, after Albert Memmi, 'heterophobia' (i.e. fear of the different): 1) the primary response to the stranger, outsider or foreigner, frequently characterized by antipathy; 2) a secondary, 'rationalized' response, typified by xenophobia or ethnocentrism, that can lead to social exclusion or discrimination; and 3) racism, of which antisemitism is a subset, based on a biological argument, that organizes negative images into a world-view or ideological system in which Jews are identified as the evil force and absolute enemy. See Taguieff, *Rising from the Muck*, 122n3.

and Judaism in paranoid or diabolical terms.[16] The new Judaeophobia refers more clearly to the mixture of fascination with and demonization of Jews and Judaism today.[17] For, as Bartov put it, the constellation of the fellow-travellers of the new Judaeophobia are those 'whose fears and phobias about present conditions, utopian dreams of a better future, and nostalgic fantasies of a mythical past all converge in a bizarre and increasingly frightening way on a single figure, a single cause: "the Jew"'.[18]

But even the notion of a 'new Judaeophobia' as a label for this compulsive obsession with 'the Jew' runs the risk of conflating the five major vectors of transmission that are sometimes identified as new threats, or their confluence as a new convergence, none of which proves distinctive of the new millennium.[19] Each of these vectors have a longer history that needs to be understood in terms of its specifics and in terms of its transformations in the post-Second World War period: 1) Holocaust denial, 2) Judaeophobia in the Islamic world, 3) the anti-Israel bias of the extreme left, 4) anti-Israel anti-racism, and 5) anti-Zionism as antisemitism. Anti-Zionism or anti-Israelism is the key point of contact between these different strands that otherwise are largely differentiated by crosscutting cleavages. Part of what needs to be understood, therefore, is when anti-Zionism becomes Judaeophobic. For, as Walter Laqueur sums it up, the issue of the new antisemitism 'boils down to the question of whether antisemitism and anti-Zionism are two entirely distinct phenomena or whether anti-Zionism can turn into, in certain circumstances, antisemitism'.[20]

16 As such, the new Judaeophobia overlaps with the 'new racism'. Both clearly employ a coded language that ultimately depends more on cultural rather than on racial differentiation. On the 'new racism', see Martin Barker, *The New Racism: Conservatives and the Ideology of the Tribe* (London: Junction Books 1981); Amy E. Ansell, *New Right, New Racism: Race and Reaction in the United States and Britain* (New York: New York University Press 1997); Eduardo Bonilla-Silva, *Racism without Racists: Color-Blind Racism and the Persistence of Racial Inequality in the United States* (Lanham, MD: Rowman and Littlefield 2003); and Patricia Hill Collins, *Black Sexual Politics: African Americans, Gender, and the New Racism* (New York: Routledge 2005).

17 The term 'Judaeophobia' should not be understood literally as a fear of Jews or Judaism. Fear and fascination are intertwined in the history of all demonization; indeed they are at the heart of the image of Satan. I believe the term was first coined by Leo Pinsker in his 1882 pamphlet *Auto-emancipation* and, in Pinsker's analysis, the roots of Judaeophobia are broadly construed; Leo Pinsker, *Auto-emancipation*, trans. from the German by D. S. Blondheim (New York: National Education Department, Zionist Organization of America 1948), esp. section 2.

18 Bartov, 'The new anti-Semitism', 15.

19 Taguieff therefore argues that the origins of the new Judaeophobia are properly dated to the aftermath of the Six Day War. In addition to *Rising from the Muck*, see his enormous tome, *Prêcheurs de haine: traversée de la judéophobie planétaire* (Paris: Mille et une nuits 2004), 341, as well as *L'Imaginaire du complot mondial: aspects d'un mythe moderne* (Paris: Mille et une nuits 2006), 142.

20 Walter Laqueur, *The Changing Face of Antisemitism: From Ancient Times to the Present Day* (Oxford and New York: Oxford University Press 2006), 7.

Denying the Holocaust

Holocaust denial has operated in different guises from the end of the Second World War. The bedrock of claims that the Holocaust was a hoax perpetrated by Jews in order to secure funding and legitimacy for the Jewish state was put in place in a series of works published from 1948, first by the prominent French fascist Maurice Bardèche, and then by the Buchenwald survivor of the Resistance and former Communist Paul Rassinier. 'Holocaust denial [then] found a receptive welcome in the United States during the 1950s and 1960s', writes Deborah Lipstadt, 'particularly among individuals known to have strong connections with antisemitic publications and extremist groups'.[21] The assault on historical reality by the deniers was compounded by an assault on the memory of the Holocaust following the Soviet occupation of Eastern Europe: the official Communist version of the Second World War contended that all perpetrators of the Holocaust were 'fascists' and its victims were 'anti-fascists', while the remnant of surviving Eastern European Jews were suffering from discrimination and defamation often as 'Zionists'.[22]

In the 1960s and 1970s, the radical right in Western and Central Europe began its resurrection. These groups were racist, nationalist and not only anti-Jewish, but anti-black, anti-Asian, anti-Arab and hostile to non-European immigrants in an era of rising immigration. Holocaust denial or diminution became one plank in their ideological platforms, as when the leader of the French Front National, Jean-Marie Le Pen, said of the gas chambers that they were 'a minute detail of Second World War history'. Arthur Butz's *The Hoax of the Twentieth Century* (1976) created a controversy that made Holocaust denial much more visible, and the Institute for Historical Review in California convened the first Revisionist Convention in the summer of 1979, treating and promoting denial as a respectable scholarly pursuit. Those who attended were 'a conglomeration of Holocaust deniers, neo-Nazis, philo-Germans, right-wing extremists, antisemites, racists, and conspiracy theorists'.[23] In the 1980s the Canadian Ernst Zundel, aided infamously by David Irving and Robert Faurisson, began to focus on the technical challenges of the Nazis' use of gas chambers and zyklon-B as their method of industrialized extermination. When famed American intellectual Noam Chomsky penned a defence of Faurisson's right to free speech in his book *The Rumor of Auschwitz*, he lent denial the veneer of his cultural acclaim, to his discredit. By the 1990s deniers sought to open a front on college campuses by taking out ads in college newspapers entitled 'The Holocaust Story: How Much is False? The Case for Open Debate'. And, by

---

21 Deborah Lipstadt, *Denying the Holocaust: The Growing Assault on Truth and Memory* (New York: Free Press 1993), 65.

22 See Lucy S. Dawidowicz, *The Holocaust and the Historians* (Cambridge, MA: Harvard University Press 1981).

23 Lipstadt, *Denying the Holocaust*, 137.

the new millennium, the global web of the marginalized Holocaust denial community could be linked, and denial literature and arguments were easily disseminated via the Internet.

The activists who deny the Holocaust are zealous warriors in a crusade. Their denial might, in fact, be regarded as the final stage of genocide. They are the bureaucrats of the next solution to the Jewish Question, the 'paper Eichmann', as Pierre Vidal-Naquet has appropriately tagged them.[24] The geography of denial is worldwide, with key nodal points in Orange County and Lyons, and its banner has been exported to diverse locations in the Arab and Islamic world, including, of course, Iran. Its linchpin is a certain irrefutability, since denial is a closed system. As Nadine Fresco explains:

> A document dating from the war is inadmissible because it dates from those years. The deposition of a Nazi at his trial is inadmissible because it is a deposition from a trial. This is applicable to all Nazis who were tried. If, as is the case, not one of them denied the existence of gas chambers, it is not because the gas chambers existed ... but because the witnesses believed that if they assisted the victors, the judges would reward them with clemency. As for the testimonies and depositions of some hundreds of thousands of Jews who pretended to be survivors of the genocide, they are inadmissible because given by people who could only be instigators or, at best, accomplices in the rumor that led to the swindle from which they benefited.[25]

Like the epicentres of denial, its ideology is multiple, underpinned by diverse motives: 1) neo-fascist and neo-Nazi antisemitism; 2) German and East European nationalisms; 3) far-right anti-communism since, for both ethno-nationalists and anti-communists, 'Judaeo-Bolshevism' remains a vivid spectre still haunting Europe; 4) fringe groups of the extreme left; and 5) absolute anti-Zionists, including those in the Islamic world.[26] Whatever the expression or the motive, however, this form of Judaeophobia is not new, although its dissemination on websites and, more recently, in Iran through a state actor is novel.

Islamist Judaeophobia

The second vector, Islamist Judaeophobia, has a much longer history. In an era of rampant Islamophobia, it is important to say that the Islamic world is

---

24 On Holocaust denial, see Pierre Vidal-Naquet, *Les Assassins de la mémoire: 'Un Eichmann de papier' et autres essays sur le révisionisme* (Paris: La Découverte 1987); Alain Finkielkraut, *L'Avenir d'un négation: réflexion sur la question du génocide* (Paris: Seuil 1982); and Lipstadt, *Denying the Holocaust*.

25 Nadine Fresco, 'The denial of the dead: on the Faurisson affair', trans. from the French by Audri Durchslag, *Dissent*, vol. 28, no. 4, Fall 1981.

26 As will become evident below, I distinguish between ideological or absolute anti-Zionists and principled anti-Zionists or post-Zionists.

obviously complex and highly variegated. There are forty-six countries with a Muslim majority and approximately 1.3 billion adherents to Islam (one in five humans is a Muslim). While there are many Islams across this landscape and even variants of Islamism—the political mobilization of Islam—it is the anti-Jewish strand within this mixed Islamic tapestry that we need briefly to outline. While unquestionably historically less malicious than traditional Christian anti-Judaism, in which Jews are represented as the murderers of God and the spawn of the devil, there are textual roots of contemporary Islamist Judaeophobia in the Qur'an and the Hadith. Jews are depicted in the Qur'an as 'corrupters of Scriptures' (3:63), and accused of falsehood (3:71), distortion (5:85), as well as cowardice, greed and chicanery. Jews are even accursed by God and metamorphose into apes.[27] Some recent Islamist interpreters, such as Sayyid Qutb, as central to their theology, have developed this series of epithets into the heart of an anti-Jewish world-view.

Since Jews and Christians are both described as *Ahl al-Kitab* (People of the Book), in the pre-modern era they were legally defined as *dhimmis* (protected people), whose religious freedom in the Muslim world was tolerated as long as they—adherents of substandard and distorted religions—maintained a clear sense of their subjection. A series of measures, symbolic for the most part, were instituted: *dhimmis* were required to pay a *jizya* (poll tax), to wear distinctive clothing, to live and worship in inferior places, and were prohibited from riding on horses or camels, though not donkeys. 'A social framework of discrimination and disabilities that constantly emphasized the superiority of Muslims' was instituted.[28] As Bernard Lewis explains, the most vociferous anti-Judaic calumnies, like the blood libel, entered the Islamic world 'during the reign of the Ottoman sultan Mehmed the Conqueror, and it [the blood libel] almost certainly originated among the large Greek-Christian population under Ottoman rule'.[29] In the period in which Nicholas II (1868–1894) called the Ottoman Empire 'the sick man of Europe', antisemitic literature began to enter the Middle East. By the 1930s and the Second World War, fascists in Europe inspired a number of parties and movements in the Arab world.[30] The most famous figure to emerge from the nexus of Nazi ideas and the Arab world was Haj Muhammad Amin al-Husseini, the Grand Mufti of Jerusalem, who orchestrated anti-Jewish riots in mandate Palestine to oppose Jewish settlement and then, to aid his opposition to the Vishuv, he allied with Hitler, who became a financial patron. The Mufti in turn broadcast pro-Axis propaganda to the Arab world from Berlin in the period of the Final Solution.

27 For the Qur'anic sources, see Bernard Lewis, *The Jews of Islam* (Princeton, NJ: Princeton University Press 1984), 11–14.
28 Robert Wistrich, *Muslim Anti-Semitism: A Clear and Present Danger* (New York: American Jewish Committee 2002), 6.
29 Lewis, *The Jews of Islam*, 158.
30 See Matthias Küntzel, *Jihad and Jew-Hatred: Islamism, Nazism and the Roots of 9/11*, trans. from the German by Colin Meade (New York: Telos Press 2007).

But clearly the establishment of the state of Israel in the heart of what was previously *Dar al-Islam* (Islamic lands) marked a major turning-point. For some Muslims, the victories of the Israelis in the wars since 1948 have become, in Gabriel Shoenfeld's words, a

> wellspring from which to draw conclusions about the 'Satanic' nature of the Zionist victories. Wicked unseen forces were the only conceivable explanation for such an inexplicable outcome, in which the noble and courageous Arabs were defeated by those whom the Qur'an itself taught were 'inferior and wretched'.[31]

During the Cold War, the Soviet Union's influence in the region began to supplant the lexicon of the right with the phraseology of the left. The Zionist movement, using Yasser Arafat's words as a quintessential example, was depicted as 'racist and fanatic in its nature, aggressive, expansionist, and colonial in its aims, and fascist in its methods'.[32]

If 1948 and its aftermath was an open wound in which anti-Jewish motifs festered, the lesions have not healed due to the massive inequalities of wealth and gender, institutionalized underdevelopment and political un-freedom throughout much of the Muslim world. As the two United Nations Development Prorgamme reports authored by Arab social scientists in 2002 and 2003 make clear, this is compounded by ongoing strife between sects and ethnic groups, secularists and religious adherents, between Shi'ites and Sunnis, and by stagnant economic growth in the Middle East. Throughout the Islamic world, there is an effort to achieve rapid modernization and industrialization, which inevitably entails enormous social dislocation. Accordingly, in Shoenfeld's formulation: 'If the Jew in a modernizing Europe became, in the words of one historian, "the symbol of modernization and modern society, and was hated as such," in the modernizing Arab world the state of Israel plays an equivalent role.'[33]

The decisive crossroad for this was, of course, June 1967. The over-whelming victory of Israel in the Six Day War marked the decline of pan-Arab nationalism and Islamism began to emerge as an alternative ideology both to the corruption and failures of Arab leaders and to the hypocrisy of the West. But the cultural, historical and political Arabism that, in Olivier Carré's characterization, 'has haunted [Arab public opinion] since the earliest days of the independence struggle against the Ottomans and then against the British, the French, the Zionist movement, Israel, and finally "American imperialism"' has endured.[34] Militant Islamism from the Muslim

---

31 Gabriel Schoenfeld, *The Return of Anti-Semitism* (San Francisco: Encounter Books 2004), 31.

32 Quoted in ibid., 20.

33 Ibid., 30.

34 Olivier Carré, *L'Orient arabe aujourd'hui* (Brussels: Complexe 1991), 194. English translation in Taguieff, *Rising from the Muck*, 64.

Brotherhood to al-Qa'ida seized on this cluster of factors to make Judaeophobia a central strand of its platform.[35] In parts of the Islamic world, Israel has been transformed, as Fiamma Nirenstein put it,

> into little more than a diabolical abstraction, not a country at all but a malignant force embodying every possible negative attribute—aggressor, usurper, sinner, occupier, corrupter, infidel, murderer, barbarian. As for Israelis themselves, they are seen not as citizens, workers, students, or parents but as the uniformed foot soldiers of that same dark force.[36]

This representation of Israel is disseminated in sermons in mosques and shared on tape recordings, on television, on the Internet, in newspapers and broadsheets, and via graffiti that adorns the walls of some of the Islamic enclaves of European cities. There has clearly been a rise in the number of assaults on Jews and Jewish property, including the firebombing of synagogues, the desecration of cemeteries and attacks on identifiable Jewish establishments in Western and Central Europe committed not by neo-Nazis or the extreme right but by Muslim youth.[37] These young men, who often suffer from institutionalized discrimination, identify with the struggles of Palestinians or other insurgent Muslims around the world.

35 See Küntzel, *Jihad and Jew-Hatred*.

36 Fiamma Nirenstein, 'How suicide bombers are made', *Commentary*, September 2001.

37 The *Report on Global Anti-Semitism* by the US Department of State, released 5 January 2005, which documented this spike in antisemitic activity, restated the findings of the French Commission Nationale Consultative des Droits de l'Homme that concluded after an extensive analysis that 'disaffected French-North African youths were responsible for many of the incidents, which French officials linked to tensions in Israel and the Palestinian territories'; the report is available online at www.state.gov/ g/drl/rls/40258.htm (viewed 19 July 2008). In the cases where the perpetrators of antisemitic acts are known, there are similar findings across Western Europe and Britain. But the matter of these findings is complicated, as the FRA working paper concludes: 'In the course of the rise in anti-Semitic incidents in Europe over the past years, there has been a shift in the public perception of the "typical" anti-Semitic offender, particularly in countries like Belgium, Denmark, France, Germany, Sweden, and the UK, from the "extreme right skinhead" to the "disaffected young Muslim", "person of North African origin", or "immigrant" and member of the "anti-globalisation" left. This shift, although widely reported, is difficult to substantiate on the basis of the available statistical evidence and the situation is probably far more complex. One has to point here to the difficulties in verifying classifications of perpetrators based on the perceptions of victims or witnesses, rather than a formal and objective process for determining identity. Furthermore, in a number of countries it is not legally possible to investigate the ethnic or religious background of perpetrators'; 'Anti-Semitism: summary overview of the situation in the European Union 2001–2007', updated version, January 2008, available at http://fra.europa.eu/ fra/material/pub/AS/Antisemitism_Overview_Jan_2008_en.pdf (viewed 4 September 2008). See also Paul A. Silverstern, 'The context of antisemitism and Islamophobia in France', *Patterns of Prejudice*, vol. 42, no. 1, February 2008, 22–3.

In the case of France, for example, both Jews and Muslims emigrated from the Maghreb and West Africa in the period of decolonization, often to the same neighbourhoods. Both communities have similar patterns of religious observance (20 per cent pray regularly) and active communal affiliation (20 per cent belong to community organizations). The Jewish experience in the metropole, however, has been characterized by educational and economic success, while that of their African counterparts has been marked by vastly higher rates of educational failure, unemployment, jobs in low-paying, low-prestige enterprises and higher rates of incarceration.[38] These social facts help to explain why some French Muslims displace and misplace their frustration and anger on to Jews and Jewish sites that symbolically express the iniquities they daily experience. So an Islamic anti-Jewish streak is hardly new, but Israeli independence and especially the Six Day War, combined with the movement of Muslims back to the metropole and the rise of radical jihadism, has supercharged this anti-Jewish element.

The extreme left in the age of globalization

If the Six Day war indicated a shift in some Islamic discourses, then June 1967 marked a categorical rupture between many on the radical left and Israel. To avoid homogenizing a phantasmic 'left' that runs through many works on the 'new antisemitism', it is important to distinguish between the streams on the extreme left and the socialist and social-democratic left in Europe and elsewhere, and the progressive and liberal left in the United States that makes up the mainstream of leftist opinion. For some on the extreme left, as Taguieff explains:

> Judeophobia answer[s] with remarkable symbolic efficiency, the demand for meaning and the mobilization of causes felt by ... those orphans of 'revolution' who continue to think and find guidance in the traditional Communist element of revolutionary myth, in one of its many Marxist (Leninist, Trotskyist, Third Worldist) or anarchist (neoleftist, 'neoradical') variants. For these 'radical' milieux ... Israel is the devil incarnate, 'Zionism' is the absolute enemy.[39]

38 On Muslims in Europe, in addition to Taguieff's *Rising from the Muck* and Shoenfeld's *The Return of Anti-Semitism*, 57–73, see in particular the chapter 'Anti-Semitism among Muslims and the rise of *communautarisme*', in Jonathan Laurence and Justin Vaisse, *Integrating Islam: Political and Religious Challenges in Contemporary France* (Washington, D.C.: Brookings Institution Press 2006). The most comprehensive picture of antisemitism in France today is Michel Wieviorka, *La Tentation antisémite: haine des juifs dans la France d'aujourd'hui* (Paris: Robert Laffont 2005).

39 Taguieff, *Rising from the Muck*, 8. Here, as at other points in Taguieff's book, since he adds no qualifiers to his statements, he veers from sound analysis to a vitriolic castigation that mirrors the object of his analysis. What is true of Taguieff here can also be said of many of the other alarmist accounts of the new antisemitism.

Anti-Zionism began to creep into the core values of the revolutionary left during the Cold War and the various struggles for decolonization. This was exacerbated as the Palestinian struggle began to replace the national liberation movements of the 1950s and 1960s in the postcolonial era as the central front in the struggle against the inequities of the neo-colonial order, especially after the apartheid regime in South Africa ended in the 1990s.

Anti-Zionism was also wedded to a vociferous anti-Americanism in the Cold War,[40] during which, in the struggle against the Soviet Union and as a result of its anti-Communist alliances, the United States often supported authoritarian and repressive regimes clinging to power, in addition to its slow response to dealing with its own 350-year racist past during the civil rights struggles. The confluence of anti-Americanism and anti-Zionism reached a new peak with George Bush and Ariel Sharon at the helms of state. Beginning with Sharon's visit to the Temple Mount in September 2000, the fallout from 9/11 and then the incursion into Iraq in March 2003, American and Israeli unilateralism and unbridled mutual support has led to the exacerbated co-opting of images culled from the antisemitic past to portray both regimes.

In the process, the rhetoric of 'Judaeo-Bolshevism' as the paragon of far-right antisemitism following the First World War has morphed into what we might call 'Judaeo-Americanism' as the archetype of what many on the extreme left oppose. A paradigmatic example of this: a demonstrator at the 2003 World Economic Forum in Davos wore a mask of Donald Rumsfeld with a large yellow star and 'Sheriff' inscribed on it, and was driven forward by a cudgel-wielding likeness of Ariel Sharon, both being followed by a huge model of the Golden Calf. 'The message', as Josef Joffe commented, was that

> America is in thrall to the Jews/Israelis, and both are the acolytes of Mammon and the avant-garde of pernicious global capitalism. ... Having captured the 'hyperpower,' Jews *qua* Israelis finally do rule the world. It is Israel as the *Über-Jew*, and America as its slave.[41]

Indeed, the iconography of globalized antisemitism is no longer carried by static entities like the cathedral but by ephemeral markers like the cartoon,

40 Paul Hollander's definition of anti-Americanism is useful. For Hollander, the term denotes a 'particular mindset, an attitude of distaste, aversion, or intense hostility the roots of which may be found in matters unrelated to the actual qualities or attributes of American society or the foreign policies of the United States. In short ... anti-Americanism refers to a negative predisposition, a type of bias which is to various degrees unfounded... It is an attitude similar to [such other] hostile predispositions as racism, sexism, or anti-Semitism'; Paul Hollander, *Anti-Americanism: Critiques at Home and Abroad 1965–1990* (New York: Oxford University Press 1992), viii. See also Alvin H. Rosenfeld, *Anti-Americanism and Anti-Semitism: A New Frontier of Bigotry* (New York: American Jewish Committee 2003).
41 Josef Joffe, *Nations We Love to Hate: Israel, America and the New Antisemitism* (Jerusalem: Vidal Sassoon Center for the Study of Antisemitism, Hebrew University 2005), 1.

since, as Joffe points out, 'cartoons are drawn editorials. Surely they are also the shortest road to the subconscious.'[42] One might elaborate on Joffe's point by suggesting that the television melodramas in the Arab world that re-enact the *Protocols of the Elders of Zion* as a mini-series are little more than animated cartoons played by real actors.

Television, and especially the Internet, have thus become the global vehicles for the dissemination of age-old anti-Jewish motifs in the post-industrial era, often reworked around the nexus of Judaeo-American world domination. Within this nexus, there are two key motifs. First, the 'cabal' of neo-conservatives dominated by Jews, including Paul Wolfowitz, Richard Perle, Douglas Feith, Elliott Abrams, Lewis 'Scooter' Libby and William Kristol, among others, who have turned the United States into a client-state serving the interests of Israel.[43] Second is 'the Jewish lobby' or 'the Zionist lobby', which is said to dominate American foreign policy.[44] For some within the left who parrot these stereotypes and prejudices, anti-Zionism has become a central site encapsulating the harmful institutional forces at work in the age of globalization.

Shulamit Volkov has persuasively argued that antisemitism is a cultural code and that anti-Zionism is the recalibration of this code to fit the present. By arguing that antisemitism is a cultural code, Volkov meant two things:

> The first is that cultural as well as social and political views come in packages, in the form of ideational syndromes; the second, that only relatively minor issues, though of the kind that are common enough in public discourse, can serve as codes, signifying larger, more important syndromes.[45]

Antisemitic codes thus serve as a short cut to explain the operational forces of anxiety in people's lives, when they do not have the language or analytic sophistication to name them properly. While most of the signs and signifiers that make up the ideational syndrome of the new Judaeophobia are not new,

---

42 Ibid., 8.
43 See Joshua Muravchik, 'The neoconservative cabal', in Ron Rosenbaum (ed.), *Those Who Forget the Past: The Question of Anti-Semitism* (New York: Random House 2004), 365–84. Attention to the ways in which 'the neoconservative cabal' as an antisemitic motif reinscribes mythical conspiratorial accounts of the Jewish desire for world domination in the *Protocols* certainly does not foreclose a critical view of how neoconservative ideologues, both Jews and non-Jews, as well as the institutions that have advanced their perspective, like the Project for the New American Century, American Enterprise Institute and the *Weekly Standard*, have exerted a profound influence on American foreign policy.
44 On these points, see Rosenfeld, *Anti-Americanism and Anti-Semitism*, 14–16. The most nuanced articulation of this argument is John Mearsheimer and Stephen Walt, 'The Israel lobby', *London Review of Books*, 10 March 2006.
45 Shulamit Volkov, 'Readjusting cultural codes: reflections on anti-Semitism and anti-Zionism', in Jeffrey Herf (ed.), *Anti-Semitism and Anti-Zionism in Historical Perspective: Convergence and Divergence* (London and New York: Routledge 2007), 43.

the cultural code has readjusted to new geo-global circumstances. 'Anti-Semitism has become a signal, an indication, a yellow flag', Fiamma Nirenstein maintains, 'signaling a pestilence spreading in the very heart of the phenomenon of globalization itself, [and] in its institutions (the UN, the NGOs, the European Union, the media)'.[46] As Daniel Jonah Goldhagen puts it: 'Always protean in quality, always changing to take on the idiom of its day, anti-Semitism in our globalized era has been globalized.'[47]

Indeed, antisemitism *per se* arose alongside globalized capitalism from the late eighteenth century. Antisemitism on the right defined itself against the dark, satanic mills of modernity. But antisemitism on the left also tracked alongside the rise of globalization: from the English Deists to the *philosophes* and through the thinkers of the *Aufklärung*, from the so-called utopian socialists through the early Marx and into the writings of Ferdinand Tönnies and Werner Sombart, the threats of global modernization were projected on to Jews and Judaism. Postmodern globalization, including 'the opening of borders to the greater movement of ideas, people, and money', Mark Strauss avers, 'has stirred familiar anxieties about ill-defined "outside forces"'.[48] The result has on occasion produced strange bedfellows among some ultra-nationalists, parts of the populist green movement and various segments of the orphans of the revolution.[49]

This alliance is hardly one of an elective affinity, since there have been vicious turf battles, both literal and virtual, among these differing contenders within the anti-globalization movement. But there have also been overlaps between their visions about who is responsible for the dark side of globalization. These conjunctures are, paradoxically, a function of the disjunctures within the global cultural economy. Arjun Appadurai has compellingly argued that 'the new global cultural economy has to be seen as a complex, overlapping, disjunctive order that cannot any longer be understood in terms of existing center–periphery models'.[50] Rather than any linear configuration of the flow of Judaeophobia from Europe to the Islamic world and back again, Appadurai's model of the five dimensions of global cultural flows is useful in accounting for the global forces contributing to the dissemination of the new Judaeophobia since, as Goldhagen rightly states, today 'there are many anti-Semitic centers and multidirectional flows'.[51]

46 Fiamma Nirenstein, 'Israel, globalization, and anti-Semitism in Europe', in Kertzer (ed.), *Old Demons, New Debates*, 48.
47 Daniel Jonah Goldhagen, 'The globalization of anti-Semitism', in Kertzer (ed.), *Old Demons, New Debates*, 180.
48 Mark Strauss, 'Antiglobalism's Jewish problem', in Rosenbaum (ed.), *Those Who Forget the Past*, 271–85 (275).
49 For some examples, see ibid., 274.
50 Arjun Appadurai, 'Disjuncture and difference in the global cultural economy', in Arjun Appadurai, *Modernity at Large: Cultural Dimensions of Globalization* (Minneapolis: University of Minnesota Press 1996), 32.
51 Goldhagen, 'The globalization of anti-Semitism', 181.

What shapes global cultural processes today, Appadurai maintains, are the intersections of *ethnoscapes* (the flow of people, refugees, immigrants, exiles), *technoscapes* (the flow of technology), *financescapes* (the flow of money and currency markets), *mediascapes* (the flow of images from newspapers, magazines, television stations, films and the Internet) and *ideoscapes* (the flow of ideas). The forces that generate these cultural flows condition global cultural formations, a quintessential example of which is the syndrome of the new Judaeophobia.

Anti-Israel anti-racism

Among the paradoxes of these flows is the way in which the new Judaeophobia has marshalled anti-racism to underpin criticism of Israel. As Alain Finkielkraut put it, 'it is born of this ... anti-racist exuberance that recodes all dramas—current or ancient—into the terms of one of only two alternatives: tolerance and stigmatization', reducing the complexities of the world into 'Nazis' and 'victims'.[52] Here, its origins go back to the 1975 campaign to pass UN Resolution 3379, which declared 'Zionism is a form of racism and racial discrimination'. The resolution was passed with the sponsorship of the Soviet Union in alliance with Arab states. It was rescinded in December 1991, through Resolution 4686. But, at the UN-sponsored World Conference against Racism, which took place in Durban, South Africa in 2001, Israel was once again singled out with charges of ethnic cleansing, racism, war crimes and crimes against humanity. The agenda of establishing international standards to combat racism was hijacked by the Non-Governmental Organization Forum and Youth Summit whose activists consistently disrupted the conference with Israel-bashing. 'At a deeper level, the charge of "racism" (and therefore of "apartheid," "genocide," etc.)', Taguieff writes, 'turns against Jews-Zionists-Israelis the old negative interpretation of the election of Israel: that is, the denunciation of the "chosen people" as a people giving itself every right to dominate, conquer, oppress, and destroy'.[53]

But it is not only the new demonization of Israel and Zionism in the name of anti-racism, but also the fight against it that benefits from the multidirectionality of globalized media technologies. Today, as instantly as an antisemitic canard enters the flow of mediascapes, an army of Jewish and democratic institutions, media and campus watchdogs, journalists and academics combat it, including groups mobilized by the state of Israel. 'For the first time in history', Fiamma Nirenstein affirms, 'a Jewish state can fight anti-Semitism in the international arena, and this has made things very different'.[54] Each side

---

52 Alain Finkielkraut, *Au nom de l'autre: réflexions sur l'antisémitisme qui vient* (Paris: Gallimard 2003), 26. Unless otherwise stated, all translations from the French are by the author.
53 Taguieff, *Rising from the Muck*, 67.
54 Nirenstein, 'Israel, globalization and anti-Semitism in Europe', 44.

marshals the discourse of racism to advance their perspective on Jews-Israel-Zionism and the complex of charges that are ascribed to these signifiers.

Anti-Zionism versus antisemitism

But if, as we have seen, none of the factors that constitute the so-called 'new antisemitism' are new to the new millennium, then alarm about the new antisemitism is not new either. In the immediate aftermath of the Six Day War, publications appeared by several writers that explicitly argued that the new code for antisemitism was anti-Zionism. For example, Jacques Givet's examination of the left's opposition to Israel, published in 1968, was subtitled *Essai sur le néo-antisémitisme*.[55] The Yom Kippur War in 1973 once again gave rise to books warning of *The New Anti-Semitism*, the title of Foster and Epstein's rebuke, for example.[56] Again, after the Israeli incursion into Lebanon in 1982, volumes were produced signalling a rise in antisemitic rhetoric hiding behind the shield of anti-Zionism, like Alain Finkielkraut's *La Réprobation d'Israël*.[57] Moreover, all these works raised the alarm about a confluence of anti-Zionism within part of the radical left and within the Islamic world, which is what many observers signal as the most significant new danger of the new antisemitism.

55 Jacques Givet, *La Gauche contre Israël? Essai sur le néo-antisémitisme* (Paris: Jean-Jacques Pauvert 1968). See also, for example, 'Contre une certaine gauche', *Les Nouveaux Cahiers*, no. 13–14, Spring–Summer 1968, 116–19.

56 Foster and Epstein, *The New Anti-Semitism*. In addition, one might cite, by an Israeli scholar, Shmuel Ettinger, 'Le Caractère de l'antisémitisme contemporain', *Dispersion et Unité*, no. 14, 1975, 141–57. Norman Finkelstein's diatribe, *Beyond Chutzpah: On the Misuse of Anti-Semitism and the Abuse of History* (Berkeley and Los Angeles: University of California Press 2005) does not address the earlier French works on neo-antisemitism, but is not wrong that Foster and Epstein's book 'came to serve as the template for subsequent productions' in English. Finkelstein's book is the recapitulation of his argument in *The Holocaust Industry: Reflections on the Exploitation of Jewish Suffering* (New York: Verso 2000) as applied to antisemitism. His core contention is that the 'new antisemitism' is merely a meticulously orchestrated media extravaganza 'not to fight anti-Semitism but rather to exploit the historical suffering of Jews in order to immunize Israel against criticism' (*Beyond Chutzpah*, 22). It is based on the overly simplistic argument that the only factor accounting for recent attacks against Jews and Jewish institutions is the territorial displacement and dispossession of Palestinians and the Israeli-Palestinian conflict, even though this is unquestionably a central source of aggravation. His position is the mirror-image of the alarmists he seeks to denounce.

57 Alain Finkielkraut, *La Réprobation d'Israël* (Paris: Denoël 1983). See also Nathan Perlmutter and Ruth Ann Perlmutter, *The Real Anti-Semitism in America* (New York: Arbor House 1982); Léon Poliakov, *De Moscou à Beyrouth: essai sur la désinformation* (Paris: Calmann-Lévy 1983); Robert S. Wistrich, 'Anti-Zionism as an expression of antisemitism today', in Robert S. Wistrich, *Between Redemption and Perdition: Modern Antisemitism and Jewish Identity* (London and New York: Routledge 1990), 214–24; and Michael Curtis (ed.), *Antisemitism in the Contemporary World* (Boulder, CO: Westview Press 1986).

Léon Poliakov, the doyen of historians of antisemitism, was among the first to locate and historicize the emergence of a new epistemic and political configuration that materialized in the aftermath of the period between June 1967 and May 1968, and that indicated shifts in the index of Judaeophobia.[58] Poliakov narrated, with his inimitable clarity, the emerging crystallization of anti-Zionism as antisemitism. In *De l'antisionisme à l'antisémitisme*, he was concerned with establishing the distinction between anti-Zionism and antisemitism by tracing the history of the myth of the 'Zionist plot', fabricated first in Prague in 1952, that from its beginnings absorbed the antisemitic myths that preceded it.[59] August Bebel's quotation about antisemitism as 'the socialism of fools' aside, Poliakov shows that—within Marxist *theory*, from its genesis,[60] and explicitly developed as *policy* within the Soviet Union from October 1918—a principled anti-Zionism was perfectly reconciled with a strong stance opposing antisemitism.

But, beginning with Stalin's persecution of Jews from 1949–53, which continued after his death 'under the pretext of a critical attitude toward the Jewish State and its partisans', the discourse of anti-Zionism within the Soviet sphere of influence was slowly infused by an ancient hatred.[61] Concomitantly, in the Middle East, from the first Arab-Israeli war in 1948, anti-Zionism was animated by a desire to destroy the Jewish state. After 1968 Poliakov maintains that the revolutionary left, committed to the radical transformation of all existing structures, began to share the Arab perspective of eliminating the structures of the Jewish state.[62] Zionism began to be treated as coterminous with colonialism, racism, apartheid and crimes against humanity. Associated with these evils, it was deemed illegitimate and merited destruction. As he always did, Poliakov situated this position within the *longue durée*, arguing that from Voltaire and Fichte, through Fourier, Proudhon, Marx and Stalin, there has been a long tradition of anti-racist anti-Israelism that opposed Jewish particularity to universality, the carnal Jew to the spiritual humanist, Jewish materialism, legalism and anachronistic superstition to the true faith and reason of humanity.

However, Poliakov was not always careful to avoid collapsing all forms of critique of Israel or Zionism into antisemitism. A vociferous debate within and outside Israel has included, and does still, numerous voices that decry the occupation of the West Bank, the ongoing building of settlements, the

---

58 Léon Poliakov, *De l'antisionisme à l'antisémitisme* (Paris: Calmann-Lévy 1969).
59 Ibid., 10.
60 On Marxism and the Jewish Question, see Robert S. Wistrich, *Socialism and the Jews: The Dilemmas of Assimilation in Germany and Austria-Hungary* (East Brunswick, NJ: Associated University Presses 1982); Jack Jacobs, *On Socialists and 'the Jewish Question' after Marx* (New York: New York University Press 1992); Enzo Traverso, *Marxists and the Jewish Question: The History of a Debate (1843–1943)*, trans. from the Italian by Bernard Gibbons (Atlantic Highlands, NJ: Humanities Press 1994).
61 Poliakov, *De l'antisionisme à l'antisémitisme*, 11.
62 Ibid., 167.

injustices by the Israeli military and the violation of human rights without ever casting opprobrium on Jews as a group and without recycling classical anti-Jewish stereotypes. 'If Israel does not treat its non-Jewish citizens equally and humanely', Walter Laqueur maintains,

> if it persists in holding on to territories occupied in 1967 against the will of the local population, if it illegally seizes land elsewhere, if a racialist-chauvinist fringe inside Israel defies the law and elementary human rights and to considerable degree dictates its outrageous behavior to a government, if some people in Israel are unwilling to accept the rights of others, such behavior invites condemnation.[63]

Condemnation of Israel includes lots of groups and individuals that are critical of Likud or Kadima's unilateralism or the specifics of Israeli state policies regardless of which political party holds power. These include many Jewish critics and organizations such as Jewish Voices for Peace, Jews against the Occupation, Jews for Peace in the Middle East, Brit Tzedek, *Tikkun*, Women in Black, B'Tselem, Gush Shalom and Yesh Gvul. Such vigorous debate is the sign of a healthy democracy and at the heart of both the prophetic and talmudic traditions of Judaism.

Moreover, as David Myers has shown, there is also a long tradition of 'principled Jewish anti-Zionism' that has shadowed Zionism from its origins. Before the Holocaust, he notes, 'the Bund, the Autonomists, Reform Judaism, the Agude (i.e. Agudat Yisrael)—all saw Zionism as a competitor whose underlying rationale and territorial ambition were fundamentally flawed'.[64] Leading Jewish thinkers, including Hermann Cohen and Franz Rosenzweig, opposed both Zionism and assimilation in insisting on exile for Jews, in Rosenzweig's words, to steel them for 'battle on behalf of the exalted life and *against descent into the contingency of land and time*'.[65] Following the Holocaust, the groups and figures opposing political Zionism dwindled but among those who continued the pre-war tradition of insisting on diaspora Judaism were Jakob Petuchowski, Steven Schwarzschild, George Steiner and Richard Marienstras, who founded Le Cercle Gaston Crémieux, which was an important influence on several contemporary French-Jewish intellectuals. Along with these Jewish intellectuals, there are also a 'diverse array of Jewish critics in the diaspora ranging from Simon Rawidowicz to Michael Selzer to groups such as the American Council for Judaism and Breira'.[66] Their mantle has been taken up most recently by the likes of Tony Judt and

---

63 Laqueur, *The Changing Face of Antisemitism*, 6.
64 David N. Myers, 'Can there be a principled anti-Zionism? On the nexus between anti-historicism and anti-Zionism in modern Jewish thought', in Herf (ed.), *Anti-Semitism and Anti-Zionism in Historical Perspective*, 25.
65 Quoted in ibid.
66 Ibid., 27.

in edited collections like Tony Kushner and Alisa Solomon's *Wrestling with Zion: Progressive Jewish-American Responses to the Israeli-Palestinian Conflict*, or Seth Farber's *Radicals, Rabbis and Peacemakers: Conversations with Jewish Critics of Israel*.[67] There has always also been a strain of Jewish ultra-orthodox anti-Zionism, the most famous representatives being Neturei Karta and the Satmar Rebbe.

There were also vigorous debates beginning in the 1980s about a group of Israeli intellectuals collected under the rubric of post-Zionism, including Baruch Kimmerling, Adi Ophir, Uri Ram, Amnon Raz-Krakotzkin and Ilan Pappé.[68] So there is clearly a long and respectable tradition of anti-Zionism and post-Zionism that has no animus against Jews and Judaism. To the contrary, they are 'principled anti-Zionists' in precisely the sense of forging their position on the basis of what they hold to be good for Jews and Judaism. Moreover, on the basis of the many strands *within Zionism* that have opposed political Zionism, like those affiliated with Brit Shalom and the Ihud faction, and those who argued for binationalism, like Martin Buber, Judah Magnes and Hannah Arendt, many of the policies of the state of Israel would be considered reprehensible to their ethical and political principles. Zionism is hardly monolithic, and it cannot be conflated with the policies of the state of Israel, which themselves have to be appreciated in a historically nuanced fashion.

It is therefore clear that not every critique of Israel is antisemitic and that not all forms of anti-Zionism are animated by Jew-hatred whether advanced by non-Jews or Jews. In fact, numerous Jewish traditions have insisted that preservation of what is most precious about Judaism and Jewishness *demands* a principled anti-Zionism or post-Zionism. Indeed, the platitude that criticism of Israel *per se* is not the problem is readily acknowledged. Even those who do not subscribe to it fully—like many on the right side of the spectrum who have engaged in a wholesale condemnation of 'the left' as antisemitic if not in intention then at least in giving support to those who *are* antisemitic when they find fault with Israel—readily utter it before they go on to condemn all those who criticize the policies of Israel.

67 Tony Kushner and Alisa Solomon (eds), *Wrestling with Zion: Progressive Jewish American Responses to the Israeli-Palestinian Conflict* (New York: Grove Press 2003); Seth Farber (ed.), *Radicals, Rabbis and Peacemakers: Conversations with Jewish Critics of Israel* (Monroe, ME: Common Courage Press 2005). For a wholesale indictment of these works and other progressive Jewish thinkers whom he charges with antisemitism in effect if not in intent, see Alvin Rosenfeld, *'Progressive' Jewish Thought and the New Anti-Semitism* (New York: American Jewish Committee 2006). This charge is discussed and deconstructed below.

68 For a good overview on post-Zionism, see Laurence J. Silberstein, *The Postzionism Debates: Knowledge and Power in Israeli Culture* (New York and London: Routledge 1999), and, for the opposing perspective, Tuvia Friling (ed.), *Critique du post-sionisme: réponse aux 'nouveaux historiens' israéliens*, trans. from the Hebrew by Fabienne Bergmann (Paris: In Press 2004).

Reflections on the new Judaeophobia: Butler, Sartre and the Frankfurt School

Judith Butler has explicitly critiqued those who claim that critics of Israel 'are anti-Semitic in their effect if not their intent', as former Harvard University President Lawrence Summers famously put it.[69] For Butler, this claim has the effect of censorship 'in effect if not intent'.[70] In developing her argument, she makes several salient points about the use of the charge of antisemitism to disarm critics of Israel or Zionism. First and most evident is that it dilutes the claim when incidents like the torching of synagogues or the desecration of Jewish cemeteries or attacks on individuals as Jews occur, since all accusations of antisemitism are flattened. Second, it contributes to conditions in which all criticisms of Israel are deemed as hate speech. Third, and most problematically for Butler, it forecloses any distinction between Jews and Israel, Jewishness and Zionism.

This failure to discriminate capitulates to the antisemitic fantasy that all Jews act together in a worldwide conspiracy, and it disables any critical distance between members of the heterogeneous Jewish community as well as between Jews and the state of Israel. 'In holding out for a distinction to be made between Israel and Jews', Butler insists she is 'calling for a space for dissent for Jews, and non-Jews, who have criticisms of Israel to articulate' while 'also opposing anti-Semitic reductions of Jewishness to Israeli interests'.[71] In making this case, Butler rightfully calls for criteria that can delimit the difference between antisemitism and anti-Zionism.[72]

When does criticism of Israel become antisemitism?

The criteria for distinguishing legitimate criticism of Israel from anti-Zionism that masks Judaeophobia are hardly self-evident and present philosophical and political quandaries. Efforts to delineate some standards focus on the language used to describe Israel and the selectivity with which Israel is constituted within the new world order.[73] The most well known of these is Natan Sharansky's '3-D test' in which he stipulates that *double standards* applied to Israel, *delegitimization* of the state of Israel and

69 Lawrence Summers, 'Address at morning prayers', in Rosenbaum (ed.), *Those Who Forget the Past*, 57–60 (59). Also in Rosenbaum's collection, see Berel Lang, 'On the "the" in "the Jews"', 63–70, which focuses on how the definite article 'the' can be antisemitic in effect if not in intent.

70 Judith Butler, 'The charge of anti-Semitism: Jews Israel, and the risks of public critique', in Rosenbaum (ed.), *Those Who Forget the Past*, 438–50 (438).

71 Ibid., 449–50.

72 To be fair to Lawrence Summers, his specific examples of the point at which anti-Zionism slips into Judaeophobia actually indicate that he did have in mind the precise distinction that Butler calls for.

73 Joffe, *Nations We Love to Hate*, 3.

demonization of Israel each contain the kernel of antisemitism.[74] These criteria are still somewhat loose, but are clarified through examples, and they were incorporated into international juridical forums like the European Monitoring Centre on Racism and Xenophobia (now the FRA).

Double standards are a form of what Zygmunt Bauman calls 'allosemitism', the singling out of Jews and Judaism as so special, different, unique and exemplary that they merit different standards of normative assessment.[75] This, Bauman asserts, is the fountainhead of antisemitism.[76] 'When criticism of Israel is applied selectively', writes Sharansky, or 'when Israel is singled out ... for human rights abuses while the behavior of known and major abusers, such as China, Iran, Cuba, and Syria, is ignored', then this is Judaeophobia. But the criteria of 'double standards' has its own double standards. Supporters of Israel often argue that Israel is unique in the region of the Middle East in many ways: it is the sole democracy (they forget Turkey when they make this argument); it is a lone island of Jewishness in a sea of Islam; and it is the only true western ally in a region dominated by non-western mores and political institutions. Israel's supporters, therefore, claim time and again that it is different, unique, singular, and that, as a result, it ought to be singled out in the region. Indeed, precisely because of these singularities and the ways in which Israel functions in practice and symbolically in the Middle East, it is not a state like any other. For religious, political and geo-strategic reasons, the Israeli-Palestinian conflict is over-determined, and therefore magnified attention on it is partly warranted.

Likewise, the criteria concerning the delegitimization of Israel have merit, especially when Israel is the only Jewish state and almost half the world's Jews are Israelis. But they can also serve to delegitimize certain arguments. On the one hand, the claim that Israel is not a legitimate state, for example because it is a lever of neo-colonialism in the Middle East, is tantamount to a rhetorical justification for the claim that Israel ought not to exist. This is a step towards what Raymond Aron famously called *étatcide*—the wholesale elimination of the people of Israel—when de Gaulle uttered his famous 'sermon to the Hebrews' on 27 November 1967, calling them 'un peuple d'elite, sur de soi-meme et dominateur' (an elite people, sure of itself, and dominators). De Gaulle's pithy rebuke of Israel is a good example of *group*

---

74 Natan Sharansky, '3D test of anti-Semitism: demonization, double standards, delegitimization', *Jewish Political Studies Review*, vol. 16, no. 3–4, Fall 2004.

75 Zygmunt Bauman, 'Allosemitism: premodern, modern, postmodern', in Bryan Cheyette and Laura Marcus (eds), *Modernity, Culture and 'the Jew'* (Cambridge: Polity Press 1998), 143–56.

76 Bernard Lewis argues that there are two factors essential to antisemitism: 'One of them is that Jews are judged by a standard different from that applied to others ... The other special feature of antisemitism, which is much more important than differing standards of judgment, is the accusation against Jews of cosmic evil'; Bernard Lewis, 'The new anti-Semitism', *American Scholar*, vol. 75, no. 1, Winter 2006, 25–36.

stigmatization, whereby the actions of Israel's political leaders are conflated with the character of Jews in general in a way that reiterates antisemitic calumnies in the context of the acts or actions of the Israeli government.[77] In fact, when de Gaulle invoked the images of Jewish arrogance, superiority, power and domination, removing the protective shield that he symbolically represented as head of the Resistance, in Aron's words, he 'authorized a new antisemitism'.[78] Delegitimization overlaps with double standards when the Jewish national liberation struggle or Jew's rights to national self-determination are denied at the same time that they are supposedly accorded to all other groups. But, on the other hand, what about the argument of Israel's delegitimacy that is coupled to a larger critique of the form of the nation-state and the inherent pathologies of nationalism? For many on the radical left, this is central to their position and, if one takes this stance consistently then there can be nothing antisemitic about the claim that Israel is an illegitimate state since all nation-states would be deemed illegitimate.

Demonization as the third test of anti-Zionist Judaeophobia takes many forms. Its most oft-cited modes are the claim that Israel is a racial state (encapsulated in the so-called 'Zionism is racism' UN resolution), the contention that Israel is an apartheid state, the assertion that Israel's dispossession of Palestinian territory in the West Bank is akin to the colonial American expropriation of native land, or instances of Holocaust banalization, instrumentalization or even Holocaust inversion that suggest that 'Israel has become like the Nazis' in its persecution of the Palestinians, the Jews of the Middle East.[79] When Manfred Gerstenfeld writes that 'Holocaust inversion manifests itself in many ways', including 'speech, writing, and visual media', as well as 'cartoons, graffiti and placards', he could be addressing any of the central tropes for the demonization of Israel. In the case of Holocaust inversion, 'it employs sinister characterization of Israel and Israelis, Nazi symbols, and sometimes takes the form of Nazi genocidal terminology to describe Israel's actions'.[80] Robert Wistrich acutely explains why Holocaust inversion is a pernicious form of the new Judaeophobia:

> 'anti-Zionists' who insist on comparing Zionism and the Jews with Hitler and the Third Reich appear unmistakably to be de facto anti-Semites, even if they vehemently deny the fact! This is largely because they knowingly exploit the reality that Nazism in the postwar world has become the defining metaphor of absolute evil. For if Zionists are 'Nazis' and if Sharon really is Hitler, then it becomes a moral obligation to wage war against Israel. That is the bottom line of

---

77 On the point about group stigmatization, see Myers, 'Principled anti-Zionism', 22.
78 Raymond Aron, *De Gaulle, Israël et les juifs* (Paris: Plon 1968).
79 See Melanie Phillips, 'The new anti-Semitism', in Rosenbaum (ed.), *Those Who Forget the Past*, 251–7 (252).
80 Manfred Gerstenfeld, 'Holocaust inversion: the portraying Israel and Jews as Nazis', *Post-Holocaust and Anti-Semitism*, no. 55, April 2007.

much contemporary anti-Zionism. In practice, this has become the most potent form of contemporary anti-Semitism.[81]

In each modality of the demonization of Israel, one can make the same arguments that Wistrich does about what is insidious about the nazification of Israel. In each case, the claim is a shorthand identification of Israel with the most grievous instances of political evil and the only morally defensible response is to wage a campaign fired by moral indignation against Israel, *if the analogy holds*. For each of these arguments that demonize Israel depend on making an analogy between practices in Israel today and other historical incidents of oppression, persecution, ethnic cleansing, crimes against humanity or even genocide. And analogic thinking is inherently fallacious when it does not consider how these historical comparisons differ. In each case—Nazi Germany, apartheid South Africa, the colonial United States—the circumstances and situations were very different from Israel's occupation of the West Bank, instituted by processes, ideologies and practices very different than those of Zionism, and producing conditions of horror on a very different scale.

But, at the same time, all comparative accounts depend on drawing out analogies, and making comparisons is intrinsic to thinking about the moral and political significance of events. There is a paradoxical logic at work here, for it is only on the basis of understanding what is unique about a historical event that one has the basis of comparison. And when one makes comparisons without attention to these singularities, there is a risk that the political mobilization made possible by such comparisons (boycotts, divestment, anticolonial struggles) themselves become unethical. This is no different when it comes to Israel, which means that all forms of comparison ought to be open for discussion but in a way attenuated to the specific circumstances of life in Israel and Palestine and without making the analogies so facile that their only purpose is to serve as a good sound-bite.

Consequently, the criteria of demonization, delegitimization and double standards for demarcating when criticism of Israel becomes Judaeophobia are a useful beginning, but they are still tenuous and pose problems. We need a more rigorous set of criteria that will enable interlocutors to argue about the issues without each side slinging arrows and epithets at the other. As Butler pointed out, it is imperative that we conceptually pull apart anti-Zionism and antisemitism, but it proves a difficult task for philosophical and political reasons.

---

81 Robert Wistrich, 'Anti-Zionism and anti-Semitism', *Jewish Political Studies Review*, vol. 16, no. 3–4, Fall 2004, 29.

Jean-Paul Sartre on anti-racist 'neo-antisemitism'

But, presuming that we can distinguish anti-Israel attitudes from antisemitism, what matters in terms of the new Judaeophobia is how such criticisms of Israel are mobilized politically and in what circumstances they become antisemitic. Jean-Paul Sartre, for his part, provided a powerful analysis of why the formula that 'Zionism is racism' proves to be antisemitic. When he accepted a degree *honoris causa* in philosophy from the Hebrew University of Jerusalem on 7 November 1976, his remarks that evening indicted those who asserted that 'Zionism is racism' as racists themselves. Those who advocate this position, he sternly suggested, align themselves with the nefarious politics of racial antisemitism by implying that 'the Jews are in their eyes a race'.[82] In the second volume of his *Critique de la raison dialectique*, he had already analysed how Stalinist anti-Zionism, which was avowedly antiracist, ultimately reinscribed racism, a phenomenon Sartre already called at the time 'neo-antisemitism'. While 'anti-Semitism in its basic form as *racism* … was obviously condemned by Marxist ideology (as indeed by mere democratic liberalism)', Sartre made the case that Stalinist anti-Zionism nonetheless 'became racist anti-Semitism through an inexorable dialectic'.[83] Sartre's dialectical analysis proves more compelling than definitional approaches in assessing the politics of anti-Zionism.

Stalin's anti-racist antisemitism was animated by political exigencies, specifically the problem of integrating Jews into 'socialism in one country'. According to Sartre, there were three main circumstances that aroused Stalin's concern. First, there were Jews dispersed across the Soviet Union and the capitalist world, and the establishment of Israel compounded this fear of the existence of a global Jewish diaspora. Second, Stalin imagined that 'the emergence of a Jewish state under the particular control of American capitalism (via the mediation of Jews in the United States), the activities of the Zionist League, etc.' constituted a threat of 'traitors within'.[84] Third, 'any specificity had to be denied them [Jews]' in the name of socialism. The result was to position Jews within the inherent contradictions of Soviet Communism: 'they were denied any cultural autonomy, because it prevented integration; but they were denied integration, because their historical past already designated them as traitors and they had to be kept under constant surveillance.' The antinomies between de-Jewification and integration led, according to Sartre, to extermination as 'the inescapable solution'. 'We shall

---

82 Jean-Paul Sartre, 'Discours de Sartre à l'ambassade d'Israël pour l'acceptation de son diplôme de docteur *honoris causa* de l'Université hébraïque de Jérusalem 7 novembre 1976', in Ely Ben-Gal, *Mardi chez Sartre: un hébreu à Paris (1967–1980)* (Paris: Flammarion 1992), 313–14 (313).

83 Jean-Paul Sartre, *Critique of Dialectical Reason*, vol. 2, ed. Arlette Elkaim-Sartre, trans. from the French by Quintin Hoare (London and New York: Verso 2006), 265, 271.

84 Ibid., 266.

recognize in his policy towards the Jews', Sartre concluded, 'a *neo-anti-Semitism* of political rather than ethnic origin'.[85]

As he had suggested was the case with the sound-bite 'Zionism is racism', Sartre explicitly argued that neo-antisemitism sprang from 'the old anti-Semitic racism', whence it derived its virulence. A circularity reinforced the Soviet regime's antisemitism, which was animated by populist fear and dislike of Jews. Popular antisemitism, Sartre maintained, had an economic foundation. But 'the campaign against the Jews once more took on that diversionary aspect that it had always had, under all governments. By reinforcing racism, political anti-Semitism ended up dissolving into it.'[86] For political antisemitism ultimately was premised on the fact that 'the Jewish group was dangerous by its nature' and this was true both for the masses and for the leaders who exploited this 'petrified web of traditions'.[87] The logic of Stalin's political anti-Zionism also reiterated bourgeois antisemitism, whose 'universalism of Reason' began with the assumption that 'Jews are *countryless*'. For Stalinists, however, their 'cosmopolitanism' was a degraded form of internationalism that was lambasted as the 'Jewish International'. Ultimately, therefore, Sartre reasoned that the assault on Zionism 'seeks to preserve racism while claiming to transcend it'.[88] Consequently, Sartre demonstrated that 'Stalin and his collaborators were retotalized as racists by the masses' and this transformation of 'neo-anti-Semitism into racism' was 'at once free and inevitable'.[89] Sartre's analysis could largely be applied *mutatis mutandis* to much of the unprincipled anti-Zionist Judaeophobia today.

The Frankfurt School and 'ticket thinking'

As was the case with Sartre's analysis of Stalinist anti-racist neo-antisemit-ism, Max Horkeimer and Theodor Adorno had already sketched the contours of what they also later pointed to as being 'neo-antisemitism'. In the last section added in 1947 of their 'Elements of Antisemitism', which concluded *Dialectic of Enlightenment*, they laid down their critique. The seventh set of theorems they explored opens with a stunning line consider-ing that it was written just after the Holocaust: 'But there are no more antisemites.'[90] In developing this point, Horkheimer and Adorno argue that antisemitism as such is no longer necessary when the logic of globalized capitalism replaces all thinking with stereotypes, clichés, jargon, stock

85 Ibid., 265.
86 Ibid., 268.
87 Ibid.
88 Ibid., 269.
89 Ibid., 269, 270.
90 Max Horkheimer and Theodor W. Adorno, *Dialectic of Enlightenment*i [1947], trans. from the German by John Cumming (New York: Continuum 2000), 200.

phrases, dogmatic adherence to ideology and, generally, to the petrification of thought, which they call 'ticket thinking'.[91] 'In the world of mass series production', they claim, 'stereotypes replace individual categories'.[92]

In a world governed by instrumental rationality, where there is only *homo economicus*, they contend that individual decisions are taken over by corporate interests: large capital, trade unions, political parties and mass culture. Modern means of communication colonize all differences and mankind is divided into power blocs. All mediations are eliminated by the 'cogwheel mechanism of industry'.[93] 'Ticket thinking', they continue, 'is a product of industrialization and its advertising machine, [and] extends to international relations'.[94] Antisemitism, they argue, is itself a symptom of the mass production of 'ticket thinking' by the culture industry. Since this is the case, the Jews could be replaced as victims, as is evident by the rampant globalized Islamophobia today. And Jews themselves can easily get caught up in the cogwheels of 'ticket thinking'. Horkheimer and Adorno thus suggest how a frenetic, paranoid and delusional neo-conservative philo-semitism serves as the reverse of Islamism's Judaeophobia, each a symptom of 'ticket thinking' in the age of digital communication in which stereotypes stand in the place of critical thought.

Their analysis also indicates the ways in which the struggle against antisemitism can paradoxically feed the symptoms it seeks to alleviate. Horkheimer and Adorno suggest that the globalized marketplace defines the production, dissemination and consumption of ideas whose logic is governed by commodification and fetishization. This 'ticket thinking' has also infused political struggles. This means that those who seek to gain publicity to promote their positions can do so by referencing the pre-packaged reservoir of anti-Jewish images and, in so doing, provoke an immediate response from the army of NGOs who combat antisemitism.

Since their fundraising depends on using the Internet constantly to show their supporters that they are marshalling resources in the struggle, they disseminate petitions against petitions, for example, those calling for boycotts against Israel. They ostracize books and articles that they claim cross the line between criticism of Israel and antisemitism by publicizing books and articles that respond point by point to the charges, which often helps to spur sales or leads to the wider circulation of what they oppose (through alternative Internet media and the blogosphere). Two good examples here are the campaign against Jimmy Carter's *Palestine: Peace Not Apartheid* and John Mearsheimer and Stephen Walt's *The Israel Lobby and U.S. Foreign Policy* (and the *London Review of Books* article that preceded it). In

---

91 On this point, in relation to the work of Hannah Arendt, see Jeremy Waldron, 'What would Hannah say?', *New York Review of Books*, 15 March 2007, 8–12 (12).
92 Horkeimer and Adorno, *Dialectic of Enlightenment*, 201.
93 Ibid., 204, 205.
94 Ibid., 205.

the media-driven frenzied war of words, the medium is often the only message, since in many discussions in the public sphere the only thing that people often have read are the emails or blogs that have pre-scripted their response. The global flow thus helps to publicize political causes, draws together—albeit largely only virtually—unlikely alliances, and helps to generate funding for the next skirmish. All this leads to little more than the propagation of the 'ticket thinking' that is the very source of the Judaeophobic imagination.

So what's new?

In these glosses on the work of the Frankfurt School, Sartre, Butler and Poliakov, therefore, it becomes apparent that not only is the so-called 'new antisemitism' not very new, but its outlines had already been identified and discussed by some of the leading theorists of antisemitism. What they discerned was a shift in the epistemic and political configuration of Judaeophobia from biological towards cultural arguments, or even explicitly anti-racist positions that nonetheless reinscribed the logic of racism in castigating the inherently malevolent tendencies of 'the Jewish character' and in defaming Judaism and Jewishness. But at the same time, the code of anti-Zionism and its antithesis—anti-anti-Zionism—has come to replace the need for antisemitism *per se* in the age of 'ticket thinking', when political mobilization, whether by the left or the right, often depends on the reduction of a critical perspective to a sound-bite or a visual image. The spectacle of the Jewish body within the programmes outlined for the body politic draw on a litany of figures and clichés that are sometimes irresistible to those whose political exigencies seek a shortcut to achieving utopian solutions to the dark side of globalization. And the conflicts of the Middle East and the Arab-Israeli struggle—for this is often the imaginary, symbolic and real site where the tensions of globalized capitalism play out—are the perennial reference points. But this should hardly be surprising, since visions of political salvation have focused on this site for two thousand years.

"Black Intellectuals in America: A Conversation with Cornel West"[1]

INTERVIEWERS: JONATHAN JUDAKEN AND JENNIFER GEDDES

JJ: Just about a decade after you were born, Richard Hofstadter published the 1964 Pulitzer Prize-winning book, *Anti-Intellectualism in American Life.* About 30 years later as Robin Kelly puts it, "1993 was a period when the so-called black public intellectual came into being prompted largely by the publication of Cornel West's *Race Matters.*" So what happened in those three decades that laid the groundwork for black intellectuals emerging as perhaps the most important cadre of intellectuals in the national landscape today and how do you see your role in that?

Cornel West: That's a good question. We must pay dues to our dear brother from Buffalo, Richard Hofstadter because he is somebody who means so much in terms of his style and genre and somebody who himself exemplifies the fusion of synoptic vision, synthetic analysis, as well as his own intellectual witness. There's a new biography on Richard Hofstadter that situates him much more in the center than historically he has been viewed. I spend a little time on Hofstadter principally because what you actually have is a superb communicator.

What happened between 1964 and 1993 was certainly structural transformations that had to do with de-industrialization that had to do with the capitalist economy being restructured in such a way that communities now are scattered and dispersed. You no longer have the basis for the older kind of public intellectuals and you had new public intellectuals who were good at communicating literately as well orally because of television, because of radio, because 1980 is C-Span.

It's a whole different world. Can you imagine listening to Lionel Trilling lecture on Jane Austen on C-Span? You're talking about being a public intellectual in a way he could not conceive of and a way that Hofstadter could not conceive of. So that on the one hand, you've got some structural transformations that certainly Russell Jacoby and others have talked about, but on the other hand, you've got the problem of how do you preserve effective forms of communication.

To put it in highbrow terms, Hofstadter was an eloquent writer. I don't care what he wrote. *Age of Reform*…we can go right across the board. [David] Hume writes an essay on the decline of eloquence way back in the eighteenth century. Now, he understands eloquence the way Cicero and Quintilian understand it—wisdom speaking, *ars topica*, a sense of the whole, synoptic view, synecdochic imagination, relating parts and wholes.

What you have in the 1990s are those persons who are attempting to enact a certain kind of Humean eloquence in terms of speaking clearly, being able to give people a sense of the whole, and do it in a language that's intelligible to them. Hofstadter did it by the page. In the 1990s, people are doing it on the page but also orally, coming out of oratorical traditions.

We have to keep in mind that in the 1950s and 60s, you've got towering public intellectuals like Sinclair Drake, but nobody talks about them. He writes *Black Metropolis* in 1945 before he finishes his Ph.D. thesis. It's introduced by Richard Wright who's just been a number one best seller in 1940 with *Native Son* and then Wright comes back with *Black Boy* in 1945. He introduced the *Black Metropolis* and Drake's still a graduate student. He's a celebrity in Chicago. Nobody talks about Sinclair Drake. Why? Invisible.

It's part of the challenge of black intellectuals. Nat Hentoff wrote an essay in *The Chicago Review* in 1955 called "Jazz and the Intellectual, Someone Goofed." It is a powerful critique of the New York intellectuals' refusal to come to terms with white supremacy and its legacy. It's powerful. It would have been nice if Russell Jacoby had read that essay because in his story that dimension is gone.

JJ: So if a whole group of black intellectuals emerge in public life, let's say as a kind of a new version of the New York intellectual...

Cornel West: It's not a new version, though. It's different, but it's connected.

JG: Could you explain how it's different? Why is it not just a new version of the New York intellectuals?

Cornel West: The New York intellectuals had their own problematic. They were wrestling with modernism and Marxism and urbanism and what it is to be new immigrants who voluntarily came here vis-à-vis the goyim, vis-à-vis the WASPs, the white Anglo-Saxon Protestants. Whereas the black intellectuals are actually dealing with the night side of American democracy. They're dealing with the problematic of the forms of death—social death and civic death, spiritual death and psychic death in America—and so it's a very different context in which they're working; they have a very different relation to the world.

Look at W. E. B. DuBois—his relation to the world is so very different. It's Africa. It's the Bandung Conference. It's China. Whereas for the New York intellectuals, it's Berlin—its ugly memory, but also its grand achievements. It's Goethe, it's Beethoven. But it's also concentration camps. Now, there's nothing wrong with that problematic. I actually have great respect for many of the great New York intellectuals. I understand them to be both towering figures and children of their age. Black intellectuals are in conversation with them but we're in a very different space and have a very different kind of problematic.

The sad thing is that the children of the New York intellectuals are the ones who bash us. They have difficulty taking seriously the new because they only understand the new in light of their fathers, in light of the old. It's understandable.

JJ: So, this new visibility of a whole number of figures, does this mean that in the 1990s, de facto racially segregationist intellectual practices were beginning to be eroded or come to an end? Or are we still sort of suffering under the legacy of an intellectual segregation?

Cornel West: That's a good question. You know, the irony is that you probably had as much or more black presence in *Commentary* in the 1940s and '50s under Elliot E. Cohen. He was the editor when *Commentary* was very progressive. The same would be true for *Partisan Review* with James Ball. So even though in those days you had New York at the center of things, you had the new immigrants basically providing guidance for the modernist Marxist problematic. They had an openness to black voices and black intellectuals.

These days you've got a kind of de facto racial segregation in the life of the mind. For example, *Times Literary Supplement*: I read it regularly but it's very sad when it comes out. *New York Review of Books*: I read regularly but it's very sad. So that what you actually have is a kind of thoroughly marginalized black presence. And by black presence I don't even mean just black writers, but black subject matter. If someone were to come down from Mars and read these major journals of the last 30 years, you'd think there's hardly a black intellectual tradition at all because they're still writing about Ellison and Baldwin.

I mean, you've got a whole host of folk out there doing important things but they're below the radar screen and it's probably because there are so many other texts to look at that come from different parts of the world. I can understand that, but it's a kind of Jim Crow Jr. in the life of the mind. Jim Crow, Esq.—a professional and sophisticated and subtle segregation. They're not racists at all, but when you actually look at their de facto practices, they're very segregated.

JJ: In your interview with Bill Moyers, 'A World of Ideas', you said, 'I understand the vocation of the intellectual as trying to turn easy answers into critical questions and putting those critical questions to people with power. The quest for truth, the quest for the good, the quest for the beautiful, all require us to let suffering speak.'[2] In light of this, what do you see as the ethical burden of the intellectual?

Cornel West: Well, you know that the notion that the condition of truth is to allow suffering to speak actually comes from the next-to-last line of the section called "The Speculative Moment" in Theodor Adorno's Introduction to *The

Negative Dialectics. He said the condition of truth is to allow suffering to speak.[3] It's Adorno's grounding in Jerusalem even though he's a critical theorist. That's very Hebrew scripture, profoundly Judaic, and I resonate with that even though he's got a secular mode of it and a very sophisticated, negative, dialectical way of conceiving it. But he's always looking for the defeated. You remember on page 151 of *Minima Moralia* where he also tries to focus on the most vulnerable, the widow, the stranger. It comes very much out of Hebrew scripture, couched in their very stories and narratives.

Now, why is that important? It's important for me first as a Christian because I understand that we Christians are a rich footnote to prophetic Judaism, that for us to be human is to practice a certain kind of loving kindness or steadfast love that highlights the most vulnerable or the least of these and actually finds joy in serving others and believes that love itself is a desirable mode of being in the world even though it's absurd given the kind of world in which we live. That's just Christian. So you either decide that you don't love and become part of the living dead or you love and love intensely and end up being crushed. Now, that may be a crude way of putting it, but that's a Christian modality and you can hold to that whether you believe that Jesus is the Son of God or not. It's just a way of being that this first generation Palestinian Jew enacted as a representative of prophetic Judaism that other people then jumped on. Paul invents the whole movement around this particular Jewish life and death.

Now, what does that mean for me? It means then as an intellectual with this Christian baggage, I'm going to be free because the world is not going to determine who I am. I have a definition of who I am that cuts over against the world. I'm in the world but not of it. And so I'm free to do what? Be Socratic. Try to tell the truth. *Parrhesia*, plain speech, frank speech, and so forth. I'm free to do what? I'm free to love across the board. As you speak a truth, you can do it with a generosity but also with a bite, expose the lies, but most importantly, you bear witness.

JJ: So, in your affirmation of this Christian prophetic tradition, of the prophetic tradition in general—

Cornel West: In general. Christian is just a version. It's generic. That's my tradition but I talk about it in a broader terms.

JJ: Would you even go so far as to say that Christ was a model of the public intellectual?

Cornel West: No, not really because he wasn't Socratic enough. He did not believe in the kind of intense interrogation, including his own convictions. Jesus doesn't embody that. You don't get a critique of slavery. He's not an abolitionist. There's a whole host of things that that particular Jew who means so much to me didn't do so I don't want to in any way impose some kind of modern category on this first generation Palestinian Jew. He did some other things but he's not a model of the public intellectual.

In fact I don't believe there's one such model. The great public intellectuals for me would by Erasmus, it would be Hume, it would be Adorno, it would be Said, it would be Virginia Woolf. Actually in some ways, it would be Anton Chekhov, a much more quiet dignified public intellectual. Takes a stand on Dreyfus and against antisemitism in that way. But all of these represent different models.

JJ: But the model that you represent is defined by the insurgent black intellectual. This is not a quiet model.

Cornel West: Absolutely. That's right.

JJ: So can you just reprise what you mean by that notion and the ways in which you've sought to embody it?

Cornel West: I think that it's a combination of things, really. One would be what it really means to be a jazz man in the life of the mind and a blues man in the world of ideas. A jazz man is someone who tries to find his or her own voice. This is crucial. To find your own voice means you have to have enough courage to discover who you are, what your own vocation is, such that the vocation is never to be reduced to your profession, your calling never reduced to your career. But you don't find your voice unless you bounce it up against other voices.

Ralph Waldo Emerson says the greatest genius is also the most indebted person. By 'genius' he doesn't mean some romantic notion of isolated individuals conquering the world, but he means geniality, largeness of mind and heart and spirit. But if you're a genial person in that sense you're listening to so many other voices. You're indebted which is his definition of piety, right—being indebted to those who came before you to help you make your move from womb to tomb, so you acknowledge what came before. Emerson was always quoting and quoting and quoting and quoting—he's just embedded. He's showing you this is what Montaigne means to me. This is what Plato means. And yet the configuration of those voices generate a voice that's just his, just Ralph's and that for me is fundamental. That's why Emerson means a lot, but for me, it's primarily a jazz model, you see. That's one.

Another model is the black church model, which we talked about already. The third has to do with the New York intellectuals. See, the irony is that the New York intellectuals—not all of them—but, I mean, the Michael Harringtons, and the Lionel Trillings, and Jacques Barzuns and the Richard Hofstadters—they mean much to me precisely because they were emerging when the academy itself was beginning to consolidate and they could dig into the academic specialization but tease out of it something that provided a broader view. I loved that about them.

JJ: And fourth would be what you've talked about in terms of the role of the organic intellectual, which has to do with the sort of links between the role of intellectuals and communities in struggle, right?

Cornel West: Yes, the fourth would actually be both the black church on the one hand and progressive social movements on the other. You're absolutely right. The black church has to do with speaking boldly, clearly, passionately as a form of service that empowers and inspires others. And the progressive movements would have to do with trying to be non-dogmatic in one's language so you don't speak a language that excludes others religiously or politically. When I say exclude, what I mean is that it's broad enough to speak of issues of justice, not just tied to one religious tradition, it is tied to freedom and equality, not just tied to one religious interpretation. So in that sense, it's open-ended even though it still takes a stand.

JJ: Now, one of the things you have said is that in taking a stand you have to allow different voices to resonate and echo through a process of quotation and citation. But one way in which you've been criticized in some of your writing is for namedropping: articulating a position but not necessarily indicating all the complex arguments that go along with that. And that has to do with the style of writing for a public audience. Do you want to talk about that a little bit?

Cornel West: Yes, I think there are two sides to it, though, and I'm glad you raised that. I mean, one is that I come out of a tradition, like Emerson, where the namedropping is a way of signifying a whole position, a moment in a tradition, so it does assume a certain set of references that people would have in reading it. But it is also a way speaking to yourself in terms of what that name signifies, how that name relates to various positions, and viewpoints and orientations and so on. So that I think some of that criticism is warranted.

But if you're going to unpack every particular allusion and reference, then you end up not being able to get to your point or give people a sense of what the whole is. This is, of course, in Emerson. *Essays* is the great example of that, but this is also true for the New York intellectuals.

My God, you read Trilling's great essay on Keats's letters. He's got allusions across the board he never fleshes out. Why? Because he's on the move and he drops these things. It's enabling him to make the connections and he hopes that you have enough knowledge to know what's going on. That's part of their style.

JJ: And you've left the breadcrumbs so that people can follow the path that you're on.

Cornel West: If they want to. That's exactly right.

JJ: Is there an element of the critique, though, that bothers you in the sense that people don't read you generously when they make that critique, with the acknowledgment that if you wrote texts that were loaded with footnotes, you could tease those connections out? Those critics are not reading your works between the lines, appreciating the sort of multiple affiliations that are created in the whole.

Cornel West: I think you're right about that. I think it also has to do with the fact that the texts that do footnote richly, like *The American Evasion of Philosophy* very few people actually allude to. *Keeping Faith* is another text that very few people ever refer to. So you see that many of my essays do unpack things the way *Race Matters* might not or parts of *Democracy Matters* might not. But this is true for our culture as a whole. It's not just me.

I mean the level of charitable readings and generous interpretations has decreased exponentially in the last few decades and that is one of the sad features of intellectual life that there is always going to be a pettiness and jealousy in the life of the mind. But it has become so pervasive that it's hard to feel as if you ever get a fair hearing because of the polarization of our intellectual and ideological life. It's not just an individual like me. It's true across the board.

JG: Can I ask you about the antagonism of the academy towards doing work for the general public? For example, it's actually bad for an assistant professor's tenure case to have written books oriented towards the public. And also, why do you think people in the academy have such a hard time speaking in ways that people outside the academy can hear or understand?

Cornel West: I think it goes partly back to Hofstadter. Hofstadter's point is that America is a business civilization and deeply anti-intellectual. America fears intellect but loves intelligence. It is a creative critical faculty that they are afraid of, because it's too Socratic and asks terrifying questions. American intelligence is about achieving ends and objectives. So Americans love intelligence; intellect, they fear.

And if you are going to actually make a choice of being an intellectual, it means that you are going to hit up against most of the civilization and culture. Therefore you create your own world to reaffirm your sense of calling which becomes very insular and yet helps you sustain your project because so much of the rest of the culture looks at you like you have lost your mind.

Because the business of America is business, we know that the academy itself has become corporatized, more business oriented, modeled on markets, and we have to come to terms with that. Markets are here to stay. Intellectuals have to deal with markets. The question is how do you use these markets in such a way that you still hold up non-market values like integrity and playfulness of the mind and the intrinsic pleasure of intellectual engagement.

JG: What does the life of the mind have to offer to our broader culture today? What do you think our society needs from those who are engaged in the life of the mind?

Cornel West: I think the life of the mind is fundamentally about a sense of awe, wonder, openness, exploration, and adventure. The kind of adventure the great Alfred North Whitehead talked about. It's an adventure in exploring different views and viewpoints, different arguments and perspectives. There is a certain capaciousness that goes with it, an expansiveness of heart, mind, and soul that has its own exhilarating joy and is a desirable way of being in the world. It is still worldly in the way Said puts it. It's rooted in circumstances, but it still has its own intrinsic joy.

I say joy rather than pleasure because I don't think it's hedonistic. I think joy is something much deeper. Joy has to do with a connection with others. You can have pleasure all by yourself, and when Montaigne is sitting there in dialogue with Plato, or Emerson's in dialogue with Montaigne, it really is a community across time that is being established even though it's a voice of a dead man and a reader who's alive.

JG: How would our culture be transformed if the life of the mind was engaged in contemporary American culture and people who lived the life of the mind were more committed to speaking out in our culture?

Cornel West: Well, see the thing about the life of the mind is that it is not intrinsically moral. I don't believe that if the life of the mind became a mass movement that America would necessarily be a better place because you've got virtues among those outside of the intellectual world that are quite precious and you have got virtues and you have got vices inside the intellectual world that are quite vicious, so I don't want to romanticize the life of the mind, that somehow it carries within it these wonderful political effects and consequences.

My conception of *paideia*—this formation of attention and cultivation of self and maturation of soul—goes beyond a life of the mind. It's really more a shaping of a kind of a person and the life of the mind is just one dimension of that person. So I would not want to over-freight the talk about life of the mind within the larger backdrop of *paideia*. A democratic *paideia* includes a Socratic life of the mind, but without the prophetic, and a certain moral shaping, and without empathy and sympathy and so forth—I mean some of the most fascinating people I have ever met in the life of the mind, who I love to talk to, are not decent persons. I hate to say that...

JJ: It goes beyond the life of the mind then in the sense of not only an ethical vocation that demands attention to the downtrodden and the wretched of the earth, but a political effort to work at creating community, and institutions that are able to duplicate themselves, to create conditions that enable people to continue the process of the life of the mind. So the life of the mind should not be fetishized or idolized because there are other forms of knowledge or wisdom that are crucial.

Cornel West: Absolutely.

JJ: Can you talk more about the fact that some of your political praxis has focused on the university itself as an important site of struggle. What are the ways in which the university helps to support oppositional and insurgent black intellectuals? And what are the ways in which the university is complicit with hegemony and with power?

Cornel West: I think the university at its best constitutes a space within liberal society in which there is supposed to be a robust and uninhibited dialogue taking place. And therefore it allows for a divergence of intellectual and ideological perspectives that one might find difficult enacted in other spheres in American society. That's a beautiful thing because there has to be a space where there is some robust discussion going on, investigations, interrogations. Now, that's the ideal. It certainly doesn't always happen, but its justification is a quest for truth (small 't'), and for knowledge (small 'k').

That is not true for corporations concerned with producing X product or Y product. Now, what that means is that persons like myself can find a place and position to both work and engage young precious minds of all colours, classes, genders, and sexual orientations wedded to that fundamental mission: the quest for truth, knowledge unbound. You never really possess the truth, but we're after it and to me that is very precious.

Now, I know that universities are still shot through with all the different prejudices and problems as the larger society, but universities have a certain legitimation in light of this ideal. So even if you bring critique to bear on the university, they have to somehow justify what they're doing in light of that quest. Not a McCarthyism or the escalating authoritarianism now evident at certain universities; they can just say explicitly, 'Well, you know, we don't take that quest for truth that seriously'.

JJ: But even more insidious, I think, is the way in which the university is itself one cog within a larger capitalist structure. And that the logic of instrumentality in the humanities in particular becomes the only way you can articulate what it is that you're doing that's of worth. And part of what you're saying is that non-instrumental ends are the very root of what it is that we are doing in producing citizens in a democracy.

JG: Is it possible that there is a politicization of knowledge that actually destroys what you find so precious about the life of the mind? What are the possible relations between public life and the life of the mind? What are the dangers? How do we keep what's precious about the life of the mind but also see that intellectual life does have a public role?

Cornel West: Well, I think three things. One is that within the university itself there has to be a full-fledged pluralism regarding the conversation. You have to have a variety of different voices, methodologically, ideologically, politically and so forth and so on. Now, there is always a politics that goes along with pluralism, but it's a form of politics that doesn't allow for vulgar politicization, that trumps conversation, that doesn't allow for certain viewpoints.

Now, even still—the larger point—there still has to be the acknowledgment that the university is part of a larger set of interlocking institutions connected to our economy, connected to the capitalist world economy that cannot be overlooked. The university cannot survive outside of the world, outside of the economy, outside of the big donors, outside of federal support, be they private or public university, and so forth and so on. The question is: how do you preserve that rich space of robust inquiry given all of those structural realities that are characterized by dirty politics. It is a matter of acknowledging the way in which the political economy of the university impacts what happens in the university that can be quite precious.

JJ: Part of this has to do with the university's division of labor into disciplines and the university disciplining people through those disciplines. One of the things about your work is that it has from the very beginning cut across disciplinary boundaries. Your work operates in different genres: philosophy, religion, literature, black history, oratory, spoken word. You've also embraced the dialogical in your work with others; You have not only written alone. You have spoken about this Emersonian way of invoking your ancestors. So, how central is it, in fact, to the very task of the intellectual to speak in different idioms, to dialogically engage with others, to speak to different audiences? How central is that to the role of the intellectual, to be a true public intellectual.

Cornel West: I think there are so many different ways of being an intellectual: be it a democratic intellectual, a public intellectual, however wants to define it. I don't believe there is one model or one paradigm of the public intellectual. There are so many different ways of being.

I think Steven Sondheim was one of the great public intellectuals of our day. He's the greatest playwright in song that we have ever had, but he does it in a certain kind of way. He's not out there all the time. You just listen to *Passion.* Go see *A Little Night Music, Company, Sunday in the Park with George,* and above all, *Sweeney Todd.* That's one way of being a public intellectual. Gary Will is another I have great respect for. Very different. See, we can go right across the board in that regard.

For me, see, I come out of a tradition, and here it's close to Ralph Ellison. You know, Ralph Ellison or James Weldon Johnson, they always understood themselves as renaissance men. A renaissance person is just a humanist, concerned about the fact that human beings are going to die, concerned about what you going to do before you die, what kind of a person are you going to be before your body's a culinary delight to terrestrial worms. That's what the humanist tradition is, going back to Erasmus. So I act as if I live in a de-disciplinized world, where disciplines don't exist. It's not a matter of being interdisciplinary. That still presupposes disciplines.

I'm trying to make sense of how to live, to get a sense of the whole, which is a question of learning how to die, so that what happens is that you have a variety of different venues. Ellison tried the trumpet, then he tried the novel, then he tried essays. Then he became a magnificent interviewer. His interviews are works of art. Coltrane's the same way. He's reading Einstein. He's reading the Kabala. He's got the Koran. He's got the Bible. He's listening to Stravinsky. He's trying to make sense in light of his own calling. Trying to impose some order on what Samuel Beckett called 'the mess'. I mean, that's really what he's trying to do. That's all I'm trying and so I just pull from all these different venues to communicate.

JJ: So if you have to choose one word to define your orientation, would it be wrong to choose the term existentialist?

Cornel West: Yeah, because existentialist tends to be associated with Sartre.

JJ: But you have advocated a Chekhovian existentialism, a Christian existentialism. There's an existentialist Marxist tradition. It seems to me a useful way of grouping your orientation in the way in which it focuses on the struggles of people's lives, the nature of the human condition, our struggle to be fully human.

Cornel West: That's right. I mean that's humanism. Christian humanism, humanist Christian, Chekhovian Christian. Existentialist might be a little too abstract. Let me put it this way. But, see, that's why I would never be a jazz critic or a blues scholar. I'd rather be a jazz man and a blues man, you know, a participant in the ongoing tradition and just a spectator checking it out. You want to be a shaper and a molder of the culture or civilization in which you're a part—you know what I mean?

Let me put it this way. If there's one thinker in the twentieth century who speaks to me out of the European tradition it is Walter Benjamin. You remember that wonderful essay by Adorno: the specific weight of the concrete setting the center as a periphery; permanence of danger; catastrophe; wrestling with the angel of history. Benjamin has the same sensibility as I do. Actually, it is a deeply Jewish sensibility. In that sense, I have a very profound elective affinity to certain thinkers out of the Jewish tradition who have that problematic of the catastrophe, the monstrous, the scandalous, the traumatic. Kafka has it probably more than any of them. And I resonate deeply with that even though it's within my own context of a black intellectual and political tradition.

JJ: So let's turn a little bit to the catastrophic in the contemporary context and to your work in *Democracy Matters*. For me, the most brilliant insights of *Democracy Matters* emerge when the lens of race informs the moral and political diagnosis of the arrested development of democracy. Why is the lens of race such an informative perspective on *Democracy Matters* post-9/11?

Cornel West: It's because we often talk about American democracy without talking about white supremacy. These white supremacist roots are deeply illuminating in terms of trying to look at subsequent developments of American democracy.

All Americans feel unsafe, unprotected, subject to random violence and hated for who they are after 9/11. And I say to be a nigger in America for 400 years is to be unsafe, unprotected, subject to random violence and hated for who you are. Now, we know this is not an identical relation. But there is enough overlap there to say now the whole nation's niggerized, walking around fearful, walking around feeling an object of hate, walking around anxiety-ridden, feeling intimidated, feeling helpless and impotent and feeling as if they can't shape their destiny any longer.

Well, what is a democracy? Democracy is a condition in which everyday people feel as if they can lift their voices and shape their destiny. But to niggerize is to de-democratize. That's what America did to black people. It made sure they could not be citizens. What was left? Well, their bodies, their voices could be used. They can amuse you. Stimulate you. Titillate you.

Now how did Martin Luther King resist niggerization? Unbelievable courage. Refusal to give in on democratic ideals. And in the most undemocratic conditions he remained a radical democrat. What a model for Americans as they undergo niggerization.

JJ: But to take it one level deeper, part of what's illuminating is also the ways in which race shows how American history and values from their very origins have been implicated in imperialism. So, can you talk a little bit more about this tension within the American tradition itself: between American efforts to establish a democratic tradition and American imperialism?

Cornel West: That's a deeper question in terms of indigenous peoples, their land and their bodies being the very site for the expansion of American democracy. And you have still got black and brown as part of the American imperial project.

I think one of the important dimensions of *Democracy Matters* is the centrality of empire tied into race in a way that was not true in *Race Matters*. This has been a challenge of every democracy going back to Athens. Every democracy we know has been predicated on some kind of imperial project. So the question becomes how does one engage in a critique of democracy with democratic ideals that are suspicious of the imperialism which often are the preconditions for your democracy. It's a real paradox.

And I don't think that we really have an answer. I think that it is one of the night sides of any democratic experiment and I think that Melville and others force us to look at this night side all the time, as does Toni Morrison and Eugene O'Neil and Robert Penn Warren. You have to confront it and yet you know there's a genocidal dimension of your identity.

JJ: The chapter in *Democracy Matters* on the Arab-Israeli conflict is extraordinary because you are negotiating a minefield and it seems to me that the antimonies in the Arab-Israeli conflict are, as you say, central to suturing the wound within the Middle East, but how one negotiates those antimonies is very complicated. Can you talk about how you see the role of the intellectual in bearing witness to those kinds of conflicts?

Cornel West: I think that the intellectual has to not just speak truth, expose lies, but bear witness in such a way that they are sensitive to the histories of the various peoples' conflicts you are talking about so that, for example, in that chapter, I tried to let the various communities know I understand their paranoia even as I refuse morally to justify the various excesses, whatever the form they take.

On the one hand, you have got a Jewish community with a variety of different perspectives, having its own internal conflicts. But one has to understand the history of anti-Jewish hatred and antisemitism.

But I am also coming out of a tradition that highlights those who are subjugated, a tradition that includes the Hebrew Bible. As a Christian, I understand the centrality of the Hebrew Bible to Judaism from my own personal faith. But the Palestinians cannot but be crucial in terms of my understanding of the Middle East given their role as a subjugated people.

So the question becomes how do you tease out the best of the prophetic voices of both sides to build some bridges in light of the U.S. imperial presence and the history of the British imperial presence. How do you tell that story in such a way that you can open up first the various people to listen and then to try to make a strong case when they decide to listen to persuade and convince them?

JG: That seems to be a parallel to the discussion about abortion in America where very little public debate happens. It is primarily name-calling and slogans. So how can you get people to actually have the kinds of conversations that democracy is supposed to be about in which they really do debate and talk when public discourse is at such a low level?

Cornel West: It's a tough thing and part of it is just a matter of will and imagination where you try to conceive of what it is like to be in your opponent's world. Look at the world from their perspective and even if you radically reject it, you could try to see some of the things that drive them to justify why they think what they think and do what they do. I know that is a little cliché. But when it comes down to it, Shelley's right: poets are the unacknowledged legislators of the world and if you don't have will and imagination, you're going to end up arbitrating with power and force alone.

JG: It seems to me that you are also modeling a kind of public discourse. In the way you talk about what is at stake for the Israelis and what's at stake for the Palestinians and what the history is and what psychologically each sides brings to the table. You are trying to model a way of talking about very controversial issues that says what is really at stake for each side and let's actually have a conversation about it?

JJ: But I also think the citation of Shelley is very interesting because you're saying that poets being the unacknowledged legislators means that it is not only a rational discourse that can articulate precisely what each side needs to suture these wounds. It is specifically in terms of a kind of religious or poetic language that we have to respond to these issues. My question is whether there is still a universal framework of meaning that can address these kinds of conflicts or is Jean-François Lyotard right that all we can do in the post-modern condition is bear witness to the differend: to the paranoia and psychic foibles and political history of the sides that are competing.

Cornel West: Yes they are competing and there is an increasing incredulity towards metanarratives as Lyotard talks about. So in one sense, he is right. In another sense, however, he is deeply wrong because there are still significant overlaps within all of the various narratives such that you find in all variety of different cultures a consensus that the violation of a child or the rape of a mother is morally horrific, even if this is articulated in a variety of different ways. There is a consensus that cuts across cultures and civilizations that constitutes a certain kind of framework or at least the raw material for a conversation.

JG: Like human rights?

JJ: Or a set of ethical imperatives that most people agree to, which are embodied in the Ten Commandments

Cornel West: Or legal systems and religious beliefs and so forth. Now, I don't want to exaggerate the overlap but I do think there is enough overlap so that it is not like Alasdair MacIntyre's portrait of ruin at the beginning of *After Virtue* or Lyotard's description in *The Postmodern Condition*, though I think they are on to something. I don't want to downplay that critique, but I think they overdo it in terms of what can bring us together.

That's one of the reasons why somebody like Martin King or Mandela or Gandhi constitute universal symbols. They embody something that speaks to all of us even though everybody knows Martin was a Christian. Very few people knew Mandela was, but he was a Christian and, of course, Gandhi was a kind of an ecumenical religious figure who pulled from a variety of different traditions. But all of us resonate so deeply because we have got this deep human concern for babies and rights and liberties and dignity and even the sanctity of sentient beings.

JG: If you had a vision of what intellectual life would be like in 20 or 50 years—we have talked about the segregation of intellectual life right now—do you have a vision for what it would be like?

Cornel West: An intellectual life? Wow, that's a good question. Well, we would be reading and attending more Chekhovian plays and listening to more of Coltrane's music, which is to say we would be looking at our lives and saying:

'My God they can be so much richer. We are wasting our time engaged in superficial diversions. We ought to be involved with substantive questioning and the pursuit of joy, not just pleasure, as we interrogate and examine ourselves like Coltrane does in "A Love Supreme."

Now, what institutional form would that take? Probably fewer disciplines and more intellectual discussion and conversation, more cosmopolitan forms of inquiry that transcend the national, the tribal, the racial, and so on.

But, you know, the twenty-first century will probably be a contest between the United States and China, so we have to always understand the limits of the historical context since we have two leviathans emerging. China is going to have to learn some deep democratic lessons from America, just like we have got to learn some deep lessons from China regarding how you sustain community and get beyond vicious, rapacious individualism. But I have a dream for how we might get beyond these dichotomies if only poets were in fact the legislators of the world.

(Endnotes)

1   A truncated version of this interview first appeared as 'Black Intellectuals in America: A Conversation with Cornel West', *The Hedgehog Review* 9.1 (Spring 2007): 81-91

2   Cornel West, 'A World of Ideas', *The Cornel West Reader* (New York: Basic Civitas, 1999), 294.

3   Theodor Adorno, *Negative Dialectics*, trans. E.B. Ashton (New York: Continuum, 1973), 17-18.

Index